BONES, BOATS, & BISON

E. JAMES DIXON

BONES, BOATS,

& BISON

Archeology

and the First

Colonization

of Western

North America

Albuquerque

THE UNIVERSITY

OF NEW MEXICO

PRESS

© 1999 by the University of New Mexico Press
All rights reserved.
First edition, second printing 2001

Design and composition by B. Williams & Associates

Library of Congress Cataloging-in-Publication Data
Dixon, E. James.
Bones, boats & bison : archeology and the
first colonization of western North America /
E. James Dixon. — 1st ed.
    p.   cm.
Includes bibliographical references (p.   )
and index.
ISBN 0-8263-2057-0 (alk. paper). —
ISBN 0-8263-2138-0 (pbk. : alk. paper)
1. Paleo-Indians—North America.   2. Paleo-
Indians—West (U.S.)   3. Indians of North
America—Antiquities.   4. Indians—Origin.
5. North America—Antiquities.   6. West
(U.S.)—Antiquities.   I. Title.   II. Title:
Bones, boats, and bison.
E77.9.D58   1999   99-41913
970.01—dc21   CIP

This book is dedicated to my wife, Mim.
Without her love and support
I couldn't have finished this work.

Contents

Figures

Tables

Preface

THIS BOOK is intended to provide a framework to organize a large volume of archeological data and to provide a foundation for future research and interpretations. It attempts to articulate archeological information between adjacent regions of western North America. To keep the book readable and useful, it has been necessary to select information that illustrates the defining characteristics of archeological traditions and complexes. Consequently, much information about individual sites has been excluded, and many sites have not been discussed or even cited. These omissions are not intended to diminish the significant excavations and analyses of the many excellent archeologists whose work has contributed to our understanding of the early archeology of western North America.

To avoid possible inaccurate conversions of ^{14}C determinations to calendar years and make this work correspond to the large body of extant literature, the ^{14}C determinations have been left uncalibrated in this presentation. Many scientists have reservations about the accuracy of the calibration curve beginning about 10,000 ^{14}C years B.P., the time period that is the focus of this book. During this time it becomes impossible to rely on the annual growth cycles recorded in tree rings and consequently it is necessary to use other less reliable organisms for calibration. Furthermore, the vast majority of the literature contains dates which are not calibrated. The radiocarbon dates are reported as they appear in the literature or as they have been reported by radiocarbon dating laboratories. They are presented first by the date, followed by the statistical error of the measurement and laboratory numbers when possible.

Regional and topical summaries pertaining to the early archeology of western North America have appeared in recent years which are relevant to the early archeology of western North America. These works have served as important references for the preparation of this manuscript. The fourth edition of Marie Wormington's 1957 *Ancient Man in North America* remains a classic reference for Paleoindian archeology and New World archeology in general. More recent works have been written by multiple authors and have been published as edited volumes. Topical volumes include: *Early Man in America from a Circum-Pacific*

Perspective (1978) edited by Alan Bryan; *Peopling of the New World* (1982) edited by Jonathon E. Ericson, R. E. Taylor, and Rainer Berger; *Early Man in the New World* (1983) edited by Richard Shutler; *New Evidence for the Pleistocene Peopling of the Americas* (1986) edited by Alan Bryan; *Megafauna and Man: Discovery of America's Heartland* (1990) edited by Larry D. Agenbroad, Jim I. Mead and Lisa W. Nelson; *The First Americans: Search and Research* (1991) edited by Thomas Dillehay and David Meltzer; and *Prehistoric Mongoloid Dispersals* (1996) edited by Takeru Akazawa and Emőke J. E. Szathmáry. My earlier book, *Quest for the Origins of the First Americans* (1993), may also be included in this list.

Significant regional syntheses focusing on the early archeology of western North America include: *Prehistoric Hunters of the High Plains* (1978 and 1991) by George Frison; *California Archaeology* (1984) by Michael J. Moratto; *Early Human Occupation in Far Western North America: The Clovis-Archaic Interface* (1988) edited by Judith Willig, Melvin Aikens, and John Fagan; *Early Hunter-Gatherers of the California Coast* (1994) by Jon Erlandson; *Early Human Occupation in British Columbia* (1996) edited by Roy Carlson and Luke Bona; *The Prehistory of the Northwest Coast* (1995), by R. G. Matson and Gary Coupland; and *American Beginnings: The Prehistory and Paleoecology of Beringia* (1996) edited by Frederick Hadleigh West. Brian Fagan's *The Great Journey: The Peopling of Ancient America* (1987) also represents an important contribution to the body of literature on the early archeology of North America. In addition, there are many important synthetic articles and specific issues of regional and topical journals devoted to the early archeology or paleoecology of a region.

All of these works have provided important contributions to our knowledge regarding the earliest occupation of western North America and each provides important insights into regional archeology. The variety of perspectives and the wealth of data from these sources, as well as individual site reports, were extremely valuable in preparing this synthesis. I am indebted to these, and other, scholars for their efforts which helped establish our knowledge and understanding of the early archeology of western North America.

Synthesis is an ongoing process in archeology. It necessitates moving from the security of well-known small-scale phenomena within restricted areas into the less secure realm of defining patterns of information derived by many researchers from many different archeological sites and diverse regions. A work of this nature requires modifying some existing interpretations to accommodate recent discoveries, the application of new methods, and the progress of ongoing research. While this book relies heavily on the excellent work of many scholars and researchers spanning more than a hundred years, the responsibility for this synthesis and associated interpretations rests solely with the author.

Acknowledgments

MARIE WORMINGTON completed the last edition of her 1957 book, *Ancient Man in North America*, while at the Denver Museum of Natural History. Her work laid the foundation for all subsequent synthesis and analysis of the early archeology of North America, particularly western regions of the continent. I am proud to have had the opportunity to help continue the tradition of Paleoindian archeology at the Denver Museum of Natural History begun by Jesse Figgins and continued by Marie Wormington. I wish to express my appreciation to many of my friends, colleagues, and volunteers at the Denver Museum of Natural History for their help. Bob Pickering, Chairman of the Anthropology Department, and Jane Day, former Chief Curator, supported my application to the National Endowment for the Humanities and my leave from the Museum to work on this book.

Kathie Gully, Kathy Honda, Liz Clancy, and Kris Haglund of the Denver Museum of Natural History library and archives provided valuable help in locating references and archival material. Rick Wicker, Nancy Jenkins, and Dave Schraeder provided important photographic assistance. Figures 1.3, 1.6, and 5.1 are reproduced with permission of the Denver Museum of Natural History Photo Archives and with the assistance of Liz Clancy, photo archivist. David Overstreet provided Figure 3.15. James Watts helped prepare Figures 3.16 and 3.23. Special thanks goes to Eric Parrish for his patience and skill in drawing and computer graphics in the preparation of Figures 2.1, 2.4, 2.5, 2.6, 2.7, 3.1, 4.1, 5.3, 6.1, 6.3, 6.4, 6.6, 6.7, 7.1, 7.4, 7.7, 8.1, 8.2, 9.1, 9.3, 9.6, 10.1, 10.2, and 10.3. His ability to visually portray my abstract concepts coupled with his artistic talent greatly enhanced the text.

I thank Dennis Stanford for permission to use Figures 3.17, 3.18, 3.26, 6.2, 9.2, 9.4, and 9.8. Mort Turner provided Figures 3.14 and 4.8, and Tom Dillehay provided Figure 4.6. I thank Frederico Solorzano for permission to modify his slides to produce Figure 4.2 and for permission to use Figures 4.3, 4.4, and 8.6. Roy Carlson and Michael Waters graciously provided Figures 5.5 and 5.9, respectively. Douglas Owsley provided Figures 5.6 and 5.7. Richard McNeish gave permission to use Figure 4.5. Steve Holen kindly shared Figure 3.20, and Larry Agenbroad provided Figure 3.22.

During the course of conducting research for this book, I examined collections and archival material at several museums. I wish to express my appreciation to the late John Cotter and the library and archival staff at the University of Pennsylvania Museum for their assistance. David Hurst Thomas and the staff at the American Museum of Natural History provided valuable help during my research there. Douglas and Wanni Anderson extended their hospitality during my visit to the Haffenreffer Museum of Anthropology, providing access to collections, as well as stimulating and thought provoking conversations. I am indebted to Dennis Stanford and Pegi Jodry at the Smithsonian Institution for their hospitality and for giving so generously of their valuable time to help me examine collections, locate and share photographs and illustrations, and facilitate my archival research.

My special thanks to Tom Stafford for sharing unpublished radiocarbon information. He provided valuable consultation regarding specific ^{14}C dates and ^{14}C dating in general. Amy Dansie of the Nevada State Museum generously shared prepublication copies of the research on the Nevada mummies. Thomas Green graciously provided prepublication data describing the Buhl burial.

I truly appreciate the time and attention given by Dennis Stanford, Tom Stafford, and Adam Bennett to review the entire first draft of this manuscript. I also thank Doug Anderson for his review of an early version of Chapter 7, Tom Dillehay for reviewing drafts of Chapters 1–4, Betty Meggers for her comments on an early draft of Chapter 4, and Bonnie Pitblado for reviewing an early draft of Chapter 8. Patrick Olsen and Heidi Manger provided editorial assistance and helpful insights to clarify the manuscript. Although not always heeded, the valuable comments and constructive criticism of all these individuals helped improve the quality of the final manuscript.

The research and preparation of this book has been made possible by a Fellowship for College Teachers and Independent Scholars from the National Endowment for the Humanities (FB-33053-96). I remain deeply indebted to the National Endowment for the Humanities for their vision and support.

My family has been extraordinarily supportive throughout this project. I wish to thank my children Colleen, Denbigh, and Bryan who tolerated my obsession with this book. Very special thanks goes to my wife, Mim Dixon, who patiently reviewed the entire manuscript. Without her support, it could not have been completed.

1 The Dawn of Paleoindian Archeology

IN 1923–1924, two distinctive stone projectile points were discovered among the bones of extinct bison at Lone Wolf Creek, near Colorado City, Texas. The site was being excavated by a field crew under the supervision of H. D. Boyes. Boyes was a local rancher who was supported by Jesse D. Figgins, the first director of the Denver Museum of Natural History (then the Colorado Museum of Natural History). This paleontological excavation had been undertaken for the purpose of collecting bones of extinct animals, and the excavators were not expecting to find artifacts.

Although the evidence suggested that the projectile points (Figure 1.1) had been used to hunt the extinct bison found at Lone Wolf Creek, none of the original specimens was found in situ. That is, they had been displaced from their original locations and their association with the bison bones was not recorded and observed by trained scientists. Because they had not been examined in their primary context by qualified archeologists and geologists, the discovery was considered equivocal. Although it appeared that the projectile points had been used to kill the bison, definitive proof was lacking.

The importance of this discovery can only be appreciated when one has a larger understanding of the history of American archeology. By the late 1800s, the debate over the antiquity of human occupation in the Americas had become involved in "a complex interplay of discoveries, personalities, national and state politics, and sociological trends in American science, which together polarized geological and archaeological opinions (although not on disciplinary lines)" (Gifford and Rapp 1985:412). Some scientists believed humans had come to the Americas only a few thousand years ago, and others believed that they had arrived tens, and possibly hundreds, of thousands of years ago. Particularly vocal in this debate were two respected scientists: W. H. Holmes, who was in charge of the Smithsonian Institution's Bureau of American Ethnology, and Aleš Hrdlička, who led the Smithsonian's Division of Physical Anthropology (Figure 1.2).

Based on his extensive analyses of human skeletons from the Americas, Hrdlička knew that all known human remains from the Americas were fully modern. The remains of earlier types of archaic humans, such as the Neander-

Figure 1.1 Projectile points found at Lone Wolf Creek, Texas in 1924. (Photograph by Rick Wicker, Denver Museum of Natural History.)

thals found in Europe, had not been discovered anywhere in North or South America. This evidence indicated to him that all the human remains from the Americas were postglacial in age and that humans had not arrived in the Americas until after the last Ice Age. Given his knowledge of physical anthropology, he did not consider it likely that human remains or artifacts could be associated with the bones of Ice Age animals. His conclusions were formulated prior to the introduction of radiocarbon dating in the late 1940s and were necessarily based on geological interpretations. During the early 1900s, most geologists and archeologists believed that the last Ice Age did not end until sometime between 20,000–60,000 years ago (Krieger 1964).

Holmes based his objections on his analysis of recent stone artifacts that he had excavated from quarry sites. He clearly recognized that just because New World artifacts superficially resembled Old World specimens, they were not necessarily as old (Holmes 1893). This research led him to question claims of alleged Pleistocene (Ice Age) antiquity based solely on the similarity of some American artifacts to Pleistocene specimens from the Old World. To complicate the debate, numerous claims of Pleistocene age for the human occupation of the Americas were based on poorly documented, excavated, and analyzed discover-

Figure 1.2 Alěs Hrdlička conducting field research in Alaska, 1929. (National Anthropological Archives, Smithsonian Institution.)

ies throughout the United States (Gifford and Rapp 1985; Meltzer 1991; Whitney 1867, 1880). This debate created an atmosphere in which respected and well-trained American archeologists, geologists, and natural historians remained skeptical of claims of Ice Age antiquity for American artifacts because definitive proof resulting from in situ discoveries excavated by qualified professionals was lacking.

As a result of the discovery at Lone Wolf Creek, Figgins suspected that humans and extinct forms of Ice Age bison had been contemporaneous. Less than two years had passed when an African American cowboy, George W. McJunken, discovered the bones of extinct bison eroding from Wild Horse Arroyo near Folsom, New Mexico. He told residents of nearby Raton, New Mexico of his discovery, and Fred J. Howarth and Charles Schwacheim, two avocational naturalists, later collected some of the bison bone from McJunken's site near Folsom. They in turn brought the discovery to the attention of Figgins, who immediately replied in a letter that "the Bison is very similar to the Texas material [meaning the Lone Wolf Creek bison bones]. If not the same species, then it is a closely related form, apparently considerably larger than our example" (February 6, 1926 letter from J. D. Figgins to Fred Howarth, Raton, New Mexico in the Denver Museum of Natural History Archives). The similarity of the bison remains from Folsom to those of Lone Wolf Creek must have made Figgins suspect that the site near Folsom might also contain artifacts associated with early humans. In a subsequent letter Figgins wrote, "I have a hunch that creek and its laterals will produce something worth while. At a depth of 10 feet, or even less, they are almost sure to prove highly interesting and I should not be the least surprised to find some poor Indian in the same Locality. The conditions there are ideal hunting ground for the paleontologist." (March 31, 1926, letter from J. D. Figgins to Fred Howarth, Raton, New Mexico in the Denver Museum of Natural History Archives). Folsom would soon provide an opportunity to demonstrate a direct association between humans and these extinct Ice Age animals.

Figgins endorsed and financially sponsored the excavations at Folsom, along with other local investigations, by providing $300 from the CMNH. With the approval of the state of New Mexico, the CMNH purchased the rights to the fossils for the sum of $50. Excavations began in earnest in the summer of 1926 (Figure 1.3), and the field notes of Charles Schwacheim indicate that the discovery of the first Folsom point occurred on July 14, 1926 (Schwacheim 1926; Folsom and Agogino, 1975).

Later that year, Figgins traveled to the East Coast and presented the discoveries to the eastern academic establishment, including Aleš Hrdlička at the Smithsonian Institution. Hrdlička commented that it was unfortunate that the specimens had been removed from their original context before being verified by qualified scientific experts. This infuriated Figgins who vowed in a fiery letter to his assistant Harold Cook (the Museum's field representative at the Folsom site) that he (Figgins) would forcefully prove his point to the "Hrdličkas" [as it appears in the original] (1926 letter from J. D. Figgins to H. J. Cook., Denver Museum of Natural History Archives).

Hrdlička's demand for in situ evidence that could be examined by outside researchers led Figgins and Cook to leave additional specimens discovered in 1927 in situ. Telegrams were sent inviting national experts to examine the site for themselves. Frank H. H. Roberts, Jr., examined the site on behalf of the Smithsonian Institution's Bureau of American Ethnology and reported back to Holmes and Hrdlička that the discovery was genuine. A. V. Kidder represented the Peabody Museum, Andover, Massachusetts, and Barnum Brown came as the scientific representative of the American Museum of Natural History in New York. As a result of these visits and direct field observations, there emerged professional consensus that the distinctive Folsom points and bones of the

Figure 1.3 H. J. Cook (left) and F. J. Howarth (right) at the Folsom site, circa 1927. (Denver Museum of Natural History Photo Archives.)

Pleistocene bison (*Bison antiquus*) were contemporaneous. There was little doubt that the Folsom points had been used to kill the bison.

The Lindenmeier site proved to be another important Folsom site. Although the site had been known since 1924, it wasn't until 1930 that E. B. Renaud, a faculty member at the University of Denver, recognized that the points from the site were similar to those recovered from Folsom, New Mexico (Coffin 1937). The Smithsonian Institution began excavation at the site in 1934 under the direction of Frank Roberts (Roberts 1935, 1937) (Figure 1.4). Several groups excavated at the site concurrently including the Coffin family, who had originally discovered and leased the excavation rights from the land owner, William Lindenmeier. In 1935, the Smithsonian took over part of the lease from the Coffins who also continued to work next to Roberts's field crew from the Smithsonian until 1938 (Wormington 1957:31). In 1935, John Cotter (1935) also led a field party sponsored by the cmnh and excavated at the site as well. The excavations at Lindenmeier, particularly the Smithsonian excavations under the direction of Roberts, broadened understanding of Folsom culture. The original Folsom site in New

Mexico was a kill site, but the excavations at Lindenmeier revealed a campsite. As a result, work at Lindenmeier greatly expanded knowledge of the types of artifacts and lifeways of Folsom people. In 1959, C. Vance Haynes and George Agogino (1960) returned to Lindenmeier and together devoted about 700 man hours (Wormington 1960) collecting small pieces of charcoal that were ^{14}C dated to 10,780 ± 375 B.P. (L-24a) (Haynes and Agogino 1960). This was the first radiocarbon date for Folsom culture.

The first suggestion of archeological material that might predate the Folsom was the discovery of a mammoth skeleton near Angus, Nebraska. Figgins (1931) reported this discovery, which was allegedly associated with a fluted projectile point (Figure 1.5). H. Marie Wormington (1957:43) stated that geologists subsequently examined the site and believed it to be mid-Pleistocene in age thus demonstrating that the fluted projectile point and mammoth bones were not associated. This led her to suggest that the artifact may have been a forgery deliberately introduced into the deposits. Agogino and Ferguson (1978) suggest that it is unlikely that the artifact was planted because the find predates the discovery of the Clovis site. Based on a later reanalysis of the stratigraphy at the site and

Figure 1.4 Excavations at the Lindenmeier site, 1935. (Photograph by Frank H. H. Roberts. National Anthropological Archives, Smithsonian Institution.)

Figure 1.5 Double exposure photograph showing both sides of the fluted projectile point found near Angus, Nebraska. (Photograph by Rick Wicker, Denver Museum of Natural History.)

a single thermoluminesence (TL) date, Holen and May (1996) concluded that the Angus Mammoth site is not an archeological site and concur with Wormington that the artifact may have been planted.

The possibility that this artifact was a forgery is supported by the fact that at the time it was reported, all fluted points were considered to be Folsom or Folsom-like. In 1931, possible forgers would probably have assumed that if Folsom-like points were associated with extinct bison, they might also be the type of projectile point associated with mammoths. Recent microscopic analysis of this point (Calvin Howard, personal communication 1998) indicates that the specimen lacks surface characteristics normally found on artifacts that have been buried or exposed on the surface for long periods of time. The weight of evidence suggests that this point may be one of the earliest forgeries of a Paleoindian artifact.

In 1933, Figgins joined Fr. Conrad Bilgery, S.J., a faculty member at Regis College in Denver, in the excavation of mammoth remains that had been exposed by erosion near the Dent train depot north of Denver (Figure 1.6). The year before (1932), Bilgery had recovered a stone projectile point among the mammoth remains, and the following summer another point was found. Figgins realized that the points were larger than the points that had been found at Folsom, the workmanship was not as refined, and they were fluted somewhat differently (Figgins 1933).

Although Dent was the first well-documented discovery of tools associated with mammoth remains in North America, the excavators were apparently reluctant to provide a type site designation for Dent, as had been done for Folsom.

Figure 1.6 F. Howarth excavating at the Dent mammoth site, Dent, Colorado, 1932. (Denver Museum of Natural History Photo Archives.)

Only two projectile points were found during excavation (one of which was subsequently lost), and a third point that was found at the site in 1932 but not reported until 1955 (Wormington 1957:44). There was also uncertainty whether the boulders, the mammoth bones, and the artifacts found at the site had been redeposited. Had researchers been confident enough of the discovery and aware that the artifacts were significantly different in age and technology than Folsom, Dent may have been the type site for what subsequently became known as the Clovis complex (Cassells 1997:64).

In the summer of 1932, A. W. Anderson, a resident of Clovis, New Mexico, showed archeologist E. B. Howard a Folsom point he had found at Blackwater Draw, located approximately 22.5 km (14 mi) southwest of Clovis near the Texas–New Mexico border (Hester 1972). Howard briefly investigated the site and planned to return the following summer. Before he returned from the University Museum in Philadelphia, the New Mexico State Highway and Transportation Department used the area as a barrow pit to supply sand and gravel for road construction. The Highway Department excavations soon uncovered artifacts and the bones of extinct Ice Age animals including mammoth, bison, camel, and horse (Hester 1972:3).

Howard returned to the site the following summer to investigate the gravel pit and nearby blowouts. In 1934, along with geologist Ernst Antevs, Howard focused excavations on the gravel pit (Antevs 1936; Hester 1972; Howard 1935).

Little archeological field research was undertaken in 1935, but in 1936 and 1937, Cotter served as field director for Howard. It was during this period that Cotter (1937, 1938) was able to make the first clear distinction between Clovis and Folsom projectile points based on typological differences. From field observations, Cotter (1938:117) reported that the Clovis points were associated with mammoth bones and were stratigraphically superimposed by typologically distinct Folsom points found with bison bones.

The 1920s and 1930s were exciting times for North American archeology. Not only were chronological barriers crumbling, but the human associations with the magnificent Pleistocene megafauna were also firmly established. In addition to the projectile points and other lithic artifacts, Cotter reported two cylindrical bone tools that had been beveled at the end. Characteristic Clovis projectile points, bone shafts (believed by archeologists to be foreshafts), beveled-based bone points, and scrapers were recognized as important artifacts associated with Clovis sites. Earl Green (1963) added blades (long, thin parallel-sided stone flakes struck from prepared stone cores) to the Clovis tool kit. This suite of artifacts has become the hallmark of Clovis technology. Blackwater Draw Locality 1 became recognized as the type site for the Clovis complex. Later radiocarbon dating demonstrated that Clovis people occupied the western Great Plains from circa 11,500–11,000 B.P., and Folsom sites were dated between circa 11,000–10,000 B.P. (Haynes 1964).

Following the pioneering breakthroughs of the 1920s and 1930s, Roberts (1940) introduced the term Paleoindian to North American archeology. He used Paleoindian in referring to sites containing the remains of extinct Ice Age animals found in association with artifacts and cultures adapted to conditions unlike those that exist today (Roberts 1940:54). However, the term did not get broad application until 1957 when it was used by Wormington in the fourth edition of her book *Ancient Man in North America* (Holliday and Anderson 1993: 80; Wormington 1957).

A symposium to address problems of archeological terminology and chronological distinctions was held in 1941 in Santa Fe, New Mexico. As a result of this meeting, Clovis and Folsom were defined as types. The group also attempted to grapple with the problems created by the growing number of unfluted lanceolate projectile points found throughout the West that were being lumped under the catchall term Yuma (Holliday and Anderson 1993; Howard 1943; Krieger 1947; Wormington 1948, 1957).

These pioneering efforts established a sequence of cultural succession on the Great Plains and set the stage for the introduction of radiocarbon dating. Radiocarbon dating was developed during World War II by Willard Libby as a result of wartime research on cosmic radiation. He published the first radiocarbon dates in 1949. Archeologists were now armed with a new and powerful dating technique to more firmly order the sequence of cultural development in North America.

Scientists understand that when a previously undocumented archeological culture is first discovered, the discovery in all probability does not represent the earliest or latest occurrence of that culture. Over time, additional research will establish temporal and geographic parameters for particular types of artifacts and the way of life associated with them. Once a temporal barrier in archeology is broken, similar discoveries that conform to the type site are more readily accepted. The age and geographic distribution of both Clovis and Folsom cultures have been defined, tested, and confirmed, and archeologists no longer demand the level of proof required of the original discoveries. However, archeologists continue to ask: Where did these early people come from? They did not just appear spontaneously, and researchers have continually looked northward toward Alaska and eastern Beringia for the answer.

Incorporating new discoveries with the existing body of knowledge was desperately needed. In 1933, the eminent Canadian archeologist Diamond Jenness (1933) organized a symposium that was held in Canada in conjunction with the Fifth Pacific Science Congress. Scholars synthesized the state of research from their respective disciplines and applied that knowledge to develop insights regarding the antiquity and origins of humans in the Americas. The resultant interdisciplinary volume, *The American Aborigines: Their Origin and Antiquity*, established the paradigm for the first colonization of the Americas that would persist for the next sixty years. It also created a format used repeatedly by subsequent generations of interdisciplinary scholars sharing data and perspectives from their respective fields in an attempt to address these questions.

It was at this symposium that W. A. Johnston, a geologist with the Geological Survey of Canada, outlined Pleistocene glacial and sea level relationships and how they resulted in the emergence and submergence of the Bering Land Bridge. He postulated that humans could have moved through Canada into southern regions of the Americas during interglacials, times during which the continental glaciers had melted. He thought that people were probably prevented from doing so during glacial periods. He also cautiously introduced the concept of a possible ice-free corridor between eastern Beringia and the more southern regions of North America during the last glacial period, the Wisconsin. This concept was important to those who thought humans may have entered the southern regions of the Americas prior to the end of the last Ice Age. It is also important to mention that Johnson (1933:14–15) perpetuated the assumption of Ernst Antevs (1929) that glacial ice had extended to the Pacific and Atlantic Oceans. This excluded the possibility of human movement along the coasts of North America either via the North Atlantic or along the North Pacific rim.

At the 1933 symposium, Alfred S. Romer, a leading vertebrate paleontologist, examined the evidence suggesting the association of artifacts and extinct Ice Age animals and concluded that the association at several localities, including the finds at Folsom, were valid (Romer 1933). However, he recognized the possibility that many of these species may have survived until the end, and possibly after the end, of the last Ice Age. He concluded that there was no compelling evidence for humans in the Americas until the end of the last Ice Age. Nels Nelson (1933), an archeologist with the American Museum of Natural History, examined a broad array of archeological evidence including paleontology, depth of archeological deposits and their geological context, artifact typology, human physical characteristics, and cultural traits from both the Old and the New Worlds. He concluded that humans had not reached the American continents until the end of the last Ice Age, possibly sometime between 5,000–10,000 years ago. Other contributions on the topic were offered by the leading anthropologists of the day including Franz Boas, Roland B. Dixon, E. A. Hooton, Erland Nordenskiold, Herbert J. Spinden, and Clark Wissler. However, it was clear that the answers to the origin and antiquity of humans in the Americas would have to come from additional archeological and geological research.

While exciting developments were taking place in the western United States, discoveries also were being made in Alaska. In 1933, unusual artifacts turned up on the campus of the University of Alaska in Fairbanks. In 1934, some of these specimens were sent to Nels Nelson at the American Museum of Natural History in New York. Nelson immediately recognized the distinctive core and blade technology that was "identical in several respects" with specimens from the Gobi Desert that had been collected by the Central Asiatic Expedition in 1924–1928. Nelson realized that the specimens were technologically related to similar paleolithic specimens from Eurasia and were evidence of an early migration from Eurasia to the American continent (Nelson 1935, 1937). His observations provided the first objective archeological evidence to support the Bering Land Bridge hypothesis for the colonization of the Americas from Eurasia (Mobley 1991; Nelson 1935).

Also in the 1930s, artifacts and the remains of extinct Ice Age animals were reported by miners working in the Fairbanks area (Rainey 1939). They were discovered as massive deposits of overburden were removed in order to expose underlying gold bearing gravels (see Chapter 3). In several cases, the artifacts appeared to be associated with the remains of mammoth, horse, and bison. Many of the bones of these extinct animals appeared to have been broken and otherwise modified by humans. However, like the very early discoveries to the south, these locales were not observed and documented in situ by trained professionals.

These early Alaskan discoveries tended to support the Bering Land Bridge migration hypothesis and the idea that humans and Ice Age animals were contemporaneous in Alaska. These concepts were further reinforced in 1948 when

R. W. Thompson reported finding a fluted projectile point in northern Alaska (Thompson 1948). The specimen was similar in form to the Clovis and Folsom points reported from the Great Plains. This and subsequent discoveries of similar points led to speculation that Ice Age hunters using fluted (or similar) projectile points crossed the Bering Land Bridge from Eurasia on their way to colonizing the Americas. This concept was supported by the fact that Upper Paleolithic sites in Eurasia documented hunting of Pleistocene animals, including mammoths, and that these sites were similar in many respects to Clovis sites in North America.

However, it was unclear how the fluted points reported throughout northern Alaska and Canada were related to the distinctive core and blade technology originally identified by Nelson. The core and blade assemblages proved difficult to date, and it was not until the 1960s and 1970s that the age of these sites began to be understood (Dixon 1985; Giddings 1964, 1967; West 1967, 1975). The northern core and blade sites turned out to be younger than the Clovis sites to the south. To make things even more confusing, the archeological sites where the northern fluted points had been found could not be reliably dated.

Retrospectively, it might be fair to state that the conflict pitting Hrdlička and Holmes against those who believed that humans had arrived in the Americas much earlier has been somewhat overemphasized by later historians. Holmes and Hrdlička were countering exaggerated claims of antiquity for archeological discoveries in the Americas based on comparisons of gross similarity to artifacts found in Europe during the 1800s. For example, Charles Abbott (1876, 1883, 1889, 1892) had found artifacts in glacial gravels near Trenton, New Jersey. He believed the artifacts were virtually identical to the Paleolithic hand axes being found in Europe that dated to the Pleistocene. This led to a brief but widespread belief among archeologists and geologists in an American Paleolithic period comparable in age to the European Paleolithic (Meltzer 1991:15).

However, the antiquity of the "American Paleolithic" artifacts was not evident by their geologic context. Holmes (1890, 1892, 1893) subsequently refuted the concept that the artifacts from the Trenton gravels were Pleistocene in age. He demonstrated that although superficially they appeared to be similar to European specimens, they were much younger and only appeared crude (i.e., ancient) because they were unfinished or rejected during manufacture. Holmes successfully demonstrated that crudeness did not necessarily equal oldness, and artifacts could not be cross dated across vast areas based merely upon superficial physical similarities.

Scholars from different disciplines were approaching the problem from different perspectives. As a physical anthropologist, Hrdlička (1912, 1925, 1937) recognized that all human remains discovered in the Americas were those of modern humans. He could find no physical anthropological evidence indicating an earlier human form, such as Neanderthal found in Europe. Both Holmes and Hrdlička insisted on greater scientific rigor in demonstrating the nature and age of New World archeological remains. In the absence of reliable dating methods, it was extremely difficult for these early researchers to accurately determine the age of New World archeological discoveries, particularly those dating to about 10,000 years ago, the approximate time the last Ice Age came to an end.

Christy Turner (1992:7–8) has emphasized that as early as 1925, Hrdlička wrote that the first human migration to the Americas did not occur prior to about 15,000 years ago because no anatomically "archaic" human remains had been found in the Americas. While it was true that the work of Figgins, Cook, Howard, Cotter, and others had demonstrated that humans and Pleistocene fauna were contemporaneous in North America, it remained for later radiocarbon dating to reveal that these discoveries were restricted to the very end of the last Ice Age, or Pleistocene. Today most taxonomists regard the Ice Age *Bison antiquus* as a slightly larger version of the modern bison (*Bison bison*).

It retrospect, all participants engaged in the debate over the antiquity of humans in the Americas were correct based on the evidence each brought to the problem. Each scientist approached the issue using the tools and evidence derived from their respective disciplines and experiences. The major problems were that the Pleistocene was undated and that the early evidence of humans in the Americas turned out to have occurred at the very last dying gasp of the last Ice Age. This was the time when many Pleistocene animals, such as the mammoth, were becoming extinct.

If there were excesses on the part of the those, such as Hrdlička, who could not find evidence to support an American Paleolithic, there were also excesses on the part of those who took credit for breaking the barrier. For example, in January 1935, Figgins (1935) received a fragmented human skull and other human skeletal parts from J. C. McKinley of Branson, Colorado. Figgins believed the preservation of the human remains was similar to that of the bison bones found at Folsom and the mammoth bones found at Dent (Figgins 1935:1), thereby suggesting that the human bones and the bones of the extinct animals were probably the same age. Subsequent field investigation of the site where the human remains were found led Figgins to tentatively correlate their stratigraphic position to the finds at Folsom (Figgins 1935:2). He was so convinced of the antiquity of this discovery that he was willing to introduce a new species of *Homo* into the literature that he named *Homo novusmundus* sp., or New World Man, based on analysis of the published photographs that he acknowledged "fail to reveal the rugosity . . . of the skull" (Figgins 1935:3). The reconstruction of the *novusmundus* skull and its description exaggerated the individual's "archaic" attributes. Retrospectively, Figgins wanted a fossil "archaic" human to correspond in age to the fossil bison at Folsom. Given our knowledge of the range of variation among modern humans, *novusmundus* is clearly a modern human, *Homo sapiens*.

The scope of the earliest archeology in North America has expanded to include a wide variety of topics and an array of researchers based in many different institutions (Figure 1.7). Although research has continued to refine chronology building and dating, the early archeology of western North America is addressing research topics such as the relationships between cultural and environmental change, lithic sourcing and analysis, subsistence studies, social organization, ritual and belief systems, and many other fascinating subjects.

The years following the Second World War have also been a time of synthesis. In 1952, E. H. Sellards published his work *Early Man in America* and introduced the term Llano complex (after the Llano Estacado, or Staked Plains of Texas and New Mexico) to encompass fluted projectile points and other Paleoindian artifact assemblages (Sellards 1952). In 1957, Marie Wormington completed the fourth edition of her classic work, *Ancient Man in North America*, which was most recently reprinted in 1964 (Wormington 1957). Wormington's

Figure 1.7 Prominent researchers of western Paleoindian archeology on a field trip at the Clovis type site, 1986. *From left to right*: Harold Malde, Glenn Evans, Eileen Johnson, George Agogino, Dennis Stanford, Grayson Mead, Vance Haynes, and Vance Holliday.

work was extremely influential because it provided the most comprehensive review of the early archeology of North America. Through the various editions, she developed the northern Great Plains typology for sites younger than Folsom that were characterized by lanceolate projectile points.

Progress toward synthesis was somewhat slower in Canada and Alaska. It wasn't until 1967 that David M. Hopkins of the Alaska Branch of the U. S. Geological Survey coordinated and edited *The Bering Land Bridge*, the first broad synthesis of the early archeology and paleoecology of eastern Eurasia, Alaska, and northwestern Canada (Hopkins 1967). These pioneering works have been augmented by single authored works, such as George Frison's *Prehistoric Hunters of the High Plains* (1978, 1991), and by numerous edited volumes with contributions by leading researchers presenting new discoveries and insights into the nature of the early archeology and environments of western North America. Growing national interest in the earliest archeology of the Americas led to the establishment of a Paleoindian research program at the Smithsonian Institution under the direction of Dennis J. Stanford in 1972.

One of the most controversial issues in North American archeology is the time when humans first colonized the Americas. This issue focuses on evidence from a variety of archeological sites that tend to confirm human occupation of the Americas prior to 11,500 B.P. The term pre-Clovis has been widely used by North American archeologists when discussing sites that are older than circa 11,500 B.P. However, Meltzer (1989) suggests the term pre-Clovis is inappropriate, because it implies a historical connection between Clovis people and cultural groups that may be older than Clovis.

No clear professional consensus exists regarding the validity of pre-11,500 B.P. human occupation in North America or the first human colonization of the Americas. Many archeologists are intellectually open to a wide array of possibilities but regard much of the evidence presented for many pre-11,500 B.P. archeological sites as equivocal. The rigorous criteria for proof demanded by Hrdlička and met by Figgins and others provided the foundation for developing criteria necessary to evaluate claims of pre-11,500 B.P. occupation of the Americas. Although these criteria are perhaps more rigorously adhered to in North America than in other parts of the world, they are widely employed to evaluate New World archeological sites suggested to be older than circa 11,500 B.P. These criteria have probably been best expressed by C. Vance Haynes (1969:714) when he defines what must constitute acceptable scientific evidence for human presence in an archeological context:

> For establishing man's presence, the minimum requirements met for the Folsom site still apply for future excavations. The primary requirement is a human skeleton, or an assemblage of artifacts that are clearly the work of

man. Next, this evidence must lie in situ within undisturbed geological deposits in order to clearly demonstrate the primary association of artifacts with stratigraphy. Lastly, the minimum age of the site must be demonstrable by primary association with fossils of known age or with material suitable for reliable isotopic age dating. [Haynes 1969:714]

The primary requirement is human skeletal remains, or an assemblage of artifacts that are clearly the work of humans. Next, this evidence must be in situ within undisturbed geological deposits in order to clearly demonstrate the primary association of artifacts with stratigraphy. Lastly, the minimum age of the site must be demonstrable by primary association with fossils of known age or with material suitable for reliable isotopic age dating. These same criteria for proof of pre-11,500 B.P. age sites have been proposed and endorsed by other researchers (Griffin 1979; Jennings 1978a; Stanford 1979c).

Because of the difference in historical development between New World and Old World archeology, there exist important differences in evaluating evidence from these two areas. Hammer stones, flakes, pebble tools, and other simple stone artifacts that may be commonly accepted by Old World archeologists as artifacts characteristic of the Paleolithic and dating to the Pleistocene are frequently rejected as Ice Age artifacts by North American archeologists. If they have been found out of context in the Americas, the artifacts might be regarded as noncultural in origin or as simple tools possibly made by later (post-Pleistocene) people.

The uniquely North American set of historical events and the intellectual polarization that has surrounded the earliest archeology of the Americas have led to a somewhat unique American view of Pleistocene archeology. When evaluating the time of entry of humans into the Americas, it is reasonable to assume that the absence of archeological evidence probably means the absence of people. Conversely, the earliest archeological sites should indicate the time of colonization. While on the surface this seems to be very simple and straightforward, it is a difficult and complex problem. Consequently, North American archeologists have adopted a rigorous set of criteria for accepting or rejecting archeological sites and artifacts that are alleged to be older than 11,500 B.P. In the absence of datable human remains, the debate over whether or not pre-11,500 B.P. sites exist in the Americas revolves around two fundamental issues: (1) distinguishing between objects that have been modified by humans and objects that have been modified by other processes, and (2) establishing the correct age of archeological sites and artifacts.

The answer to the simple questions of when and how did humans first arrive in the Americas requires knowledge of complex and sometimes conflicting information. Any discussion of pre-11,500 B.P. sites in the Americas must take into consideration the manner in which people may have been able to come to the Americas. This requires knowledge of many subjects, including technological and cultural development in adjacent parts of the world, the geology and paleo-ecology of Beringia, and the history of North American glaciation before, during, and after the last Ice Age.

2 The First Colonization of North America

Origins

The human colonization of the Americas was the final continental dispersal of the human species on earth. This epic in human history required specific types of adaptation to enable humans to move through the high-latitude environments of northeastern Asia into North America. Social and ecological factors were involved that influenced the character and timing of this great event.

Humans evolved in the Old World beginning in Africa, and subsequently colonized Asia and Europe. Many archeologists believe that the first humans to enter the Americas came from northeastern Asia about 12,000 years ago. However, this is not the only possible time for humans to have reached the New World. Some archeologists (Carter 1952, 1957; Irving et al. 1986; Jopling et al. 1981; Simpson et al. 1986; and others) believe humans may have come to the Americas 150,000–200,000 years ago. Still others (Griffin 1979; Haynes 1969; Hrdlička 1928; and others) are of the opinion that humans first arrived in the Americas within the last 50,000 years or more likely within the last 14,000 years. At least one linguist (Nichols 1990) suggests that the Americas may have been inhabited possibly as early as 35,000 years ago.

Biological and Linguistic Evidence

While archeologists attempt to understand and interpret this complex problem based on the artifacts they find buried in the earth, biological anthropologists approach questions of cultural origins by comparing the similarities and differences of physical characteristics between groups of people. Some of these characteristics are obvious traits, such as skin, hair, and eye color. Other characteristics are far more subtle, such as the shape of teeth or very specific genetic markers of populations revealed only by sophisticated analysis of deoxyribonucleic acid (DNA).

Language also has been used as a means to compare the relationships between people. Most people are identified with a specific cultural group based on the language they speak. By comparing how similar, or dissimilar, languages are to one another, linguists assume varying degrees of historic relationship between groups of people.

These two fields of inquiry, linguistics and biological anthropology, demonstrate that ancestors of living Native Americans most likely came to the Americas from northeastern Asia. For example, Christy Turner (1983) has studied the dentition of prehistoric and living Native Americans and northeast Asians. Based on about twenty dental traits, such as the shape of tooth crowns and the number of tooth roots, he has defined an overall dental pattern that he calls "Sinodonty." This pattern includes three-rooted lower first molars and "shovel shaped" incisors (Figure 2.1). This distinctive dental pattern is shared among most Native Americans and people from northeastern Asia. However, Sinodonty is not found in people who originated in southern Asia, Africa, or Europe. Another less complex dental pattern called Sundadonty is shared among the people of Southeast Asia and is also found in prehistoric American populations. Turner (1992:6) concluded that because less dental evolution has occurred in the Americas, the New World has been occupied for less time than Asia. Turner be-

Figure 2.1 Line drawing of a human three-rooted lower first molar compared to a human two-rooted lower first molar and a shovel shaped incisor compared to a non-shovel shaped incisor (Redrawn from Turner [1983:148]. Graphic by Eric Parrish.)

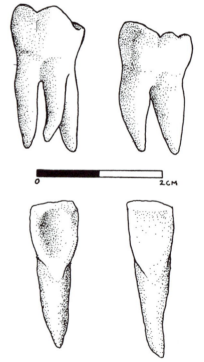

lieves that widespread Sinodonty demonstrates a northeast Asian origin for most Native Americans.

Turner (1983, 1985, 1992) recognizes three major subdivisions of Sinodonty based on the dental characteristics of Native Americans. He proposes that colonization of the Americas occurred in three distinct migrations. The first migration according to Turner included ancestors of the people of South America and southern North America. The second migration included the ancestors of Native Americans residing in interior Alaska and along the Northwest Coast of North America. The third migration included the Aleut-Eskimo who occupy the coastal fringes of Alaska. Some genetic research (Williams et al. 1985) may support Turner's "three-wave" model for human migration to the Americas.

These data appear to correspond with linguistic data compiled by Greenberg (Greenberg 1987; Greenberg et al. 1986). By applying a process called mass comparison, he lumped Native American languages into three groups called Amerind, Na-dene, and Eskimo-Aleut. The linguistic data appears to correlate well with the dental evidence. This could lead to the conclusion that the first "wave" of migrants included the ancestors of the Amerinds, the second "wave" included the ancestors of the Na-dene, and the last "wave" to immigrate to the New World included the Eskimo-Aleut (Greenberg et al. 1986). This three-migration theory based on linguistic evidence has been revised to indicate that there were a minimum of three, and possibly more, migrations (Greenberg 1996:529).

Another hypothesis suggests that the glacial barriers could possibly explain the three postulated linguistic and biological groups (Rogers 1985a; Rogers et al. 1991). If humans already occupied the Americas at the onset of the last glacial, they may have been isolated into three ice-free refugia, one in eastern Beringia, another along the Northwest Coast, and a third south of the continental ice. This hypothesis suggests that the observed differences in dental traits and languages could result from isolation rather than migration.

Other researchers have begun to study DNA, the genetic material that contains the "code" outlining the physical composition of every individual. Genes are composed of DNA and carry the hereditary characteristics required to create various forms of life and to define specific individuals. There are two types of DNA: nuclear and mitochondrial. Mitochondria are contained within each cell for the purpose of providing energy for metabolism. Mitochondrial DNA (mtDNA) is more abundant and less complex than nuclear DNA and is passed from one generation to the next through the maternal line (Giles et al. 1980). Because it is transmitted to a child from the mother, scientists can compare similarities between mtDNA from various populations and identify groups of people who share a common lineage through their maternal ancestors.

In analyzing mtDNA from Native Americans, Schurr et al. (1990) recognized four basic mtDNA lineages, or haplogroups, that they labeled A, B, C, and D. The fact that only four lineages could be identified suggests that the founding populations may have been very small. All four lineages occur in all Native American populations and have been identified in ancient human remains (Kaestle 1997). However, it is not clear how this information can be properly interpreted. Based on mtDNA analysis, Torroni et al. (1992) conclude that Amerind and Na-dene populations were founded by two separate migrations. However, research by Horai et al. (1996) draws the conclusion that the four lineages, or clusters, are evidence of four distinctive ancestral populations that migrated to the Americas gradually in different "waves." Because all four founding lineages are found in all Native American populations, Merriwether et al. (1995) reason that this is best explained by a single migration and that all four lineages are derived from the original founding population. Other researchers (Bailliet et al. 1994; Lorenz and Smith 1996) report evidence suggesting there may have been at least one more haplogroup in Native American populations prior to contact with Europeans. This haplogroup has been designated lineage X, which is rare and has only been found in Europe and Asia Minor and is not reported from Asia (Morell 1998). Emőke Szathmáry (1996:160) states that it is impossible to determine whether a haplotype results from mutation or migration, thus rendering these types of analysis inconclusive. However, she (Szathmáry 1996) suggests that the biological data may best fit a single migration of people from Asia who were subsequently isolated into northern and southern groups by continental glaciation. These data indicate there is no consensus among researchers and that colonization of the Americas may have been a complex process. It possibly included some influences from Europe or possibly from early people that shared some European characteristics and who may have entered the Americas via Asia.

Although the conclusions drawn from genetic research are controversial, analysis of mtDNA raises serious challenges that question the "three-wave" migration model based on the analysis of contemporary languages and prehistoric dental traits. Archeologists have long recognized the great difficulty in recognizing genetic, ethnic, and linguistic "signatures" in the archeological record. Although much work remains to be done, it is clear that to establish migration of people, it is necessary to document a culture in one region and subsequently document it in another. To do this, it is necessary to identify material traits that can be reliably attributed to a specific culture. The early archeology of eastern Beringia and North America is so poorly understood that it is impossible to describe these cultures except at general levels of comparison.

Linking language to specific genetic or technological traits is difficult and probably misleading. The use of language and technology are learned, while genetic traits are biologically inherited. There are a number of ways by which one language might be abandoned and another adopted. For example, one method might be the acceptance of a trading language, or "lingua franca," that gradually becomes widespread throughout a region, ultimately replacing the local languages. Another mechanism might be what is known as "elite dominance," whereby a group in power imposes their language on others causing local languages to be replaced by the language of the dominant elite culture. To determine if these linguistic concepts are applicable in explaining cultural interactions during the late Pleistocene is difficult. Greenberg (1996:529) acknowledges that if New World immigrants left no linguistic relatives in their homeland and died out in the Americas, there would be no linguistic evidence of their presence in the Americas. It is quite possible that groups, particularly if they were small, speaking a particular language or dialect may have simply died off and consequently there might be no linguistic connection between America's earliest colonists and contemporary Native Americans.

Archeological Evidence

From an archeological perspective, the problem becomes even more complex. Toth (1991:55) has suggested that if we assume a model for the colonization of the Americas that uses an ever-increasing population over time, the odds of documenting the very earliest evidence of human occupation are very slim. Furthermore, there is no need to think of human migration as a specific event. Humans may have populated the Americas in small numbers, or migratory "dribbles," over long periods of time (Meltzer 1989). Some migrations may have been successful, and others may not have been. Some of these small groups of early migrants could have been genetically swamped by later groups, exterminated by warfare, or eliminated by the introduction of disease. Groups may have been too small to be viable, or may have died out because they were unable to adapt to new environments.

If the earliest immigrants were few in number and used artifacts primarily manufactured from perishable organic material that survived for only a short time, the evidence of their presence would be extremely difficult to detect in the archeological record. This would be even more difficult if these early people lacked what archeologists consider to be diagnostic artifact types, such as fluted stone projectile points. There would be no genetic or linguistic evidence among modern Native Americans if the colonists did not survive. As a result, a continuous archeological record may not exist from the Ice Ages to later, well-documented North American archeological sites. It is possible that sporadic colonization events occurred that are not reflected in the subsequent development of New World archeology. Thus, tracing the migration of specific groups of people is extremely difficult in the archeological record.

The Bering Land Bridge

The concept of a land connection between Asia and North America is deeply rooted in American science. In 1589, Fray de Acosta (1604) first suggested a land connection as an explanation of how humans and some plants and animals may have first entered North America from Asia. He suggested that there was, or had been at some time in the past, a land bridge between Asia and North America in the high northern latitudes. The reason he held this premise was that he believed that the human species had originated in the Old World based on the teachings of the Bible. He fully accepted that all humans had descended from Adam and Eve and that they had been created in the Old World. He reasoned further that early humans and many of the animals found in the New World were not capable of crossing the vast expanses of oceans. Consequently, humans and some types of animals could have only reached the Americas via a land connection with the Old World. He lacked firm scientific evidence for his hypothesis and relied on the Judeo-Christian doctrine of his time as the foundation for this interpretation.

Although subsequent scientific discoveries have demonstrated that the human species did originate in the Old World and developed over a period of almost four million years, this evidence was not available to de Acosta. Since de Acosta's time, the concept of the Bering Land Bridge has been invoked repeatedly over hundreds of years to explain the human migration route to the Americas. It has become deeply imbedded in New World scholarship and has been bolstered by a vast amount of scientific research.

In 1728, Vitus Bering established that there was not a land connection between North America and Asia. It was later realized (Dawson 1894) that the Bering and Chukchi Seas were relatively shallow and that the continental shelf stretching between Siberia and Alaska was exposed as dry land at various times during the Pleistocene when the sea level was lower (Figure 2.2). By 1933, enough data had been compiled for Johnston (1933:31–32) to use estimates of a lower sea level to demonstrate that a land bridge existed between Asia and North America during the last glaciation. As the melting continental glaciers discharged their stored water into the oceans, the sea level rose, flooding the Bering Land Bridge and establishing the Bering Strait that separates North America and Asia. By 1967, enough geologic evidence had accumulated to enable Hopkins (1967:464–465) to speculate that the Bering Land Bridge was inundated by the rising sea level for the last time sometime shortly after 10,000 years ago. Hopkins (1973, 1979, 1982) revised his estimates of the sea level history of Beringia and suggested the final inundation of the Bering Land Bridge occurred sometime shortly after 14,000 years ago (Hopkins 1982).

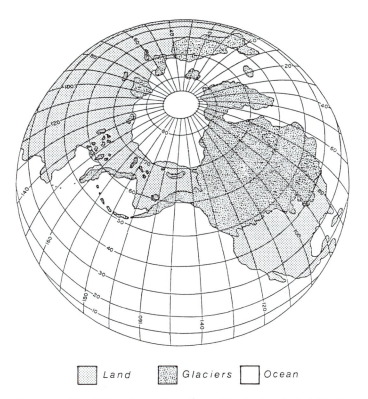

| | Land | | Glaciers | | Ocean |

Figure 2.2 North America and northeast Asia during the height of the Wisconsin glaciation (from Dixon 1993:5).

Direct evidence that proves the existence of the former land bridge has been discovered in recent years. The remains of extinct animals have been dredged from the ocean floor (Dixon 1983). In addition, ancient river channels that could only have formed by water flowing across the surface of the land have been documented on the sea floor (McManus et al. 1983). Cores taken from the sediments beneath the Bering and Chukchi Seas contain deposits, such as peat, that could only have been formed when the continental shelf was exposed as dry land (Elias et al. 1992; Hopkins 1967; McManus et al. 1983). Radiocarbon dating of beetles that had to have lived in a subaerial environment were recovered from sediment cores from the Bering Land Bridge. This led Hopkins to revise his 14,000 B.P. estimate and demonstrated that the land bridge was not flooded until sometime shortly after 10,000 years ago (Elias et al. 1996) (Figure 2.3).

The broad land connection between Alaska and Asia came into existence and disappeared during the Ice Age, or Pleistocene. During the Pleistocene, vast amounts of snow fell on the continents. The snow was derived from water evap-

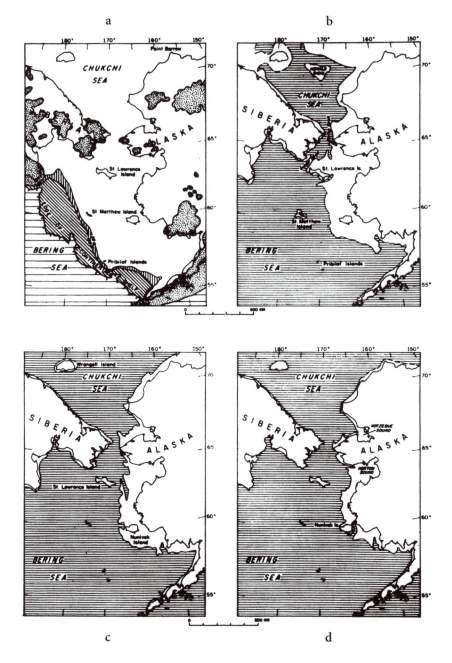

Figure 2.3 Sequence of sea level rise in the Bering Sea area. (a) The Bering Land Bridge at the height of the last glaciation circa 18,000 B.P.; (b) partition of the land bridge, shortly after 10,000 B.P. (c, d) stages of Holocene sea level rise in Bering Strait, at minus 38 meters and minus 30 meters respectively. (Hopkins 1973:524, reproduced with permission of *Quaternary Research* and the author.)

orating from the oceans. This caused the sea level around the world to drop almost 200 m (650 ft). The snow gradually became glacial ice in the northern regions of the northern hemisphere and at high elevations in the southern hemisphere. When the continental glaciers melted due to the warmer climate at the end of the Ice Age, the water was transported back to the oceans by the earth's rivers and calving glaciers. This caused the sea level to rise.

For some people, the thought of the Bering Land Bridge conjures up a vision of a narrow strip of land connecting Alaska and Siberia in the area that is now the Bering Strait. However, the Bering Land Bridge was a vast region of low topography stretching between North America and Asia. At the height of the last Ice Age, it was more than 1,000 km (620 mi) wide from north to south. A few mountains, which are today islands in the Bering Sea, were widely spaced across the land and rose abruptly above the flat landscape.

The land bridge and adjacent areas of North America and Asia form a geographic area called Beringia. This region has been divided further into two provinces: western Beringia and eastern Beringia. Western Beringia is situated in Asia extending eastward from the Verkhoyansk Range to the Bering Strait. When scientists speak of eastern Beringia, they are referring to the region that is today Alaska and adjacent areas of Canada that were not covered by the massive continental glaciers. Eastern Beringia was not covered by glacial ice during the Pleistocene probably due to low precipitation.

Approximately 18,000 years ago, most of the continental shelf was exposed as dry land. This occurred during the height of the last major glaciation, called the Wisconsin, after the state where it was first clearly identified and described. At the close of the Wisconsin, beginning about 14,000 years ago, sea level began to rise and the configuration and size of the Bering Land Bridge began to change dramatically (see Figure 2.2). The most recent evidence from sediment cores from the Bering continental shelf indicates the land connection between Alaska and Siberia was severed for the last time by approximately 10,000 B.P. (Bobrowsky et al. 1990; Elias et al. 1992).

David M. Hopkins (1982), the leading international expert on the history of the Bering Land Bridge, has named the interval between 14,000–8,500 B.P. the Birch Interval, because of the high percentage of birch pollen found in sediment cores. Prior to the Birch Interval, the environment probably was dryer and grassier, with tundra plants. Different environmental zones probably existed in different areas depending on elevation, effective moisture, temperature, and shelter (Schweger 1982). It was also cooler than today with less vegetative cover and windswept with sand dunes forming in some areas. The Birch Interval (14,000–8,500 B.P.) marks a period of dramatic climatic change that irreversibly altered the geography and environment of eastern Beringia. Continental glaciers receded rapidly and the sea level rose, covering the Bering Land Bridge for the last time. During the Birch Interval, the unique and complex environment of the last Ice Age was replaced by a predominantly shrub tundra dominated by dwarf birch.

The climate and environment during the Birch Interval were different than Alaska's modern climate and environment. Eastern Beringian pollen cores have been interpreted (Ager and Brubaker 1985; Barnosky et al. 1987; Ritchie 1984; Ritchie et al. 1983) to demonstrate that *Populous* spp. predominates in the pollen record between 11,000–9,000 with spruce (*Picea* spp.) becoming common by 9,000 B.P. The rise of *Populous* spp. is interpreted to indicate warmer summer temperatures (Edwards and Dunwiddie 1985; Lev 1987), and the beginning of peatlands formation (Hopkins 1982) suggests increased moisture. The sea level continued to rise, and the coastlines of Alaska and northeastern Siberia retreated. The Arctic and Pacific Oceans were connected permitting the exchange of marine species between them. The first firmly documented archeological evidence demonstrating human occupation of eastern Beringia during the Birch Interval appears at several archeological sites in interior Alaska (Powers and Hoffecker 1990).

In eastern Beringia, there exist a series of well-dated sites in Alaska's Nenana and Tanana River Valleys that document human occupation beginning possibly as early as 11,800 B.P. (Hamilton and Goebel 1999; Holmes 1990, 1996; Holmes et al. 1996; Powers and Hoffecker 1989). They are essentially contemporaneous with the earliest well-dated sites in more southern areas of North America characterized by fluted projectile points and frequently associated with the remains of mammoth and other extinct Ice Age animals. The differences between the types of artifacts from these sites and Clovis sites to the south suggest to some archeologists that these early sites are not directly related.

Human Migration Routes

Some archeologists believe southward migration from Beringia into the Americas may have begun as early as 150,000–200,000 years ago, or possibly even earlier (Carter 1952, 1957; Irving et al. 1986; Simpson et al. 1986; and others). Still others are of the opinion that humans first arrived in the Americas within the last 50,000 years and more likely within the last 14,000 years (Griffin 1979; Haynes 1969; Hrdlička 1928; and others). Knut Fladmark (1983) has provided what is probably the most comprehensive review of the possible routes by which humans may have first entered the Americas. Careful review of the paleoenvironmental literature and glacial geology led him to conclude that the two most plausible routes are: (1) the Beringian midcontinental route, and (2) the Beringian northwestern coastal route.

Midcontinental Route

During the last glaciation (the Wisconsin), an enormous glacier called the Laurentide ice sheet formed in eastern Canada. Concurrently, glaciers in the Canadian Rockies began to flow out of the mountains; they coalesced and spread eastward, forming another massive ice sheet called the Cordillera. These massive Laurentide and Cordilleran glaciers expanded until they met in the areas that are today Alberta and northern British Columbia, Canada.

The merged Cordilleran and Laurentide ice would have formed an impenetrable barrier stretching from the Atlantic Ocean to the Pacific Ocean and more than 800 km (500 mi) from eastern Beringia to southern Alberta. For human groups who survived on an economy based on hunting, gathering, and fishing, the massive continental glacier would have presented a lifeless, dangerous, and seemingly endless icescape. Archeologists agree that the merged continental glaciers would have formed a barrier so severe that it would have been impossible for humans to cross it during the late Pleistocene.

The Beringian midcontinental route proposes that people moved south from eastern Beringia through central Canada east of the western mountains. There exist two versions of the midcontinental route. The first and more accepted concept suggests that southward migration could not have begun until the continental glaciers had melted enough to permit people to move southward, sometime between 11,000–12,000 years ago. The other theory suggests an earlier migration through a hypothetical ice-free corridor that some scientists believe may have existed sometime during the last Ice Age. Although little evidence supports this theory, it is popular among some archeologists because some archeological sites in North America that may be more than 12,000 years old.

The concept of an ice-free corridor stretching between eastern Beringia and the unglaciated southern areas of North America was suggested by W. A. Johnston in 1933 and reinforced by geologist Ernst Antevs (1937) and others. The archeological need for such a theory arose because some scholars felt it was necessary to explain the possible evidence for the presence of humans south of the continental ice before the melting of the continental glaciers. The term ice-free corridor is applied to a hypothetical, relatively narrow strip of unglaciated land that was thought to exist between the Laurentide and Cordilleran ice sheets. For many years, researchers agreed that these two ice sheets joined in western Canada; however, some believed that this may have been a very brief event and that the ice soon melted, leaving a relatively narrow strip of unglaciated land between these huge glaciers. It was further theorized that this narrow corridor would have provided an avenue through which plants, animals, and humans could have passed from Beringia into other unglaciated regions of North America. Other species could have moved from south to north through the corridor.

Belief in an ice-free corridor began to crumble when Canadian paleoecologist Glen MacDonald (1987a) demonstrated that some of the most important radiocarbon dates used to support the existence of an ice-free corridor were incorrect. He persuasively argued that an ice-free corridor did not exist until the very end of the Wisconsin glaciation, when the continental ice began its final retreat (MacDonald 1987a, 1987b). Other evidence suggests that even if an ice-free corridor did exist, it would have been inhospitable for human colonization (Burns 1990, 1996; Mandryk 1990).

Geologic research (Jackson et al. 1996, 1997; Leboe 1995) appears to have finally resolved the issue of existence and timing of an ice-free corridor. Passage between Beringia and the unglaciated areas of North America remained blocked until sometime shortly after 11,000 B.P. (Jackson and Duk-Rodkin 1996; Jackson et al. 1996, 1997). Because the earliest Clovis sites are dated between 11,500–11,000 B.P., this late date for the establishment of a deglaciation corridor suggests that Clovis people were south of the continental glaciers prior to the melting of the midcontinental ice.

Glacial erratics are rock fragments carried by glacial ice and deposited some distance from the outcrop where they originated. By tracking the distribution of distinctive quartzite erratics derived from the headwaters of Alberta's Athabaska River, geologists have been able to document the coalescence of the Cordilleran and Laurentide ice over an extensive area in southern Alberta (Jackson et al. 1997). Using a relatively new dating method, called the cosmogenic ^{36}Cl method, Jackson and his colleagues were able to date the time the erratics were deposited. Their research appears to demonstrate that the merged continental glaciers did not melt in southern Alberta until sometime about 11,000–12,000 years ago (Jackson et al. 1997).

The dating of a deglaciation corridor at the end of the last Ice Age is supported by a series of radiocarbon dates on the bones of large mammals found throughout Alberta, Canada. These dates range from about 40,000 years ago (the approximate reliable limit of ^{14}C dating) to about 21,000 B.P. There is a significant gap between 21,000 B.P. and about 11,500 B.P. This gap in the radiocarbon dates indicates that the region was covered by glacial ice during that time. It wasn't until sometime around 11,500–11,000 B.P. that the ice had melted sufficiently to enable animals to reoccupy the region (Burns, 1996).

By about 11,000 B.P., the glaciers had melted enough to form what might be called a deglaciation corridor between the ice sheets. This would have enabled people to move from eastern Beringia southward into the more southern areas of North America (Clague et al. 1989; Jackson et al. 1996b, 1997; Rutter 1984). Conversely, if humans were already south of the continental glaciers, the melting of the ice would have enabled humans to move northward into the region that is now northwestern Canada and Alaska. Scientists agree that as the ice melted, plants, animals, and humans soon colonized the new land. Many archeologists believe that humans first entered the southern areas of North America by gradually moving into and settling the new environment created by the melting ice. This process would have enabled people to move gradually southward to places south of the continental ice.

If this scenario were correct, the North American continent south of eastern Beringia would not have been colonized by humans until sometime after the glaciers had melted enough to permit people and animals to pass between the melting ice sheets, sometime about 11,000 years ago (Figure 2.4). The interior migration route requires an economy based on hunting terrestrial mammals, gathering limited plant products, and probably on freshwater fishing. This type of subsistence adaptation, characteristic of high-latitude environments, would have been an essential factor for colonizing recently deglaciated lands.

Northwest Coast Route

Support is growing for the theory that people using watercraft, possibly skin boats, may have moved southward from Beringia along the Gulf of Alaska and then southward along the Northwest Coast of North America possibly as early as 16,000 years ago. This route would have enabled humans to enter southern areas of the Americas prior to the melting of the continental glaciers.

Until the early 1970s, most archeologists did not consider the coast a possible migration route into the Americas because geologists (Antevs 1929; Coulter et al. 1965; Johnson 1933; Nasmith 1970; Prest 1969) originally believed that during the last Ice Age the entire Northwest Coast was covered by glacial ice. It had been assumed that the ice extended westward from the Alaskan/Canadian mountains to the edge of the continental shelf. This would have created a barrier of ice extending from the Alaskan Peninsula, through the Gulf of Alaska and southward along the Northwest Coast of North America to the area that is today the state of Washington.

The most influential proponent of the coastal migration route has been Canadian archeologist Knut Fladmark (1979, 1986). He theorized that with the use of watercraft, people gradually colonized unglaciated refugia and areas along the continental shelf exposed by the lower sea level. Fladmark's hypothesis received additional support from Ruth Gruhn (1988) and R. A. Rogers (1985b) who pointed out that the greatest diversity in Native American languages occurs along the west coast of the Americas suggesting that this region has been settled the longest.

More recent geologic and paleoecologic studies (Blaise et al. 1990; Bobrowsky et al. 1990; Josenhans et al. 1995, 1997) documented deglaciation and the existence of ice-free areas throughout major coastal areas of British Columbia by 13,000 B.P. Research now indicates that sizable areas of southeastern Alaska along the

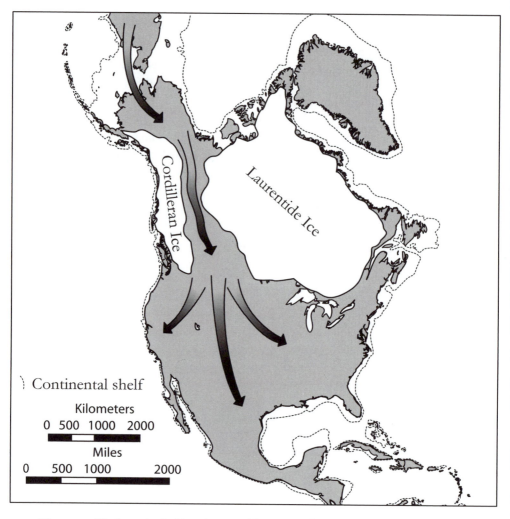

Figure 2.4 The hypothetical interior, or midcontinental, migration route. (Graphic by Eric Parrish.)

inner continental shelf were not covered by ice toward the end of the last Ice Age (Dixon et al. 1997; Heaton 1995, 1996; Heaton and Grady 1993; Heaton et al. 1996). Mann and Peteet (1994) suggest that except for a 400 km (250 mi) coastal area between southwestern British Columbia and Washington state, the Northwest Coast of North America was largely free of ice by approximately 16,000 years ago. Vast areas along the coast may have been deglaciated beginning about 16,000 B.P. possibly providing a coastal corridor for the movement of plants, animals, and humans sometime between 14,000–13,000 B.P. (Josenhans et al. 1997).

The coastal hypothesis has gained increased support in recent years because the remains of large land animals, such as caribou and brown bears, have been found in southeastern Alaska dating between 10,000–12,500 years ago (Heaton and Grady 1993, 1994; Heaton et al. 1996). This is the time period that most scientists formerly believed the area to be inhospitable for humans. It has been suggested that if the environment were capable of supporting breeding populations of bears, there would have been enough food resources to support humans (Dixon 1995). Fladmark (1979, 1983) and others (Dixon 1993; Easton 1992; Gruhn 1988, 1994) believe that the first human colonization of America occurred by boat along the Northwest Coast during the very late Ice Age, possibly as early as 14,000 years ago (Figure 2.5). The most recent geological evidence indicates that it may have been possible for people to colonize ice-free regions along the continental shelf that were still exposed by the lower sea level between 13,000–14,000 years ago.

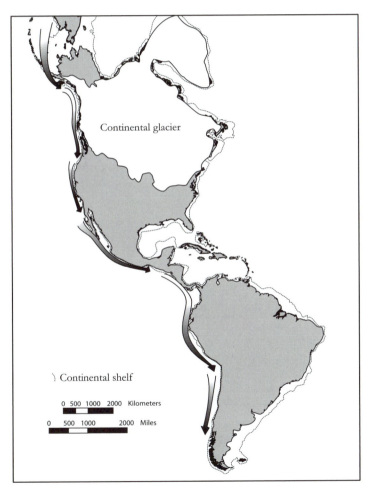

Figure 2.5 The hypothetical coastal migration route (Graphic by Eric Parrish.)

The coastal hypothesis suggests an economy based on marine mammal hunting, saltwater fishing, shellfish gathering, and the use of watercraft. Because of the barrier of ice to the east, the Pacific Ocean to the west, and populated areas to the north, there may have been a greater impetus for people to move in a southerly direction.

Transoceanic voyages across the Atlantic or the Pacific also have been considered as a possible means by which humans may have first colonized the Americas. However, some writers have abused the concept in an attempt to explain cultural traits between the two hemispheres, including similarities in art, pyramid building, and ritual practices. Recent archeological discoveries in Australia and western Polynesia indicate that ocean-going watercraft have been in existence for the past 35,000–40,000 years (Allen et al. 1988, 1989; Jones 1989; Mulvaney 1964; Specht et al. 1981; Wickler and Spriggs 1988) and possibly more than 100,000 years (Fullagar et al. 1996). Although people were to reach the islands of Oceania during mid- to late Holocene times (Gibbons and Clunie 1985; Irwin 1989; Irwin et al. 1990), it has not been demonstrated that humans were capable of making transoceanic crossings while carrying enough people and provisions to make colonization of the Americas possible. While New World archeologists keep their minds open to the possibilities of transoceanic voyages across both the Pacific and Atlantic, currently there is not adequate archeological evidence for watercraft capable of crossing the broad expanses of the oceans during the Pleistocene.

Colonization

During the past few decades, knowledge of world colonization by modern humans has increased at a phenomenal rate. Major advances in paleoenvironmental studies are expanding our understanding and interpretation of paleogeography and past environmental conditions. This new knowledge enables archeologists to view colonization as a larger cultural and biological phenomenon. Identifying and understanding the processes of colonization are important to the disciplines of anthropology and the natural sciences in general. By focusing on the earliest human colonization of the New World, archeologists can provide significant insight into the nature of humans as colonizers, their impact on pristine environments, and the influence of different environments on cultural development.

Aquatic metaphors, such as waves, trickles, dribbles, and drifts, are frequently used to describe the peopling of the Americas. However, these terms tell us little, if anything, about the actual processes of human colonization. Currently very few models for the peopling of the Americas exist. The New World may be viewed as a laboratory where the response of humans to environments that were new to them and the human impact on those environments may be analyzed. For example, some researchers believe that ecological disequilibrium may result in human dispersals and that initial contact between humans and select species of animals may result in their extinction. Paul S. Martin (1967, 1973, 1984) has postulated that the first human hunters to enter the Americas were responsible for the extinction of approximately 70 New World genera, including the large elephant-like mammoth and mastodon, and the horse. According to this scenario, as humans moved into the Americas, they encountered large animals that had developed no effective means of evading intelligent and sophisticated human predators. Theoretically, this enabled humans to quickly hunt these large mammals to extinction. This theory explaining Pleistocene extinctions is called the overkill hypothesis.

J. E. Mossimann and Paul S. Martin (1975) theorized that humans could have colonized both North America and South America in approximately 1,000 years and concurrently killed off the large Pleistocene mammals (Figure 2.6). However, Wormington (1983:192) believed that human colonization of the Americas took much longer than the model proposed by Mossimann and Martin. In her view, early hunters and gathers needed more time to develop familiarity with their environment and its resources, and once they had gained this knowledge, they were reluctant to move. She regarded environmental change and population pressure as the mechanisms causing human groups to move. This type of model requires a much longer time for humans to colonize the American continents than that advocated by Mossimann and Martin.

Robert L. Kelly and Lawrence C. Todd (Kelly 1996; Kelly and Todd 1988) have advanced a variation of Martin's model. They suggest that the first Paleoindians were technologically based foragers. Unlike modern foragers who are geographically based and generally confined by neighboring foraging groups, they suggest that the earliest human groups in North America may have relied more on knowledge of animal behavior and technology rather than knowledge of geography. This may have enabled them to move from region to region exploiting various species, some of which may have been preferred over others. According to Kelly and Todd, such a foraging strategy could result in comparatively rapid human migration and the extinction of select species.

Some scientists (Graham 1990; Guthrie 1990) counter that a dramatic change in climate caused the extinction of Ice Age mammals, while others suggest that a combination of both climatic change and predatory humans were the cause. A third hypothesis suggests that selective extinction resulted from disease introduced by humans, rather than over hunting (MacPhee and Marx 1997a, 1997b). This theory proposes that humans introduced a "hyperdisease" into North America capable of adapting to new hosts, in this case large mammals. Theoretically, this disease swept rapidly though the mammalian population resulting in the extinction

Figure 2.6 The hypothetical "Bow Wave" model for the human colonization of the Americas from North to South (modified from Mossimann and Martin 1975). (Graphic by Eric Parrish.)

of select species. To test this hypothesis, it will be necessary to discover evidence of the pathogen in the remains of the species that date to the time of extinction (MacPhee and Marx 1997a:91).

Martin's overkill hypothesis and data are frequently cited as a historic precedent demonstrating the negative impact of humanity on the natural environment. The hyperdisease theory is also used to support this point of view. However, these hypotheses can only be evaluated scientifically by establishing the chronology for the colonization of the Americas, the time of regional extinction for each species, and the archeological associations between artifacts and the remains of extinct fauna.

In their attempt to model the human colonization of the Americas, Mossiman and Martin (1975) rely heavily of the work of Birdsell (1957) who derived his statistics from his research of human population expansion on uninhabited Pacific islands, specifically Pitcairn, and later Australia (Birdsell 1977). While these data may be correct and useful in the context of the ecology of small islands, John Beaton (1991a) suggests it is not applicable for Australia, a large landmass of continental proportion similar to the Americas. It may be inappropriate to extrapolate to continental land masses the human impact on the environment based on evidence derived from the colonization of a small Pacific island.

Furthermore, it is necessary to emphasizes that the scale of investigative resolution must fit the scale of the problem (Beaton 1991a:220). In other words, at the continental level of analysis, such as the initial peopling of the Americas or Australia, it is more useful to look at large, or macro, environmental zones, such as coastlines. These macroenvironmental zones are what Beaton (1991a) refers to as megapatches. Megapatches are essentially biomes, or large environmental zones or areas, such as coasts, forests, deserts, and mountains. Obviously environmental classification on such a gross scale begs important questions, such as what types of forests.

The problem of explaining New World colonization is continental in proportion, so it must be approached with a large scale of analysis. For example, it is clear from the archeological record that the first Americans must have been hunters and gathers because at the end of the last Ice Age, the earth's human population relied on hunting and gathering as its economic mainstay. Since that time, hunting and gathering has declined, until only a few isolated human groups continue this life style in marginal habitats unsuitable for other economic pursuits. Based on our knowledge of available migration routes, genetics, and language, the first immigrants to the Americas most likely came over the Bering Land Bridge or along its southern coastal margin using some form of watercraft. Hence, knowledge of relatively contemporary northern hunter-gather settlement patterns may provide important insight essential to understand factors that might lead to migration.

Some European and North American archeologists may operate under a set of implicit assumptions that view cultural development as a series of developmental changes leading to increased "cultural progress." According to John Alsoszatai-Petheo (1986), this set of intellectual premises, or paradigm, has prevented North American archeologists from considering that hunters and gatherers view themselves as an integral part of a stable environment. He calls this the Steady-State Ecological Equilibrium paradigm, meaning that hunters and gatherers tend to achieve balance between the development of technology and population density for their specific environment. According to this perspective, many thousands of years prior to the end of the last Ice Age, there could have been an extremely low human population density, and material cultural remains, consisting largely of naturally available materials lacking technological sophistication, could have been readily discarded after use.

A universal aspect of hunters and gatherers is that these societies must maintain a territory, or range, from which the essential resources to sustain life are derived. Frans Boas, the founder of American anthropology, clearly recognized the important role of natural resources in determining human settlement patterns during his field research among the Inuit in the central Canadian Arctic in 1883–1884. He wrote:

> All depends upon the distribution of food at the different seasons. The migrations or accessibility of the game compels the natives to move their habitations from time to time, and hence the distribution of villages depends, to a great extent, upon that of the animals that supply them with food. [Boas 1964:11]

Within each territory, resources are not distributed uniformly. Certain resource concentrations play a more important role in subsistence activities than others. Because the harvest of these resources is essential for human survival, their distribution and the timing of harvesting them result in concentrations of human populations. Furthermore, collective efforts enable hunter-gatherers to maximize their harvests. For example, Robert McKennan (1969) analyzed the ecological basis for Northern Athapaskan band composition and identified two major technological devices that required collective effort to harvest large numbers of animals: the fish weir and the caribou fence. As a result of these cooperative activities, an economic surplus was generated that facilitated human settlement for extended periods of time. These types of subsistence activities led to predictable settlement locales that were restricted to specific geographic locations for a specific duration of time.

Although each group, or band, maintains a geographical range, or territory, there is "communication between groups, including reciprocal visiting and marriage alliances, so that the basic hunting society consisted of a series of local 'bands' that were part of a larger breeding and linguistic community" (Lee and DeVore 1968:11). The major limiting factor on band size is how many people can be supported, or carried, by the harvest of the resources within their territory. The maximum number of people that can be supported by the environment is called the carrying capacity, which is a general ecological term referring to the number of living things an environment can sustain (Odum 1975). Human carrying capacity is determined by the resources that can be harvested within the territorial range given a group's level of technology.

There are many controls on carrying capacity. For example, a technological innovation, such as a shift from simple spear fishing to using fish weirs to concentrate the fish and force them to swim past one spot or into a trap, could greatly increase a harvest and the number of people that might be supported. It is not only the total amount of resources within a given environment that is important, but also the ability of the people to perceive and harvest them. This is called the effective environment and is limited to the resources conceptualized and utilized by the band (Kaplan and Manners 1972:79). The band's potential to harvest resources is dependent to a large degree on their specific level of technology and their knowledge of their territory's resources. Environmental factors also affect carrying capacity, such as unusually cool summers that might alter the migration routes of caribou or high water that might reduce salmon harvests. Gradual and more efficient adaptation to the effective environment could conceivably take hundreds of years or more following colonization before the carrying capacity of a specific territory is reached.

Considerable ethnographic evidence shows that social conflict, frequently over resources, causes groups of people to break away from the larger group and relocate. Anthropologists call this phenomenon fissioning. Given our knowledge of hunter-gatherers, a hypothetical colonization model for the Americas can be constructed. Very simply stated, as a group approached or exceeded the carrying capacity of their territory, fission occurred. Although adjacent bands might be able to absorb some of the splinter population, this would also create increased competition for resources. To successfully colonize and settle adjacent unoccupied territory, the splinter group separating from the parent band would have to be a viable breeding population containing at a minimum adult males, young adult females, and possibly children.

This model is based primarily on environmental criteria and views colonization as a process characterized by a series of stages. The first stage is exploration by humans of unoccupied regions adjacent to a settled area. Exploration provides knowledge of the adjacent region's geography and resources, but the area remains unsettled by humans. Fission is the second stage: it requires that a viable breeding group break away from an existing parent population. The third stage, migration, is the actual process of the splinter group moving from the parent settlement to the known, but unoccupied, region to be colonized. The fourth stage is colonization. Colonization is the establishment of residential locales, or frontier settlements, in a territorial range that provides the resources essential to sustain life. The final stage is settlement, the process by which the colonizing population expands to fully exploit and occupy the effective environment of the new territory. As the splinter group adapts to and settles new territory, they would be expected to extend their exploration to adjacent unoccupied territory. Exploration may have been undertaken primarily by young

adult males able to travel long distances unencumbered by children, pregnant females, and the elderly.

As adaptation to the new territory becomes increasingly effective, a greater
number of people are supported by the available resources. Over time the population would eventually approach or exceed carrying capacity and fission
would occur again. A subsequent migration would take place and an adjacent explored but unoccupied territory would be colonized. The absence of competition
would tend to promote colonization of unoccupied territory.

This model favors colonization within the same general type of environment, or megapatch, such as coastal margins, or high-latitude/high-altitude
tundra, or forests. Once adapted to a major environmental type, such as coastal
margins, a group would have the technology and knowledge essential to harvest
specific types of resources already familiar to them. This type of colonization
would be safer and more predictable than colonizing new environments when
establishing frontier settlements, because it requires less risk. Furthermore, it
maintains a linguistic, cultural, and genetic bond to the parent bands still occu-
pying adjacent territory. This bond would tend to enhance the survival of the
frontier settlement because it would establish opportunities for trade, various
types of alliances, and exchange of marriage partners. In many respects this conceptual model is similar to the modified concept of stem groups discussed by
Dillehay (1997:810) and Beaton (1991a), whereby the splinter group maintains
contact and possibly shares overlapping territory with the parent band.

The "bow wave" model illustrated in Figure 2.6 is characterized by bow
shaped horizontal lines, or waves, symbolizing the sequential advance of the
human population at approximately the same latitude (Mossiman and Martin
1975). By comparison, the macroenvironmental zone model illustrated in Figure
2.7 is characterized by vertical (north to south) lines along major environmental zones, such as the coasts and the western Cordillera. When observing the
major physiographic and ecological regions of the Americas, they tend to be oriented vertically from north to south. For example, the western Cordillera of
North America is a huge mountainous spine extending from Alaska to Arizona, the plains extend from Canada to northern Mexico, and the western
coastal coniferous forest stretches from Alaska to California. Figure 2.7 presents
the abstract concept for colonization of the Americas and is not a map depicting human New World colonization.

North to south colonization also could have occurred along ecotones,
which are zones of transition between two or more biomes. These transitional
environments may have been the megapatch of choice, possibly being more
productive than either of the adjacent biomes and possibly permitting people
access to resources in adjacent biomes. On a very large (continental) level of

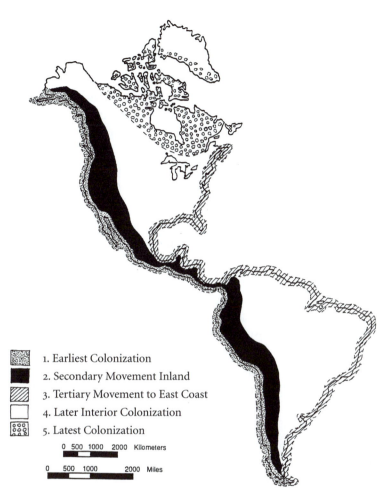

1. Earliest Colonization
2. Secondary Movement Inland
3. Tertiary Movement to East Coast
4. Later Interior Colonization
5. Latest Colonization

0   500 1000   2000   Kilometers

0   500   1000   2000   Miles

Figure 2.7 Hypothetical sequence for the colonization of the Americas by macroenvironmental zones. (Graphic by Eric Parrish.)

analysis, the coastal zone, the interface of the plains and mountains, and other analogous environmental zones could be regarded as ecotones.

It is difficult to estimate how long the first colonization of the Americas may have taken. If an ecological model similar to the one suggested here is applicable to the Americas, the length of time it takes to approach or exceed carrying capacity and the distance moved to establish a new territory or range would have to be known. In relatively linear environmental zones, such as river systems or coastal margins, colonization might be expected to be rapid, possibly resulting in high-velocity migration in conjunction with the use of watercraft. In other types of ecological settings, colonization may have happened at a much slower rate. With colonization occurring along major environmental zones, it may be reasonable to assume that different environmental regions of the Americas were colonized at different times and possibly at different rates of speed. Some territories may have been occupied for hundreds of years before fissioning occurred. For example, coastal zones may have been inhabited long before the interior plains or deserts. Given the current level of knowledge regarding the very early archeology of the Americans, attempts to mathematically model this process would be extremely speculative.

This model attributes fissioning primarily to the growth of a population to approach or exceed the carrying capacity of their immediate environment. However, it is essential to evaluate a variety of theoretical explanations and combinations of explanations when attempting to understand the processes of human colonization. Social, cultural, and economic factors probably played important roles in colonization. For example, banishment following the violation of cultural taboos, such as incest or murder, could cause fission without the carrying capacity being reached. Thomas Dillehay (1991) has pointed out the importance of disease ecology in initial human migration. The complex problems of medical and economic adjustments to new environments may have had dramatic impacts on social cohesion and survival of groups.

There are other incentives for the colonization of unoccupied territory. The first people to occupy a region have first pick of the resources. Such resources might include easily obtained high quality stone, such as obsidian, for manufacturing tools, rich unharvested shellfish beds, or large herds of mammals not previously subjected to human predation. Furthermore, large cultural and geologic events, such as social conflict, climate change, volcanic eruptions, or floods, may have had dramatic impacts on the carrying capacity, possibly resulting in the movement of entire groups of people.

The term migration implies a deliberate, planned movement by people with an understanding of a specified destination. The use of this term alone tends to confuse and possibly distort our attempts to understand the underlying processes that explain the colonization of the continents. An ecological model suggests that migration was an important stage in a gradual process of colonization consisting of several phases that occurred throughout similar types of environmental zones. It is different than the "bow wave" model (Birdsell 1957; Mossiman and Martin 1975) that proposes relatively rapid human colonization of unoccupied lands at a relatively uniform rate based on estimates of human population growth forcing population movement that crosscuts all major ecological areas.

If colonization is viewed as a process consisting of several stages, it is reasonable to assume that the archeological sites resulting from each stage of the process may be different. Archeologists should be able to recognize them based on their characteristics. For example, most if not all, artifacts used during the migration stage should originate from the territory of the parent band. Because migration requires reproducible groups of people, it would be expected that artifacts would be those used by both men and women and possibly children. Because migration is a transitory process, archeological sites would reflect short periods of occupation, possibly only a day or two in many cases. Archeological sites formed during the colonization stage might be smaller and exhibit a less intensive resource utilization than subsequent settlements. It should be possible to order these types of sites temporally. During the process of colonization within any given region, sites formed as a result of exploration should be expected to be the oldest and settlements would be the most recent and most complex. Archeological sites resulting from exploration of unoccupied territory would be expected to be ephemeral, possibly containing small amounts of food refuse, occasional evidence of fire, and possibly an occasional tool used by transients engaged in travel, survival, and subsistence activities.

Although the archeological evidence for the actual processes of New World colonization remains poorly understood, the peopling of the Americas was one of the great colonizing achievements of humanity. It stands as an important event in human history and poses fascinating questions. For example, what are the earliest reliable archeological "signatures" documenting initial colonization of the Americas? Can this evidence be used to define the timing and geographic sequence of colonization? What characterized the cultures of the first colonists, and are these characteristics shared across geographic and temporal boundaries? What were the environmental impacts of human colonization on the pristine New World environments, and can they be documented archeologically? What was the impact of new environments on cultural development? These are some of the intriguing questions that may only be answered by evidence from America's oldest archeological sites.

3 North America's Oldest Sites

Introduction

Once a chronological barrier in archeology has been broken, archeologists ask: Is there anything older yet to be found? To accurately address this question, the types of evidence to be considered as proof must be clearly defined and understood. It is extremely unlikely that the first archeological discovery of a particular cultural tradition will represent either the oldest or the youngest example of its kind. Consequently, archeologists generally assume that there are probably older and younger examples of the types of artifacts and ways of life.

Chapters 3 and 4 review sites from North and South America that some researchers believe are older than circa 11,500 B.P. It is essential to evaluate the archeological evidence at the continental, and even inter-continental, level in order to establish reliable limiting dates for the colonization of the Americas. Site by site evaluation also helps determine whether specific sites, or groups of sites within a region, can be used reliably as baselines from which to build subsequent cultural chronologies. The following review demonstrates that a few well-known sites do not provide reliable evidence for early human occupation of the Americas. However, others indicate colonization took place prior to 11,500 B.P.

Nature has an uncanny knack for producing objects that are virtually identical to similar objects resulting from human activity. For example, fresh, or green, long bones of large mammals tend to fracture in a spiral fashion. Spirally fractured bone is commonly found at campsites where hunters have cracked the bones to extract the nutritious marrow. However, virtually identical specimens may be found in noncultural contexts where large mammal bone has been spirally fractured by other agents, such as nonhuman predators or accidental breakage while the animal is alive. By comparing the patterns and frequency of bone fracture, researchers have developed methods to distinguish between bones broken by carnivores and those fractured by humans (Binford 1981). Bones can also be fractured by massive blocks of churning ice in northern rivers (Thorson and Guthrie 1984), or by rockfall in caves and rockshelters (Dixon 1984). Other examples of the physical alteration of stones and bones include faceting, striation, abrasion, and even flaking by the actions of gravity, carnivores, rivers, and glaciers. Numerous specimens created by these and other noncultural processes are virtually identical to artifacts manufactured by humans.

Taphonomy is the study of the physical, biological, and cultural processes that result in the modification of mammalian remains, especially bones, including the processes of preservation and destruction as fossils (Behrensmeyer and Hill 1980; Brain 1981; Dixon and Thorson 1984). Advances in taphonomic analysis have made it possible to reinterpret some pre-11,500 B.P. sites. Today researchers can more accurately distinguish culturally modified bone from nonculturally modified specimens.

In some instances, pseudoarcheological sites can be created by noncultural processes. For example, charcoal resulting from noncultural forest fires can be introduced into caves by porcupines carrying wood. Packrat middens in rockshelters and near cave entrances can burn from noncultural fires, creating hearth-like features. The bones of animals that have died from natural causes in caves and bones that have been carried into caves and rockshelters by nonhuman predators can be spirally fractured by rockfall from the ceiling and gnawing by carnivores. Rocks falling from the roof of a cave or the cliff above can be flaked or fractured in ways that resemble stone artifacts made by humans. Occasionally, aggregates of these types of objects can be found in locations such as river gravel bars, or in caves and rockshelters. Associations of burned wood, spirally fractured bone, and even pieces of stone resembling stone tools may be found together. These aggregates of noncultural objects can create the appearance of an archeological site; however, they do not result from former human habitation or activity. Consequently, archeologists must be extremely careful to excavate and interpret these deposits properly. To do so requires a broad understanding of many disciplines, including geology and biology, in addition to archeology.

There is a fascinating array of sites throughout North America (Figure 3.1) that some researchers consider to be older than 11,500 B.P. Curiously, the integrity of many of these sites has been questioned by subsequent research. Frequently information refuting their validity is spread through the professional community as a result of conversations, field trips, and papers presented at professional meetings. Yet, comparatively few publications in the scientific literature explain why particular sites do not meet the criteria necessary to be accepted as valid archeological sites and that they are no longer considered to be older than 11,500 B.P. Many sites simply either fade into obscurity, and archeologists cease discussing them in classrooms, publications, and other forums because the evidence is often too ambiguous to accept or refute their age or context.

One of the objectives of this chapter is to evaluate these types of sites and share research regarding their possible age, interpretations about the recovered

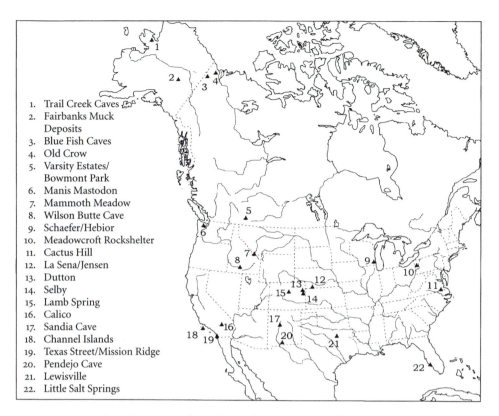

1. Trail Creek Caves
2. Fairbanks Muck Deposits
3. Blue Fish Caves
4. Old Crow
5. Varsity Estates/ Bowmont Park
6. Manis Mastodon
7. Mammoth Meadow
8. Wilson Butte Cave
9. Schaefer/Hebior
10. Meadowcroft Rockshelter
11. Cactus Hill
12. La Sena/Jensen
13. Dutton
14. Selby
15. Lamb Spring
16. Calico
17. Sandia Cave
18. Channel Islands
19. Texas Street/Mission Ridge
20. Pendejo Cave
21. Lewisville
22. Little Salt Springs

Figure 3.1 Map of North America depicting the locations of significant sites presented in the text that are possibly older than 11,500 B.P. (Graphic by Eric Parrish.)

artifacts, and the current professional consensus regarding their validity. This chapter focuses on those sites that are best known, most controversial, or have the highest potential for being older than about 12,000 B.P. Some sites, such as Tule Springs, Nevada (Wormington and Ellis 1967) and Friesenhahn Cave, Texas (Stanford 1983) have been excluded from this presentation because it has been adequately demonstrated that they are not archeological sites dating earlier than circa 12,000–11,000 B.P.

Early assumptions regarding the possible pre-11,500 B.P. artifacts and human remains were based on a variety of evidence including imprecise geologic correlations, interpretations that lacked chronological accuracy, and dating methods that are now recognized to be inaccurate. Advances in radiocarbon dating and laboratory techniques now make it possible to reanalyze and accurately date well-preserved bone containing adequate bone collagen (Stafford 1994; Stafford et al. 1990, 1991; Taylor 1992). Using rigorous chemical pretreatment and accelerator mass spectrometry (AMS), it is possible to radiocarbon date extremely small organic samples. These new and more reliable dating methods have made it possible to reexamine important early human skeletal remains and to date artifacts made of organic materials, such as bone, antler, and ivory. Many artifacts and human remains originally believed to be older than 11,500 B.P. are now being accurately redated.

Five criteria are employed to evaluate potential pre-11,500 B.P. sites in the Americas, following the criteria outlined by C. Vance Haynes (1969:714) and subsequently Stanford (1983:65). The most definitive evidence for demonstrating humans were present in the Americas prior to 11,500 B.P. would be reliably dated human remains. In the absence of human skeletal remains (or indirect evidence of fossil humans such as preserved footprints), all of the first four following criteria must be met. The criteria are:

1. Are the artifacts clearly the product of human manufacture?
2. Is the recovered material within clear stratigraphic context?
3. Are there reliable, concordant, and stratigraphically consistent radiocarbon dates from the deposit?
4. Are paleoenvironmental studies consistent with ages assigned to the site?
5. Are there human remains that are reliably dated older than 11,500 B.P.?

Some archeologists recommend that more than one archeological site meeting these criteria must be found before the evidence for pre-11,500 B.P. occupation of the Americas can be fully accepted. They advocate expanding these criteria to include recovery of an adequate sample of cultural remains to characterize a cultural pattern and to recognize recurrent and similar patterns in the archeological record (Griffin 1979; Toth 1991).

Each of the following sites is evaluated briefly using these criteria. These sites are presented geographically, beginning with western Beringia, followed by eastern Beringia, and then southward from North America to South America.

Beringia

There are numerous sites reported from western Beringia that have been ascribed to the Paleolithic and possibly date to the Pleistocene (Dikov 1993). However, the presumed antiquity of many of these sites is based on typological considerations. As of 1998, they have not been reliably dated based on their stratigraphic context or by the application of reliable chronometric methods such as radiocarbon dating.

In western Beringia, the area east of the Verkhoyansk Range in northeastern Siberia, there are two sites, Berelekh and Ushki I (Figure 3.2), that are firmly dated to the last Ice Age. A third site, Uptar, is undated but contains a fluted projectile point considered by some researchers to be a possible precursor to Clovis technology in North America. These three sites are considered important to some researchers because they suggest the presence of humans in western Beringia prior to the first human colonization of North America.

Berelekh is located on a tributary of the Indigirka River near the Arctic Ocean and is dated to approximately 13,000 B.P. (Michael 1984; Powers 1973). The site apparently contains bifacial projectile point fragments and lacks microblades (Mochanov 1977; Powers and Hoffecker 1989). However, Vereshchagin (1977) believes that the Berelekh bone assemblage is not cultural in origin. The actual archeological site is located 100–200 m (328–656 ft) from what appear to be noncultural bone accumulations, and no artifacts have been found in the bone deposit (G. Haynes 1991:213). Because of the conflicting reports and interpretations, there does not appear to be conclusive evidence of human predation of mammoth and other Ice Age animals at the site. Consequently, the dating of the human occupation and association with the extinct Pleistocene fauna is questionable.

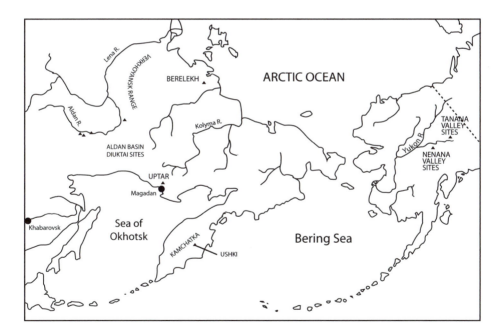

Figure 3.2 Map of Beringia depicting the locations of key late Pleistocene and early Holocene archeological sites (modified from the *Desert Research Institute News*, Winter 1996:5).

Ushki I is a prehistoric settlement containing a stratigraphic level, Horizon VII, that was reportedly dated by radiocarbon to circa 14,000 B.P. (Dikov 1977, 1979). Ushki I is located on the shore of Ushki Lake in central Kamchatka (Figure 3.2). Horizon VII contains a bifacial lithic industry consisting primarily of stemmed projectile points. More recently, the age of Horizon VII at Ushki I has been revised and is believed to be circa 11,500 B.P. based on several radiocarbon dates (A. V. Lozhkin, personal communication 1991). According to the site's excavator, N. N. Dikov, Horizon VII lacks microblades and is superimposed by Horizon VI that contains microblades and dates to circa 10,500 B.P. (Dikov 1977, 1979, 1993; Dikov and Titov 1984; Powers 1990).

The Uptar site (King and Slobodin 1996) is located approximately 40 km (25 mi) north of Magadan and the Sea of Okhotsk (Figure 3.2). Although the Uptar site has not been firmly dated, it lies beneath volcanic ash, or *tephra*, dated to circa 8,300 B.P., and some of the artifacts had been heavily weathered prior to deposition of the tephra, thus suggesting the site is considerably older. While King and Slobodin (1996:635) report a few microblades from the site, the assemblage apparently does not contain other evidence of microblade manufacture, such as microblade cores or core tablets. The bifaces in the Uptar collection are lanceolate in outline but are smaller in size than typical North American specimens and lack edge grinding characteristic of New World Paleoindian specimens.

A single fluted bifacial stone projectile point has led King and Slobodin (1996) to suggest possible affinities between Uptar and North American fluted projectile points. However, this correlation is highly speculative, and it is premature to postulate intercontinental historical connections based on superficial comparison of a single artifact. The specimen is not edge ground as are New World examples. The flute probably results from an impact fracture, which is caused by a projectile point striking an object or surface that results in the detachment of a longitudinal flake creating a flute-like flake scar on the artifact. Although the Uptar site documents an early bifacial technology and contributes to understanding the diversity of the early archeology of northeastern Siberia, it probably has little if any relationship to fluted projectile point sites in North America.

Trail Creek Caves

The Trail Creek Caves are located on Alaska's Seward Peninsula and were excavated under the supervision of Danish archeologist Helge Larsen in 1949 and 1950. Although the first artifacts were recovered from the caves in 1928, excavations began only after a geological field party under the direction of David M. Hopkins in 1948 reported finding subsurface artifacts and preserved mammal

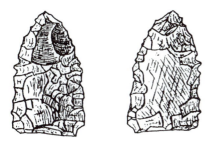

Figure 3.3 Chalcedony biface, from Layer III (110 cm below the surface), Trail Creek Cave 2 (reproduced from Larsen 1968a:56 by permission of Arktisk Institut, Copenhagen, Denmark).

bones. There are several small caves in the vicinity, but only Caves 2 and 9 contained evidence of human occupation.

In the lower levels of Caves 2 and 9, Larsen reported what he believed were culturally modified Pleistocene faunal remains. These included the right scapula of a horse (*Equus* sp.) from Cave 9, fractured bison calcanei from Cave 2, and fractured dog teeth from both caves. Based on replicative experiments and comparison of the bison bones with similar examples of bison recovered from the muck deposits in the vicinity of Fairbanks, Alaska, Larsen concluded that the bison bone and possibly the horse scapula had been broken by humans. He further postulated that the dog canines had been broken by humans possibly to prevent the dogs from damaging the hides of animals while hunting. The modified bone of the extinct Pleistocene animals and two ^{14}C determinations, one on a horse scapula (15,750 ± 350 B.P., K-1210) and another on a bison calcaneus (13,070 ± 280 B.P., K-1327), led Larsen to speculate that Arctic big game hunters had utilized the caves between 13,000–15,000 years ago when the Bering Land Bridge still connected Asia and North America (Larsen 1968a:57–63,76). In addition to the modified faunal material, Larsen reported a chalcedony projectile point (Figure 3.3) from levels containing the Pleistocene faunal material. He was cautious in associating it with the Pleistocene faunal remains (Larsen 1968a:75).

Subsequent reanalysis of the dog canines demonstrated that they had been misidentified and were actually deciduous bear canines that lacked cultural associations (Dixon and Smith 1986). Vinson (1993) conducted additional excavations at two caves near Larsen's Caves 2 and 9. By analyzing taxonomic abundance and diversity, bone damage, and skeletal element survival, he concluded that there is little, if any, evidence that the Pleistocene bones were modified by humans. The single stone projectile point derived from the Pleistocene level has not been accurately dated but may be typologically related to Chindadn points of interior Alaska (Cook 1996) probably dating to between circa 11,500–10,500 B.P. (Dixon 1993).

Fairbanks Muck Deposits

In the vicinity of Fairbanks, Alaska, several potentially important locales were discovered during the process of removing perennially frozen Pleistocene silt that covered gold bearing gravels. The silt, called muck by the miners, is actually silt that was deposited (and redeposited) throughout the region by wind and other agents during the Pleistocene. These sediments were removed by the miners by spraying water on the silt with large hydraulic nozzles, called giants. This melted the ice within the deposits and flushed away the unwanted overlying silt. During this process of removing the muck, the hydraulic mining unearthed a spectacular array of mummified Pleistocene animals, thousands of bones, and some artifacts.

These archeological specimens were collected by local miners as well as students from the University of Alaska under the supervision of the University's first president Charles Bunnell and the self-taught naturalist Otto William Geist. Much of this work was sponsored by Childs Frick, a paleontologist based at New York City's American Museum of Natural History. Although some portions of the collection remained at the University of Alaska, the majority of this material was shipped to the American Museum of Natural History. Several of the students working for Bunnell and Geist became respected scientists. Their correspondence and other documents associated with these finds contain recurring themes; the specimens were believed to be deeply buried, associated with Pleistocene fauna, and in situ.

The muck deposits contained a variety of spirally-fractured and modified bones. There are several possible, but poorly documented, associations of Pleistocene fauna and artifacts; at least four localities are known from the muck deposits and some may be older than 11,500 B.P. Recent advances in AMS ^{14}C dating of bone makes it possible to accurately determine the age of some of these localities and artifacts for the first time.

The following four localities contained Pleistocene fauna that may have been associated with artifacts: (1) Goldstream Pit 1-G, located approximately 12 km (8 mi) north of Fairbanks; (2) the Ester Stripping Pit, located near Ester, Alaska, approximately 16 km (10 mi) west of Fairbanks; and (3) two different localities on Fairbanks Creek approximately 32 km (20 mi) northeast of Fairbanks. Separate finds of mummified mammoth remains were discovered in 1940 and 1948. Early human skeletal remains have not been reported from the Fairbanks muck.

Goldstream Pit 1-G. In 1933, two beautifully made bone projectile points (Figure 3.4) were recovered from the muck being removed from an area designated Pit 1-G on Goldstream Creek about 6 km (4 mi) downstream from the town of Fox. Other specimens from Pit 1-G included the left mandible of a beaver, the right tibia of a wolf or dog, and mummified remains of two horse (*Equus* sp.) left metatarsals with the hide, muscle, and hooves preserved. However, the association between the bone projectile points and animal remains is unclear. The fact that there were two left metatarsals indicated that at least two individual horses were preserved at the site. Rainey (1939:393) suggests the specimens were from thin gravel lenses about 12–14 m (39–46 ft) below the original surface.

In 1995, samples of bone were carefully extracted from each of the two bone projectile points. AMS ^{14}C radiocarbon determinations were run on the bone removed from the points (Stafford, personal communication 1995). Both points appear to be manufactured from large mammal metapodials, and the marrow cavity of the original bone forms what appears like a flute along one side of each specimen. The longer of the two points (#34701) produced a ^{14}C determination of 8,490 ± 60 B.P.(CAMS-16008) and the shorter specimen (#34700) dated to 8,590 ± 70 B.P. (CAMS-16009). The resultant dates overlap at one sigma, suggesting the points were made at the same time, possibly from the same animal, and possibly by the same individual. The age of the projectile points indicates that they are attributable to the Northern Paleoindian tradition. Both points lack slots for microblade insets. Accurate dating of both specimens provides an important addition to understanding early Holocene bone technology in eastern Beringia and demonstrates rather conclusively that these artifacts are not older than Clovis sites found in the more southern regions of North America.

The Ester Stripping Pit. In 1939, Froelich Rainey reported a number of archeological finds from the Fairbanks muck deposits, suggesting the possible association of humans and Pleistocene fauna in eastern Beringia. The discover-

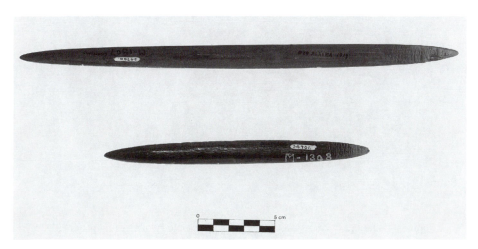

Figure 3.4 Bone projectile points from Goldstream Pit 1-G, Alaska.

ies included a partial maxilla (the bones of the lower skull containing the upper teeth) of a young probocidean (either a mammoth or mastodon), which was apparently associated with two stone Yuma projectile points (Figure 3.5). The find was reported to have come from approximately 20 m (65 ft) below the original ground surface. Although one of the projectile points is missing, the one reportedly frozen in the ice and in direct contact with the maxilla (Rainey 1939:397) is illustrated in Figure 3.5, along with the maxillary bone that is in two fragments, each containing a small erupting tusk of a probocidean calf.

Rainey (1939:398) compared the point to similar specimens found at Clovis, New Mexico, associated with mammoth remains. However, by 1948 Wormington (1948) demonstrated that the term Yuma encompassed many different projectile point types that were difficult to characterize temporally and morphologically. Re-examination of the point based on its overall morphology, including lateral edge grinding near the base, suggests that it closely resembles Paleoindian forms, rather than later Holocene types. Four AMS ^{14}C radiocarbon determinations on bone, two on each half of the maxilla (Stafford, personal communication 1995) indicate the specimen dates to circa 12,300 B.P. The two samples from the right half of the maxilla were dated to 11,310 ± 120 B.P.(CAMS-13301) and 12,270 ± 70 B.P. (CAMS-17126) and the two from the left half dated to 12,220 ± 70 B.P. (CAMS-13303) and 12,380 ± 70 B.P. (CAMS-17127).

Figure 3.5 Dark gray chert projectile point and maxillary of a young probocidean with erupting tusks found in the Ester Stripping Pit, approximately 10 mi west of Fairbanks, Alaska.

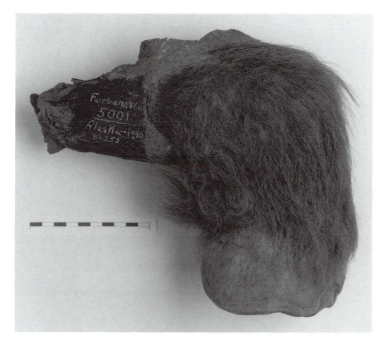

Figure 3.6 Mummified foot of a mammoth calf, Fairbanks Creek, Alaska, 1940.

These age determinations demonstrate that the maxilla dates to the very late Pleistocene. The projectile point's general typological similarity to other Paleoindian projectile points dating to the late Pleistocene/early Holocene and the four relatively late ^{14}C determinations suggest the probocidean calf and projectile point may have been associated. These data are not conclusive because the original association was not documented in situ. However, if the original stratigraphic association and interpretations were valid, this could be one of the earliest dated associations for humans and probocideans in North America.

Fairbanks Creek 1940. The well-preserved foot of a mammoth calf (Figure 3.6) (specimen #255–5001) was found by Dick Osborne, then a University of Alaska student working for Charles Bunnell and Otto Geist. The specimen was imbedded in a lens of gravel in the muck on the left limit of Fairbanks Creek near the terminus of Snow Gulch. Because much of the muck had already been removed as a result of hydraulic operations, it was impossible to determine how far the mammoth foot was below the original surface. The following day Osborne found a gray chert biface (Figure 3.7) that may have been associated with the mammoth foot. The biface appeared to have come from the same gravel lens in which he had found the mammoth foot (Osborne, personal communication 1993).

Figure 3.7 Gray chert biface recovered near the Fairbanks Creek mammoth foot, 1940.

The foot is exceptionally well preserved and includes hide, muscle, bone, and even reddish golden hair. It exhibits no evidence of butchering or other types of cultural modification. The specimen had been dated by conventional radiocarbon methods in 1968 to 15,380 ± 300 B.P. Two AMS ^{14}C radiometric dates were run on the mammoth foot in 1995, one on hair and the other on muscle. The resultant date for the muscle is 17,550 ± 80 B.P. (CAMS-19250) and for the hair is 17,170 ±70 B.P. (CAMS-19253) (Stafford, personal communication 1995). The circumstances of the discovery make it impossible to determine whether the artifact and mammoth remains were contemporaneous.

Fairbanks Creek 1948. In 1948 the head, trunk, and left forelimb of a juvenile mammoth (Figure 3.8) was found in the drain used to carry off the overburden resulting from hydraulic removal of the muck along Fairbanks Creek. An early ^{14}C determination run on skin and flesh dated to 21,300 ± 1300 B.P. (L-601) was reported by William Farrand (1961:732). In 1968, a subsequent date run on muscle attached to the skin of the head was dated to 24,140 ± 1200 B.P. (Guthrie 1990). Guthrie (1990) named this specimen Effie, a pun relating to the Fairbanks Exploration (F. E.) Company. The day prior to the discovery of this incredible specimen, George O. Schuman, another student working for Geist and Bunnell, discovered a scraper made of a large flake of fine-grained red-brown chert (Figure 3.9). Schuman believed the specimen was in situ deeply buried approximately 15 m (50 ft) from the exposure from which the partial carcass of the mammoth calf was washed. Although it is possible that the mammoth (or possibly other Pleistocene faunal material) from this deposit may have been associated with the scraper, it is now impossible to verify the association. If the artifact and mammoth were deposited at the same time, this site would be the oldest evidence for direct association of humans and mammoths in North America.

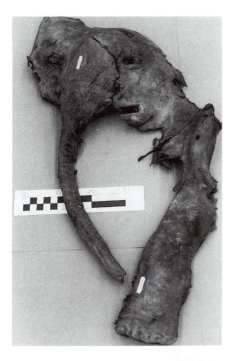

Figure 3.8 The partially preserved face, trunk, and left foreleg of a mammoth calf recovered from Fairbanks Creek, Alaska, 1948.

Figure 3.9 Scraper possibly associated with the 1948 Fairbanks Creek mammoth.

Old Crow

Near the Athapaskan village of Old Crow and the surrounding areas in the Canadian Yukon Territory, researchers have collected a wide variety of faunal remains and some bone artifacts that have been interpreted to be older than 11,500 B.P. (Bonnichsen 1978, 1979; Harington et al. 1975; Irving and Harington 1973; Morlan 1978, 1979, 1980, 1983; Morlan and Cinq-Mars 1982). These specimens are largely from the Old Crow, Blue Fish, and Bell Basins, which were lakes during the late Pleistocene. These lakes were formed by advancing glacial ice that blocked stream outlets and caused the water level in the basins to rise. At the end of the Pleistocene, the glaciers melted and the lakes drained, leaving massive lacustrine deposits (sediments formed in a lake) that have been downcut and eroded by rivers. An important result of these geologic events is that the bones of Pleistocene animals have been exposed, eroded, and redeposited along the Old Crow and upper Porcupine Rivers. International attention was drawn to the Old Crow region in 1973 when William Irving and C. R. Harington reported dating a bone hide-working tool, called a flesher (Figure 3.10), to circa 27,000 B.P. The ^{14}C date was derived from bone taken from the flesher. Irving (Irving et al. 1977) also reported a human mandible that was redeposited with Pleistocene faunal remains and that they suggested was also Pleistocene in age. Subsequent ^{14}C dating of the mandible and flesher demonstrated that they were late Holocene in age.

The specimens recovered from these locales fall into two primary categories. First, a vast array of bones that have been flaked, polished, striated, faceted, and otherwise altered in ways that appear to be the result of human modification exists (Figure 3.11). While it is possible that some of the specimens may have been manufactured by humans, equally plausible noncultural processes may explain their appearance, including processes such as carnivore breakage, rodent gnawing, trampling by large mammals, fracture resulting from geologic overburden, and modifications resulting from the actions of rivers and river ice.

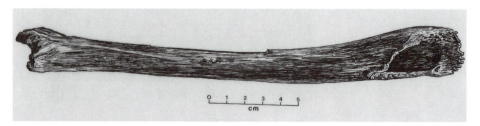

Figure 3.10 Caribou tibia flesher from the Old Crow area, Yukon Territory, Canada (redrawn from Bonnichsen 1979:161 and Morlan 1980:128).

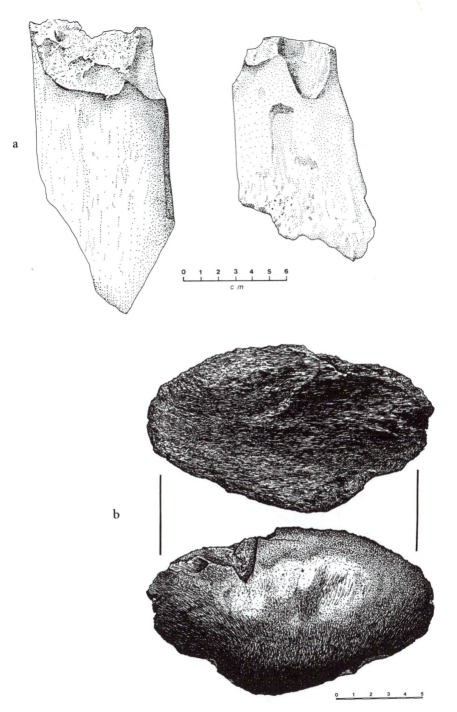

Figure 3.11 (a) Spirally fractured and flaked probocidean bone core and (b) probocidean bone flake. Both examples from the collections of the University of Alaska Museum (from Dixon 1993:47).

The second group of specimens is bone artifacts. Four of the artifacts believed to be Pleistocene in age were the flesher, a billet (a hammer-like object used for flaking stone or bone) made of caribou antler, and two wedges also made from caribou antler. The bone flesher had originally been dated by using the apatite portion of the bone, a technique that has subsequently been demonstrated to be susceptible to contamination by groundwater carbonates (Hassan and Hare 1978; Hassan and Ortner 1977). Subsequent AMS ^{14}C dating of proteins from the flesher and other tools demonstrated that the bone from which the flesher was made dated to 1,350 ± 150 B.P. (RIDDL-145), the billet to 2,930 ± 140 B.P. (RIDDL-133), and the two antler wedges were 1,730 ± 100 B.P. (RIDDL-140) and 1,880 ± 140 B.P. (RIDDL-141), respectively (Nelson et al. 1986). Clearly, the artifacts can be no older than the bone from which they have been manufactured.

Blue Fish Cave 1

Blue Fish Cave 1 (Figure 3.12) is the largest of several small caves and rockshelters at the western end of a limestone-dolomite ridge located approximately 54 km (33.5 mi) southwest of the village of Old Crow in Canada's northern Yukon Territory. The cave is approximately 250 m (820 ft) above the Blue Fish River, a tributary of the Porcupine River. Cave 1 commands a panoramic view of the upper-middle course of the Blue Fish River Valley. The site was first excavated in 1977 under the direction of Jaques Cinq-Mars (1979) who defined seven stratigraphic units (I–VII) and four cultural components (A–D) (Cinq-Mars 1979: 7–8, 27–29). Lithic artifacts were recovered from cultural components A and B and microchips from components C and D. The deposits contain fine-grained wind blown (eolian) sediments, abundant faunal remains, discontinuous organic lenses, and floral and faunal remains intermixed with bedrock rubble. Age estimates for the deposits have been derived by comparing the faunal remains, fossil pollen, and sedimentary sequence with records from adjacent regions. Cinq-Mars suggests that the oldest artifacts from the site could possibly be as old as 14,000 B.P. Organics within the stratigraphic units have not been directly dated in order to define the chronology for the stratigraphic units.

Based on analysis of the faunal remains, Cinq-Mars (1979:27) concludes that the predator most likely to explain the accumulation and modification of the faunal remains is *Homo* sp. The evidence for human occupation from the two oldest cultural units (units C and D) is based on the recognition of microchips that are only identifiable under microscopic examination. It is assumed that the microchips are the product of lithic manufacture or use by humans. Similar specimens (microchips) have been recovered from geologic deposits of Tertiary age that are clearly noncultural. Cinq-Mars (1979:21) acknowledges that they may

Figure 3.12 Aerial Photograph of Blue Fish Caves looking east.

have been created by noncultural mechanisms, such as eolian-induced percussion, sediment movements, or frost fracturing. Such specimens are so small that they can also be subject to eolian transport.

Although movement of sediments as a result of freezing and thawing, known as cryoturbation, has disturbed the stratigraphy to some degree, pollen diagrams from Blue Fish Caves 1 and 2 correspond roughly to lake records elsewhere in the region (Cinq-Mars 1979; Ritchie and Cwynar 1982). Carnivore remains, including red fox, Arctic fox, ermine, wolf, American marten, mountain lion, and American lion, have been recovered from the Blue Fish Caves (Cinq-Mars, personal communication 1989, cited in Harington 1989; Sattler 1991:86). Sattler (1991:87) suggests that the quantity of bone recovered from Blue Fish Cave 1 is a stellar example of a bone deposit resulting from long use of a cave by northern carnivores. Beebe (1983) asserts that the pattern of ungulate longbone breakage is caused by canid (wolf, fox, dog, etc.) gnawing, although she acknowledges the possibility that the initial opening of the marrow cavity possibly could have been made by humans. Dixon (1986) has suggested that rockfall from the rock face directly above the cave entrance and solifluction may explain impact fracture and rubble scarring on some of the Pleistocene bone. This type of bone breakage and modification can be misinterpreted as evidence of cultural activity. Stratigraphic and taphonomic problems resulting from solifluction and other noncultural processes render the interpretation of late Pleistocene human occupation at Blue Fish Cave 1 equivocal.

Figure 3.13 Alan Bryan at the Varsity Estates Site pointing to the contact between the glacial gravels and the overlying lake sediments where the fractured cobbles and flakes were found, 1998.

Varsity Estates and Bowmont Park

The Varsity Estates and Bowmont Park sites are located in Canada along the Bow River Valley near the city of Calgary, in the province of Alberta. The sites were discovered by Jiri Chlachula in the early 1990s. Chlachula found three lithic specimens that he classified as "finished tools" and several others that he called cores and flakes. They were eroding from the contact of Cordilleran Bow Valley till and overlying fine grained silts deposited by glacial lake Calgary (Chlachula 1994). The in situ specimens were approximately 24 m (79 ft) below the contemporary surface and embedded within the till among glacially rounded cobbles and pebbles (Figure 3.13) (Chlachula 1994; Gruhn and Bryan 1998). Fifty specimens were recovered from the site as a result of excavations in 1996 and 1997. The investigators suggest these may be artifacts including choppers, cores, scrapers, gravers, and burinated pieces (Gruhn and Bryan 1998). No faunal remains, charcoal, or other organic material suitable for radiocarbon dating was recovered. Chlachula suggests that these specimens were redeposited in the till by advancing glacial ice during the late Wisconsin, because glacial striations are superimposed on the chipped surfaces of some of the specimens. Based on the geologic context of the site, it is estimated to be older than about 21,000 B.P. (Chlachula 1994). Gruhn and Bryan (1998) suggest that people may have used the glacial cobbles exposed on the surface of the melting Wisconsin glacial ice.

The Bowmont Park site is located on the side of a south facing roadcut about 20 m (66 ft) above the Bow River flood plain. Sixty-four possible artifacts are reported to have been excavated about 1 m (.3 ft) below the surface at or near the contact of what appear to be fluvial gravels capped by colluvial deposits of loam, silts, and sands. The possible artifacts are described as flaked pebbles and cobbles, possibly cores or choppers, and split cobbles with patterned unifacial flaking (Gruhn and Bryan 1998).

Chlachula (1994:22) states that, "the evidence for the cultural authenticity of the recorded lithic assemblages consists of the occurrence of diagnostic patterned flaking and edge-retouching attributes, which are encountered in the Old World Pleistocene . . . " that he believes are "absent on transported rocks with identical lithological composition from local high-energy fluvial and glacial environments." However, most New World archeologists are extremely reluctant to ascribe antiquity based on topological comparison with Old World assemblages. Many would question the cultural authenticity of flaked cobbles derived from high-energy glacial and fluvial deposits. Although the age ascribed to these specimens may be reasonable based on their geologic context, most New World archeologists would assert that the specimens were probably flaked by moving glacial ice, geologic compression, or moving water, rather than humans.

Manis Mastodon

The remains of a mastodon were found in a bog on the Olympic Peninsula in the state of Washington about 5 km (3 mi) south of the town of Sequim (Gustafson et al. 1979). What has been cautiously identified as the probable tip of a bone projectile point was discovered in the rib of the mastodon. Two radiocarbon dates run on associated seeds and wood and micro-organics were 12,000 ± 310 B.P. (WSU-1866) B.P. and 11,850 ± 60 B.P. (USGS-591) (Gustafson et al. 1979:158). The mastodon bones lay directly on glacial deposits, suggesting that the animal had died shortly after the retreat of the last Ice Age glacier. Thus, its stratigraphic position is consistent with the radiocarbon dates.

Bone growth around the mastodon's rib indicated that the wound had begun to heal prior to the animal's death. X-ray thin sections demonstrated that the intrusive object tapered to a point and penetrated the rib about 2 cm (.75 inch). Several pieces of worked bone and tusk were also found, including a worked bone object that was pointed at both ends. Although the left side of the animal was semi-articulated (Gustafson et al. 1979:160), the skull had been fractured and some of the animals bones were disarticulated and others were missing. This suggested that the animal had been butchered by humans. Although many large cobbles, some of which were fractured, were associated with the glacial deposits upon which the mastodon was recovered, only one flaked cobble spall was believed to have been manufactured by humans. However, its precise relationship to the mastodon remains is unclear. The bones of muskrat, duck, caribou, and bison were also recovered from the bog. Presuming that the dating of the site is accurate and that the intrusive object in the rib is actually a man-made object, this site may contain the earliest and most convincing evidence for the late Pleistocene association of humans and extinct fauna in northwestern North America.

Mammoth Meadow

The Mammoth Meadow site (Figure 3.14) is located on the northwestern bank of South Everson Creek in southwestern Montana. It is a quarry site where early people camped and excavated lithic material for the manufacture of stone tools. The stratigraphic sequence contains a series of cultural occupations, with an occupation attributable to the Cody complex (a late Paleoindian archeological complex generally dating to 9,000–8,400 B.P.) occurring between approximately 115–190 cm (45–75 inches) below the surface and stratigraphically above older stratigraphic units containing artifacts (Bonnichsen et al. 1990:5, 1992:298, Unit III; Bonnichsen et al. 1996:205, horizon 9c, Figure 13.3). The age of the Cody complex occupation is documented by two AMS ^{14}C determinations of 9,390 ± 90 B.P. (TO-1976) and 8,226 ± 84 B.P. (BX-1682) (Bonnichsen et al. 1996: 205).

The lowest cultural levels (designated units IVa and IVb in Bonnichsen et al. 1990, 1992 and horizons 9c and 10c in Bonnichsen et al. 1996) contain lithic

Figure 3.14 Excavations at Mammoth Meadow. (Photograph courtesy of Mort Turner.)

artifacts, faunal remains, and hair. These lower stratigraphic units are described as a gray/brown subangular, cobble/clay overlying stratified subangular and water-rounded sands and gravels. The hair and artifacts reportedly come from these two levels, thereby suggesting a late Pleistocene age for the occupation. The hair has been identified to species that include regionally extinct caribou and extinct Pleistocene horse and mammoth (Bonnichsen et al. 1993). Human hair has also been identified among the Pleistocene mammalian hair (Bonnichsen et al. 1996), but the human hair has not been radiocarbon dated. No direct ^{14}C determinations document the age of these stratigraphic units, and direct association of the artifacts and human hair with the Pleistocene fauna is not clear. Most researchers do not regard the presence of human hair alone as adequate proof of human occupation prior to 11,500 B.P.

Wilson Butte Cave

Wilson Butte Cave is actually a lava blister (a gas or vapor pocket formed near the surface of a lava flow that can create a hollow cave-like geologic feature) located in southern Idaho. The site was excavated by Ruth Gruhn in 1959 and 1960 (Gruhn 1961, 1965). The early excavations produced a radiocarbon date of 14,500 ± 500 B.P. (M-1409) run on small mammal bones from Stratum C, the lowest stratigraphic level containing artifacts. However, questions arose whether this early radiocarbon determination actually dated the cultural occupation because of the "complicated and perhaps confused" site stratigraphy and problems in reliably dating bone (Irwin 1971:46).

Gruhn returned to the site in 1988 and 1989 (Gruhn 1995) and resumed excavations to address these and other questions. She excavated deposits underlying Stratum C where the artifacts had been found. From this underlying level, designated Stratum E, she obtained two AMS ^{14}C determinations of 16,000 ± 140 B.P. (TO-1650) and 33, 250 ± 320 B.P. (TO-1467) and eight stone flakes made of obsidian, ignimbrite, basalt, and chalcedony. However, she (Gruhn 1995:16) suggests that based on obsidian hydration analysis, the flakes may be intrusive from the overlying Stratum C.

Thick-stemmed projectile points were recovered from Stratum C, suggesting the cave may have been occupied first by people who made artifacts attributable to the Western Stemmed Point tradition (Chapter 8). Although two of these points were dated by the obsidian hydration method to 14,600 ± 402 B.P. and 13,657 ± 389 B.P., this dating method is probably not reliable at this site, and other specimens from the same level produced hydration dates ranging between circa 8,400–6,000 B.P. (Gruhn 1995:17). Stratum C also produced concave-based and large shouldered projectile points, bifaces, scrapers, burins, and utilized flakes. Gruhn (1995:17) believes that the evidence for human occupation from Stratum

E is unclear and that the evidence for dating human occupation prior to the Western Stemmed Point tradition in Stratum C is ambiguous. The oldest ^{14}C date on charcoal from Stratum C is 10,230 ± 90 B.P. (TO-1485), suggesting that this may be a reliable date for early human occupation of this stratigraphic unit.

Schaefer and Hebior

The Schaefer and Hebior sites are located in southeastern Wisconsin. Excavations began in 1992 at the Schaefer site, where there was a pile of disarticulated bones of woolly mammoth (*Mammuthus primigenius*). The bones exhibited cut marks, fractures, and striations suggesting they had been butchered and piled at the edge of an ancient lake that gradually dried and became a bog. The bones were subsequently covered with 130–140 cm (51–55 inches) of peat that accumulated over the site (Overstreet et al. 1993).

Subsequent excavation at the Schaefer site in 1993 uncovered chipped-stone implements directly associated with the mammoth bones. A radiocarbon date on bone collagen run on mammoth bone produced a ^{14}C date of 10,960 ± 100 B.P. (Beta 62822), suggesting that the Schaefer site might be a kill site associated with the Chesrow complex. The Chesrow complex is an early archeological complex identified at several sites in southeastern Wisconsin. It is characterized by a variety of lanceolate projectile points characteristically manufactured from local cherts and is contemporaneous with the Clovis complex on the Great Plains (Overstreet 1993; Overstreet et al. 1995).

However, two radiocarbon dates on wood deposited at the site shortly after the mammoth bones dated to 12,220 ± 80 B.P. (Beta 62823) and 12,480 ± 130 B.P. (Beta 62824). This suggests the first bone collagen date was too recent. A highly purified sample of the mammoth bone collagen was subsequently dated to 12,310 ± 60 B.P. (CAMS-30171), and is consistent with the earlier dates run on wood.

The Hebior site is located near Kenosha, Wisconsin. Approximately 25 m^2 (270 ft^2) of the site was excavated in 1994. The Hebior mammoth was an adult male, and like the Schaefer mammoth, the bones exhibit signs of butchering. Several stone artifacts including flakes, a chopper, and two flaked-stone bifaces were found among the bones (Figure 3.15) (Hall 1995). Two AMS ^{14}C determinations run on purified samples of mammoth bone collagen from the site produced dates of 12,480 ± 60 B.P. (CAMS-28303) and 12,520 ± 50 B.P. (CAMS-24943). These results led Overstreet and Stafford (1997) to conclude that both the Schaefer and Hebior sites resulted from human hunting or scavenging of mammoths in the southwestern Lake Michigan basin by at least 12,500 B.P.

Both the Schaefer and Hebior sites occur in low energy depositional environments, and are located in primary depositional contexts. In these types of depo-

Figure 3.15 Chipped-stone biface associated with mammoth bones at the Hebior site. (Reproduced by permission from *The Wisconsin Archeologist,* 79(1)(1998):43; photograph courtesy of D. F. Overstreet.)

sitional environments, there is little reason to attribute either the bone modifications or the lithic artifacts to noncultural processes. Both sites have been professionally excavated, recorded, and reliably dated by the ^{14}C method. Based on the available evidence, both the Schaefer and Hebior sites appear to provide evidence indicating human interaction with mammoths prior to 11,500 B.P.

Meadowcroft Rockshelter

The Meadowcroft Rockshelter is a deeply stratified site located in southwestern Pennsylvania. Excavations were conducted under the direction of James Adovasio from 1973–1977 (Adovasio et al. 1977; Adovasio, Gunn, Donahue, and Stuckenrath 1978; Adovasio, Gunn, Donahue, Stuckenrath, Guilday, and Lord 1978). The excavations defined 11 major stratigraphic units that span the past 16,000, and possibly 19,000, ^{14}C years. As with many limestone caves and rockshelters, the organic preservation at the site was exceptional. The rockshelter contained rare and well-preserved examples of basketry and other organic material. In addition, the earliest cultural occupations in the rockshelter have been dated to 19,100 ±810 B.P. (SI-2062) and 19,600 ± 2400 B.P. (SI-2060). Another suite of ^{14}C dates from this same level suggests another occupation approximately 16,000–12,000 ^{14}C years B.P. (Adovasio et al. 1977:32–33). The oldest artifacts come from Stratum IIa, which had produced 13 lithic tools and more than 300 stone waste flakes and pieces of flaking debitage as of 1977. The three most diagnostic specimens are a medial section of a retouched blade, a fragment of a flake knife, and a triangular biface (Figure 3.16). Although it is not clear if they are food remains, faunal and floral remains from the middle and lower Stratum IIa include white-tailed deer, possibly small game, hickory, walnut, and hackberry (Adovasio 1993:211-213).

The stratigraphy at the site is well defined and separates episodes of cultural occupation. Although large standard deviations are associated with many of the early ^{14}C determinations, they are stratigraphically consistent. However, other researchers (Dincauze 1981; Haynes 1977, 1980; Mead 1980) have questioned the age of the earliest cultural material. They note that older Pleistocene levels do not contain extinct Ice Age animals, suggesting that these levels might actually be Holocene in age and that the radiocarbon dates from the lowest levels might have been contaminated by coal or other ancient organic matter. This could possibly cause the resultant dates to be older than the actual time of human occupation. Adovasio and his colleagues (Adovasio, Gunn, Donahue, and Stuckenrath 1978; Adovasio, Gunn, Donahue, Stuckenrath, Guilday, and Lord 1978; Adovasio et

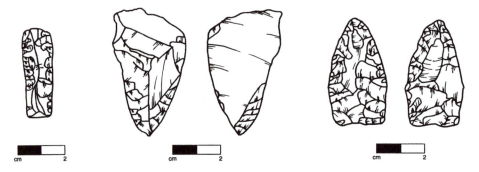

Figure 3.16 Artifacts recovered from the lowest levels at Meadowcroft Rockshelter. (Redrawn from Adovasio et al. 1997 by James Watts.)

al. 1980) have attempted to address these issues through additional interdisciplinary research, and they conclude that the dating of the site is reliable. If the ^{14}C chronology is correct, Meadowcroft Rockshelter may contain the longest occupational sequence yet discovered in North America.

Dutton and Selby

The Dutton and Selby sites are approximately 27 km (17 mi) apart and are located on the High Plains of eastern Colorado, southwest of Wray, Colorado. Both sites were extensively excavated by the Smithsonian Institution under the overall direction of Dennis Stanford during the summers of 1976, 1977, and 1978. Because of their proximity and similarity, Stanford (1979c, 1983) and Graham (1981) have consistently reported these two sites together, and that format is followed here.

The sites are shallow depressions eroded into the Peorian loess (>17,000 B.P.) and contain the bones of Pleistocene mammals (*Camelus* sp., *Equus* sp., and *Bison* sp.). Lying disconformably upon the loess are a series of lacustrine strata dating between approximately 17,000–12,000 B.P. (Figure 3.17). At both Dutton and Selby, a gleysol (dated to 11,710 ± 150 B.P. [SI 2877] at the Selby site [Stanford 1979b:105, 1983]) overlays lacustrine units. Each unit contains an array of Pleistocene fauna, including mammoth, horse, bison, camel, sloth, peccary, and several species of small mammals. The lacustrine deposits apparently resulted from ephemeral ponds, or playas, that existed during the late Pleistocene. Many of the bones recovered from these levels have polished edges, impact fractures, breakage apparently for marrow extraction, striations, and flake scars and indentations possibly the result of cutting or chopping (Figure 3.18). These modifications are strikingly similar to those reported from the Old Crow basin and to some ethnographic specimens (Stanford 1979a:120, 1983:67).

At the Dutton site, a Clovis horizon associated with a buried soil stratigraphically overlays older levels containing modified Pleistocene bones. Seven small, impact lithic flakes were recovered from screen washed lacustrine sediments at the Dutton site. Several flakes were thermally altered, and they were angular, not rounded, suggesting they did not originate from the gravels in the lacustrine deposits. A scraper was also found in the Peorian loess among disarticulated camel bones at the bottom of a rodent burrow.

Stanford (1983:65) regards the data from both Dutton and Selby as equivocal in terms of demonstrating the presence of humans in North America prior to 11,500 B.P. Although these sites may be noncultural in origin, it has not been demonstrated that noncultural mechanisms can account for all types of bone modification recovered from these low energy depositional environments.

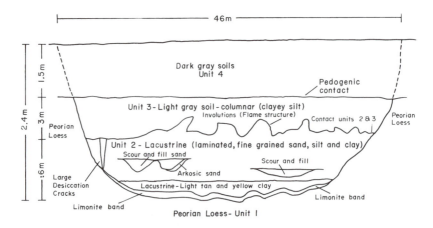

Figure 3.17 Generalized geological cross section of the Dutton site (from Stanford 1979b:104). (Courtesy of Dennis Stanford.)

Figure 3.18 Modified bones from the Lacustrine Unit at the Selby site (from Stanford 1979b: 110). (Photograph courtesy of Dennis Stanford.)

Lamb Spring

Lamb Spring is located approximately 3.2 km (2 mi) east of the Front Range of the Rocky Mountains in Douglas County, Colorado approximately 11 km (7 mi) southwest of Littleton, Colorado. The South Platte River is approximately 1.6 km (1 mi) west of the spring. The site was a natural spring that attracted large mammals and human predators during the late Pleistocene and early Holocene. The site was discovered by the landowner Charles Lamb, who exhumed the bones of extinct Pleistocene mammals while attempting to expand the spring for use as a stock pond in the summer of 1960. The spring is now dry.

Lamb Spring has been the subject of repeated archeological excavations by the Smithsonian Institution, first under the overall direction of Waldo Wedell in 1961–1962 and later by Dennis Stanford in 1981–1982 (Rancier et al. 1981; Scott n.d.; Stanford, Wedel, and Scott 1981; Wedel 1965). Wedel's excavations documented eight stratigraphic units and two primary bone beds. A Cody complex (a late Paleoindian complex generally dating between circa 9,000–8,400 B.P.) bison kill is stratigraphically above an older sedimentary unit deposited in channels cut by a slow moving stream fed by an aquifer (McCartney 1980). A single collagen date on mammoth bone of 13,140 ± 1000 B.P. suggested the lower level may be older than Clovis sites. Although Wedel's excavations did not find any artifacts in the level containing extinct Pleistocene fauna, he believed that the manner in which the bones had been modified, flaked, and stacked suggested that the mammoths may have been butchered by humans (Wedel 1965).

Stanford placed a test trench at the site in 1979. This revealed more of the Pleistocene bone bed and a 15 kg (33 lb) boulder that showed signs of battering indicative of use as a hammer stone, which Stanford suggested could have been used to break the massive mammoth bones. The nearest source for this manuport (a culturally unmodified object transported to an archeological site by humans) is the South Platte River, which is at least 1.6 km (1 mi) west of Lamb Spring. Excavations in 1980–1981 focused on exposing and interpreting the possible pre-11,500 B.P. level as well as excavating the Cody complex bison kill. Two buried channels were defined, one containing the mammoth and other Pleistocene faunal remains and another containing the Cody bison kill. The lower, and older, channel contained the skeletal remains of mammoth (*Mammuthus columbi*) (Figure 3.19), camel (*Camelus* sp.), horse (*Equus* sp.), canids, cervids, birds, and other small vertebrates (G. Haynes 1991:226; Rancier et al. 1981).

Four crudely flaked chalcedony specimens were found with the mammoth bones. However, the investigators could not ascertain with certainty whether they were manufactured by humans, resulted from trampling by animals, or were somehow geologically modified by the spring. Further excavation also revealed

Figure 3.19 Lamb Spring Mammoth (*Mammuthus columbi*) crania and tusks, in situ, in 1982. (Photograph courtesy of Dennis Stanford.)

that the large boulder came from an area of the site where the Cody channel had cut into the level containing the mammoth bones. Consequently, it is possible that stratigraphic mixing in this particular area of the site was responsible for its association with the mammoth bones. Although the boulder could have been used as an anvil to fracture bison bone, it is more suitable as a hammer stone for breaking larger, more massive mammoth bone. The biological age range and composition of the mammoths excavated from the site suggest to G. Haynes (1991:204, 227) that the mammoth remains represent an assemblage that is not typical of human kill sites and may be more reminiscent of assemblages accumulated as a result of both cultural and noncultural factors.

In 1995, Lamb Spring was purchased by the Archaeological Conservancy, an organization dedicated to the acquisition and preservation of important archeological sites. Renewed investigations by the Denver Museum of Natural History in cooperation with Dennis Stanford and the Smithsonian Institution included a subsurface coring, stratigraphic mapping, and AMS dating program under the direction of Thomas Stafford. Stafford defined the limits of the spring deposits that contain both the Cody complex age bison bones and the Pleistocene faunal remains. These studies revealed that substantial portions of the site remain unexcavated. Preservation of collagen in many of the bones from the Pleistocene levels is highly variable probably rendering some bone dates from this level unreliable. Consequently, it is difficult to use ^{14}C to determine whether the bones were deposited abruptly or over a relatively long period of time. However, individual sunflower seeds collected from the Pleistocene bone bed have been dated by the AMS method and provide exceptionally accurate dating of the Pleistocene spring deposits. These determinations suggest that sediments dating to the Clovis period circa 11,300 B.P. may disconformably overlie sediments that contain older mammoth remains (Stafford, personal communication 1997). If the older mammoth remains represent a noncultural accumulation as G. Haynes suggests, the younger deposits may contain evidence of Clovis occupation. Additional research is necessary to answer these questions.

La Sena and Jensen

The La Sena site is located on the shore of Medicine Creek Reservoir in Frontier County, Nebraska. The disarticulated, fractured, and flaked bones of a mammoth have been excavated under the direction of Steve Holen, University of Nebraska. Radiocarbon samples indicate the site dates to between 19,000–18,000 B.P. The mammoth bones are buried approximately 3.35 m (11 ft) deep in fine-grained wind-blown loess. The bones apparently exhibit little if any evidence of carnivore gnawing (Figure 3.20).

Although no stone tools have been found at La Sena, the thick shafts of the mammoth limb bones have been fractured by forces that have left distinctive impact fractures similar to those recognized at a number of Clovis sites. Holen (1994) suggests that the bones were then flaked to produce sharp-edged flakes that were used as tools and discarded at the site. He has also recognized a similar pattern of bone breakage and flaking at the nearby Jensen mammoth site, which has been dated to circa 13,000 B.P. At both the La Sena and Jensen sites, there is no geologic evidence of former high-energy environments, such as rivers, streams, or rock slides that could have broken the mammoth bones. Because the bones are wholly contained within the loess, which has been deposited relatively gently over long periods of time, it is difficult to explain how these massive mammoth bones were broken and subsequently flaked by any other mechanism than human intervention.

Cactus Hill

The Cactus Hill site is located on the eastern bank of the Nottoway River in southeastern Virginia. Work began at the site in 1993, and four distinct localities have been identified and designated A, B, C, and D. Area B is reported to contain

Figure 3.20 Photograph of "stacked" probocidean ribs at the La Sena site. (Photograph courtesy of Steve Holen.)

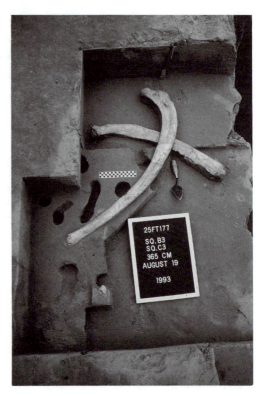

the oldest dated archeological remains (McAvoy and McAvoy 1997). The site contains a long record extending from sometime between approximately 15,000–11,000 B.P. until historic times. The cultural materials are found within an eolian (wind blown) sand that overlays older deposits of fluvial (stream deposited) sands and gravels, which in turn overlays gray clay. The site apparently has a long history and was preferred as a campsite because of its location near the Nottoway River, its elevation above the adjacent terrain, and good drainage by the underlying sand and gravel (Jones and Johnson 1997; McAvoy and McAvoy 1997).

The stone tools from the pre-11,500 B.P. level are manufactured from local stones probably collected from the bed of the nearby Nottoway River. In area B, a variety of flakes and blade-like flakes made of quartzite has been recovered from a stratigraphic unit underlying a Clovis occupational horizon at this site. Although the assemblage is relatively small, McAvoy and McAvoy (1997) describe the lithic artifacts as triangular projectile points, waste flakes, retouched flakes, retouched blade-like flakes, and cores from which the blade-like flakes were struck (Figure 3.21). Some of the blade cores appear to have been used as tools.

The earliest use of the site appears to have been for very brief periods of time.

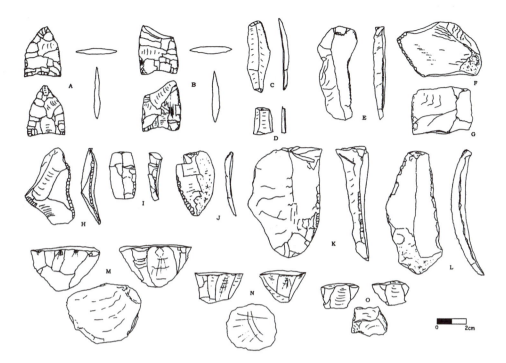

Figure 3.21 Artifacts from the oldest stratigraphic levels of the Cactus Hill site: (a) and (b) projectile points; (c)–(e), (h)–(l) blades and blade like flakes; (f) and (g) retouched flakes; (m)–(o) blade cores (modified from McAvoy and McAvoy 1997:157).

The lithic remains were recovered around the charcoal apparently resulting from a fire built directly on the surface. Charcoal has been identified as white pine, a species that no longer grows in the region. Two radiocarbon dates from hearth-like features have produced dates of 16,670 ± 730 B.P. (Beta 97708) (fine carbon particles collected by flotation) and 15,070 ± 70 B.P. (Beta 91590) (New Dates at Old Site 1997). No faunal remains were recovered from this level, but analysis of residual protein, presumably preserved on lithic tools, suggest that rabbit may have been exploited by these early people (McAvoy and McAvoy 1997: 179).

The earliest evidence for human occupation at Cactus Hill, locality B, is stratigraphically below a later Clovis-like fluted point occupation dated to 10,920 ± 250 (Beta 81589). The geologic context of the cultural material and concordant ^{14}C determinations for the site as a whole indicate that this occupation is older than 11,000 B.P. Although the assemblage of artifacts is small, the site has been professionally excavated and appears to contain a well-documented human occupation that occurred prior to Clovis times.

Texas Street and Mission Ridge

Several localities near Texas Street in San Diego, California, have produced crudely flaked-stone artifacts that George Carter (1952, 1957, 1980) suggested may date to mid-Pleistocene times. Most of the artifacts are made of local quartzite and were recovered from fluvial deposits along the San Diego River. The specimens are sometimes associated with oxidized hearth-like features that can be up to 30 m (100 ft) in diameter and over half a meter thick (Wormington 1957:223). Wormington (1957:223) found it difficult to accept the interpretation that these large burned areas were hearths and believed that they are the result of noncultural factors. Because the sites are located along an active geological fault, Stanford (1983:71) suggests that the cobbles may be bipolarly crushed in situ by geologic pressure and subsequently retouched after they were eroded and as they moved down the steep embankments.

Reeves et al. (1986) report similar specimens from a mid-Pleistocene terrace of the San Diego River called Mission Ridge, and they compare these specimens to Carter's Texas Street assemblage. Reeves et al. (1986) argue that the geologic processes that Stanford (1983) suggested may have created the Texas Street specimens may not explain the production of the Mission Ridge assemblage. Reeves attributes both assemblages to a Middle to Late Pleistocene cobble core/unifacial flake cultural tradition. However, they conclude that most of the bipolar cores and flaked cobbles result from noncultural mechanisms (Reeves et al. 1986:76–78). The Mission Ridge assemblage is not directly dated, and no empirical evidence indicates that the Mission Ridge and Texas Street assemblages are contemporaneous. It is highly probable that both assemblages result from noncultural geologic processes.

Channel Islands

The Channel Islands, located off the coast of southern California near Santa Barbara, are divided into two groups: the northern and southern Channel Islands. During the Pleistocene when the sea level was lower, the northern islands formed a single land mass called Santa rosae Island, which was approximately 8 km (5 mi) from the mainland (Orr 1968:18). However, as sea level rose at the end of the last Ice Age, Santa rosae was separated into several smaller islands. The mammoths recovered from the Channel Islands are very small, or pygmies (Figure 3.22). It is believed that in an effort to adapt to the limited island habitat, natural selection favored smaller animals, resulting in a substantial reduction in size over time.

Since the early 1950s, Phil Orr and R. Berger have reported what they believe

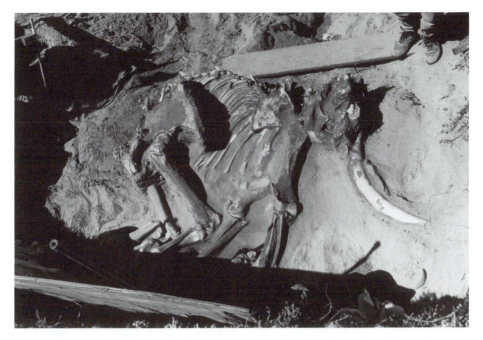

Figure 3.22 Articulated skeleton of a pygmy mammoth, in situ, Santa Rosa Island. (Photograph courtesy of Larry Agenbroad.)

are in situ associations of mammoth remains, stone tools, and hearths on the Channel Islands (Berger 1980, 1982; Berger and Orr 1966; Orr 1951, 1967, 1968; Orr and Berger 1966). However, other researchers have questioned the cultural origins of these deposits (Cushing et al. 1986; Erlandson 1991; Glassow 1977, 1980; Moratto 1984). Sediment and magnetic analyses have been employed to test whether the hearth-like sediments exhibit physical changes resulting from heating. The results indicated that the modifications to the sediments were not characteristic of fire areas (Cushing et al. 1986). Further analyses indicated that the dark discoloration on the bones resulted from mineral staining rather than burning and that carbonized wood believed to be charcoal had actually been carbonized by ground water, not by fire. The analysis concluded that many, if not all, of the so-called fire areas were created by water moving through (and possibly on the surface of the sediments before they were buried). This created ocherous areas resulting from concentrations of iron, manganese, and other minerals, that created areas of red, orange, and black coloration. This same processes was also responsible for carbonizing wood and other plant material and staining bones. As a result of these analyses, the association of early humans and pygmy mammoths in the Channel Islands is not accepted by most scientists.

Calico

The Calico site is located approximately 8 km (5 mi) north of the Mojave River in San Bernardino County, California. Excavations at the site were an outgrowth of archeological surveys of Pleistocene Lake Manix. These discoveries ultimately led Ruth DeEtte Simpson to show the site and its artifacts to the famous African archeologist Louis Leakey in 1963 (Simpson 1979:9). Oxidized cobbles thought to be the remains of a hearth were found at the site, but charcoal was not present. Based primarily on lithic technological analysis and typological comparisons with Pleistocene collections from Asia, the deeply buried position of the specimens within the sediments, and the geologic dating of the deposits, Leakey, Simpson, and others concluded that Calico was a legitimate archeological site containing artifacts (Figure 3.23) that were more than 150,000 years old

Figure 3.23 Line drawings of bifacially flaked stone specimens from Calico. (Redrawn from photographs [Simpson 1979:39] by James Watts.)

(Leakey et al. 1968; Schuiling 1979; Simpson et al. 1986). However, these conclusions have not been broadly accepted by archeologists.

The artifacts were excavated from a massive alluvial fan, called the Yermo Fan, which is located along the ancient shorelines of Pleistocene Lake Manix. Duvall and Venner (1979) conducted a statistical analysis of the artifacts from the Calico site and concluded that the artifacts were not manufactured by humans. Stanford (1983) has suggested that their statistical analysis may not be applicable to this particular problem because it is based on comparison with much later New World bifacial technologies, rather than Old World pebble tool lithic technologies.

Alluvial fans are formed by rocks and finer-grained sediments that are transported by water and gravity from a relatively narrow mountain valley onto a broader flatter area. Most of the artifacts from the Calico site are made of chalcedony, which outcrops in the canyon above the alluvial fan. Chalcedony cobbles have been deposited in the fan along with other sediments (Clements 1979:26). Given this geologic context, the artifacts may have been formed (chipped and flaked) by noncultural geologic processes during the natural formation of the Yermo Fan, rather than having been manufactured by humans (Haynes 1973). The artifact assemblage probably represents selective sampling and retention of non-culturally flaked stones from the millions of rocks moved downslope, many of which have been chipped by geologic processes.

Pendejo Cave

Pendejo Cave is located on Fort Bliss, a U. S. military reservation in south-central New Mexico not far from the community of Orogrande. The north-facing cave appears to have been formed by mechanical weathering along a small anticline in dolomite (Figure 3.24). Downslope dislocation and movement of the weathered rubble has formed a short cave approximately 4 m (13 ft) wide by approximately 8–10 m (26–33 ft) into bedrock from the dripline.

The cave contains stratified deposits that provide an extensive paleoecological record. Evidence of human use of the cave is demonstrated by hearths, lithic artifacts, textiles (Adovasio and Hyland 1993), modified bones, human hair, and clay artifacts. According to the investigators, 57 radiocarbon determinations demonstrate that the deposits span more than 55,000 years (Chrisman et al. 1996; MacNeish 1991, 1992, 1993). No chert inclusions occur in the dolomite bedrock, and consequently, any cherts or other exotic lithic material must have been transported into the cave by humans or animals.

The cave was occupied by humans during Archaic (later than circa 8,000 B.P.) and possibly Paleoindian times (between 11,500–8,000 B.P.). However, the evidence for occupation prior to 11,500 B.P. rests on the discovery of fractured and modified bones of Pleistocene animals, human fingerprints and handprints pre-

Figure 3.24 The entrance to Pendejo Cave, New Mexico, 1995.

served in fire hardened clay, and burned zones interpreted as hearths or culturally generated fires. The cave deposits contain seven to nine major, and many more minor, periods of packrat occupation. Packrat nests contain large amounts of vegetation including grasses, sticks, twigs, and other organic debris. Many of the burned zones thought to be cultural in origin are actually burned packrat middens. They were probably ignited by noncultural fires spreading into the cave from adjacent areas. These burned areas contain charred macrofossil remains that include packrat feces and other packrat midden material and do not appear to be anthropogenic.

To compound the interpretative difficulties at Pendejo, the deposits have been extensively bioturbated (the churning or mixing of sediments by animals or plants) (Dincauze 1997) during thousands of years of packrat nesting and burrowing. Despite descriptions suggesting the stratigraphic units are well defined, not mixed, and that they demonstrate "acceptable geological and stratigraphic integrity" (Chrisman et al. 1996:362–64, 373; Chrisman et al. 1997), many units have been repeatedly crosscut by rodent burrowing and nesting (Stafford, personal communication 1995). The cultural hearths dating to the Pleistocene have been interpreted by other investigators as burned packrat nests and middens (Stafford, personal communication 1995).

The identification of human skin impressions and fingerprints preserved in clay has been questioned by other researchers. They suggest the preserved print ridges are not human prints based on the number of ridges in a given area (Shaffer and Baker 1997). However, Chrisman (1997) argues that the prints have been distorted because the photographs are of curved surfaces and because baking and drying the clay after the impressions were made modified them. Even if the prints are legitimate artifacts, the extensive bioturbation at the site makes their association with Pleistocene age botanical and faunal specimens questionable.

There are also equally plausible noncultural explanations for the modified Pleistocene bone, such as desiccation fracturing, carnivore fracture and flaking, rodent gnawing, rockfall, and rubble scaring. Jagged blocks of dolomite that have fallen from the ceiling of the cave are large enough to fracture, flake, or scar any bone lying on the surface. Many of these large blocks have fallen a distance of 1–3 m (3–10 ft), and some rocks weigh more than 40 kg (100 lb). Johnson and Shipman (1993) conducted scanning electron microscopic analysis of a sample of bone from the Pleistocene levels and were not able to identify evidence of cultural modification on any of the specimens.

In the absence of clearly identifiable bone tools, such as awls or projectile points, a complex taphonomic setting such as Pendejo Cave requires detailed bone by bone description and analysis that analytically excludes other possible means of noncultural alteration. Although Pendejo Cave contains a wealth of archeological and paleoecological data, evidence of human activity prior to 11,500 B.P. cannot be documented satisfactorily. Noncultural taphonomic processes, noncultural fires, bioturbation, weathering, and rockfall best explain the earliest suite of specimens and other evidence from Pendejo Cave.

Sandia Cave

Sandia Cave is located in central New Mexico in Las Huertas Canyon in the northern Sandia Mountains. Frank Hibben (1937, 1940, 1941a, 1941b) originally postulated that Sandia Cave contained the oldest cultural complex in North America that predated Clovis and that exhibited typological similarities to Solutrean sites of the European Paleolithic. Controversy has surrounded the interpretation of the discoveries at Sandia Cave since the first reports began to appear in the 1930s and early 1940s (Bliss 1940a, 1940b; Hibben 1937, 1940, 1941a, 1941b). The controversial issues range from the stratigraphic integrity of the artifacts (Bliss 1940a, 1940b; Brand 1940; Byers 1942; Haynes and Agogino 1986; Hibben 1937, 1940, 1955, 1957; Stevens and Agogino 1975) and the accuracy of the radiocarbon dates (Crane 1955; Johnson 1957; Krieger 1957; Stevens and Agogino 1975) to the professional integrity of the principal investigator (Preston 1995). This protracted debate over a period of more than fifty years has resulted in diverse opinions regarding the age and nature of Sandia Culture.

Hibben (1937, 1940, 1941 a, 1941b, 1942) described the cave stratigraphy from the surface downward beginning with a recent layer containing Holocene age artifacts, modern fauna, and ground sloth. Underlying this lay a calcium carbonate crust extending from the front to the rear of the cave. Directly beneath this was a layer containing Folsom artifacts and a consolidated mixture of bone, limestone fragments, and other debris including the remains of extinct Pleistocene animals. Below the Folsom level was a layer of culturally sterile yellow ochre that was in turn underlain by the Sandia deposit that also contained the bones of extinct mammals, limestone fragments, and other sediments. Below this was a culturally sterile "clay," or limestone residuum, resting on top of the limestone bedrock. Hibben believed the stratigraphic units were undisturbed and the relative chronological sequence correct. However, other archeologists believed the stratigraphic units were disturbed and the chronology as interpreted by Hibben was incorrect.

The issues surrounding Sandia cave remained largely unresolved until painstaking and detailed reinvestigation of the site was begun in 1961 by C. Vance Haynes and George Agogino. Their research continued sporadically from that time until 1986, when their results and conclusions were published. Their field research focused on remnants of the stratigraphy adhering to the side walls of the cave and portions of the deposits that had not been excavated during the earlier work, analysis of faunal remains, and additional ^{14}C dating. Their reanalysis of the stratigraphic unit from which the Sandia artifacts were derived (called unit X by Haynes and Agogino) demonstrated that the site had been heavily disturbed by rodent burrowing and that the artifacts, including the Sandia points had been introduced into the lower levels by bioturbation (Haynes and Agogino 1986). Fifty percent of the mandibles collected by Haynes and Agogino were pocket gopher and 20 percent were pack rat. They found that ^{14}C dates on these remains spanned the interval circa 13,500–8,500 B.P. demonstrating that these animals inhabited the cave in large numbers during the time when the artifacts and stratigraphic units containing them were being deposited.

The classic Sandia points frequently illustrated in the literature (Figure 3.25) seem to be restricted to north and central New Mexico. They have also been discovered at the Lucy site in New Mexico (Wormington 1957) and from some surface sites in the region. Specimens that are somewhat similar and date to the early Archaic period in New Mexico are called Bahada points (Irwin-Williams 1973). It has been suggested (Tony Baker, personal communication 1996) that the Sandia points found throughout the region may be reworked Bajada points. Haynes and Agogino (1986) have also suggested that the distinctive Sandia points may be specialized tools made and used by Clovis people to mine ochre at the cave. No matter what the origin or function of Sandia points, there is no historic relationship between the development of Sandia and Solutrean artifacts. Sandia points are technologically distinct from Solutrean points, which were

Figure 3.25 Casts of Sandia points housed at the Denver Museum of Natural History. *From left to right*: (a) Sandia Cave, Type I; (b) Sandia Cave, Type II; and (c) Fluted Sandia point, from the Lucy site. (Photograph by Rick Wicker, Denver Museum of Natural History.)

made by unifacially flaking true blades to form a shouldered projectile point. Today the artifacts from Sandia Cave are no longer accepted as being older than Clovis sites found elsewhere in the region, and Sandia Culture is no longer regarded as a viable cultural complex.

Lewisville

In the early 1950s, numerous hearths were discovered in a barrow pit near Lewisville, Texas. The site is located within the impoundment of a local reservoir Lewisville Lake and rising water flooded the site in 1957. The site contained numerous burned areas that were associated with Pleistocene faunal remains including probocidean, bison, horse, and camel, as well as the bones of extant species. A Clovis projectile point was recovered from one hearth that yielded a ^{14}C date of circa 37,000 B.P.; subsequent radiocarbon dates from the other hearths were all greater than 37,000 B.P. (Crook and Harris 1957, 1962). Because these early ^{14}C determinations did not correlate with similar artifacts from other sites, the dating of the Lewisville site has been controversial (Heizer and Brooks 1965; Wormington 1957).

The site remained an enigma until 1978 when a drought reduced the water level in Lewisville Lake to expose the area in which the hearths were located. The site was immediately investigated by archeologists from the Corps of Engineers who discovered that it was still intact. A more comprehensive reinvestigation was undertaken by Dennis Stanford from the Smithsonian Institution who began work in 1979, only to be stopped after a few weeks by rising water. However, the lake level dropped and exposed the site again in 1980 (Stanford 1983).

Excavations by Stanford (Figure 3.26) recovered additional bone from the hearths and smaller features. Laboratory analysis of the carbonized material from one of the hearths revealed that the prehistoric occupants of the site had burned lignite (coal) in the hearths. Lignite occurs naturally in the underlying stratigraphic unit. This analysis indicates that the extremely early dates at Lewisville result from contamination of the ^{14}C samples by older (dead) carbon contained in the underlying lignite (Stanford 1983:70).

To further complicate matters, stratigraphic analysis by John Albanese re-

Figure 3.26 Excavations at the Lewisville Site. (Photograph courtesy of Dennis Stanford.)

vealed that an unconformity, a break in the depositional sequence caused either by lack of deposition or erosion, was present at the site (Stanford 1983:70). In this case, the unconformity was the result of erosion of the original occupational surfaces, leaving only the bottom of the hearths.

The reinvestigation revealed that the hearths had been excavated into older stratigraphic units. Analysis of bone and other organic remains found within the burned features identified the remains of small mammals, egg shells, reptiles, amphibians, roasted mud dauber nests, and hackberry seeds. On the other hand, the remains of the large megafauna commonly associated with the Clovis complex were not identified. This evidence supports an interpretation of Clovis people as generalized gatherers as well as big game specialists (Stanford 1995).

Little Salt Spring

Little Salt Spring is located near Charlotte Harbor in southwestern Florida. It is frequently discussed in relationship to nearby Warm Mineral Springs (Chapter 5), which also has produced early archeological material and human remains. Little Salt Spring is a freshwater cenote (a vertical shaft in limestone that contains water and is open to the surface). During the Pleistocene, sea level was lower and this in turn lowered the water level within the cenote. Because the regional climate was dryer at that time, the spring attracted humans and animals. The lower water table exposed a rockshelter-like ledge about 26 m (85 ft) below the modern surface of the spring, which was used by early people.

Clausen et at. (1979) report finding the collapsed shell of an extinct tortoise that had been impaled with a sharp pointed wooden stake on the 26 m (85 ft) ledge. A bone from the tortoise dated to 13,450 ± 190 B.P. (Tx–2335), and the wooden stake apparently used to kill the animal was dated to 12,030 ± 200 B.P. (Tx–2636). Some of the tortoise bones and part of the shell were carbonized suggesting the animal was killed with the stake and cooked in its shell. Other artifacts recovered from the ledge include a socketed antler projectile point and a unique nonreturning oak throwing stick, or boomerang. Several sharpened wooden stakes and a wooden mortar dating between 10,000–9,000 B.P. were also recovered. The remains of other extinct Pleistocene animals were found on the submerged 26 m (85 ft) ledge including bison, mammoth or mastodon, wood ibis, ground sloth, and two species of freshwater turtle (Clausen et al. 1979).

Many archeologists have regarded Little Salt Spring as a Clovis site that has slightly anomalous early dates. However, it is equally plausible that the occupation of the ledge predates the Clovis interval, circa 11,500–11,000 B.P. Rigorous AMS ^{14}C dating of the artifacts and fauna from the 26 m (85 ft) ledge is essential to resolve this question.

Summary

The preceding review demonstrates that several different types of depositional settings occur for sites that are reported to be older than 11,500 B.P. in North America. These include: (1) caves and rockshelters; (2) eolian (wind blown) deposits; (3) spring, bog, and lake sediments; and (4) fluvial (stream) deposits. To correctly interpret potential archeological evidence in these contexts, scientists must apply a broad interdisciplinary perspective to each site and its associated environment.

Because many of these depositional settings are extremely complex, researchers can no longer responsibly investigate sites using only the methods and principles of a single discipline. Today competent and professional excavation and analysis require interdisciplinary teams of experts trained in archeology, geology, and paleobiology to properly excavate, analyze, and interpret potential archeological remains. If research teams can not be formed, sites should not be excavated until the resources and personnel are available to do it properly.

Interpretation of possible cultural remains must be made in conjunction with an understanding of the ecological and geologic processes that operate at each of these types of sites (Table 3.1). The methods employed to evaluate the evidence must be appropriate to problems posed by each type of setting. These methods encompass a wide range of disciplines and types of analysis including radiometric and relative dating, taphonomic analysis, environmental reconstruction, forensic analysis, investigation of the geologic processes, knowledge of animal behavior, and numerous other research approaches. It is no longer considered sound science to approach these complex types of sites from the perspective and training of a single discipline.

Cave and rockshelter deposits are notoriously plagued with a variety of factors making analysis of the deposits and the specimens recovered from them extremely complex and difficult to interpret. These settings attract a variety of carnivores and other animals, in addition to humans. Frequently the same cave will be shared by different species depending on the season of the year. It is challenging to distinguish the physical evidence resulting from animal activity (such as various types of bone modification and transport) from evidence resulting from human occupation. Bioturbation and rockfall can further complicate the archeological record, making it extremely difficult to separate the cultural from noncultural evidence and chronology.

Other high-energy environments, such as river systems, glaciers, springs, and lake margins, can modify bone and other objects in ways that exhibit an uncanny resemblance to artifacts made by humans. Flowing water and ice can entrain, polish, facet, striate, flake, and fracture rocks and bones in a variety of ways that can be mistaken for artifacts by the most seasoned scientists. Bioturbation,

Table 3.1

Evaluation of Pre-11,500 B.P. Sites in North America

| Site Name | Criteria | | | | | # of Criteria Met |
	Artifacts	Stratigraphy	Dating	Environmental Context	Human Remains	
Blue Fish Cave 1	x	?	?	x	o	2
Bowmont Park	?	x	x	?	o	2
Cactus Hill	x	x	x	x	o	4
Calico	?	x	x	x	o	3
Channel Islands	x	?	?	?	o	1
Dutton	?	x	x	x	o	3
Ester Stripping Pit	x	?	x	?	o	2
Fairbanks Creek 1940	x	?	x	?	o	2
Fairbanks Creek 1948	x	?	x	?	o	2
Goldstream Pit G2	x	x	Holocene	x	o	4
Hebior	x	x	x	x	o	4
La Sena	?	x	x	x	o	3
Lamb Spring	x	?	x	x	o	3
Lewisville	x	?	?	?	o	1
Little Salt Spring	x	?	x	x	o	3
Mammoth Meadow	?	x	x	x	Hair?	3
Mannis Mastadon	?	?	x	x	o	2
Meadowcroft	x	x	?	?	o	2
Old Crow Basin	?	?	x	x	o	2
Pendejo Cave	x	?	?	x	Hand Prints?	2
Sandia Cave	x	?	?	?	o	1
Schaefer	x	x	x	x	o	4
Selby	?	x	x	x	o	3
Texas Street	?	x	?	?	o	1
Trail Creek Caves	?	?	x	x	o	2
Varsity Estates	?	x	x	?	o	2

Total Sites **26**

Key:	x = acceptable evidence present	1 Criterion Met	4
	? = evidence questionable	2 Criteria Met	11
	o = absent	3 Criteria Met	7
		4 Criteria Met	4

solifluction, earthquakes, landslides, and a variety of other sediment moving processes can disturb, and even reverse, stratigraphy and relocate cultural objects and organic material used for radiometric dating. The physical and biological world is capable of combining many of these processes in a virtually infinite array of contexts that necessitate careful interdisciplinary research if the data are to be accurately interpreted. At some sites, like Sandia and Pendejo Caves, the excavators failed to recognize important evidence of bioturbation, specifically rodent burrowing that has mixed artifacts from higher levels into lower deposits.

In lower energy environments such as loess deposits, playas, and peat bogs, noncultural modification of lithic and faunal material is subtle and difficult to explain. At present, there are no satisfactory alternative taphonomic explanations for sites such as Manis, La Sena, Schaefer and Hebior, Cactus Hill, and Little Salt Spring. It appears that some, if not all, of these locales may have been visited by humans prior to 11,500 B.P.

Another possible explanation for some sites may be that Clovis, or even later, people may have scavenged bone for utilitarian purposes from animals that may have died hundreds or even thousands of years earlier. These long-dead animals may have provided quarries where bone could be easily scavenged, disarticulated, flaked, stacked, and used to make expedient tools. This type of adaptation might be particularly useful in landscapes where lithics were not readily available or during winter when perhaps only bones protruded from the snow or when the frozen earth made subsurface quarrying difficult. Evidence for scavenging mammoth remains by later people has been suggested for some Beringian sites, including Broken Mammoth, Mead, Swan Point, and Berelekh. This type of scavenging could produce anomalous bone beds that exhibit human use of the faunal remains but lack other definitive archeological evidence. Quarrying ancient bone could explain the contradictory evidence of cultural activity and anomalous early ^{14}C determinations derived from bone. While scavanging might explain some sites, at other sites, like La Sena and Schaefer, mammoths appear to have been buried shortly after they died.

There is an increasing trend to use forensic and microscopic evidence to establish human occupation. Such evidence includes the presence of human fingerprints, hair, lithic microchips, blood, and other residues. Many of these methods used to detect this evidence are derived from other disciplines, primarily microscopy, microbiology, and physics, fields in which many archeologists are often poorly trained. Although these methods hold great promise to increase our ability to recognize the presence of early humans in the Americas, they also introduce new problems. Archeologists, for the most part, must rely on others who have the requisite training but may lack appreciation for problems of contamination in prehistoric settings. Most archeologists will not accept forensic evidence alone, such as residues on a stone, hair fragments, or fingerprints, in the absence of other recognizable cultural objects or features. Until professionally acceptable protocols have been established for sampling and identifying these types of evidence, the results will remain questionable.

Reliable AMS dating (on osseous materials, such as bone, antler, and ivory) has enabled archeologists to solve complex chronological problems associated with many of these early sites. For example, AMS dating methods resolved the age of Holocene cultural objects that had been mixed with modified Pleistocene faunal remains from the muck deposits near Fairbanks, Alaska and Old Crow in Canada's Yukon Territory. The eloquence of this technique is that it enables researchers to accurately date small amounts of bone and other organic materials without destroying entire specimens. Thus, researchers are able to preserve what may be some of the oldest and rarest artifacts in the Americas.

The analysis of the specimens recovered from Varsity Estates and the Calico Hills is strikingly similar to the discovery by Charles Abbott (1876, 1883, 1889, 1892) of Paleolithic artifacts among the Trenton gravels approximately 100 years earlier and later discredited by W. H. Holmes (1890, 1892, 1893) (see Chapter 2). Calico Hills may be an excellent example of how Old World criteria, i.e. typological comparison, has been applied in a New World archeological context in the absence of the rigorous tests required of early New World sites. Even the initial endorsement of the site by such an eminent scholar as Louis B. Leakey was not sufficient to persuade most North American archeologists regarding the authenticity of the artifacts.

Discovering and evaluating archeological evidence resulting from the first colonization of a continent may be very different than evaluating archeological evidence from regions that have been settled for long periods of time. It is theoretically possible that some areas of North America were explored long before they were settled. Sites resulting from exploration might be very difficult to detect. For example, archeological evidence might consist of only a stone flake or two, possibly some stacked or fractured bones, and occasional fires of short duration. This is the type of archeological signature recorded at many North American sites older than 11,500 B.P.

This chapter has reviewed the evidence from more than 30 sites in Beringia and North America. None of these sites contains human remains. Analysis of sites from North America indicate that at least three sites appear to meet four of the criteria required for acceptance, seven meet three, ten meet two, and four meet only one. Taken collectively, these data indicate to many researchers pre-11,500 B.P. occupation of North America. Their analysis emphasizes the need for continued and rigorous research directed toward resolving the timing of the first human colonization of the Americas. The next chapter (Chapter 4) discusses several Central and South American sites possibly older than 11,500 B.P. that are best known to North American archeologists.

4 Early Sites in Mexico, and Central and South America

Introduction

This chapter presents and discusses selected sites south of the southern border of the Unites States. Although Mexico is part of North America, most of the archeological reports are published in Spanish, and archeological research is often analyzed in association with data from countries in Central and South America. Sites from Mexico, and Central and South America are considered by some archeologists to exhibit the most convincing evidence for human occupation prior to 11,500 B.P. (Figure 4.1). Beginning as early as the 1800s, archeological sites have been reported from South America suggesting the association of extinct Pleistocene mammals and artifacts.

By circa 11,500 B.P. a wide array of environmental zones and environments throughout South America were already settled by humans. Many of these sites are contemporaneous with, and possibly older than, Clovis sites in North America. This evidence indicates that the initial colonization of South America must have occurred prior to Clovis times.

Although several presentations and discussions of Mexican, and Central and South American sites considered to be older than 11,500 B.P. have been published (Bryan 1983, 1986; Bryan et al. 1978; Gruhn 1987; MacNeish 1983), much of the evidence supporting them has been questioned (Lynch 1991a, 1991b). Lynch (1974) suggests that although extraordinary caution has been exercised in evaluating the age and integrity of archeological sites in North America, similar restraint has not characterized the late Pleistocene and early Holocene archeology practiced by some North American researchers working in South America. While this evaluation may be applicable in a few cases, it is not shared by most New World archeologists.

This chapter focuses on archeological sites from Central and South America that are best known to North American archeologists and for which the strongest claims of human occupation prior to 11,500 B.P. have been made. As in Chapter 3, the sites are presented sequentially from north to south. This section

1. Chapala Basin
2. Tlapacoya I and II
3. Valsequillo
4. Taima-Taima
5. Las Vegas
6. Pedra Pintada
7. Pedra Furada
8. Pikimakay Cave
9. Santa Elina
10. Lapa do Boquete
11. Lapa Vermelha IV
12. Quebrada Tacahuay
13. Quebrada Jaguay
14. Monte Verde
15. Los Toldos
16. Mylodon Cave
17. Fell's Cave

Figure 4.1 Map of Mexico, and Central and South America depicting the locations of early sites presented in the text. (Prepared by Eric Parrish.)

is followed by a brief presentation of other, less well-known sites, dating to, and prior to, circa 11,500 B.P. The chapter concludes with a general discussion of the evidence for the occupation of both North and South America prior to 11,500 B.P.

Chapala Basin

Chapala Basin is located in the state of Jalisco, Mexico (Figure 4.2). Another nearby sedimentary basin containing Lake Zacoalco shares a similar geologic context with the Chapala Basin. Work has been carried out in this region of Mexico since the 1950s by Federico A. Solorzano, Museo Regional de Guadalajara and Institutio Nacional de Antropologia e Historia, Guadalajara, Mexico. Solorzano (1990) reports 11 localities around Lake Chapala and another near Lake Zacoalco from which an impressive assemblage of upper Pleistocene fauna has been recovered. Species include antelope, armadillo, bear, bison, camel, capybara, coyote, several species of deer, glyptodont, hare, sloth, horse, jaguar, llama, mammoth, otter, peccary, raccoon, saber-toothed tiger, skunk, tapir, and wolf. More than a half a million specimens have been recovered (Haley and Solorzano 1991), and the faunal assemblage has been estimated to date within the last 50,000–80,000 years (Solorzano 1990:500). The fossil Pleistocene bone from the Chapala Basin is characteristically black, probably resulting from manganese staining, while specimens from Zacoalco are stained brown.

Among the vast assemblage of Pleistocene mammal remains are a wide array of spirally fractured, cut, polished, perforated, and otherwise modified bone, antler, and ivory. While some of these specimens clearly result from such noncultural agents as carnivore fracture and gnawing, others have been modified by humans, and some are complete artifacts. In the opinion of Solorzano (1990), the bones were modified prior to fossilization because the modified surfaces (cuts, perforations, polishing, etc.) exhibit the same black patina, or staining, as the unmodified surfaces. He believes that the processes of fossilization for both the culturally modified and unmodified portions of the same bones must have taken the same length of time.

Some human remains have also been found. These include: cranial frag-

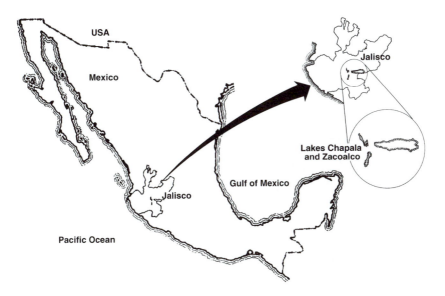

Figure 4.2 Map depicting the location of the Chapala Lake Basin, Mexico. (Courtesy of Frederico Solorzano.)

ments, isolated molars and incisors, and mandible fragments from different individuals. One specimen, believed to be a supraorbital ridge (Figure 4.3), has been the focus of considerable attention because it is similar to examples from archaic humans in the Old World (Figure 4.4). Such a discovery would be of international significance because it would suggest that the Americas were once colonized by earlier human forms. However, Solorzano cautions that this identification has been made on a small fragment of bone. Other researchers suggest that this bone may not be human but rather derived from the remains of another, as yet unidentified, species.

Figure 4.3 Photograph of possible Archaic human supraorbital ridge, Chapala Basin, Mexico. (Photograph courtesy of Frederico Solorzano.)

Figure 4.4 Possible human supraorbital ridge inset in a cast of a European *Homo erectus* skull, demonstrating how it might be derived from a similar specimen. (Photograph courtesy of Frederico Solorzano.)

The assemblage from the Chapala and Zacoalco Basins bear many striking similarities to the Old Crow Basin in Canada's Yukon Territory. For example, both assemblages are heavily mineralized and stained suggesting that the bones were fossilized prior to modification. Both assemblages lack lithic artifacts. At both sites specimens range from nonculturally modified bone to clear examples of osseous artifacts. Small, but significant, amounts of human skeletal material have been recovered from both the Old Crow and Chapala Basins. Unfortunately, the Chapala bone is so heavily mineralized that it lacks adequate collagen for ^{14}C dating by the AMS method (Stafford, personal communication 1996).

Although similarities between Old Crow and the Chapala Basin are striking, there are also significant differences. For example, in the warmer climate of the Chapala Basin, river ice does not appear to have played an important taphonomic role. The lower energy environment of Chapala Basin may minimize the abrasive and fracturing action compared to the high-energy environments of the Old Crow and Porcupine Rivers. While many of the bone aggregates in the Old Crow Basin appear to have been formed by river deposition, those in the Chapala Basin may have resulted from rapid runoff and flash floods during the rainy season from May to July (Haley and Solorzano 1991). These processes may have redeposited, modified, and concentrated sediments and artifacts at some locals in the Chapala Basin.

Another important question is the rate of staining. It was discovered in the Old Crow Basin and interior Alaska that artifacts and other objects, such as cow bones butchered during historic times, could be stained rapidly. Although the unmodified and modified areas of bones displayed the same degree of fossilization proving that the artifacts were made prior to fossilization, the fossilization process occurred relatively rapidly and neither the artifacts nor bones were extremely old. If this is the case in the Chapala Basin, then the human remains and artifacts could all be Holocene in age. A reliable method of dating the human and modified bone is essential to establish the age of the Chapala specimens.

Tlapacoya I and II

The Tlapacoya sites are located about 20 km (12 mi) southeast of Mexico City and are two of eighteen localities investigated by Lorena Mirambell and José Luis Lorenzo between 1965–1973. (Lorenzo and Mirambell 1986, 1999; Mirambell 1978). Tlapacoya I and II are localities with possible evidence of human occupation prior to 11,500 B.P. Tlapacoya I is a deeply buried stratified site situated on a hill near the ancient shoreline of Pleistocene Lake Chalco. Although the lake is now dry, the excavators suggest that people lived next to the lake during the last Ice Age because many of the 2,500 stone flakes made of andesite have rounded edges. This suggests they had been polished by waves at the edge of the lake and that the site may have been occupied for several seasons (Mirambell 1978:224).

Two trenches were excavated at Tlapacoya I. They were designated Alpha and Beta. Trench Alpha cut through what appeared to be a reddish oxidized stratigraphic zone containing charcoal and animal bones. A hearth was found in this stratigraphic unit that contained two flakes of obsidian (which is not found locally) and additional flakes and blades made from local rocks. The hearth was radiocarbon dated to 24,000 ± 4,000 B.P. (A-794), and a pile of anatomically unrelated animal bones was discovered nearby. Two pieces of worked bone and two additional hearths were discovered adjacent to trench Alpha, and charcoal from them was dated to 21,700 ± 500 B.P. (I-4449). Adjacent to these hearths were two additional piles of animal bones, some of which were those of extinct Pleistocene animals. A waterworn quartz scraper was recovered from the same stratigraphic unit dated to circa 22,000 B.P. in trench Beta.

Although it is possible that the wave action of the ancient lake may have fractured and otherwise modified local stones, the occurrence of nonlocal obsidian indicates that this material was transported to the site by humans. Use of the site by nonhuman carnivores and/or scavengers might provide alternative explanations for the piled and worked bone. C. Vance Haynes (1967) indicates that the obsidian artifacts were found in screens and probably originate from rodent burrows, and the in situ flakes are manufactured from local rock that may not have been fractured by humans. Waters (1985) suggests that the circular hearth-like areas may have been created by animals "rooting" in the sediment. However, it is difficult to attribute the uncanny aggregations of bones, lithics, and charcoal entirely to noncultural agents. Additional research employing contemporary analytical and dating techniques could provide new insight into the Tlapacoya I assemblage.

Tlapacoya II is adjacent to a small cave located near the ancient beach of Lake Chalco. A trench 60 m (197 ft) long and 1 m (3.3 ft) wide was excavated from the ancient lake sediments toward the cave. The trench encountered the trunk of a large tree that was radiocarbon dated to 23,150 ± 950 B.P. (GX-0950). Mirambell (1978:228) reports that an obsidian blade was found beneath the trunk of the tree. However, she further implies that the tree might not accurately date the blade because the artifact might have "fallen in place" sometime before or after the deposition of the tree trunk. C. Vance Haynes suggests that it may have intruded into the lower sediments through compaction fault cracks extending downward from the surface (Haynes 1967). Although it is possible that the obsidian could be intrusive into the lower levels from later occupations, Mirambell

(1978:229) indicates that obsidian from both Tlapacoya I and II exhibit the same degree of hydration, indicating that they are approximately the same age.

Valsequillo

Cynthia Irwin-Williams (1967, 1969, 1978) reported several sites near the Valsequillo Reservoir, Puebla, Mexico. These sites were brought to her attention by Camacho J. Armenta who had previously reported the possible association of mammoth remains and artifacts from the region (Armenta 1959). Several of these sites were associated with extinct Pleistocene fauna including horse, camel, and mastodon. One site in particular, Hueyatlaco, excavated by Irwin-Williams contained five periods of stratigraphically superimposed human occupation. The oldest contained several stone artifacts, including three projectile points, two were manufactured on blades and a third from a flake. Patterns of bone modification recovered in association with the lithic artifacts suggested to Armenta (1978) that humans had modified them.

Although detailed stratigraphic work was carried out at the site by several geologists (Malde and Steen-McIntyre 1981; Steen-McIntyre et al. 1981), their conclusions regarding the antiquity of the archeological remains has been questioned (Irwin-Williams 1978, 1981; Szabo et al. 1969). Because the Pleistocene bone associated with the artifacts is heavily mineralized, it was not possible to use the available ^{14}C methods for dating bone at that time. Attempts to date a camel pelvis associated with the bifacial tools by the uranium-series method produced a date of 245,000 ± 40,000 years. Attempts to date two overlying tephra (volcanic ash) units using fission track dating produced ages of 600,000 ± 340,000 and 370,000 ± 200,000 years (Steen-McIntyre et al. 1981:14–15). These dates are so extreme for the peopling of the Americas (and even for the development of similar sophisticated bifacial projectile points anywhere in the world) that such an early age is essentially impossible (Irwin-Williams 1978, 1981). Attempts to date the site using paleomagnetism were also unsuccessful (Liddicoat et al. 1981).

A subsequent analysis of the faunal assemblage from the Hueyatlaco locality by paleontologist Russell Graham (in preparation) demonstrates that the faunal assemblage is characteristic of other late Pleistocene assemblages. Graham's analysis supports Irwin-Williams's opinion that the earlier dating of the site was inaccurate. Based on the results of his analysis, it is highly probable that the early Valsequillo deposits associated with extinct Pleistocene mammals may be Clovis or possibly slightly older in age. The locality warrants additional research and renewed efforts to accurately date the deposits using contemporary dating techniques.

Taima-Taima

Taima-Taima is located at a spring in the arid coastal zone of northern Venezuela about 1 km (.6 mi) south of the Caribbean coast near the town of Coro (Ochsenius and Gruhn 1979). It was discovered in 1961 and excavated discontinuously throughout the 1960s under the direction of José M. Cruxent. The remains of mastodons, glyptodonts, and horses have been unearthed at the site, along with artifacts. Even though the site was fenced and posted, two busloads of visitors plundered and vandalized the site in 1967, destroying much of Cruxent's careful work.

Taima-Taima is one of several sites considered to be characteristic of the El Jobo complex (Cruxent 1956, 1957, 1970). The El Jobo complex is characterized by stone tools including lanceolate projectile points with tapering convex bases usually made of quartzite. The complex also includes knives, scrapers, and flakes found at several sites in the state of Falcón in northern Venezuela (Cruxent and Ochsenius 1979; Rouse and Cruxent 1963). Two North American researchers, Ruth Gruhn and Alan Bryan, resumed excavations at the site in 1976 with support from Venezuelan colleagues José Cruxent and Claudio Ochsenius. Bryan (1979) defined four stratigraphic units (Units I–IV) overlying a natural pavement of cobbles at the site. Under the cobbles is an ancient Miocene sand that contains coal (Bryan and Gruhn 1979). Unit I, a dark gray sand, contains extinct fauna associated with artifacts. The stratigraphic sequence is dated by 27 radiocarbon dates ranging between 14,440 ± 435 B.P. (IVIC-191-2) and 9,650 ± 80 B.P. (VIC-675); however, three of the dates appear to be anomalous (Bryan and Gruhn 1979:53–58).

Gruhn (1979a:32) describes the in situ discovery of an El Jobo point in the right pubic cavity of a partially disarticulated juvenile mastodon. Many of the animal's bones exhibited cut marks and striations interpreted to be evidence of butchering. Bryan and Gruhn (1979) believe the four radiocarbon dates ranging between 12,980 ± 85 B.P. (SI-3316) and 14,200 ± 300 B.P. (UCLA-2133) run on twigs sheared at both ends and believed to the remains of the stomach contents of the juvenile mastodon most accurately date human occupation at the site. The radiocarbon chronology indicates Unit I was deposited between circa 13,400–12,600 B.P., and Bryan and Gruhn (1979:58) estimate that the mastodon kill occurred circa 13,000 B.P.

Most of the cultural remains from Taima-Taima are tools of expediency (objects selected from the natural environment and used as tools). This, and the fact that some of the site sediments have been turbated by the action of the spring has led other researchers (Haynes 1974; Lynch 1974) to question the primary association of the artifacts with the remains of extinct Pleistocene fauna. Because the underlying bedrock contains coal, the possibility has been raised that the ^{14}C samples may be contaminated by older "dead" carbon originating from the underlying coal (Haynes 1974; Lynch 1974).

The questions raised regarding the stratigraphy and radiocarbon dating at Taima-Taima cast doubt on the reliability of the interpretations about the site. However, the suite of approximately 20 concordant ^{14}C determinations from the site and the reports by Gruhn (1979a, 1979b) of finding and recording an El Jobo point in situ during the course of controlled systematic excavations are persuasive. Based on the data presented, Taima-Taima appears to provide valid evidence of human association with extinct Pleistocene fauna in South America circa 14,000 B.P.

Pedra Pintada

Pedra Pintada is a sandstone cave located on the north bank of the Amazon River in north-central Brazil (Roosevelt et al. 1996). The site is well dated by 56 ^{14}C determinations and 13 thermal luminescence dates. Although this site has received considerable attention for being older than Clovis sites in North America, the argument put forth by the researchers is that it is *contemporaneous* with North American Paleoindian sites, not older than these sites. In their opinions, Pedra Pintada documents a contemporaneous, yet different technology and adaptation that requires earlier (pre-11,500 B.P.) archeological sites to explain the different, yet contemporaneous, adaptations. Fiedel (1996) points out that only a few of the ^{14}C determinations are contemporaneous with Clovis and that they are statistical outliers indicating that the site is probably younger than Clovis sites elsewhere. Dillehay (1996) and Meggers (1996) conclude that Pedra Pintada is an example of early Brazilian Holocene cultural adaptation and is not the same age as Clovis culture. While Pedra Pintada represents a well-excavated site and an important contribution to the archeology of South America, it is not older than 11,500 B.P. The site does provide another example of early Holocene cultural diversity in South America that implies that settlement had to have occurred much earlier, possibly prior to Clovis times (Roosevelt 1995; Roosevelt et al. 1996).

Pikimachay Cave

Richard S. MacNeish excavated Pikimachay (flea) Cave in 1969–1970. The site is about 2,850 m (9,350 ft) above sea level and is situated about 14 km (8.7 mi) north-northwest of the town of Ayacucho in the south-central highlands of Peru. The cave has three main rooms (Figure 4.5) that MacNeish (1979) named the North, South, and Central Rooms. Each room has a distinct stratigraphic sequence. In the South Room, MacNeish discovered levels dating back to the

Pleistocene. As a result of his excavations, MacNeish (1979:16, 18–21) defined 15 stratigraphic zones and 43 episodes of human occupation spanning more than 20,000 ^{14}C years. These were subsequently lumped into seven layers used to define three pre-11,500 B.P. cultural "complexes": the Pacaicasa (>20,000–16,000 B.P.), the Ayacucho (16,000 –12,000 B.P.), and the Huanta (<12,000 B.P.). These are followed by two Holocene complexes, the Puente and Jaywa (MacNeish 1971:73).

Reports of the research at Pikimachay Cave are confusing and difficult to interpret (MacNeish 1971, 1979, 1980). The oldest materials from the site are ascribed to the Pacaicasa and Ayacucho complexes. The artifacts in these complexes consist of very simple flakes and flaked stones that have been given a variety of functional typological names, such as "hammer core chopper," "scraper plane," and "double edge spokeshave." Modified and possibly butchered bones, some of which are extinct Pleistocene species, are associated with these early complexes.

Although some archeologists suggest human occupation of Pikimachay Cave is demonstrably older than 11,500 B.P. (Bryan 1983), others question the ev-

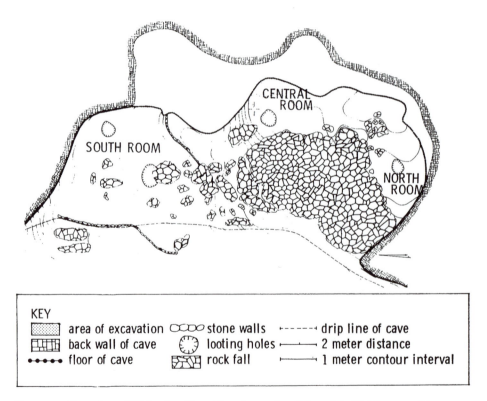

Figure 4.5 Plan view of Pikimakay Cave, Peru (reproduced from MacNeish 1979:9, **Figure 4**, courtesy of R. S. MacNeish).

idence for occupation prior to 11,500 B.P. (Dillehay 1985; Lynch 1980, 1983; Toth 1991). The major problem is that the "artifacts" from the lowest levels are made of the same rock that forms the cave. Consequently, the crude "tools" possibly result from rocks falling, shattering, and flaking as they strike other stones on the floor of the cave. Rockfall, rubble scarring, and carnivore gnawing are possibly responsible for the modifications observed on faunal remains. MacNeish (1979, 1980) reports massive and repeated rockfall throughout the cave deposits in all of the rooms.

Monte Verde

Monte Verde is possibly the most significant pre-11,500 B.P. site to be documented in the Americas. It is situated on the north bank of Chinchihuapi Creek, a tributary to the Maullin River in south-central Chile (Figure 4.6). Unlike other potential early sites, Monte Verde is a campsite reflecting a wide range of human activity and includes residential structures and exceptionally well-preserved organic remains, including bone, wood, and other materials. The site has been scientifically excavated under the overall direction of Thomas D. Dillehay with cooperation from a number of South American colleagues (Dillehay 1997). A series of eight stratigraphic units from most recent MV-1 to oldest MV-8 have been described at the site and are dated by at least seven concurrent ^{14}C determinations. The artifacts and other evidence of human occupation have been recovered from MV-7, which is capped by a layer of peat that has sealed and preserved the archeological materials.

Dillehay (Collins and Dillehay 1986; Dillehay 1984, 1986, 1988, 1997; Dillehay et al. 1983) reports the remains of at least 12 dwellings symmetrically aligned along the northern bank of the creek. The remains of animal skin, presumably used to cover the dwellings, were found along with shallow clay-lined braziers in the dwellings. In other areas of the site, large communal hearths were found with the remains of edible seeds, nuts, fruits, and berries.

About 30 m (98 ft) west of the cluster of dwellings were the remains of a wishbone-shaped structure. Most of the mastodon bones and stone tools from the site were recovered here. Along with other floral material, the excavators found masticated leaves of the boldo plant, which currently is used by local residents to brew a tea believed to have medicinal value. The unique shape and positioning of the structure along with the associated artifacts suggested to Dillehay that it may have served as a center for dressing meat from large animals, making and using stone tools and perhaps for medicinal practices.

Because organic preservation is exceptional, wood artifacts have been recovered, including mortars, several wooden hafts containing stone flakes, an assortment of digging sticks, a pointed lance or spear about 1.5 m (4.9 ft) long, vast

Figure 4.6 Photograph of Monte Verde looking across Chinchihuapi Creek. (Photograph courtesy of Thomas Dillehay.)

amounts of worked wood, and other small objects. A wide variety of plant remains had been transported to Monte Verde including the remains of various tubers, such as the wild potato. Although there are a few well-made bifacially flaked stone tools, most of the lithic industry consists of individual flakes, split pebbles, and other stones exhibiting little modification from their natural states. There are many nearly spherical forms; a few are grooved and were possibly used as bola weights and/or stones for slings. Although no human remains were recovered, footprints of a child or small adolescent were preserved on the surface of MV-7.

Several concordant ^{14}C determinations indicate that the occupation at Monte Verde occurred about 12,500 B.P. The faunal remains document a minimum of seven different mastodons. The presence of these late Pleistocene animals is significant because it further supports the ^{14}C chronology and indicates the deposits are older than about 11,000 B.P., the approximate time when mastodons became extinct. The artifacts were found and recorded in situ. No geologic or other noncultural processes have been identified to suggest this suite of evidence could have been produced by any mechanism other than human occupation (Meltzer et al. 1997). Based on the evidence from the excavations, Monte Verde meets, or exceeds, the criteria for establishing the validity of sites proposed to be older than 11,500 B.P. in the Americas.

Two hearth-like features were discovered stratigraphically below the base of unit MV-7 about 70 m (230 ft) north of the main occupation area (Dillehay 1997;

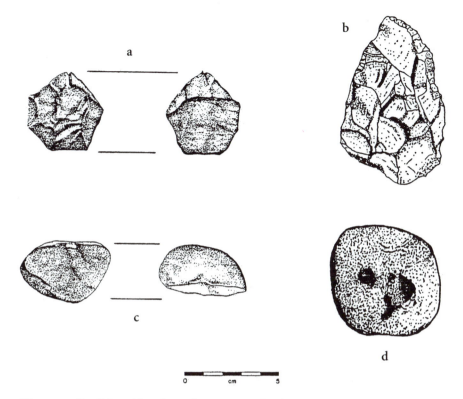

Figure 4.7 Possible artifacts from the 33,000 B.P. level at Monte Verde: (a) percussion-split basalt pebble, (b) unifacially flaked basalt core, (c) percussion flake made of basalt, and (d) edge-battered basalt cobble (reproduced with permission from *Nature*, Vol. 332, 10 March 1988, and the author, Dillehay 1988: Figure 2, p. 151.)

Dillehay and Collins 1988). Two ^{14}C determinations from these hearth-like features are 33,370 ± 530 B.P. (Beta 6754) and >33,020 B.P. (Beta 7825). Scattered about these features were 26 naturally fractured stones (Figure 4.7) that appear to have been used by people. In the absence of additional data, the investigators are not certain that these features present unequivocal evidence of human occupation.

Pedra Furada

Boqueirao do Sitio da Pedra Furada, or "Pedra Furada," is located in northeastern Brazil. This exceptional site is well known for its rock art as well as for its claim of being older than 11,500 B.P. The site is a rockshelter located along the base of a sandstone cliff (Figure 4.8). The deeply stratified sediments are primarily sand and clasts derived from the gradual weathering of the sandstone.

Within the rockshelter, 10 major stratigraphic units have been recognized (Delibrias et al. 1988). The Pleistocene levels have been dated by at least 19 ^{14}C determinations that range between circa 17,000 B.P. to three dates of about 40,000 B.P. (Delibrias et al. 1988; Guidon and Delibrias 1986; Parenti et al. 1990). The oldest ^{14}C determinations are possibly finite dates, suggesting that the deposits may exceed the limits of radiocarbon dating, which under ideal conditions is generally considered to be about 50,000–48,000 B.P. Stratigraphically above the Pleistocene levels are well-dated early and mid-Holocene human occupations containing bifacially flaked stone tools. The site also contains a human burial dated to 9,670 B.P. (Peyre 1993).

A fragment of rock bearing paint made from red ochre was detached from the rockshelter wall and incorporated into sediments dated to circa 17,000 ± 400 B.P. (no lab number reported) (Guidon 1986). Although this might provide a minimum limiting date for the rock art, it is also possible that the fragment might

Figure 4.8 Photograph of the sandstone cliff, Pedra Furada. (Photograph courtesy of Mort Turner.)

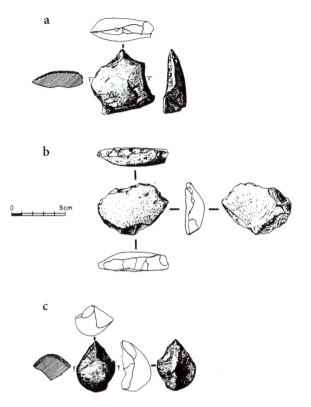

Figure 4.9 Line drawing of artifacts from Pleistocene levels at Pedra Furada (from Dixon 1993).

a

b

0   5cm

c

have worked its way into the older sediments from above. Possibly as many as 150 hearth-like features have been reported from the Pleistocene levels (Bahn 1993). They are semicircular/elliptical formations of sandstone blocks and quartzite pebbles. Some of the areas contain charcoal, and some stones are discolored suggesting they have been heated (Parenti et al. 1990).

Some researchers have questioned the artifactual nature of the flakes and other simple stone tools (Figure 4.9) and the cultural origin of the charcoal (James 1989; Lynch 1990). They suggest that the charcoal resulted from noncultural fires. The lithics found in the Pleistocene levels at Pedra Furada are made from quartz and quartzite pebbles derived from a conglomerate layer above the sandstone cliff. They postulate that cobbles eroded from above and fractured upon impact with the surface, creating flakes and flake cores that resemble pebble tools. Because it had been suggested that cobbles may not be cultural in origin, an extensive research project was undertaken by Fabio Parenti to resolve this issue. Parenti concluded that the stone specimens were made and used by humans (Bahn 1993).

Other Sites

At two sites in Chile, Fell's Cave and Mylodon Cave, extinct Ice Age animal remains have been reported associated with artifacts. At Fell's Cave distinctive "fishtail" projectile points were recovered with the bones of extinct ground sloth and horse (Bird 1938, 1946, 1988; Clutton-Brock 1988; Markgraf 1988). At Mylodon Cave, also located in Chile, artifacts have also been reported in association with ground sloth remains (Bird 1988; Borrero 1995). Ten radiocarbon dates ranging between 13,560–12,300 B.P. and three between 10,830–10,200 B.P. reliably date the ground sloth remains (Borrero 1982, 1995; Mengoni Goñalons 1986). Although initial interpretations suggested that these sites may have had great antiquity, reanalysis demonstrates that these Ice Age species (sloth and horse) persisted somewhat later in southern South America than in other parts of the western hemisphere, possibly until circa 10,000 B.P.

The results of excavations at Lapa Vermelha IV in Brazil were reported in the late 1970s and early 1980s (Laming-Emperaire 1979; Laming-Emperaire et al. 1975 cited in Gruhn 1991; Prous 1986a, 1986b cited in Gruhn 1991, 1997). The site is a solution cavern in which quartz and limestone artifacts were recovered from levels dated to 15,400 B.P. This is underlain by an older, and apparently noncultural, level dated to circa >25,000–22,400 B.P. (Gruhn 1991, 1997). Stone artifacts and worked wood are reported (Vialou et al. 1995 cited in Gruhn 1997) from another Brazilian rockshelter, Santa Elina, apparently dated by radiocarbon to circa 22,500 B.P. Ten artifacts are also reported to have been found in a lower level of this site dated with the U-Th method (a dating method based on the rate of radioactive decay of uranium and thorium to lead) to circa 32,000 ± 5,000 B.P. However, the context of these discoveries has not been adequately described.

The lowest level, Level 11, of Los Toldos 3 has the oldest radiocarbon date for an archeological site in Argentina. Unifacial tools were found with the fossil remains of horse and extinct camel (Cardich 1978). However, the chronology of the site has been questioned by Borrero (1989, 1995) and Lynch (1990). Borrero (1995:208) indicates that the radiocarbon date of 12,600 ± 600 B.P. (FRA 98) from Level 11 was derived from "pooled" carbon samples and that the circa 12,600 B.P. date for this level needs to be tested by additional radiocarbon analysis (Borrero 1995:211).

Gruhn (1991, 1997) presents several sites from Brazil that have not been published in English that are possibly dated to 11,500 B.P. or earlier. Lapa do Boquete is a rockshelter apparently containing unifacial flake tools associated with radiocarbon dates ranging between circa 12,000–11,000 B.P. (Gruhn 1991, 1997 citing Fogaça and Lima 1991; Prous 1991; Prous et al. 1992). Faunal remains from this site include freshwater mussels, fish, and mammals along with the remains of burned palm nuts. A radiocarbon date of circa 12,000 B.P. is reported from a hearth associated with ochre and "exotic" flakes of quartz from Abrigo de Santana do Riacho (Gruhn 1991, 1997 citing Prous 1981, 1986a, 1986b).

Sites are also reported along the Pacific Coast of Ecuador (Stothert 1998; Wisner 1999) and Peru (Keefer et al. 1998; Sandweiss et al. 1998) that demonstrate early maritime adaptations along the western coast of South America by circa 11,000 B.P. At the Las Vegas site in southwestern Ecuador, marine fish and shell fish have been recovered from a habitation site dating between 10,840–10,100 B.P. (no lab numbers reported) (Stothert 1998; Wisner 1999). Farther south at Quebrada Tacahuay, Peru, located less than .5 km (.3 mi) from the Pacific Ocean, an occupation dating between 11,000–10,500 B.P. contains the remains of marine fish, marine birds, and lithic tools. The site would have been approximately .7–.9 km (.4–.6 mi) from the sea at the time it was occupied (Keefer et al. 1998). At another Peruvian site, Quebrada Jaguay, the remains of marine fish, shells, crustaceans, and mollusks have been recovered along with fragments of knotted cordage (possibly fish net), stone flakes, and a few broken and unfinished stone tools characteristic of a bifacial technology (Sandweiss et al. 1998). At the time of occupation, the site was located approximately 7 or 8 km (4 or 5 mi) from the sea. Obsidian from the oldest stratigraphic level, which has been radiocarbon dated to circa 10,000–11,000 B.P., is from a source approximately 130 km (80 mi) inland (Sandweiss et al. 1998).

Politis et al. (1995) note evidence of mastodon predation dating between 13,000–11,000 B.P. from several parts of "northern" South America. Documented sites include Monte Verde in southern Chile (Dillehay 1997), Tagua-Tagua in central Chile (Montané 1968), Tibito in Columbia (Correal Urrego 1981 cited in Politis et al. 1995), and at Taima-Taima in Venezuela (Bryan et al. 1978). These data suggest that at the end of the last Ice Age, people were hunting (and probably scavenging) these large elephant-like animals in many interior regions of the continent.

Summary

Table 4.1 presents the data from the major Mexican, and Central and South American sites suggested to be older than 11,500 B.P. The table evaluates the sites using the criteria defined in Chapter 3 to establish the validity of pre-11,500 B.P. sites in the Americas. These criteria are:

1. Are the artifacts clearly the product of human manufacture?
2. Is the recovered material in clear stratigraphic context?
3. Are there concurrent radiocarbon dates from the deposit?

4. Do paleoenvironmental studies support the chronological placement of the site?
5. Are there human remains that are reliably dated older than 11,500 B.P.?

Table 4.1 illustrates that:

1. three sites may be improperly dated or the dating is controversial,
2. two sites contain noncultural specimens that may have been misinterpreted as artifacts,
3. all but one site appear to match the associated paleoecological data or the paleoecological context, however
4. three sites have little or no stratigraphic context or the stratigraphic interpretation is questionable.

Table 4.1
Evaluation of Pre-11,500 B.P. Sites in Mexico, and Central and South America

		Criteria				
Site Name	Artifacts	Stratigraphy	Dating	Environmental Context	Human Remains	# of Criteria Met
Chapala Basin	x	?	?	x	brow ridge?	2
Monte Verde	x	x	x	x	foot prints	4
Pedra Furada	?	x	x	x	o	3
Pedra Pintada	x	x	x	x	o	4
Pikimakay Cave	?	x	?	x	o	2
Taima-Taima	x	?	x	x	o	3
Tlapacoya I	x	x	x	?	o	3
Tlapacoya II	x	?	x	x	o	3
Valsequillo	x	x	?	x	o	3

Total Sites **9**

Key: x = acceptable evidence present	1 Criterion Met	o
? = evidence questionable	2 Criteria Met	2
o = absent	3 Criteria Met	5
	4 Criteria Met	2

Only two South American sites satisfy all the criteria. One is Pedra Pintada, which dates to the early Holocene and is not older than 11,500 B.P., and the other is Monte Verde. Monte Verde meets all the criteria and has indirect physical evidence of humans in the form of footprints.

In some respects, the South American data suggesting very early occupation of the Americas are more convincing than the data from North America. For example, even though Taima-Taima does not fully satisfy all the criteria, the reported associations between mastodon and the El Jobo artifacts are convincing. At Monte Verde, Pedra Furada, and to some degree Taima-Taima, much of the lithic tool kit is derived from rocks that were used with little or no modification by humans. This suggests similar technological adaptation might encompass a vast region and may have existed for a very long period of time. This also underscores the extreme difficulty in distinguishing between cultural and noncultural lithic assemblages in the absence of other artifactual materials, particularly when organic materials are absent. For example, if the organic artifacts and remains were not preserved at Monte Verde by the fortuitous deposition of peat, few lithic artifacts exhibiting cultural modification would be recognizable. If the lithic specimens had been discovered in an erosional context, such as an elevated area subject to deflation, the site might only meet only one, instead of four, of the test criteria.

Archeologists agree that the most conclusive evidence of human presence in the Americas prior to 11,500 B.P. would be reliably dated human remains. With the exception of a single fragment of possible human bone from the Chapala Basin in Mexico and the illustration of an "archaic" calvarium observed in Brazil by Bryan (1978), which since has disappeared, no human remains that are "ancient or archaic" in appearance have been reported from the Americas (Chapter 5). Unlike the Old World, the New World appears to lack archaic human forms. However, at Monte Verde, a human footprint provides exceptional fossil evidence for human presence prior to 11,500 B.P.

Some archeologists argue that, as in a court of law, a "preponderance" of evidence is required, while others demand proof "beyond a shadow of doubt." To many New World archeologists, there already exists a preponderance of evidence, but others demand that the issue must be resolved beyond a shadow of doubt. Given these different requirements for proof, it is difficult to achieve professional consensus for the arrival of first humans in the Americas. For example, some archeologists argue that Monte Verde meets all the requisite requirements demonstrating human occupation of the Americas prior to 11,500 B.P. Others counter that a single site alone can not establish absolute proof, and occupation will not be demonstrated until a clear pattern is established by repeated discovery and excavation of several sites older than 11,500 B.P. Although this debate is not fully resolved, it has shifted from questioning whether Clovis is the first valid archeological evidence for human occupation in the Americas to how much earlier than 11,500 B.P. did humans arrive in the Americas? There is growing consensus among American archeologists that the 12,500 B.P. occupation at Monte Verde provides a secure minimum limiting age for human occupation and that colonization must have occurred earlier.

5 Learning from Those Who Have Gone Before

Introduction

In recent years, the discovery, excavation, and analysis of Native American human remains has been controversial in the United States and to a lesser degree in Canada. Both Native and non-Native Americans are divided on the issue. The divisions are not strictly along racial or ethnic lines. Some people believe that all human remains should be reburied and not subject to scientific investigation. Others believe that the benefits of scientific investigation are significant and that research on human remains can be conducted with respect and cultural sensitivity. Yet others feel that the antiquity of the remains makes a difference. While some people may object to recent (several hundred years old) human remains being the subject of study, they may have little or no objection to research conducted on skeletons that are thousands of years old.

For example, in the process of excavating and analyzing very old human skeletal material on Prince of Wales Island, Alaska, local Native people participated in the excavation, expressed a strong interest in their analysis, and believe the knowledge gained from archeological research is important. In this case, scientists, Native people, and government agencies worked together in a spirit of cooperation and mutual respect. Yarrow Vaara, a member of the Tlingit tribe and student intern working at the site in 1997 and 1998, said that she regarded the human remains she was helping excavate as possibly those of her great uncle who was teaching her about her history. The Tlingit people are matrilineal, and uncles have an honored role as mentors in the clan. Similar statements made by other Native people demonstrate that many recognize that this type of research can provide information that is important to them.

The Native American Graves Protection and Repatriation Act (NAGPRA), enacted by the United States Congress in 1990, requires archeologists and governmental agencies to consult with Native American tribes prior to undertaking field research on federal lands or with federal support. Museums and other organizations that receive federal support are required to inventory and report human skeletal material, grave goods, and "objects of cultural patrimony." Objects in these categories must be returned to the appropriate Native American tribe upon their request following consultation with the museum or federal agency holding them.

It has been difficult to implement this law because it was passed without adequate financial support to enable Native Americans, government agencies, and museums to comply. In some instances, NAGPRA has polarized opinion, created resentments, and reduced cooperation. In other cases, it has resulted in better communication between Native Americans, federal agencies, and non-Native entities sponsoring archeology and holding archeological collections.

Although North American archeologists recognize the study of ancient human remains is a sensitive issue for some people, most share the conviction that the knowledge gained from the study of human remains is extremely important. Furthermore, there is a vast amount of scientific information in the literature from the past century. This information provides important knowledge about human physical and cultural development, and human origins, as well as insight into the lives of ancient people.

During the late 1800s and early 1900s, scientists largely studied human remains by measuring human skeletons, particularly crania, (Figure 5.1) and comparing measurements to define different groups of people. Since this rather simple beginning, scientists have developed a vast array of sophisticated technology and analysis that can be used to better understand our species and interpret the life history of individuals.

The human body is an encyclopedia of the events it has experienced. If an individual suffers a period of malnutrition, or even worse, starvation, the bones and teeth will record this event, particularly if the individual is young and still growing. Every time a person suffers from an infection or disease, the body produces and stores antibodies to fight the disease. Human DNA provides a record of an individual's ancestry. By examining and studying human remains, trained scientists can read a fascinating record that is unique for every individual.

Some nondestructive studies focus on the comparison of physical traits, such as bone structure, to determine the gender of skeletons. Studying dental patterns, the sequence of tooth eruption, and dental wear provides insight into an individual's relationship to other groups as well as an estimate of the age at the time of death, the diet, and other factors that were important while alive (Powell and Steele 1994; Smith 1984). Scientists can identify periods of malnutrition or famine, certain types of disease, injuries such as bone fractures, and other events recorded in the human skeleton as individuals develop, grow, and heal. By examining areas where muscles attach to bones, researchers can tell how muscular an individual may have been.

As science has progressed, the techniques for analysis have become increasingly refined and less destructive. Endoscopes (small fiber optic tubes) can be

Figure 5.1 Jesse D. Figgins measuring a human cranium, circa 1935. (Denver Museum of Natural History Photo Archives.)

inserted into small spaces and enable examination and photography of interior regions of the skeleton, such as the brain case and marrow cavities in bones. Phytoliths (tiny growths of silica produced by plants that have distinct morphology for each plant species) can be removed from dental calculus, or plaque, and provide insight into the plants that may have been an important part of an individual's diet. Surface characteristics of bones and teeth can be analyzed and photographed under high magnification by using both conventional as well as scanning electron microscopes. Other noninvasive techniques include X-rays and computerized axial tomography (CAT) scans that provide three dimensional views and pictures of the interior areas of the body. Many of these techniques are standard methods of examination used routinely on living individuals during medical and dental exams.

Contemporary analytical techniques include the extraction and replication of DNA that can be preserved in small amounts of bone. DNA provides a "blueprint" of an individual's genetic make up, the traits that make them unique and that they share with others as a member of a larger genetic group. DNA analyses are useful to objectively compare the genetic relationship of an individual to other individuals and groups of individuals. DNA analysis also can provide important cultural insight. For example, it is possible to determine whether individuals buried in the same locale, or even the same grave, were blood relatives. This type of evidence can help scientists interpret social structure, residence patterns, disease, and cultural practices of ancient people.

Probably the single most important breakthrough for Paleoindian archeology in recent years has been the ability to reliably date bone by AMS ^{14}C methods (Stafford et al. 1991; Taylor et al. 1985). Dating by this method can accurately determine when an individual died. Stable isotope analysis of carbon and nitrogen are measured from bone samples in conjunction with the same sample used for AMS dating. Isotope analysis can provide important insight into an individual's diet and can, for example, determine whether they subsisted largely on marine or terrestrial foods. These tests require only a few grams and in many cases, less than one gram of bone or other material. These analyses require no more material than might be extracted by a dentist when filling a tooth, trimming one's fingernails, or getting a haircut. Samples can be removed in a respectful manner and in ways that are virtually not detectable.

Another method for studying early human skeletal remains is facial reconstruction. These reconstructions are fascinating blends of art and science. Artists trained in human anatomy begin with casts of a human cranium and mandible and carefully reconstruct, or "build," the facial characteristics of the individual from the cast outward (Figure 5.2). By adding muscle and other soft tissue to a cast of the skull and taking into consideration the gender and age of the individual, surprisingly accurate reconstructions of individuals can be made. Law enforcement officials have successfully used these techniques to help identify individuals from their remains. Computers are now employed to help recreate the physical appearance of ancient people. These reconstructions from human remains that are thousands of years old provide unique and moving portraits of people from the past.

Since the 1800s, there have been exaggerated claims of great antiquity attributed to human remains discovered in the Americas (Dickeson Exhibit Report 1846; Whitney 1867, 1880). More recently, careful geologic investigation and dating, particularly using AMS ^{14}C techniques, have led to accurate age determinations of human bone. This research has clarified much of the ambiguity and confusion surrounding many of these early finds.

Several well-known discoveries of human remains believed to be older than 11,500 B.P. have been refuted by subsequent research. Some of the more famous of these are Del Mar Man (Bada et al. 1974), originally thought to be between 41,000–48,000 years old and subsequently ^{14}C dated to circa 4,900 B.P. (Stafford and Tyson 1989; Taylor et al. 1985); the Taber Child (Stalker 1969), originally estimated to be between 60,000–22,000 B.P. and now ^{14}C dated to 3,550 B.P. (Taylor et al. 1985); and Tepexpan Man (near Mexico City, Mexico), which since the 1940s has been thought to be late Pleistocene in age and subsequently has been found to be no older than circa 3,500 B.P. (Cotter 1991; Stafford 1994; Taylor et al.

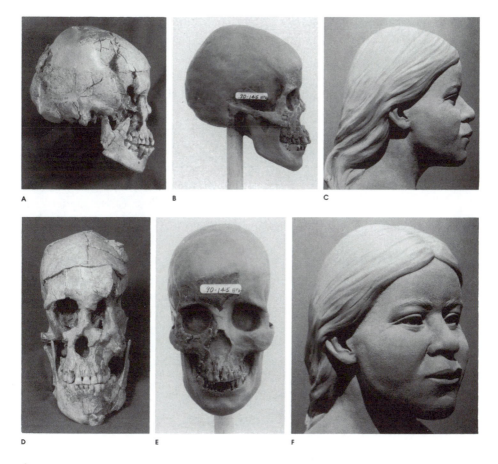

Figure 5.2 Portrait from the past. This sequence of photographs illustrate a facial reconstruction by Betty Pat Gatliff. The cast is of a young woman from the Wilson-Leonard site (10,000–9,600 B.P.). The reconstruction is illustrated in three stages; first by reconstruction of the cranium and mandible (a and d) from which a cast was made, second the addition of soft tissue (clay) to the cast (b and e), and finally the addition of surficial facial features and hair (c and f). (Reprinted from Paleobiology of the First Americans by Gentry Steele and Joseph F. Powell, *Evolutionary Anthropology* 2(4):138–146, © 1993. Reprinted by permission of Wiley-Liss, Inc., a division of John Wiley & Sons, Inc.)

1985). Three bone collagen dates for the Otavalo skeleton from Ecuador indicate a late Holocene age between circa 2,800–2,300 B.P., rather than an age somewhere between 30,000–20,000 B.P. suggested by earlier dates run on argonite (Davies 1978).

Another well-known discovery, Minnesota Man (actually a female about fifteen years old), has been redated by AMS ^{14}C to about 7,850 B.P. (7,870 ± 50 B.P. [CAMS-10354] and 7,840 ± 70 B.P. (CAMS-6380)) (Stafford, personal communication 1997), and Sauk Valley Man, also from Minnesota, has been directly dated by AMS ^{14}C to approximately 4,275 B.P. (4,360 ± 60 B.P. [CAMS-6357] and 4,190 ± 70 B.P. (CAMS-6352]) (Stafford, personal communication 1997). Midland Man, a human skeleton found near Midland, Texas, is thought by some researchers to date to the Pleistocene or early Holocene (Wendorf and Krieger 1959; Wendorf et al. 1955). However, it is excluded from the following review because of the wide range of dates proposed for it and the possibility that it is mid- rather than late Holocene in age (Holliday and Meltzer 1996; Steele and Powell 1992:306).

The review that follows is not a comprehensive inventory and description of early human remains from North America but rather a synopsis providing insight into the lives, cultures, and environments of these early Americans. It presents information from human remains believed to be older than circa 8,000 B.P. Some early human skeletal remains are excluded from this review, such as the Burial 4 from the Mostin site (Kaufman 1980), and remains from the Shifting Sands site (Amick et at. 1989), because not enough data exist to adequately describe the character and context of the human remains. Other sites, such as the Renier site in Wisconsin for which only bracketing dates between 8,500–6,000

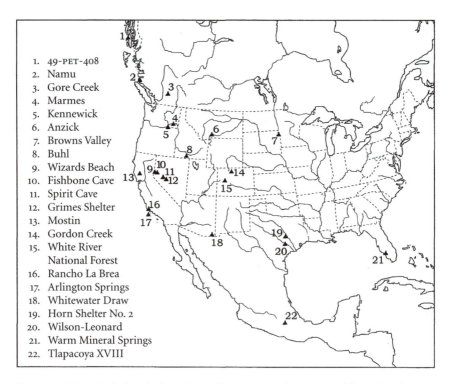

1. 49-PET-408
2. Namu
3. Gore Creek
4. Marmes
5. Kennewick
6. Anzick
7. Browns Valley
8. Buhl
9. Wizards Beach
10. Fishbone Cave
11. Spirit Cave
12. Grimes Shelter
13. Mostin
14. Gordon Creek
15. White River
    National Forest
16. Rancho La Brea
17. Arlington Springs
18. Whitewater Draw
19. Horn Shelter No. 2
20. Wilson-Leonard
21. Warm Mineral Springs
22. Tlapacoya XVIII

Figure 5.3 Map depicting the locations of human remains reported from North America that are older than circa 8,000 B.P. (Graphic by Eric Parrish.)

Figure 5.4 Yarrow Vaara and Robert Sattler excavating at 49-PET-408.

B.P. exist (Mason and Irwin 1960), have also been omitted from this discussion. They are excluded because their ages are not firmly established as older than 8,000 B.P. Although many examples of human remains thought to be more than 8,000 B.P. exist, few have been reliably dated. Even fewer have been reported in the professional literature. Sites selected for review here are those having reliable dates and stratigraphic or other reliable contextual data establishing their age. They are presented geographically from north to south (Figure 5.3).

49-PET-408

In 1996, human remains dated to circa 9,800 B.P. were discovered by paleontologist Timothy Heaton in 49-PET-408 (On Your Knees Cave) (Figure 5.4) in the northwestern portion of Prince of Wales Island, Alaska (Dixon et al. 1997). Excavations stopped immediately after the human remains were recognized, in compliance with NAGPRA. Following NAGPRA consultations, permission to study the human remains and resume excavations was granted by the Klawock Cooperative and Craig Community Associations, the local tribal governments.

As of 1998, the skeletal remains include the mandible of an adult male probably in his early twenties. The mandible (found in two fragments) contains all of the teeth, except the four incisors. Three vertebra, a partial right pelvis, and a single upper canine were found in the same passage of the cave as the mandible, about 10 m (33 ft) from the cave entrance. During the 1997 field season, another human vertebra and two rib fragments were recovered in the same passage of the cave where the remains were found in 1996. A lower human incisor was recovered from another room of the cave in 1998.

Based on estimates of age, gender, dental wear, and isotope analysis, all the human bones and teeth appear to be from the same individual. The pelvis and other bones exhibit evidence of carnivore gnawing. It is not known whether the human remains result from a deliberate burial that was later scattered by carnivores or if the individual was the victim of predation and/or scavenging. The dentition suggests that this individual suffered at least two periods of dietary stress during his childhood.

Delta ^{13}C values were –12.5 o/oo (parts per million) for the human mandible and –12.1 o/oo for the pelvis. This supports other evidence indicating that the remains are of the same individual and demonstrates that this individual's diet consisted almost entirely of marine foods. In fact, this isotopic value is so extreme that it falls within the range for marine carnivores, such as ringed seal, sea otter, and marine fish, all of which range between circa –15 o/oo and –9 o/oo.

Two AMS ^{14}C dates were run on the human bone. A sample extracted with a microdrill from the mandible dated to 9,730 ± 60 B.P. (CAMS-29873). Another sample taken from the pelvis dated to 9,880 ± 50 B.P. (CAMS-32038). These two dates overlap at two sigma and suggest that the individual dates to circa 9,800 B.P. The marine diet demonstrated by the isotope analysis indicates that the marine carbon reservoir has affected the accuracy of the ^{14}C determinations. There are few specific data for the immediate vicinity of Prince of Wales Island quantifying the difference between oceanic and atmospheric carbon reservoirs. However, to the south in the Queen Charlotte Islands, a 600 year ^{14}C difference in the regional marine and atmospheric carbon cycles has been demonstrated by comparison of ^{14}C determinations run on wood and shell (Josenhans et al. 1995). These data suggest that the dates on the human remains should be corrected by subtracting circa 600 ^{14}C years. Presuming this correction is applicable to the human remains, the corrected date for the human is circa 9,200 B.P. Consequently, the human remains appear to be contemporary with a cultural occupation dated by three AMS ^{14}C determinations on charcoal (8,760 ± 50 B.P. [CAMS-43991], 9,210 ± 50 B.P. [CAMS-43990], and 9,150 ± 50 B.P. [CAMS-43989]). Obsidian microblades, bifaces, and other tools were recovered from this stratigraphic unit, and these tools are characteristic of the Northwest Coast Microblade tradition (Chapter 6). Some of the stone artifacts are made from types of rock that do not occur on the island.

This site is significant because this is the first firm association of human physical remains with distinctive early microblades in Alaska or the Pacific Northwest. Between 9,500–9,000 B.P. at the end of the last Ice Age, the elevation of the rising sea level on Prince of Wales Island was 4–6 m (13–20 ft) above the modern sea level. Farther south in the Queen Charlotte Islands, Josenhans et al. (1995, 1997) demonstrate the sea level was approximately 145 m (475 ft) higher around 9,300 B.P. than today. This indicates that the sea level was higher on Prince of Wales Island at the time the human bones were deposited in 49-PET-408 and the Island was not connected to the mainland. Discoveries at this site inferentially demonstrate that humans living along the coast of Southeast Alaska were using watercraft, were primarily dependent on marine foods, had established trade networks, and were capable of intercoastal navigation by 9,200 B.P.

Namu

The Namu site is located on the central coast of British Columbia, Canada, near the junction of Burke Channel and Fitzhugh Sound. Carlson (1996:3) reports that the only human osteological remains consist of tooth crowns (Figure 5.5), the oldest of which date between 9,000–8,000 B.P. Although isotopic analyses have not been done on the tooth crowns, the site is situated at the mouth of a salmon spawning stream and, thus, strongly suggests a marine adaptation and diet by circa 9,000–8,000 B.P. (Carlson 1997). The dental remains exhibit the Sinodont pattern described by Turner (1983) and characteristic of northeast Asian and New World populations.

Gore Creek

The remains of a human skeleton were found at the Gore Creek site in the vicinity of Kamloops, in central British Columbia. A male skeleton missing the cranium was recovered from beneath the Mazama tephra (volcanic ash), which dates to circa 6,800 B.P. The skeleton was radiocarbon dated to 8,250 B.P. (Cybulski et al. 1981). Carbon isotope values suggest that most of the protein in the individual's diet was derived from terrestrial sources with about 8–10 percent derived from marine (salt water) fish (Chisholm 1986; Chisholm and Nelson 1983). Because this individual's remains were located inland, the isotope analysis suggests that anadromous fish (possibly salmon) were already an important

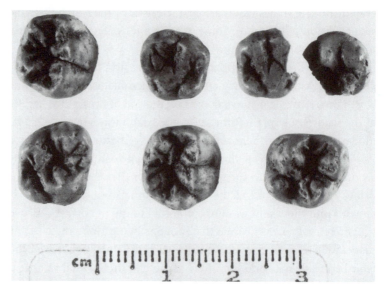

Figure 5.5 Human molars from the Namu Site, British Columbia. (Photograph courtesy of Roy Carlson.)

and possibly stable part of the diet of people living inland from the coast by that time.

Browns Valley Man

In 1933, William H. Jensen noticed human bones and artifacts in a load of gravel dumped on the driveway of a grain elevator in Minnesota. He immediately went to the gravel pit where he located additional artifacts and human bone. He subsequently recognized the burial pit-like feature from which the artifacts and bones were originally derived. He called his discovery to the attention of Albert Ernest Jenks, who investigated the site the following summer with a field party from the University of Minnesota. Jenks was able to find additional skeletal material in situ and ascertain the correct stratigraphic position of the burial.

The burial had been dug into gravel from the discharge of Glacial Lake Agassiz, estimated to have been deposited about 12,000 years ago. Consequently, the skeleton had to be younger than 12,000 B.P. Undisturbed overlying deposits were estimated to be about 8,000 years old, and the human remains were assumed to be between 12,000–8,000 years old. A subsequent ^{14}C determination of 8,700 ± 110 B.P. (no lab number) is reported by Powell and Steele (1994:181) confirming the original estimate of age. The bones had a reddish tint, and the pit was reported to be "lined" with red ochre. The remains were those of an adult male between 25–40 years of age at the time of death. His teeth were heavily worn, and the dentine was exposed in some places (Jenks 1937:18).

Although no organic artifacts were found associated with the burial, there were stone tools including two rectangular sandstone abraders, three concave-based projectile points exhibiting basal edge grinding, a straight-based projectile point (probably a resharpened projectile point fragment), and two large asymmetrical bifaces described by Jenks (1937:31) as knives lacking edge grinding. Further typological comparison of the bifacial stone projectile points suggested to Jenks (1937) that the find was roughly contemporaneous with Folsom and Yuma types reported from the western United States.

Anzick

The Anzick site is a rockshelter located in Montana that was accidentally discovered in 1968 (Jones and Bonnichsen 1994). The site and context of the artifacts and human remains were largely destroyed by construction activities before they could be examined by trained scientists. The burial contained two individuals and an assemblage of more than one hundred stone and bone artifacts. Both individuals are described as subadults (Wilke et al. 1991). Two very small pieces of human crania, one from each individual, were directly dated by the AMS method. One was bleached white and the other was stained reddish brown with hematite (red ochre). Seven AMS ^{14}C determinations were run on the bleached crania. Two of the seven dates were discounted because of the large standard deviations (about 400 years). The average of the remaining five dates was 8,610 ± 90 B.P. The same procedure was applied to the ochre stained bone and the average of five ^{14}C AMS dates was 10,680 ± 50 B.P. (Stafford 1994:49–51). More recently another AMS ^{14}C date of 11,550 ± 60 B.P. (CAMS-35912) has been obtained on gelatin from the ochre stained crania (Stafford, personal communication 1997). It is difficult to explain the difference in these dates, and resolution of this problem will require additional research.

Presuming the ^{14}C determinations are correct, the rockshelter was used for burial during two different periods separated in time by almost 2,000 years. Many of the artifacts are stained with ochre suggesting that they were intentionally included in the burial for ceremonial or metaphysical reasons. The ^{14}C determinations support the assumption that the ochre stained Clovis artifacts, including the large thin bifaces, fluted points, and foreshafts, are associated with the ochre stained human bones. As of 1998, there was not a scientific report thoroughly documenting and analyzing the human remains. Thorough analysis of the human remains and the associated and spectacular collection of artifacts could provide important new insights into the lives of Clovis people.

Marmes Floodplain

The partial remains of an individual consisting of crania, rib, mandible, and vertebrae fragments were discovered buried approximately 2 m (6.5 ft) below the surface on the floodplain adjacent to Marmes Rockshelter in southeastern Washington. The site is located on the Palouse River about 2.4 km (1.5 mi) from of its confluence with the Snake River (Fryxell, Bielicki, Daugherty, Gustafson, Irwin, and Keel 1968; Fryxell, Bielicki, Daugherty, Gustafson, Irwin, Keel, and Krantz 1968). The human remains were found accidentally in 1965 when a bulldozer trench was cut to correlate sediments from Marmes Rockshelter with those from the adjacent floodplain. By tracing the sediments exposed by the bulldozer cut directly back to the Marmes Rockshelter, Fryxell believed the human remains were from deposits underlying a stratigraphic unit in the rockshelter dated by four ^{14}C determinations to 11,000–10,000 B.P.

Prior to 13,000–12,000 B.P., the Palouse Valley contained a lake. The sediments containing the bones were deposited immediately after the lake had drained and the Palouse Canyon had been formed. Based on this excellent geologic context, the age of the human remains and associated artifacts were estimated to be between circa 13,000–11,000 B.P. (Fryxell, Bielicki, Daugherty, Gustafson, Irwin, and Keel 1968; Fryxell, Bielicki, Daugherty, Gustafson, Irwin, Keel, and Krantz 1968). At one point, C. Vance Haynes (1969:712) suggested that the Marmes remains were possibly the oldest reliably dated human skeletal remains in the New World. However, a reanalysis of the ^{14}C dates indicates that many were obtained by dating the shells of freshwater mussels. The shells probably produced ^{14}C dates that were older than they should have been because they had been contaminated by groundwater containing older carbonates. The charcoal dates from the site indicate that the skeletal material probably dates between 10,500–10,000 B.P. (Sheppard et al. 1987).

Subsequent to the original discovery in 1965, the remains of three additional individuals were recognized from floodplain excavations that continued until 1968 (Krantz 1979). They all are firmly dated to about 10,000 B.P. (Krantz 1979: 159). Fryxell's original find was labeled Marmes I, and the remaining three were labeled Marmes II, III, and IV, respectively. All remains were fragmentary, consisting primarily of cranial elements, and are presented below based on abstractions from reports by Tadeusz Bielicki (presented in Krantz 1979) and Grover S. Krantz (1979).

Marmes I. The human remains consist of more than 70 bone fragments, many of which exhibit evidence of burning. The individual was estimated to be in her late teens or early twenties at the time of death. Based on the gracile character of the bones, Krantz (1979:163) tentatively identified the individual as female. A shovel-shaped incisor and prominent, flaring cheek bones suggested to the researchers that the individual exhibited Mongoloid characteristics. Partial reconstruction of the crania suggested the individual was not long headed like some early human remains from North America.

The human bones were found among the bones of animals used for food, including rabbit, fish, elk, deer, possibly antelope, and pieces of mussel shell (Caulk 1988). This led the investigators (Fryxell, Bielicki, Daugherty, Gustafson, Irwin, and Keel 1968:513) to consider the possibility that this might be evidence of cannibalism or a cremation burial. Four pieces of worked bone, two of which rearticulated, were found among the human bones. They all appeared to be portions of a gently tapering cylindrical shaft that was flat on one side. This was interpreted to be fragments of one, or more, bone foreshafts or projectile points (Fryxell, Bielicki, Daugherty, Gustafson, Irwin, and Keel 1968; Fryxell, Bielicki, Daugherty, Gustafson, Irwin, Keel, and Krantz 1968).

Marmes II. This individual was identified as a child from a very few poorly preserved bone fragments. Four upper permanent teeth (a shovel-shaped incisor, a canine, a premolar, and a first molar) were unworn on their occlusal surfaces, suggesting that they had only recently erupted. This indicated that the child was only about six years old at the time of death. The child's gender could not be determined.

Marmes III. The remains of this individual consisted primarily of an unburned skullcap that was brought back to the laboratory along with the matrix surrounding it. In addition to the skullcap, an upper left medial incisor was recovered from the matrix. Although heavily worn, Krantz (1979:168) believes that it was shovel shaped. A pit or depression was found on the center of the left parietal indicating a healed injury about 8 mm in diameter and slightly less than 2 mm deep. The individual was tentatively identified as a male based on size and was approximately the same age as Marmes I. Marmes III is apparently an adult male who survived a blow to the head.

Marmes IV. The fourth individual from the floodplain is only represented by three small unburned fragments of a skull. The fragments were spatially separate from the other individuals and could not be rearticulated with them, indicating they were the remains of a separate individual. Estimates of age and gender were not possible, because of the very few remains recovered.

Marmes Cremation Hearth

Fragments of at least six broken and burned human skeletons were recovered from a hearth-like feature located inside Marmes Rockshelter (Krantz 1979). The primary evidence for reconstructing the number of individuals comes from more than one thousand human cranial fragments, most of which were burned. As a graduate student, James Chatters assisted Grover Krantz by meticulously rearticulating as many of these fragments as possible. It was then possible to establish that at least three fully adult humans and three children between the approximate ages of 8–14 years old were represented among the mass of bone fragments (Krantz 1979:169). Each individual was given a designation, Hearth I–VI, to distinguish the individuals from one another. Because the bone was so extensively fragmented and most of the postcranial skeletons were fragmented or missing, interpretations about the individuals are extremely limited.

Hearth I. This individual was presumed to be a male based on the thickness of the bone and comparison with Marmes III. The skull was only partially preserved, and the sutures were well fused suggesting a mature adult. The general shape of the cranial vault is somewhat round headed.

Hearth II. This individual was identified based on the preservation and partial rearticulation of the right side of the crania of an adult, who was probably not as old as Hearth I, because not all the sutures in the skull had completely closed.

Hearth III. A third adult was identified based on the bones from the back of the skull; however, no other information was available.

Hearth IV. Rearticuated skull fragments suggest the individual was a child. The bone has been burned, and about 100 similarly colored and burned pieces of bone may be from the same skull; however, they could not be refitted to one another.

Hearth V. A juvenile was identified based on the reconstruction of the right side of the face and the forehead. The individual is smaller and thinner than Hearth IV.

Hearth VI. A juvenile was also identified through the reconstruction of a separate frontal crest.

Fragments of at least three mandibles were also identified but could not be confidently assigned to any particular skull. The researchers did not attempt to match the post cranial bone fragments to the individual crania. Although numerous tooth fragments were present, they were too fragmentary to provide evidence of incisor shoveling.

The human remains recovered both within and outside the rockshelter provide the largest number of early human skeletal remains older than 8,000 B.P. from any single site in North America. A minimum of ten individuals is represented including at least four children. Marmes I, II, and probably III exhibit shovel-shaped incisors, suggesting the population as a whole may have exhibited the Sinodont dental pattern believed to have originated in northeast Asia.

Gordon Creek

The partial skeleton of a woman was found eroding from a tributary to Gordon Creek in northern Colorado (Anderson 1966). She had been buried in a flexed position on her left side with her head oriented toward the north. Her body had been placed in a shallow excavated pit .5 m (1.6 ft) deep along the southern bank of Gordon Creek (Anderson 1966). Breternitz et al. (1971:174) estimate the woman to have been approximately 150 cm (4 ft 10.75 inches) tall. She was estimated to be between 25–30 years of age. A single ^{14}C determination of 9,700 ± 250 B.P. (GX-0530) was obtained on collagen from the left ilium (Breternitz et al. 1971:170). The bones, artifacts, and burial pit were covered with red ochre.

Lithic artifacts associated with the burial include a large gray quartzite biface, a smooth stone probably used to grind ochre, a hammer stone, an end scraper, two small bifaces, and three utilized flakes. The burial also contained two worked animal ribs, a perforated elk incisor, and three secondary elk incisors that had their roots broken off (Breternitz et al. 1971; Gillio 1970). The single ^{14}C determination suggests the burial may be attributed to the early Plano period (Chapter 9). Breternitz et al. (1971:179) provide an exceptionally well-reasoned reconstruction of the burial as a ritual event.

White River National Forest

In 1989, three amateur cavers discovered human remains about .4 km (.25 mi) from the entrance of a small cave approximately 3,200 m (10,500 ft) above sea level in Colorado's White River National Forest (Finley 1995). The discovery was reported to Patty Jo Watson, who subsequently investigated the site following NAGPRA consultations between the U. S. Forest Service and the Ute tribe. The remains of a muscular 41–45 year old male were dated to circa 8,000 B.P. (Finley 1995). The individual suffered from arthritis in his neck. No artifacts were found with the remains, and the skeleton was disarticulated.

The individual's height was estimated to be approximately 165 cm (5 ft 5 inches) tall based on the height of smudge marks on the wall, presumably left by his torch. However, this is a somewhat unreliable estimate because the smudge marks could likely have been left by other cave explorers, and no evidence of a torch or charcoal was found associated with the human remains. Grooves in the man's teeth suggest he used his teeth as tools, possibly to prepare sinew (animal tendon).

Kennewick

Kennewick Man (also known as Richland Man) was discovered in July 1996 near Kennewick, Washington. The skeleton was found along an approximately 30 m (100 ft) stretch of the Columbia River, and all the bones had eroded from a river bank. Consequently, the skeleton was not recovered in situ. There are no academic publications that describe or analyze the Kennewick discovery. The following description is derived from two nontechnical publications (Chatters 1997; Slayman 1997) and from a motion filed in the United States District Court for the District of Oregon (Civil No. 96-1481-JE) with supporting affidavits by a number of scientists requesting permission to study the human remains. The suit was filed against the U. S. Army Corps of Engineers that in late 1996 prohibited access to the remains for scientific study.

The skeleton was almost complete, and although disarticulated, was missing only the sternum and a few small bones from the hands and feet. The fifth metacarpal (the bone joining the left little finger to the wrist) of the left hand was submitted for radiocarbon dating and produced a ^{14}C determination of 8,410 ± 60 B.P. (UCR-3476). This date has been recalibrated in an effort to present it in calendar years and has been frequently reported in the media as being between 9,600–9,300 B.P. There was no evidence of deliberate burial and no grave goods or other artifacts were associated with the human remains. Subsequent field investigation demonstrates that the skeleton originated from sediments underlying the Mazama tephra (volcanic ash) dated to circa 6,800 B.P.

The skeleton is that of an adult male between 40–55 years old. He was approximately 170–176 cm (5 ft 7 inches to 5 ft 9 inches) in height and of slender build. Amino acid and stable isotope analyses demonstrate that anadromous fish constituted an important part of the man's diet. Dental characteristics fit Turner's (1983) Sundadont dental pattern, rather than the Sinodont pattern indicative of later Native Americans (Chatters 1997:10). His teeth showed little wear and were all present at the time of death.

The man had endured many injuries including the compound fracture of at least six ribs, damage to his left shoulder and arm, and a stone projectile point lodged in his left hip. The projectile point is described as a Cascade point, which typologically dates between 8,500–4,500 B.P. This style of projectile is consistent with the age of the human remains. A CAT scan of the pelvis revealed that the bone had begun to heal around the wound, suggesting the man had lived for some time after receiving the wound.

The remains were examined by physical anthropologists, James Chatters, Catherine J. MacMillan, and Grover S. Krantz, all of whom noted that the skeleton's features, particularly those of the crania, exhibited Caucasoid characteristics. These anatomical features, as well as the excellent state of preservation of the bone, originally led Chatters to assume that the skeleton was that of an early pioneer of European descent who had possibly been wounded in a conflict with Native Americans.

Buhl

In 1989, a human burial was discovered on a terrace overlooking Kanaka Rapids on the Snake River in southern Idaho. The human remains were about

2.5 m (8.2 ft) below the surface when they were accidentally exposed by heavy earthmoving equipment during the excavation of a gravel pit. The Shoshone-Bannock Tribes of Fort Hall granted permission to analyze and date the skeleton and associated artifacts. A ^{14}C determination of 10,675 ± 95 B.P. (Beta 4055 and ETH-7729) was derived directly from samples of human bone (Green et al. 1998).

A 1992 analysis of the site stratigraphy identified three depositional units beneath the burial created by the flood discharge from Pleistocene Lake Bonneville; deposition is believed to have occurred between 15,000–14,000 B.P. or possibly later (Bright 1966; Malde 1968; O'Connor 1990; Scott et al. 1983). The burial was 14 cm (5.5 inches) above the Bonneville gravels, demonstrating that it post-dated that event. It was overlain by four subsequent episodes of deposition. A stemmed obsidian projectile point associated with the burial is typologically similar to other points from the Plateau and Great Basin (see Chapter 8) dating to between 11,000–7,500 B.P. (Willig and Aikens 1988). These concurrent lines of evidence suggest the ^{14}C date on human bone is accurate and that it might be slightly too young.

The skeleton had been disturbed and disarticulated sometime shortly after burial, and it could not be determined if the body had been placed in a pit deliberately prepared for the burial. In addition to the stemmed projectile point, other artifacts associated with the burial included the proximal end of an eyed needle, two fragments of an incised bone pin or awl, and a badger baculum (penis bone). The eye of the needle was made using a perforator, not a drill, and exhibits no evidence of use. The stemmed point was found under the right side of the cranium and had not been used after it was last sharpened. Green et al. (1998:450) suggest the artifacts were prepared specifically for the burial.

Although a small portion of the skeleton was probably destroyed by the heavy equipment working the quarry, the bone was well preserved. The remains were those of an adult female about 17–21 years of age who was about 165 ± 5 cm (5 ft 3–7 inches) tall. Isotopic analysis indicated a ^{13}C value of –19.5 o/oo, indicating a diet comprised primarily of terrestrial foods supplemented by marine foods, most probably anadromous fish, possibly harvested from the nearby Snake River (Green et al. 1998:448–449). The woman's teeth exhibit heavy wear interpreted by the investigators to suggest the food she ate contained a large amount of sand or grit. The results of the isotopic analysis coupled with the woman's type of tooth wear have led Green et al. (1998) to suggest that the meat in her diet may have consisted largely of processed foods, possibly some type of pemmican (a Native American food prepared from fat and dried and pulverized meat to which fruit might be added). According to Carlson (1997), the carbon and nitrogen analysis suggest that anadromous fish could have constituted less than 10 percent of the individual's diet. According to Green et al.

(1998:446), her craniofacial features are similar to those characteristic of East Asian and American Indian populations. Radiographic analysis revealed Harris lines (transverse lines in the bone) indicating that she had suffered regular (possibly as many as 15) periods of dietary or disease related stress during her childhood.

Mostin

Thomas S. Kaufman (1980) reports that human remains began eroding from the Mostin site beginning in the late 1960s and possibly as many as 100 burials may have been destroyed by erosion. The site is situated along Kelsey Creek, a stream flowing into Clear Lake in northern California. Salvage excavations undertaken in the early 1970s recovered possibly as many as 20 burials. The stratigraphic position of many of the burials is unclear, but bone collagen from several individuals was subsequently dated, including: Burial 4 dated to 10,260 ± 340 B.P. (UCLA-1795 A) (Ericson and Berger 1974), Burial 1 dated to 9,040 ± 200 B.P. (UCLA-1795 C) (Ericson 1977 cited in Kaufman 1980), and Burial 9 dated to 7,750 ± 400 B.P. (no lab number reported) (Kaufman 1980). These remains apparently have not been subject to detailed description or analysis, and further research on this early skeletal assemblage could provide important information.

In 1978, additional human remains and artifacts from the site were discovered eroding from Kelsey Creek (Kaufman 1980:98–190). The partial remains were those of an adult female who apparently had been buried within a stratigraphic unit (Stratum 5) dated to 11,250 ± 240 B.P. (UCLA-2165) (Kaufman 1980: 102). A subsequent date on bone collagen from this individual was 10,470 ± 490 B.P. (no lab number reported) (Kaufman 1980:17; Taylor et al. 1985:138). However, the accuracy of the radiocarbon dates for the human skeletal material and associated occupation has been questioned by Fredrickson and White (1988). They suggest that many, if not all, of the ^{14}C determinations from the Mostin site are too old because geothermal springs continuously feed fossil carbonates into adjacent Clear Lake. This ancient carbon may be absorbed by plants, animals, and humans living near the lake. Although the accuracy of the ^{14}C dating remains ambiguous, the human remains from the Mostin site are included here (and in Table 5.1). However, future research may conclude that the human skeletal material may be much younger than indicated by the dates run on bone collagen.

The skeletal remains included the crania, mandible, left and right humeri, ulnae and radii, part of the innominate (hip bone), and some tarsals and metatarsals. The back of the woman's head was resting down and her face was turned about 45 degrees toward her left side. A −24.5 o/oo ^{13}C measurement from the human bone suggests that her diet was largely derived from terrestrial foods. Three ground-stone artifacts, two pestles and a mano, were buried with her, and these artifacts provide evidence for processing seeds and possibly other foods (Kaufman 1980:175–188).

Arlington Springs

In 1959, Phil C. Orr found human bones eroding in a canyon about 500 m (1,640 ft) from the ocean on Santa Rosa Island off the coast of southern California. The site, named Arlington Springs, is located approximately 400 m (1,312 ft) from the shore. Orr left the bones in situ and invited scholars from around the country to visit the site. The visitors were some of the most renowned archeologists and earth scientists in North America (Moratto 1984). After the site had been examined by these experts, Orr excavated two human femora, a humerus, and an unidentified bone about 11.4 m (37.5 ft) below the surface (Orr 1962:418). Based on the size of the femora, Orr suggested that the remains were of an adult male. These remains have become known as Arlington Man. The skeleton is not complete and does not appear to be from a deliberate burial. No bone or stone artifacts were associated with the human remains.

Chemical analysis demonstrated that the bone was fossilized, suggesting considerable antiquity (Oakley 1963). Charcoal from the stratigraphic unit containing the human remains was ^{14}C dated to 10,400 ± 200 B.P. (L-568A) and 10,000 ± 200 B.P. (L-650) (Orr 1962:419). Human bone originally submitted for ^{14}C analysis was considered unsuitable for ^{14}C analysis (Morris cited in Erlandson 1994:186). However, Berger and Protsch (1989:59) were able to obtain a ^{14}C determination of 10,080 ± 810 B.P. from a long bone of Arlington Man. Controversy over the age of the human remains has focused largely on the large standard deviation and the fact that there was only one ^{14}C determination.

In an effort to address this problem, additional AMS ^{14}C determinations have been run. Johnson and Stafford (personal communications 1997, in press) have obtained an AMS ^{14}C date of 10,970 ±80 B.P. (CAMS-16810) on collagen from the human bone and another AMS ^{14}C determination of 11,490 ± 70 B.P. on *Peromyscus* sp. (rodent) bone collagen collected in direct association with the human remains. The fact that they were run on highly purified collagen suggests that these ages are more accurate than the original solid carbon dates.

Based on the ^{14}C dating of circa 11,000 B.P. and the stratigraphic position of the human remains, Arlington Man appears to be one of the oldest reliably dated humans in the Americas. Presuming the dating is correct, this discovery also provides the earliest evidence for the use of watercraft in North America. Santa Rosa Island was not connected to mainland North America during the last Ice Age (Erlandson 1994:183; Moratto 1984), so human occupation depended on watercraft. This find may also imply that humans and dwarf mammoth may have been contemporaneous on the northern Channel Islands (see Channel Islands, Chapter 3).

Rancho La Brea

In 1914, a human cranium, mandible, and some postcranial bones were recovered from Pit 10 at Rancho La Brea (the well-known California tar pits), in Los Angeles, California. The skull was that of an adult female about 25 years of age. According to Robert Heizer (cited in Kroeber 1962:416), there was apparently no inventory of the postcranial elements. A. L. Kroeber, the author of the brief manuscript describing this find, never completed analysis of the discovery, and his report was published after his death. Based on identification of avifauna also from Pit 10, it was suggested that the remains of La Brea woman may have been early Holocene in age. Subsequently, Berger (1975) has reported a ^{14}C determination of 9,000 ± 80 B.P. for the La Brea human.

Spirit Cave

Spirit Cave was excavated in 1940 by Sydney and Georgia Wheeler while doing salvage archeology for the Nevada State Park Commission (Dansie 1997a; Tuohy and Dansie 1997a). This dry cave, or rockshelter, faces west and is approximately 7.6 m (25 ft) wide, about 4.6 m (15 ft) deep and about 1.5 m (5 ft) high (Wheeler 1997). An area at the northern end of the cave was marked by a "quarter circle" made by placing rocks from the rear wall to the north wall. Under this feature, Georgia Wheeler discovered two human burials, one superimposed upon the other. The upper burial was wrapped in a mat woven from split tules (a bulrush, or tall sedge, that grows in wet places) and cord made of native hemp. The skeleton was not complete. The Wheelers reburied the bones and collected the mat. Subsequent reinvestigation of Spirit Cave recovered human bones of a young male and an adult female that were ^{14}C dated to 4,640 ± 50 B.P. (UCR-3474) and 9,300 ± 70 B.P., respectively (Dansie 1997b:17). The mat collected by the Wheelers was dated to 9,270 ± 60 B.P. (UCR-3480). The age of the female and the mat are statistically identical.

Immediately below the circa 9,300 year old skeleton, the Wheeler's discovered another burial that was completely intact. The individual was an adult male between 40–44 years of age (Jantz and Owsley 1997) (Figure 5.6). He had less overall dental wear for this age than other skeletons from the region (Edgar 1997). He was wrapped in a rabbit skin blanket and dressed in leather moccasins and a breechcloth "of fiber" (Dansie 1997b). He had broken and healed bones in his right hand (Jantz and Owsley 1997).

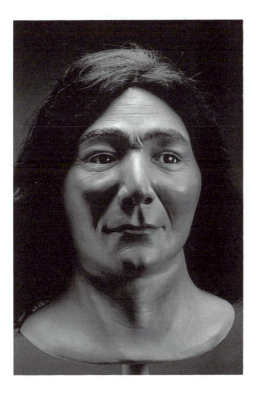

Figure 5.6 Facial reconstruction of a man in his early forties who was buried in Spirit Cave, Nevada. He survived a severe blow to the head and died about 9,400 years ago. (Reconstruction by Sharon Long in collaboration with Douglas Owsley and David Hunt of the National Museum of Natural History. Photograph by Chip Clark, courtesy of Douglas Owsley and the Nevada State Museum.)

The head was oriented toward the northeast. The individual had been buried in a semiflexed position resting on the right side with the right hand positioned under the chin and left hand in front of the pelvis, with the knees drawn slightly toward the chest. The man's shoulder-length hair was black at the time of discovery and turned reddish brown shortly after being exposed to the sunlight. The body had been placed in a deliberately excavated pit 1.8 m (6 ft) long, 1.2 m (4 ft) wide, and 1.1 m (3 ft 9 inches) deep. The upper half of the body was wrapped in a mat that had been sewn together around the head. A similar mat was wrapped around the lower body, and a large mat of tules covered the entire body. From the hips upward, the body was partially mummified.

Seven concordant AMS ^{14}C dates on human hair, bone, and tule mats provide a average (weighted mean) date of 9,414 ± 25 B.P. for this burial (Kirner et al. 1997; Tuohy and Dansie 1997b). Comparison of the cranial and facial features of the Spirit Cave mummy to other known populations suggest to physical anthropologists Richard Jantz and Douglas Owsley (1997) that the Spirit Cave mummy is more similar to some Europeans populations and the Ainu of northern Japan, than later populations of American Indians.

At the time the cave was occupied, it was probably situated near the shores of a marsh. Human coprolites (fossil feces) taken from the Spirit Cave mummy indicate the individual had consumed two species of fish shortly before his death. Fish eye lenses and otoliths (fish ear bones), animal fibers (possibly sinew) were found within the coprolites (Eiselt 1997). Coprolites also contained what were probably ground bulrush seeds (Napton 1997) and background pollen derived from the general environment, which included cattail, sedge, and the desert shrubs shad scale and greasewood (Wigand 1997).

This man had several genetic abnormalities. The Spirit Cave mummy had 34 vertebra (the average person has 33) and the extra vertebra (13th thoracic) appeared to have only one rib attached rather than the normal two. There were also abnormalities in the lower spinal column. Although not life threatening, these conditions probably caused the individual considerable discomfort (Edgar 1997). The man had suffered a severe blow to his left temple, possibly the result of violence, with two radiating fractures extended from the point of impact. The wound had healed, and bone regeneration suggested that the man lived about a year after suffering the trauma to his head. His front teeth had linear indentations suggesting his teeth were used as tools, possibly to process sinew. Three severely abscessed teeth possibly resulted in an infection that led to his death (Edgar 1997).

Five days after the first discovery, the Wheeler's returned to the cave, and Georgia Wheeler found two more burials. This time they were the remains of two individuals who had been cremated. About 51 cm (20 inches) below the surface, she found a metate (a flat stone for grinding grain) leaning against the rear wall of the cave. Ten centimeters (4 inches) below this she discovered a small twined bag of split tules and a close twined bag of hemp. Within the first bag made of tules was an inner bag made of hemp containing cremated human bones. The lower bag also contained cremated human bones. Both were at the end of a pit 1.5 m (5 ft) wide, 1.8 m (6 ft) long, and .8 m (2.5 ft) deep that S. M. Wheeler presumed was a cremation pit that had been subsequently backfilled as part of the burial. A single AMS ^{14}C determination on one of the bags of 9,040 ± 50 B.P. documents the date of the cremations (Dansie 1997b).

Fishbone Cave

Fishbone Cave is located adjacent to now dry Lake Winnemucca in western Nevada. The cave was investigated in the early 1950s under the direction of Phil C. Orr (1956, 1965). He defined a sequence of six stratigraphic units; the upper four contained cultural material. Radiocarbon dates of 11,555 ± 500 B.P. (no lab number cited) and 10,900 ± 300 B.P. (L-245) were reported by Orr (1956:3) for Level 4, which contained the oldest cultural remains at the cave. Although Levels 5 and 6 were culturally sterile, Level 4 contained the partial remains of a human skeleton consisting of the burned remains of a left foot, a clavicle, and a fibula. The burial contained the well-preserved skin of a young pelican, a piece of "fine" netting, six basketry fragments, several pieces of cordage, and a piece of matting.

Grimes Burial Shelter

In 1939, a miner entered Grimes Shelter to collect guano (bat droppings), which is used as fertilizer. There he discovered human remains that were eventually turned over to S. M. Wheeler who deposited them in the Nevada State Museum. The age and significance of this discovery was not realized until 1995 when it was realized that the diamond plaited matting was similar to that from Spirit Cave. A fragment of the Grimes shelter matting was dated to 9,470 ± 60 b.p. (ucr-3477, cams-33691). The mat had been used to wrap the remains of a child, possibly female, about 10 years old, along with a small fragment of an older individual. The crania, mandible, and about half of the postcranial skeleton of the child were preserved (Dansie 1997a).

Wizards Beach

Wizards Beach is located on the northwestern end of Pyramid Lake, Nevada. In 1968, avocational archeologist Peter Ting discovered human remains exposed by wave erosion at a time when the water level in the lake was lower than usual. The discovery turned out to be two burials, one of which (Burial A) was dated to circa 6,000 b.p. (Dansie 1997a). Four ams ^{14}C determinations dated Burial B to between 9,500–9,100 b.p., but only two of the dates have been used to determine an average age of 9,250 ± 60 b.p. for the burial (Dansie 1997a; Tuohy and Dansie 1997b). No artifacts were found with the skeletons.

Edgar (1997) describes the Wizards Beach Man (Burial B) as a robust male with well-defined muscle attachments suggesting a muscular build (Figure 5.7). The skeleton is not complete. Part of the vertebral column, the pelvis, and minor limb bones were missing. New bone deposited on the surface of his long bones indicates a reaction to diffuse infection throughout his body that lasted until the time of death. He was 40–45 years old at the time of death. His teeth were heavily worn beyond the crowns, and at the time of death tooth root stubs served as his chewing surfaces. An abscess in his lower right first molar resulted in infection of the bone probably entering through the pulp cavity of the tooth. The infection could have been the cause of his death. He also suffered from osteoarthritis in his wrists and elbows.

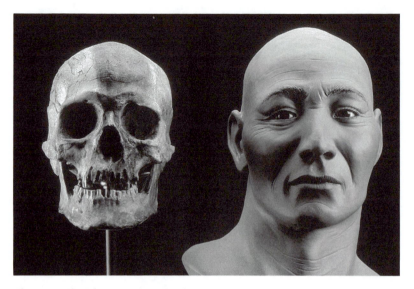

Figure 5.7 Facial reconstruction of a man who died sometime about 9,250 years ago near Wizards Beach, Nevada. (Reconstruction by Sharon Long in collaboration with Douglas Owsley and David Hunt of the National Museum of Natural History. Photograph by Chip Clark, courtesy of Douglas Owsley and the Nevada State Museum.)

Wilson-Leonard Burial II

The Wilson-Leonard site is located in central Texas, near Austin. The nearly complete skeleton of a female was recovered in situ from a shallow (22 cm [8.7 inches]) oval pit approximately 104 cm (3 ft 5 inches) long and 52 cm (1 ft 8.5 inches) wide (Figure 5.8). The skeleton was severely crushed by compaction of the sediments making physical reconstruction and anatomical analysis difficult.

The remains were of a late adolescent or young adult female, probably in her early 20s. She was discovered lying on her right side with her knees drawn upward about halfway toward her chest. Her head rested on her right hand, and her left hand was over her right wrist. Her head was oriented to the north, and she faced west. Her height is estimated to be about 158 cm (5 ft 1 inch) (Steele 1998). Although heavily fractured, reconstruction of the skull suggested the woman had a somewhat narrow cranium and face.

The young woman had lost her lower right first molar prior to her death and suffered from an abscess in the adjacent premolar. Her front teeth were heavily worn for an individual her age, suggesting she may have used her teeth for some repetitive task. Her teeth also exhibited microscopic pits and striations, which might suggest hard or abrasive foods, such as hard seeds and hulls (Steele 1998).

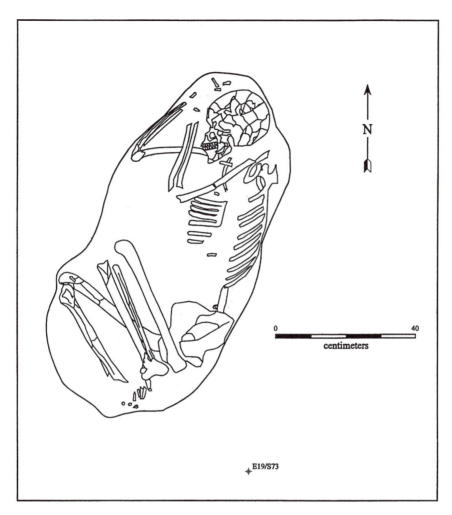

Figure 5.8 Line drawing depicting Burial II, Wilson-Leonard Site, Texas. (Modified and reproduced from Collins 1998a, with permission from Michael Collins.)

Stable isotope analysis supports the tooth wear analysis, and ^{13}C values indicate that her diet consisted primarily of c3 plants, but also included c4 plants, such as prickly pear and possibly grass seeds (Bousman 1998; Wilson 1998).

Three artifacts were recovered along with the human remains: a fossil shark tooth, a limestone cobble, and a ground sandstone mano that was later flaked and used as a chopper. The limestone cobble may have been used to hold down a cover in the burial bit (Bousman 1998). The purpose of the shark tooth is unknown. The age of the burial is between 10,000–9,600 B.P. based on several concordant ^{14}C determinations bracketing the stratigraphic position of the burial within the sedimentary units (Bousman 1998; Stafford 1998; Steele 1998).

Horn Shelter Number 2

Horn Shelter Number 2 is located on the western bank of the Brazos River approximately 16 km (10 mi) downstream from the Lake Whitney Dam northwest of Waco, Texas (Forrester 1985). The site is a stratified limestone rockshelter in which a unique double burial was discovered. Four radiocarbon determinations were derived from the stratigraphic unit designated Sub-Stratum 5G, which contained the burials. Two dates on charcoal, 9,500 ± 200 B.P. (Tx–1830) and 9,980 ± 370 B.P. (Tx–1722) suggest the burials are roughly 9,650 ^{14}C years old. Two other dates on snails from the same stratigraphic unit are slightly older (10,030 ± 130 B.P. [Tx–1998] and 10,310 ± 150 B.P. [Tx–1997]) (Redder 1985).

An adult male and female (originally identified as a juvenile) were buried together in flexed positions resting on their left sides with the female facing the male's back. Although their gender and ages were not reported by Forrester (1985) or Redder (1985), subsequent analysis by Young (Young 1985; Young et al. 1987) indicates that the adult was male. The female was originally identified as a juvenile approximately 12 years old (Young 1985; Young et al. 1987). She had a minor sinus infection in her right maxillary. The adult male is estimated to have been in his 30s to early 40s at the time of his death. He had broken a bone in his left foot (fifth metatarsal) that had subsequently healed. Well-defined areas on the bones where the muscles attach indicate he was a muscular individual. He also suffered from a sinus (left maxillary) infection. He is estimated to have been between 161–169 cm (5 ft 3 inches–5 ft 6.5 inches) tall. X-rays of the long bones of the adult revealed Harris lines suggesting he had suffered periods of dietary stress as a subadult. Neither individual exhibited signs of trauma that might have resulted in death.

The burial had been covered with limestone slabs. Three turtle shells were placed under the adult male's head and a fourth in front of his face and a fifth under his hip. Grave goods were apparently placed together near the heads of the two individuals like a cache. Included among these grave offerings were two sandstone slabs, two percussion flint-knapping tools made from the proximal ends of antlers, two sandstone abraders, an approximately 7.7 cm square (3 inches square) piece of red ochre, one flint biface, and an unidentified piece of worked deer bone. Other items included in the burial were four perforated canine pendants, possibly coyote, which appeared to have been strung around the neck of the male along with an unspecified number of perforated bird talons, possibly hawk or eagle. Another unidentified bone artifact was found in the turtle shell placed below the pelvis of the man, and a shaft wrench (see Figure 6.3) made from deer antler was positioned near his leg. An eyed bone needle appeared to be associated with the female.

The sediment filling the burial contained flint chips, turtle bones and bone fragments, deer, bird, rodent, snake, frog, at least three species of fish, and pieces of worked antler. More than 80 beads made from small marine shells (*Neritina canines*) were also recovered from the burial fill. The proximity and nature of the grave goods, the flint flakers and shaft wrench, support the identification by Young (Young 1985; Young et al. 1987) that the larger individual was male, and the needle associated with the smaller individual supports the interpretation of this individual as female. It is possible that this was a couple that died at, or about, the same time and were buried together.

Warm Mineral Springs

Warm Mineral Springs in Sarasota County in western Florida is thought by some to be the legendary "fountain of youth" sought by Spanish explorer Ponce de León. Although unable to bestow eternal youth, the Spring has exceptional powers of preservation, as archeological discoveries demonstrate. It was here in 1959 that amateur archeologist "Colonel" William Royal, a retired Air Force officer and sport diver, and marine biologist Eugenie Clark discovered a human crania that still contained brain tissue. A log from the same area (not the same stratigraphic unit) on a submerged ledge approximately 13 m (43 ft) below the surface of the spring was radiocarbon dated to circa 10,000 B.P. (Royal and Clark 1960). The skull has been subsequently dated between 7,600–7,100 B.P. (Purdy 1991:191, 200).

Because the find was made by avocational archeologists who were, ironically, being filmed for a nationally televised *Huntley-Brinkley Report* when the discovery was made, it was not readily accepted by professional archeologists. It was suspected that the discovery had been staged for publicity purposes (Purdy 1991:198–199). Consequently, the site was not given the professional attention it deserved until it eventually became clear that it was a legitimate in situ archeological discovery.

On a ledge located about 13 m (43 ft) below the surface of the spring, Royal claims to have found and removed seven human skulls (six adults and one child) and other skeletal elements representing 30 individuals over a period of many years (Clausen et al. 1975:197; Purdy 1991). Unfortunately, these specimens and associated artifacts were not professionally excavated and cataloged. Instead, they were stored in open boxes along with material collected from nearby Little Salt Spring, and some were even cemented into the stonework of Royal's fireplace (Skow 1986:82).

Between 1958–1962, geologist H. K. Brooks carefully studied and sampled the deposits. Brief professional excavations were undertaken in 1972 under the direction of Carl J. Clausen, who incorporated Brooks' earlier work. This effort resulted in a lucid scientific report about the ledge and its sediments (Clausen et al. 1975). Three stratigraphic units, or zones, containing fossil remains were defined on the 13 m (43 ft) deep ledge. An impressive series of ^{14}C determinations (Clausen et al. 1975:197–200) indicate the deposit, Zone 3, from which most of the human remains were recovered dated circa 10,500–10,000 B.P. As sea level rose at the end of the last Ice Age, water within the spring rose until the 13 m (43 ft) ledge was inundated by the rising spring about 10,500–10,000 B.P. (Clausen et al. 1975:205). Clausen theorized that the human remains and other fossils were transported to the ledge by floating on the water. As they lost buoyancy, objects, such as leaves and occasionally human remains, gradually sank to the bottom. Some rested on the ledge and others were incorporated into the debris cone at the bottom of the spring. People were attracted to the deep spring because the climate at the time was dryer and surface water was scarce. If a person fell into the spring, it was difficult, if not impossible to escape, and they would soon drown. Cockrell, who subsequently began excavation at the spring, has advanced another hypothesis. He believes that humans inhabited the ledge when it was above the water table and buried their dead there before the water level rose (Cockrell cited in Purdy 1991).

Because of the lack of secure provenience for many of the specimens and the multiple excavations at the spring, only the remains of three individuals could be positively identified as having been excavated from Zone 3, which appears to have been deposited between circa 10,500–10,000 B.P. Two of these individuals have been analyzed by Morris (1975) in an unpublished report summarized by Purdy (1991:189–192). The third individual is represented by only the ilium and vertebra from a child about six years old.

Morris describes the virtually complete male skeleton recovered by Cockrell in 1973 as a gracile young adult between 30–40 years of age, who was about 161–163 cm (5 ft 3 inches–5 ft 4 inches) tall and estimated to have weighed 50 kg (110 lbs). His teeth were heavily worn and exhibited "considerable" abscessing. His cranium was dolichocranic, comparatively long and narrow. He had a prominent square chin (Purdy 1991:189; Skow 1986:80). An atlatl hook made of shell was apparently associated with this individual.

The third individual also was recovered by Cockrell from what appeared to be the contact of Zone 3 and an underlying culturally sterile clay. This individual is only represented by a partial crania and mandible that were damaged in an attempt to restore the specimen. The skull is that of a female, possibly middle aged. The cranium tends to be long and narrow and exhibits signs of dietary deficiency. The teeth are missing.

Potentially early human remains have also been reported from nearby sites at

Vero Beach and Melbourne (Sellards 1917; Stewart 1946). The remains may also be late Pleistocene in age. Analysis of the remains by Morris (Morris cited in Purdy 1991:192) led him to suggest they may be contemporary with the remains from Warm Mineral Springs. The early collections from Warm Mineral Springs have been dispersed and mixed with those from other sites, making reliable scientific analysis extremely difficult, if not impossible. Royal justifies looting this important site because professional archeologists failed to show interest in his early discoveries and failed to participate in the excavations (Purdy 1991). However, professionals could have investigated the site 50 or even 100 years later and recovered valuable data from this unique and extremely important site. Because it was not professionally excavated, its potential significance to New World archeology will never be fully understood or appreciated.

Whitewater Draw

Whitewater Draw is located in Cochise County, in southeastern Arizona. The locality was first studied by geologist Ernst Antevs and archeologist Edwin Sayles. They defined three cultural stages, the oldest of which was associated with extinct Pleistocene fauna and called the Sulphur Spring stage (see Chapter 8) (Sayles and Antevs 1941). In 1940, Hooton (Sayles and Antevs 1941:65) described the remains of an adult human approximately 35 years old, from Sulphur Spring stage deposits at Whitewater Draw. The remains consisted of a partial and fragmented crania, mandible fragments, a partial femur, and the midsection of an ulna or fibula, and several unidentified bone fragments. Hooton described the crania as dolichocephalic. Although he was unable to determine the individual's gender with certainty, he suggested the individual might have been female.

Whitewater Draw was reinvestigated in 1982–1983 by Michael R. Waters, who discovered a second human burial during backhoe trenching (Waters 1986a, 1986b). The skeleton was located 2 m (6.6 ft) below the surface. Even though it had been partially disarticulated by the backhoe, it was possible to determine from the bones left in situ that the burial was in primary context. The remains were those of an adult female who was probably between 25–35 years old at the time of her death (Figure 5.9). She had been buried in a flexed position (knees drawn up to the chest) with her face toward the northwest. No grave goods or ochre appeared to be associated with the burial. Based on the stratigraphic position of the burial, the individual could be ascribed to the Sulphur Spring stage deposits, which were accurately dated by Waters (1986a:58) to 10,000–8,000 B.P. and possibly as old as 10,400 B.P. The woman's teeth display Turner's (1983) Sinodont dental pattern similar to that of people from northeast Asia. Her teeth exhibit heavy wear indicative of an abrasive diet.

Figure 5.9 Sulphur Springs woman. (Photograph by Gentry Steele, courtesy of Michael Waters.)

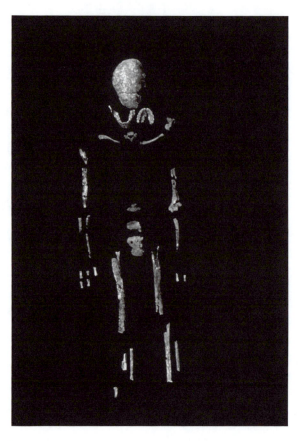

Tlapacoya XVIII

In 1968, the remains of an incomplete adult human cranium were found out of context at Tlapacoya XVIII (Lorenzo and Mirambell 1999). The remains were described as those of an adult exhibiting rather robust features. It was elongated and narrow (dolichocephalic). Subsequent to this discovery, a second incomplete human cranium was discovered in a stratigraphic unit dated to 9,920 ± 250 B.P. (I-6897). The second discovery is described as being broader (brachycephalic) (Lorenzo and Mirambell 1999). Since that time, a highly precise AMS ^{14}C date of 9,730 ± 65 B.P. (OxA-7557) has been obtained on one of the crania from Tlapacoya (presumably site XVIII) (Arroyo-Cabrales, personal communication 1998). A ^{13}C value of –16.0 o/oo may suggest a mixed diet comprised of terrestrial and marine foods. Although it appears that the two ^{14}C determinations statistically overlap, it is not clear which cranium was dated by the AMS method. They are treated as two separately dated individuals in Table 5.1.

Summary

Unlike the Old World, the New World lacks human remains that are anatomically similar to very early human forms, such as *Homo erectus*, Neanderthal, or even Archaic *Homo sapiens*. Human remains found thus far in the New World appear to be completely modern humans, *Homo sapiens*. There is some evidence possibly contradicting this, including the inconclusive identification of a human supraorbital ridge from the Chapala Basin, Mexico, (Chapter 4) and a curious report with illustrations of an archaic human calvarium (skullcap) from Brazil that has subsequently disappeared (Bryan 1978:318–321).

Since the early 1900s, physical anthropologists have recognized that the earliest human skeletons found in the Americas tended to have longer and narrower (dolichocephalic) crania. Later human remains in the Americas and current Native Americans tend to have broader (brachycephalic) heads more closely resembling Asian Mongoloid populations. Steele and Powell (1992) have concluded that the human cranial and facial characteristics from the Americas that are over 8,500 B.P. are distinctively different than later Native Americans. Based on statistical comparison with human crania from other ancient and modern populations around the world, they conclude that the earliest human remains in the Americas appear physically distinct from later people. Distinguishing features identified by physical anthropologists (Chatters 1997; Jantz and Owsley 1997; Steele and Powell 1992) for these very early New World people are: (1) longer, more narrow heads; (2) smaller and relatively more narrow faces; and (3) smaller more narrow nasal apertures.

The early human remains from the Americas tend to display craniofacial features that are more similar to southern Pacific and European populations than to later northern Asians and modern Native Americans. Morphologically, Paleoindians tend to fall between these two groups. This suggests that there may be appreciable biological and genetic differences between Paleoindians and later populations of Native Americans. However, these differences are relatively minor, and they do not necessarily mean that the populations are not related. Rapid evolutionary change could explain the differences, or the differences may result from an earlier migration to the Americas by people not closely related to later New World immigrants.

A problem that may be somewhat unique to New World archeology is that because all human remains from the Americas are completely modern *Homo sapiens*, it is very likely that potentially early (predating 12,000–11,000 B.P.) human remains might be overlooked based on the assumption that they are fully modern and consequently recent in age. This was the case for the Spirit Cave mummy from Nevada where the early association with textiles suggested to some researchers that the human remains were late Holocene in age. In addition, some of the earliest humans may exhibit some traits such as longer and narrower (dolichocephalic) crania, which possibly could be confused with the remains of later Euro-Americans. This could lead scientists to assume the remains are modern and therefore not devote the time and resources necessary to accurately date these types of remains.

The foregoing review has described all the human remains older than 8,000 years ago from North America that have been described in scientific reports. Altogether there were only 38 individuals (Namu excluded) (Table 5.1). This is a surprisingly small number considering the great length of time and the vast area from which they have been found. Of the 38 individuals, 16 were discovered accidentally by construction, erosion, or other activities. Twenty-two, or about 58 percent, of the individuals were discovered and excavated by archeologists. If the anomalous group of 10 partial individuals from the Marmes Rockshelter is excluded, only 12, or 32 percent, were found by archeologists. This suggests that in about two of every three cases, archeologist are not directly involved in the discovery of early human remains. Most sites are exposed and destroyed by natural erosion, urban sprawl, and agricultural and construction activities and do not come to the attention of scientists. Because this sample is comparatively small, encompasses a huge geographic area, and spans 3,000 years, the following summary provides only limited, yet fascinating, insights into the lives of these early Americans.

Age of Sites. Reliably dated human remains provide unequivocal proof of human presence in the Americas. The direct dating of small amounts of human bone provides minimum limiting dates for human occupation. As of 1998, no human remains from the Americas had been reliably dated to older than 12,000 B.P.

The oldest human remains appear to be from Fishbone Cave, Anzick, and possibly Arlington Springs, where they appear to be about 11,000 B.P. This suggests that by this time human population density had achieved a level sufficient to assure the survival and discovery of fossil remains over a broad geographic area and from a number of different environments. These discoveries provide a firm minimum limiting date for the occupation of North America. These people were probably descendants of earlier colonists. It is possible that prior to circa 11,500–11,000 B.P. that the North American human population may have been extremely small or geographically restricted.

Firmly dated human remains for the period between 11,000–10,000 B.P. are more common and include Buhl, Marmes, Mostin, and Warm Mineral Springs. Although well-dated human remains between 11,000–10,000 B.P. are relatively rare, there are many archeological sites throughout North America dating to this time period that do not contain human remains, suggesting that there were many more people on the landscape after 11,000 B.P.

Fourteen firmly dated occurrences of human remains are documented between 10,000–9,000 B.P. They occur from Alaska to Florida and Mexico and document diverse burial practices, regional adaptations, and probably violent interpersonal conflict. The remains of only four individuals can be firmly ascribed to the period between 9,000–8,000 B.P. Other human remains, such as the two individuals from Whitewater Draw, with broadly defined bracketing dates between 10,000–8,000 B.P. could date to this time period or earlier.

Population Characteristics. Of the 38 individuals, 11 have been identified as male and 11 as female (although two of these identifications are tentative), the remaining 16 are not identified as to gender. Of the 30 individuals for which approximations of age could be determined, nine were identified as children, subadults, or juveniles. This suggests that about one-fourth (approximately 25 percent) of the population did not survive to become adults. None of the individuals lived to be over 50, with the possible exception of Kennewick man. Most died in their 20s and 30s, and the limited data suggest that only four individuals, or about 10 percent of the population, may have lived into their 40s. The relatively early deaths of these productive people, many at or before their peak in fitness, maturity, and knowledge, must have been serious losses to early groups. As knowledgeable adults, many were important contributors (and future contributors) to the economy and safety of their bands.

Although the data are very sketchy documenting the height of these people, the tallest individual is Kennewick man who is estimated to have been about 176 cm (5 ft 9 inches) tall. The next tallest individual based on analysis of the skeleton was the adult male from Warm Mineral Springs who was approximately 163 cm (5 ft 4 inches) tall. From what little data are available, the men were short and muscular, and women were even shorter with more gracile builds.

Burial Practices. Two types of burial practices can be documented based on the limited information available. They are cremation and burial within the ground. Twelve of the individuals appear to have been cremated, and thirteen were apparently placed in graves of some type. It is interesting to note that the cremations occur in or adjacent to small caves or rockshelters and that in both instances they are in the Far West, Washington and Nevada. Cremation and shallow pit burials occur in the Great Basin. Shallow pit burials are frequently associated with red ochre and artifacts in the Great Plains region. The practice of flexed pit burials with associated artifacts and ochre is also documented at Browns Valley and Gore Creek. In five cases, the type of the burial could not be determined.

The largest assemblage of human remains is from Marmes, which exhibits

Table 5.1

Human Remains from North America Older than 8,000 B.P.

Site	^{14}C Age B.P.	Gender	Age	Height	Dentition	Pathology	Isotope Analysis	Burial Type
Anzick	11,115	?	"subadult"	NA	NA	NA	NA	ochre, artifacts
Anzick	8,600	?	"subadult"	NA	NA	NA	NA	NA
Arlington Springs	11,000	M	NA	NA	NA	NA	NA	probably accidental
Browns Valley	8,700	M	25–40	NA	heavy wear	NA	NA	pit, ochre, artifacts
Buhl	10,675	F	17–21	5'3"–5'7"	heavy wear	dietary stress	T/Ma	pit?, artifacts
Fishbone Cave	11,000	?	?	?	?	?	?	?
Gordon Creek	9,700	F	25–30	4'11"	NA	NA	NA	pit, ochre, artifacts
Gore Creek	8,250	M	NA	NA	NA	NA	T/Ma	possibly accidental
Grimes Shelter	9,470	F?	c 10	NA	NA	NA	NA	wrapped in mat
Horn Shelter 2	9,560	F	NA	NA	NA	minor sinus infection	NA	pit, flexed, artifacts
Horn Shelter 2	9,560	M	30–40	5'3"	NA	dietary stress, sinus infection, broken bone	NA	pit, flexed, artifacts
Kennewick	8,410	M	40–55	5'10"	little wear	broken ribs, damaged arm, projectile in hip	T/Ma	possibly accidental
Marmes Floodplain I	10–10,500	?	15–25	?	NA	?	NA	cremation?, artifacts
Marmes Floodplain II	10–10,500	?	6	?	shovel shaped incisor	?	NA	cremation?
Marmes Floodplain III	10–10,500	M?	15–25	?	shovel shaped incisor	blow to head	NA	cremation?
Marmes Floodplain IV	10–10,500	?	?	?	?	?	NA	cremation?
Marmes Hearth I	10–10,500	M?	adult	?	?	?	NA	cremation?
Marmes Hearth II	10–10,500	?	"subadult"	?	?	?	NA	cremation?
Marmes Hearth III	10–10,500	?	adult	?	?	?	NA	cremation?
Marmes Hearth IV	10–10,500	?	child	?	?	?	NA	cremation?

Site	Date	Sex	Age	Height	Dental	Pathology	Diet	Burial
Marmes Hearth V	10–10,500	?	juvenile	?	?	?	NA	cremation?
Marmes Hearth VI	10–10,500	?	juvenile	?	?	?	NA	cremation?
Mostin	10,470	F	adult	NA	NA	NA	NA	pit?, artifacts
Namu	9–8,000	NA	NA	NA	crowns	NA	NA	NA
49-PET-408	9,200	M	20–25	?	heavy wear, tools	dietary stress	Ma	possibly accidental
Rancho La Brea	9,000	F	c 25	NA	NA	NA	NA	probably accidental
Spirit Cave	9,400	M	40–44	NA	heavy wear, abcess, tools	blow to head, abnormal spine, broken bones	NA	pit, flexed wrapped in mat fur robe, moccasins
Spirit Cave	9,300	F	adult	NA	NA	NA	NA	pit, wrapped in mat, artifacts
Spirit Cave	9,040	NA	NA	NA	NA	NA	NA	cremation
Spirit Cave	9,040	NA	NA	NA	NA	NA	NA	cremation
Tlapacoya XVIII	9,730	NA	adult	NA	NA	NA	T/Ma	NA
Tlapacoya XVIII	9,920	NA	adult	NA	NA	NA	NA	NA
Warm Mineral Sprs	10,310	M	30–40	5'4"	heavy wear, abcess	NA	NA	probably accidental
Warm Mineral Sprs	10,250	F	?	NA	NA	dietary stress	NA	probably accidental
Warm Mineral Sprs	10,250	?	6	NA	NA	NA	NA	probably accidental
White River Forest	8,000	M	41–45	?	tools	arthritis	NA	probably accidental
Whitewater Draw	8–10,000	F	25–35	NA	heavy wear	NA	NA	pit, flexed
Whitewater Draw	8–10,000	F?	c 35	?	?	?	?	pit?
Wilson-Leonard II	9,600–10,000	F	20–25	5'1"	heavy wear, abcess, tools	NA	T	pit, flexed, artifacts
Wizards Beach	9,250	M	40–45	NA	extreme wear, abcess	osteoarthritis, systemic infection	NA	NA

M=male F=female T=terrestrial Ma=marine T/Ma=mixed diet NA=not applicable or not available ?=could not be determined or uncertain several unusual features. The fact that the bodies of at least six individuals were burned in a hearth provides important clues to the lives of these early people. A femur fragment from the cremation pit exhibits parallel cut marks 6 and 8 mm long and 2.5 mm apart as well as several less visible cut marks. These cut marks could be evidence of butchering similar to marks left on animal bones.

When the investigators attempted to rearticulate the many pieces of bone, they discovered that the degree of burning and color was not continuous across breaks. This indicated that some of the burning had taken place after the bone had been broken. In other words, the bones appeared to have been burned, then broken into fragments and then some of the fragments were burned again. This might indicate that the bodies, or body parts, were first subject to fire (as in cremation or cooking) and subsequently fragments from some of the broken bones were thrown back into the fire. Although these activities had been carried out in an area very close to the fire, the vast majority of the bones was not found in the rockshelter and had been transported elsewhere. This unusual set of circumstances led Krantz (1979:174) to suggest that "the whole picture presented is that of a cannibalistic feast during which over half of the food was removed from the immediate area and some of the leftovers thrown back into the fire."

Although the archeological evidence can be interpreted to suggest cannibalism, it seems more plausible that the pit was used repeatedly for the ritual cremation of the dead. Many cultures cremate the dead for a variety of reasons ranging from spiritual ascent of the remains carried by the fire toward the heavens and very pragmatic reasons of preventing carnivores and scavengers from desecrating the bodies of the recently deceased. A common practice after cremation is to collect the remaining bones and bury or place them elsewhere. This may account for the "missing" bones at the Marmes site. Repeated use of the cremation pit may also explain the second burning of some of the bone fragments, which may not have been completely collected after the preceding cremation.

Isotope analysis, AMS ^{14}C dating, and other contemporary analytical techniques need to be applied to the Marmes remains to accurately determine what happened at the Marmes Rockshelter and to provide insight into the lives of these early people. These types of analysis are important in attempting to determine if all the individuals were cremated at the same time or whether the cremation hearth may have been reused over a relatively long period of time, perhaps several generations. If it is preserved, analysis of DNA could possibly determine if the cremated individuals were genetically related, and isotope analysis could provide important insights regarding diet. If all the individuals were cremated at the same time, it might suggest some cataclysmic event, such as plague, drowning, social conflict, etc. had taken place. Further research is essential to accurately interpret the cultural and ecological factors surrounding this event.

Multiple burials (two individuals each) occur at Spirit Cave and Horn Shelter 2. These apparently simultaneous deaths may have resulted from events such as drowning or disease where more than one individual died or was killed at the same time. The pit burials contain grave goods indicating belief in an afterlife. The fill associated with some burials (Horn Rockshelter 2, Gordon Creek) contain faunal remains, some of which exhibit signs of burning, possibly implying additional offerings or grave-side ceremonies at which food may have been consumed.

Quality of Life. Nine individuals, almost 25 percent, appear to have died accidental deaths based on the fact that their bodies apparently were not recovered for burial or cremation. It is probable that some of the cremated and buried individuals also died as a result of accidents. This supports other evidence indicating life was dangerous and that at least one in four individuals may have died as a result of accidents.

Kennewick man, apparently not deliberately buried, provides a dramatic example of an individual who led a rough life. Long before his death, he suffered multiple fractures of at least six ribs, severe damage to his left arm and shoulder, and a severe wound in his hip from a stone projectile point, probably inflicted by a dart (small spear) propelled with an atlatl, or spear thrower. The fact that his remains were found with no grave goods or tools may imply that he also died away from his social group, and his body was not recovered for burial. His hip wound, although possibly inflicted accidentally, may be evidence of early social conflict. Marmes III and the Spirit Cave mummy suffered blows to the head, possibly delivered by other individuals.

Dietary stress, probably during periods of malnutrition or disease, is documented in at least four individuals and probably occurred in others. This probably provides evidence of periods of poor nutrition, hunger, or starvation when they were children or very young adults. The teeth of many individuals exhibit severe attrition and heavy wear causing the nerves in the teeth to be exposed. When this happened, individuals shifted to different chewing patterns to reduce the pain while chewing. This resulted in various planes, or facets, being formed where the teeth mesh. Some individuals suffered from infections and abscesses. In at least two instances (Wizards Beach and Spirit Cave) abscessed teeth probably contributed to, or caused, their deaths.

An analysis of Paleoindian dentition by Powell and Steele (1994) found the characteristics of dental wear in the oldest human remains virtually identical to that of later Archaic period Native Americans. This suggested to them that Paleoindian and Archaic diets were similar and included a broader array of foods than wild game, traditionally associated with Paleoindian hunters. Based on the polish on many of the teeth, they concluded that these early people consumed considerable amounts of plant fiber.

Different individuals from different parts of North America consumed varying amounts of grit and hard materials, suggesting differing exploitation of regional resources. Heavy wear probably resulted from a number of factors. In coastal areas an intensive diet of shell fish containing sand and grit is suggested by the human teeth recovered from 49-PET-408. At Spirit Cave, there is evidence of early seed grinding from both the artifacts and coprolite analysis. The use of grinding stones probably introduced an inordinate amount of abrasive into the diet.

Heavy tooth wear may have also resulted from eating processed foods, such as pemmican, the manufacture of which required stones to grind and pound dried meat. This is suggested by the Buhl burial, whose isotopic analysis indicated a largely meat diet while at the same time the teeth exhibited heavy wear. Isotope analysis also indicates that individuals living inland along the Northwest Coast probably relied heavily on anadromous fish, probably salmon, as an important food resource. Clothing from Spirit Cave and needles and artifacts preserved at other sites indicate they wore tailored skin clothing, moccasins, fiber sandals, and fur robes. Woven mats, bags, and baskets were also used.

These very limited and sketchy data suggest that these rugged men and women led harsh lives, periodically suffering from hunger, infections, broken bones, and violence. This limited sample indicates much shorter average life-spans for early Americans than Americans experience today. Most did not live beyond their 30s or 40s. However, just as there were times of hardship and hunger, there must have been times of comfort and abundance. Burials suggest an intellectual and metaphysical life encompassing the natural environment, the spiritual world, and belief in an afterlife.

6 Interpreting Cultural Development

THE preceding chapters have provided the historical and theoretical background important to understanding the timing, mechanisms, and evidence surrounding the first peopling of the Americas. There are many sites that some archeologists believe are older than 11,500 B.P. By about 11,500 B.P. regional cultural development had begun to take place in North America.

Archeologists employ a variety tools and concepts to interpret cultural development from the archeological record. The single most important concept is chronology. Archeologists must know the age of artifacts and archeological sites to order them in time. Various dating methods are employed based on the types of materials preserved in an archeological site and the nature of the problems being addressed.

Cultural change or innovation does not occur at the same time in all places. The change from one type of projectile point to another might occur in one area before it is adopted in another. For example, projectile points with stemmed bases appear to have been manufactured in the region of the Great Basin (in Nevada and Oregon) hundreds of years before similar forms were made on the Great Plains farther east. Although this same method of projectile point manufacture could have been developed independently, archeologists generally assume that the technology spread from one region to another if they are not separated too far geographically and in time. Understanding when and where these changes took place enables archeologists to establish time slopes for the directions and velocity of transmission of material cultural traits.

After chronological parameters have been established, a number of conceptual devices are employed to organize archeological data to compare similarities and differences within spatial contexts. The spatial units can be broad geographic areas or specific archeological sites or even features within sites. In the following chapters, the analysis of archeological similarities and differences encompasses more than 3,000 years and vast geographic regions. Because the level of analysis needs to be tailored to the scale of the research, this work uses the archeological concepts of tradition and complex to organize, compare, and interpret the archeological record of western North America prior to circa 8,000 B.P.

Tradition and Complex

The term tradition is used by most archeologists to describe groups of artifacts that are similar over a large geographic area and persist for substantial periods of time. The concept of an archeological tradition implies that a common way of life and economic pattern was passed from generation to generation over long periods of time (Willey and Phillips 1958). The beginning and end of a tradition are marked not only by a major change in the types of artifacts manufactured and used by prehistoric people but also by a change in their economy (Dumond 1982:39). When people dramatically change the way they make and use tools and the economic system upon which their lives are based, one tradition comes to an end and another begins.

The concept of an archeological complex is similar to that of tradition, but lasts for a shorter period of time and is more restricted geographically. It corresponds closely to the concept of phase advanced by Willey and Phillips (1958). Like the term tradition, it connotes technological cohesiveness but is more restricted chronologically and regionally.

Unfortunately, the terms tradition and complex are somewhat vague and consequently have been employed in different ways by different archeologists at different times. For example, how long is "a very long period of time"? To one archeologist this might be 1,000 years or more, while to another it might be 500 years or less. The term complex is equally confusing, because it relies on the same principles of definition and is based on the fact that it is a subdivision of a tradition. The only rule for its use is that it encompasses less geography and lasts for a shorter period of time than a tradition.

For example, some archeologists define the Paleoindian tradition as encompassing the Clovis, Folsom, and Plano complexes. The term tradition might be applicable because it extends throughout much of North America, shares an economy believed to be based primarily on large mammal hunting, and persists for a period of about 3,000 years. Other archeologists believe that this might be too broad a use of the concept and consider the Plano a separate tradition from Clovis and Folsom. As a result, readers will unexpectedly find a tradition nested within a tradition. Some researchers might consider Plano a complex only to realize that colleagues have defined subdivisions of Plano as complexes. This type of terminological ambiguity can take many forms and has resulted in considerable confusion.

To complicate matters even more, numerous undefined, or poorly defined, terms have been introduced into the archeological literature. Terms such as culture and stage have been used instead of, or interchangeably with, tradition and complex. Archeologists as a professional group have not attempted to impose uniformity on the application of this terminology to specific sites or assemblages of artifacts. Consequently, sites and groups of sites tend to retain the name used by the archeologist who first reported them, even though later analysis may place them within a different time period or economic system. In the following syntheses, the classificatory terms published in the literature have been retained as much as possible because attempting to reinterpret the nomenclature might unnecessarily distort further the meaning of the original research. Where possible, these have been organized under the broad categories of tradition and complex.

In the preceding chapters, it was possible to evaluate the archeological evidence site by site. However, this is not practical when synthesizing archeological data from hundreds of sites dating to different time periods and distributed over vast geographic regions. Consequently, the following chapters employ the concepts of chronology, typology, and regional adaptations to organize the archeological data. These data are in turn presented within the contexts of archeological traditions and complexes as they have been defined by regional researchers. Table 6.1 provides a general overview of the sequence of traditions and complexes for each geographic area presented in the following three chapters.

Weapon Systems

The primary weapons used for hunting in North America in early times were the lance and/or thrusting spear (which could also be thrown), the atlatl and dart, the bow and arrow, the bola, throwing sticks, and a variety of clubs. A wide array of traps, snares, and nets were also employed. Knowledge of how these tools were made and used is important to archeologists because the weapons and tools used to extract a living from the environment are often sensitive indicators of environmental and economic change.

During the Paleoindian period, the major weapon system used for hunting was based around the atlatl, or spear thrower (Figure 6.1). The spear thrower (atlatl) was sometimes equipped with an atlatl hook, which is a hook-like object attached to the back of the atlatl providing a seat for a dimple-like depression at the end of the dart. The term atlatl is the word used by the Aztec of central Mexico for spear thrower and is commonly used by North American archeologists. An early Spanish explorer Garcilaso de la Vega, described a dart propelled by an atlatl striking "with extreme force, so that it has been know to pass through a man armed with a coat of mail" (Garcilaso de la Vega cited in Swanton 1938: 358).

Although no spear throwers known to be more than 8,000 years old have been found in North America, it is probably safe to assume the discovery of atlatl hooks are reliable indicators of the use of this weapon. The preserved hooks have been found at several Paleoindian sites including Warm Mineral Spring, Florida (Cockrell and Murphy 1978) (see Chapter 5), Marmes Rockshelter (Rice 1972) (see

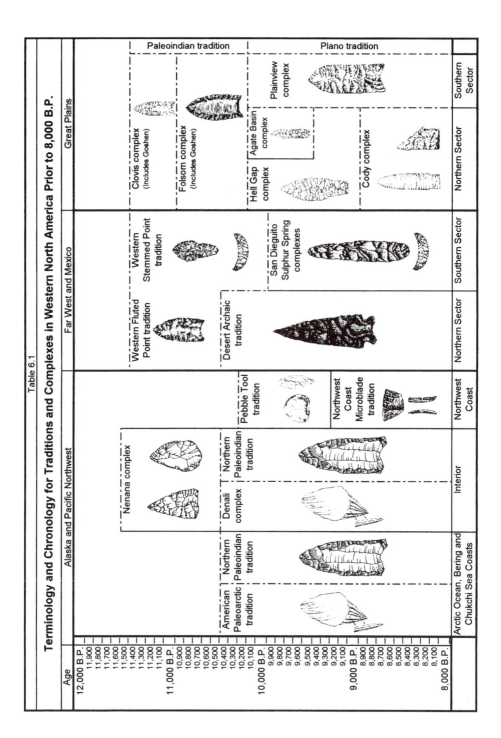

Table 6.1

Terminology and Chronology for Traditions and Complexes in Western North America Prior to 8,000 B.P.

Figure 6.1 Sketch illustrating the use of the atlatl, or spear thrower. (Graphic by Eric Parrish.)

Chapter 5), and Fort Rock Cave (Cressman 1977). Based on sophisticated analysis of the fracture patterns of Paleoindian projectile points made from glassy rock types, such as obsidian and extremely fine grained cherts, it has been demonstrated that they only could have been propelled with the use of a spear thrower (Hutchings 1997, 1998). Although the velocity of an arrow is similar to that of an atlatl dart, the mass of the dart is greater. This causes the projectile point to strike its target with much greater impact. Darts propelled by a spear thrower produce unique and distinctive fracture patterns that can only result from the force derived from the combined weight and speed of a dart thrown with an atlatl (Hutchings 1997, 1998). Consequently, the use of the spear thrower can be demonstrated in the absence of the artifact itself. In North America and some other areas of the world, the atlatl was never fully replaced by the bow and arrow. It was probably retained for selective use as the "heavy artillery" of its day that could reliably penetrate the thick hides of some large mammals and even human armor. It also has the advantage of being a weapon that can be used with one hand, thus freeing the opposing hand to use tools, weapons, or shield.

This weapon system required dart shafts most probably made of wood. Today most people envision darts as very small, but the darts used with the atlatl were intermediate in size between an arrow and a lance or javelin. Based on limited archeological information, it appears that darts were equipped with bone foreshafts upon which were seated harpoon-like dart heads (Figure 6.2). The dart heads, probably made of wood or bone, held a stone projectile point bound in a slot at the tip. A shaft wrench also made of bone or wood (Figure 6.3), is a tool used to straighten dart shafts, probably while being heat treated or steamed.

Although foreshafts are known from several sites, dart heads are extremely rare. Archeologists know that they had to exist because it is impossible to effec-

Figure 6.2 Foreshaft (Anzick Site), harpoon-like dart head (Ohio), and Clovis end blade (Anzick) used to arm atlatl darts by Paleoindian hunters. (Photograph courtesy of Dennis Stanford.)

Figure 6.3 Shaft wrench used to straighten shafts after heating or steaming by inserting them through the hole and bending until straight. (Redrawn by Eric Parrish from Forrester 1985.)

tively haft the stone projectile points on the foreshafts that have been recovered. This means that something was necessary to hold the stone projectile point and also fit onto the foreshafts. The dart heads may be rare in the archeological record because they were made of perishable materials, and when lost soon decomposed leaving only the stone projectile point. Shaft wrenches have been discovered at a number of sites, including Murray Springs in Arizona, Horn Rockshelter in Texas, and Warm Mineral Spring in Florida. Because most of this weapon system was manufactured from organic materials that decompose over time, archeologists seldom find anything but the stone projectile points used to arm the dart heads and occasionally the bone foreshafts and atlatl hooks, or pegs.

In addition to recognizing distinctive fracture patterns on some stone atlatl points, archeologists can also distinguish the difference between atlatl dart heads and arrowheads by the size and weight of the stone projectile points (Thomas 1978). By comparing measurements and weights of the stone projectile points used to tip both atlatl darts and arrows from several museum collections, Thomas (1978:471) demonstrated that in 86 percent of the cases he could correctly identify whether they had been used as dart or arrow points. Very simply stated, if the stone point is the diameter of an arrow at the point where it is attached, or hafted, to the shaft, it suggests the point was used as an arrowhead. If it is larger and heavier, it was probably used as to arm an atlatl dart.

Projectile Point Typology

Traditions and complexes are defined by changes in technology, which in turn frequently reflect changes in economy. Sometimes change is gradual and subtle, while at other times it is dramatic and swift. To detect and evaluate change or continuity in the archeological record, archeologists compare artifacts within sites and between groups of sites. In North America, stone projectile point styles, or types, have proven to be extremely useful in defining changes in material culture.

To be effective, a projectile point must have four characteristics: (1) a sharp point, (2) sharp cutting edges, (3) a hafting element that holds it to the shaft and absorbs the force of impact, and (4) a design that minimizes damage and allows the point to be reworked after it has been broken (Frison 1991:293; Musil 1988: 374). All projectile points share one attribute: a tip that comes to a point and enables it to function as a piercing implement. The primary difference between types of stone projectile points is how their bases are configured. Different types of bases reflect different hafting techniques, or ways the projectile point is attached to a shaft. Consequently, changes in projectile point types primarily reflect changes in the way they are hafted.

Robert Musil (1988) has proposed a model explaining the changes in Paleo-indian hafting techniques over time with each change leading to increased functional efficiency. This model proposes that the split-stem hafting technique is the oldest and characterizes Clovis, Folsom, and related lanceolate points. The lower sides of these points are characteristically ground along their edges to prevent them from cutting the lashing that binds them to the shaft (Figure 6.4). The split-stem hafting method requires inserting the projectile point into a slot carved in the shaft to receive the base. This hafting method was followed by stemmed projectile points that have shoulders and parallel-sided bases that are also set in a slot designed to receive the base. This is a variation of the split-stem hafting method but is more efficient than the split-stem method used for hafting Clovis and Fol-

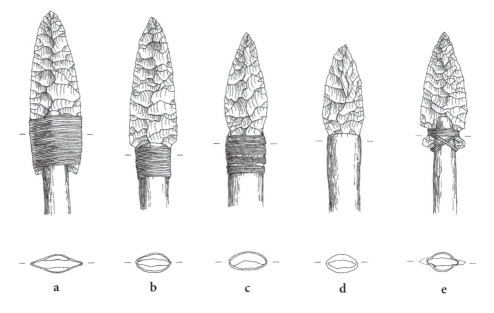

Figure 6.4 Illustration of hafting techniques: (a) split-stem, (b) parallel-sided stem inserted into slot, (c) contracting stem hafted in open, (d) closed sockets, and (e) notched (modified from Musil 1988:373 by Eric Parrish).

som points. It is more efficient because it moved the binding from the edge to the stem of the point. In addition, it enabled resharpening of points broken at the hafting location by reshaping the base and creating new shoulders farther toward the tip.

A tapering or contracting stem (Figure 6.4) indicates the third method of hafting. These points tend to be thicker and more rounded in cross section. These points were set into sockets, which are oval shaped holes or beds carved into the end of the shaft. This technique not only eliminated binding from the edge of the projectile point but also placed more surface area of the shaft in contact with the stone point providing a greater surface area to absorb thrust impact. The technique of hafting parallel-sided stemmed points appears to be derived from the split-stem hafting technique. However, the method of using sockets to haft contracting-based points is different and may be an original North American design (Musil 1988).

Notching made all previous hafting designs obsolete. It removed the lashing from the edges by insetting them in a notch chipped into either the side, corner, or base of the projectile point. It greatly increased the ease with which broken projectile points could be repaired and recycled. Notched projectile points fracture most frequently at the location of the notches as a result of forces placed on the point by thrust and impact. Because the notches may be located near the point base, the point can be recycled a number of times by simply chipping new notches closer to the tip and discarding the old broken base. According to Musil (1988), this was the most efficient hafting tradition. This explains why it was the most important hafting technique in North America beginning about 8,000 years ago and persisting in some areas until historic times.

Archeologists have attributed changes in stone projectile point types to a wide array of causes, including the migration of people, environmental changes, and changes in the species hunted. However, Musil (1988) advocates that these changes are not the result of different adaptations to specific environments or economies. Instead, they merely represent technological change of one element of material culture adopted by people of different regions because each successive design was a more effective and efficient killing implement.

Changes in hafting techniques do not necessarily mean that earlier forms were no longer used. For example, certain types of artifacts, such as lances, might be hafted using the socket method, while other types of artifacts, knives for example, might be hafted using the older split-stem technique. It is also conceivable that different techniques might be employed to haft similar types of artifacts during any given period of time. For example, when a group is making the transition from one hafting method to another, some projectile points used to tip atlatl darts might be set in sockets while others may be hafted using the split-stem method.

These changes in hafting techniques represent minor variations of a weapon system reliant primarily on bifacially flaked-stone projectile points. This projectile point technology is dramatically and conceptually different than the composite, microblade inset technology. If Deetz's (1967:48–49) two contrasting methods for manufacturing artifacts—additive and subtractive—are applied to the manufacture of projectile points, bifacially flaked projectile points typify the subtractive approach. This approach is subtractive because it requires the reduction of a lithic core by flaking away excess rock to create a flaked-stone projectile point or biface. This is the technique employed to manufacture projectile points used to arm atlatl darts.

The additive approach is characterized by composite projectile points using microblades that are thin parallel-sided stone flakes struck from specially prepared stone cores. Microblades are inset to form razor-sharp cutting edges along the margins of projectile points manufactured from organic materials (Figure 6.5). This technique is generally typified by lithic microblades inset into longitudinal groves incised in bone, antler, or ivory projectile points. By adding these elements together, technologically sophisticated composite projectile points were manufactured. The limited data available suggests that the bone points were attached to their shafts by beveling the proximal end of the projectile point and the distal end of the shaft and lashing them together (Figure 6.6). Stone burins are commonly believed to be the primary tools used to shape and grove the organic points. An interrelated set of lithic artifacts, the burin and microblade, and their associated debitage (microblade cores, core tablets, and burin spalls) provide evidence of the additive approach to projectile point manufacture in North America (Figure 6.6).

These two contrasting and fundamentally different conceptual approaches to tool manufacture suggest that other profound differences in technological and social concepts existed between people. These are fundamentally different approaches to creating very different weapon systems and each required a different sequence of complex manufacturing techniques. It is reasonable to assume that these complex concepts and technical skills are indicators of learned behavior that was passed from one generation to the next and that this knowledge was shared by a large group over a large geographic area. For example, those who used microblades to manufacture projectile points appear to be geographically restricted to Alaska and various regions of northwestern Canada.

As of 1998, there were only two cases where organic bone projectile points have been discovered in association with microblades. These are distinctive antler arrow heads slotted to receive microblade insets found in Alaska at Trail Creek Caves and Lime Hills (Ackerman 1996a; Larsen 1968a). This suggests that

Figure 6.5 Stages of manufacture to produce an antler projectile point (from Dixon 1993:56).

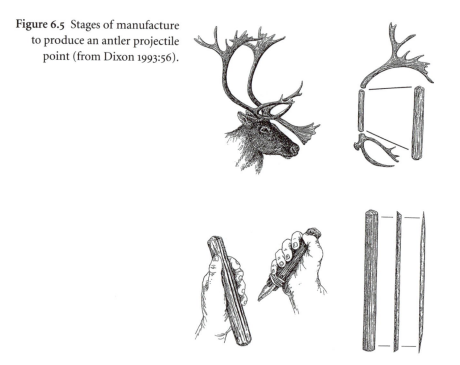

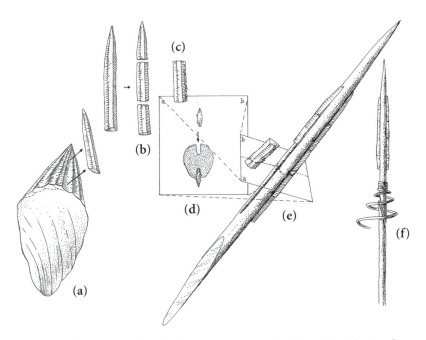

Figure 6.6 The process of producing a composite projectile point with microblade insets: (a) microblade removal from a microblade core (view from core platform); (b) microblade, proximal, medial, and distal segments; (c) medial fragment retouched or "backed" for inset; (d) cross section illustrating microblades inset into organic point; (e) the alignment of microblades in a slotted organic projectile point; (f) the beveled base hafting method. (Graphic by Eric Parrish.)

the bow and arrow may have been first introduced into North America from Asia along with microblade technology, possibly as early as 10,500 B.P.

Fluted, lanceolate, and stemmed projectile forms are assumed to have been used as tips for atlatl darts because of their size and weight. Most early fluted, lanceolate, and stemmed points are too wide at the hafted end to have been attached to arrows. The concept and use of the bow and arrow may have diffused southward from eastern Beringia to people to the south still using the atlatl during Archaic times (beginning circa 8,000–7,000 B.P.) when notched projectile points became prevalent throughout much of North America. While notched stone projectile points were used to tip atlatl darts, they were later adapted to arm arrows. The traditional methods for hafting notched stone projectile points to shafts (methods that had been used in hafting atlatl dart points for thousands of years) were adopted for arrow manufacture. The complex procedure required to make composite arrowheads by affixing microblades to separately fashioned antler projectile points characteristic of the American Paleoarctic tradition was not adopted in the south. Instead, smaller, lighter weight bifacially flaked stone projectile points were used to tip arrows.

Regional Adaptations

When analyzing human colonization at the continental level, macroenvironmental zones, or megapatches, and biomes are useful. When looking at regional adaptations, the analysis of more specific environments is required. For example, early northern adaptations to interior (noncoastal) environments were probably controlled to a large extent by duration of extreme winter temperature lows rather than mean annual temperature. In arid environments farther south, duration of extreme annual drought greatly influenced human adaptation. These extremes established fundamental constraints that to a large degree shaped unique regional adaptations and settlement patterns during the late Pleistocene and early Holocene.

For example, archeological sites in eastern Beringia are most frequently situated in microclimatic settings that minimize the extreme effects of winter climate. These settings are generally south facing slopes that optimize solar radiation effectively raising temperatures and lowering albedo (the energy reflected by snow) (Barry 1982:202). These types of warm spots are ideal settlement locales when they occur near essential subsistence resources, such as lake and river margins and constricting topographic features that tend to restrict and concentrate the movement of large mammals.

In more southerly areas of western North America, where conditions tend to be hot and dry during summer, another strategy was used. Early archeological sites tend to be located near fresh water, such as springs and Pleistocene lakes. These settings present more favorable microenvironments within larger environmental regions, or biomes. This is because they offer reliable sources of water essential for human survival and a predictable attraction for other mammals. In arid environments, the relative abundance of surface water creates unique microenvironments favoring the growth of trees, a variety of edible plants, various aquatic mammals, waterfowl, and fish. These types of diverse resources are important for foraging economies and opportunistic large mammal hunters.

High-altitude habitats tend to ameliorate the effects of aridity that placed constraints on populations living on the Great Plains and in the Far West. Water resources, stored in glaciers and snow fields, are more abundant and are commonly released over long periods of time. The high-altitude ecological settings of the western Cordillera exhibit numerous ecological characteristics reminiscent of late Pleistocene/early Holocene environments. For example, high-altitude meadows and parklands support mixed populations of bison, elk, and sheep associated with microenvironments supporting small mammals, fish, and avifauna. These regions may have served as locales where late Paleoindian technology persisted longer than elsewhere and where ecological settings may have facilitated the transition to subsequent Archaic technology and subsistence strategies (Chapter 8).

Very low winter temperatures, which result in frozen ground and extended snow cover throughout the winter, profoundly favor some types of technology over others. For example, in eastern Beringia, it is virtually impossible to obtain lithic raw material to manufacture stone tools for seven or eight months of the year because the ground is frozen and the landscape is buried beneath the snow. However, the technique of manufacturing a series of thin, parallel-sided microblades from a single piece of stone is an efficient way to produce high-quality cutting edges using a minimum amount of stone. For example, .5 kg (1 lb) of stone will produce as much as 1,300 cm (42 ft 8 inches) of cutting edges when used to manufacture microblades. However, excluding the waste material, it would produce approximately 20 cm (8 inches) of cutting edge if used to manufacture a bifacial stone tool (Hester and Grady 1982:169).

By manufacturing small, preshaped stone cores from which many microblades could be produced, a hunter could carry a compact and relatively lightweight supply of microblade cores throughout the winter. This efficient technology was ideally adapted to cold northern climates. It enabled new projectile points to be manufactured and damaged ones to be rearmed throughout the long winter when lithic resources were scarce and difficult to obtain. While this technology probably had an adaptive advantage over more consumptive bifacial industries, it probably required greater time and resources to manufacture the comparatively complex composite antler and stone projectile points. Although the bow and arrow appear to have been introduced to North America with the American Paleoarctic tradition, possibly as early as circa 10,500 B.P. (Chapter 7), it was apparently not adopted as early by the more southerly nonmicroblade using cultures in which the atlatl remained the weapon of choice into Archaic times.

Although large blades were manufactured by Paleoindian groups, true microblade technology was not adopted in most regions of North America south of Canada. This may be because rugged terrain, comparatively sparse vegetation, and comparatively warm winter temperatures assured access to numerous lithic outcrops and exposed stream beds from which lithic raw material could be obtained throughout the year. These environmental characteristics enabled technological reliance on more extravagant bifacial lithic industries, and less time probably was required to manufacture and maintain hunting implements.

Archeological surveys provide data that are useful for establishing the range and distribution of artifact types and cultural traits. These data are important in establishing the geographic distribution of traditions and complexes. They also provide broadly based information about economic and subsistence patterns. However, these data are limited, and it is necessary to rely on detailed systematic excavations of specific archeological sites and groups of sites to provide in-depth insights into culture chronology, past lifeways, social patterns, and other cultural traits. Extrapolation from well-excavated and analyzed archeological sites to broader geographic areas more fully defined by survey data, enables archeologists to synthesize archeological information over broad geographic areas during specific periods of time.

When examining specific archeological sites, archeologists can infer specific types of economic activities based on the ecological setting and physical character of the site. For example, a site situated along a salmon spawning stream at a particular point where fish may be easily trapped or speared, suggests that the site was probably a locale where people harvested anadromous fish. An archeological site located in a small cave used by bears for hibernation might suggest that it was a locale where humans hunted bears during the winter, when it was safest for them to do so. Archeological remains located in and adjacent to arroyos suitable for trapping and ambushing herds of bison probably indicate bison hunting. The remains of plants and animals preserved in archeological sites provide direct evidence of human diets, the character of the surrounding environment at the time the site was occupied, and insight into specific economic activities. The environmental settings of archeological sites and the faunal and floral remains found within them enable archeologists to identify economic patterns that help define archeological traditions.

Information from other scientific disciplines is also important in interpreting the environmental context and economic activities preserved in the archeological record. For example, geology can provide insights into trade by identifying sources of valuable materials such as obsidian, clay, and ochre. The disciplines of biology and ecology help archeologists by identifying sources and seasonal availability of biological products such as feathers, eggs, furs, fish, and various plants. Palynology, the analysis of fossil pollen, and climatology help define the environment in which early people lived and identify periods of climatic change and stress.

Archeologists also rely heavily on cultural anthropology to interpret archeological evidence. Through the use of analogy and by comparing artifacts and other evidence preserved in the earth with the behavior of living and historically recorded people, archeologists can make valid inferences about human behavior. Topics such as family and social organization, economic systems, and even the behavior of specific individuals sometimes can be best explained by drawing on the wealth of anthropological information.

Chapters 7, 8, and 9 provide summaries of the regional archeology of western North America from about 11,500 B.P. until about 8,000 B.P. Alaska and the Pacific Northwest are presented in Chapter 7. This vast area includes Alaska and

British Columbia from the Arctic Ocean to the Strait of Juan de Fuca and the watershed of the McKenzie River northward. Chapter 8 covers the Far West from the Pacific Ocean to the continental divide. Chapter 9 discusses the Great Plains, encompassing the region from the vicinity of the Peace River drainage in Alberta, Canada to the United States/Mexico border and from the Continental Divide of the Rocky Mountains to the Mississippi River. These three areas are illustrated in Figure 6.7.

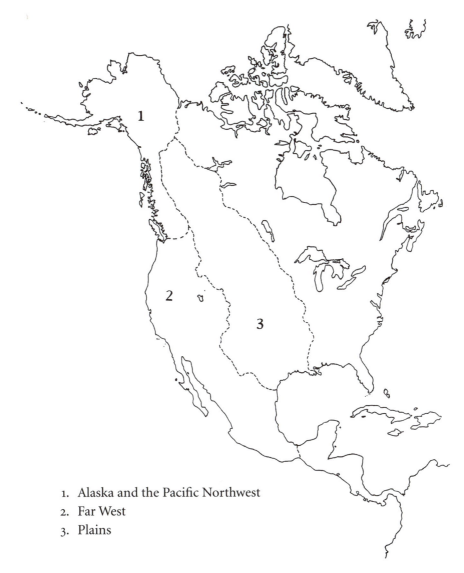

1. Alaska and the Pacific Northwest
2. Far West
3. Plains

Figure 6.7 Map illustrating the three regional divisions employed to present the early archeology of western North America. (Graphic by Eric Parrish.)

These geographic divisions of western North America are somewhat arbitrary. Boundaries between them are difficult to delineate based on environmental characteristics or shared archeological histories. Specific archeological traditions overlap different regions during various periods of time. Although each region may share a somewhat common culture history, each contains diverse environments and locally unique cultural traits.

In each region of North America, archeologists have worked on the various types of sites that have come to their attention. Many of them were chance discoveries resulting from erosion, construction, and other factors. For example, in the Great Plains, archeologists have found and excavated several spectacular mass bison kills and sites where mammoths have been hunted. In the Far West, researchers have relied most heavily on archeological evidence from caves, rockshelters, and ancient lake shorelines. In Alaska and the Pacific Northwest, most data are derived from sites located on high ground adjacent to streams in interior regions and shorelines along the coast.

Recognizing the limitations of attempting to synthesize archeological data from such broad geographic areas, environmental zones, and diverse types of archeological sites; it is still possible to identify regional cultural adaptations at the end of the last Ice Age. These distinctive regional adaptations took place in the midst of rapidly changing environments and set the stage for subsequent cultural development in western North America.

7 Alaska and the Pacific Northwest
Prior to 8,000 B.P.

THIS huge geographic region extends from the Arctic Ocean in the north to the Strait of Juan de Fuca in the south. It includes the shores of the Bering and Chukchi Seas, the Gulf of Alaska, and adjacent inland regions ranging from high latitude tundra in the north to temperate rain forest in the south. Interior regions encompass the vast boreal forest stretching from western Alaska to British Columbia, Canada. Several extensive mountain ranges, including the Brooks and Alaska Range, support high altitude alpine tundra. These diverse environments have provided a wide variety of subsistence resources and environmental conditions that have greatly influenced the development of northern cultures. It is the only area of North America adjacent to Asia and that was connected to it in the past by a land bridge. It is through Alaska that cultural traits have passed between Asia and North America.

Three distinct archeological traditions and two complexes have been identified in the vast region of Alaska and the Pacific Northwest during the period prior to 8,000 B.P. (Table 6.1). The oldest of these is the Nenana complex, which has been discovered at several sites in interior Alaska. Primarily because the geographic distribution of Nenana complex artifacts is limited to interior Alaska, it has retained its designation as a complex. Although it is still poorly defined both geographically and temporally, it appears to span the interval between at least 11,600 B.P. to possibly as late as 10,000 B.P. Archeologists have not ascertained the origins of the Nenana complex.

The second major cultural development is called the American Paleoarctic tradition. Archeologists agree that it is derived from Asia and has its technological roots in the late Upper Paleolithic microblade industries. The hallmark of this cultural tradition is microblade technology that appears to persist continuously from circa 10,500 B.P. until sometime well after 8,000 B.P. In this presentation, the American Paleoarctic tradition has been subdivided into three regional variants: (1) the first retains the original name, the American Paleoarctic tradition; (2) the second is the Denali complex; and (3) the third is the Northwest Coast Microblade tradition.

The third cultural tradition is the Northern Paleoindian tradition, which spans the interval between circa 10,500–8,500 B.P. It is believed to be a northern manifestation of the Paleoindian tradition of western North America believed to date between 10,500–8,500 B.P. Because this area is so vast, the American Paleo-arctic tradition and Denali complex are regarded as co-traditions with the Northern Paleoindian tradition. Co-traditions existed when people living in the same regions during the same period of time practiced different ways of life and made different types of tools.

Nenana Complex (circa >11,600–10,000 B.P.)

In the Nenana River Valley, several sites contain cultural remains ascribed to the Nenana complex, which dates between circa 11,300–10,500 B.P. The Nenana complex is defined on the basis of stone artifacts that occur together and date to the same time period throughout Alaska's Nenana River Valley (Powers and Hoffecker 1990). Field research in the upper Tanana River Valley in the early 1990s revealed similar artifact assemblages. As a result, the geographic area and defi-nition of the Nenana complex has been expanded to include the discoveries in

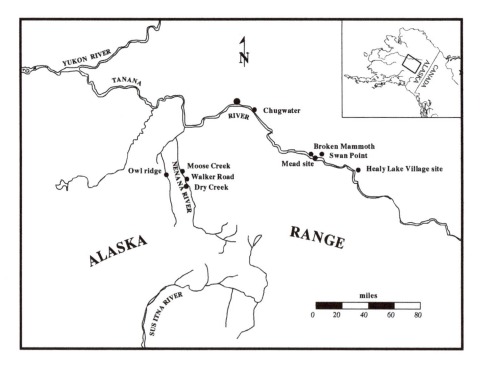

Figure 7.1 Map of interior Alaska depicting the location of important Nenana complex sites. (Graphic by Eric Parrish.)

the upper Tanana Valley (Figure 7.1), rather than to introduce a new term into an already growing and confusing array of traditions and complexes.

The types of artifacts that define the Nenana complex are: (1) triangular and teardrop-shaped projectile points and knives, (2) straight or concave-based lanceolate projectile points, (3) perforators, (4) endscrapers and sidescrapers, (5) burins, (6) hammer and anvil stones, and (7) unifacial knives and scrapers. Flakes, small stone wedges (*piece esquillée*), and lithic debitage are also associated with these sites. These diagnostic types of stone artifacts (Figure 7.2) have been found at Component I at the Dry Creek site, the Walker Road site, and the Moose Creek site. Another site in the nearby Teklanika River Valley has been dated to 11,340 ± 150 B.P. (Beta 11209), contains the same types of artifacts, and is also representative of the Nenana complex (Phippen 1988).

Radiocarbon dates from Component I at the Walker Road site and Component I at the Dry Creek site range between circa 11,800–11,000 B.P., averaging circa 11,300 B.P. (Powers and Hoffecker 1990:278). The age of the Nenana complex in the Nenana Valley was established by radiocarbon dating and by correlating the stratigraphic position of cultural deposits with the regional valley stratigraphy (Thorson and Hamilton 1977). Nenana complex sites are repeatedly found near the bottom of thick sections of windblown sediments that began to accumulate during the early Birch Interval (circa 14,000 B.P.). Faunal remains have been preserved only at the Dry Creek site, where the remains of sheep and elk were recovered. Numerous gastroliths (tiny stones from the gizzards of birds) suggest that birds, probably grouse and ptarmigan, were also important in the diet.

The earliest firmly dated archeological remains ascribed to the Nenana complex come from a series of sites located in Alaska's Tanana River Valley. These sites have been named Broken Mammoth, Mead, and Swan Point sites (Figure 7.1). Extensive excavations have not been conducted at the Mead site. The oldest paleosol identified at the site is dated to circa 11,600 B.P. A cylindrical ivory object, a scraper, as well as a few biface fragments and waste flakes and possibly a small projectile point fragment have been recovered from the site.

The nearby Broken Mammoth site (Figure 7.3) has been the subject of more thorough fieldwork and has produced considerably more information. This important site was excavated from 1990–1993 under the direction of Charles E. Holmes and David Yesner with geoarcheological support provided by Thomas Dilley and Kris Crossen. The Broken Mammoth site is important because it is well stratified, contains four major periods of cultural occupation, and exhibits concordant ^{14}C determinations. It is possibly the oldest reliably dated site in Alaska. Faunal remains are well preserved from cultural Zones II, III, and IV. Only cultural Zones III and IV (the oldest two) are relevant to this analysis.

The term cultural zone has been used to define what appear to be a series of

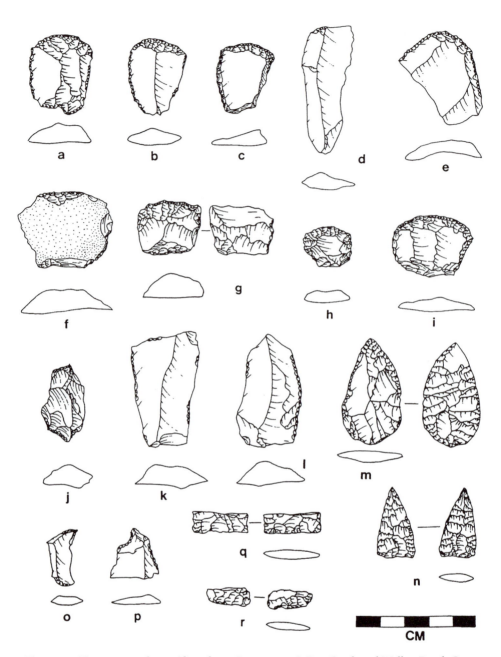

Figure 7.2 Nenana complex artifacts from Component I, Dry Creek and Walker Road, Component I: (a)–(i) end scrapers; (j) stone wedge, *piece esquillée*, Dry Creek; (k) and (l) blades, Dry Creek; (m) teardrop-shaped biface, Walker Road; (n) triangular projectile point, Dry Creek; (o) and (p) perforators; (q) and(r) basal fragments of triangular projectile points (Dixon 1993:81, courtesy of Roger Powers and Ted Goebel).

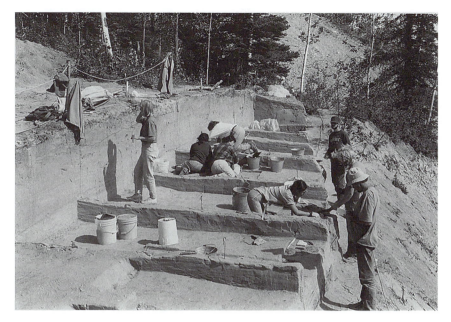

Figure 7.3 Excavations at the Broken Mammoth site, 1993.

brief occupations of the Broken Mammoth site over several hundred years. A series of nine ^{14}C determinations indicates Cultural Zone IV was occupied between circa 11,700–11,000 B.P. Cultural remains from Zone IV include waste flakes, a quartz chopper/scraper/plane, retouched flakes, biface thinning flakes, scrap fossil ivory, and a cache of tools made of fossil ivory consisting of two cigar-shaped objects, possibly points, and a possible handle. Faunal remains include bison (*Bison pricus*—a larger Eurasian form of bison), elk, swan, crane, goose, duck, ptarmigan, salmonid fish scales (possibly grayling), and bird eggshells. Small mammals include hare, marmot, otter, arctic fox, and ground squirrel. A juvenile bison mandible suggests a late summer to fall occupation and bird eggshells indicate the site was also occupied in the spring. Salmonid fish scales from these levels suggest that people fished. There is no evidence of a microblade industry from either Cultural Zone III or IV.

At Swan Point, the oldest cultural levels (circa 11,660 B.P.) contain worked mammoth tusk fragments (possibly scavenged, the fossil ivory dated to 12,060 ± 70 B.P. (NSRL-2001, CAMS-17045), microblades, microblade core preparation flakes, blades, split quartz pebble chopper/planes, dihedral burins, and red ochre. Faunal remains include goose and cervid (deer family). The next oldest occupation, dated by one ^{14}C determination to 10,230 ± 80 B.P., (Beta 56666, CAMS-4251) (Holmes et al. 1996), lacks microblades and contains small lanceolate points with convex/straight bases, thin triangular points, gravers made on broken points, and quartz pebble choppers or hammers. The remains of moose also occur in this level. Although the circa 11,660 B.P. component appears anomalous based on the presence of a microblade technology, the later occupation dating to circa 10,230 B.P. is consistent in its artifact assemblage with other Nenana complex sites.

All these sites are reliably dated based on radiocarbon dated charcoal recovered from cultural hearths surrounded by artifacts and other evidence of human occupation. The ^{14}C determinations are also in accord with stratigraphic analysis and the regional geology. However, at each site, there is mammoth ivory that predates the cultural occupation based on charcoal ^{14}C dates believed to result from the human activities. This has been interpreted by the investigators to suggest that humans were scavenging mammoth ivory from the remains of animals that died hundreds and possibly thousands of years earlier.

Swan Point is an anomaly because it appears to have a microblade industry more than a thousand years earlier than anywhere else in interior Alaska, even earlier than similar assemblages from western Beringia. The age of the Denali complex at Swan Point is derived from two ^{14}C samples. One was from mammoth ivory dating to 12,060 ± 70 B.P. (CAMS-17045) that was probably older scavenged ivory (Holmes et al. 1996:323). The other sample was willow and poplar charcoal derived from a cultural hearth apparently directly associated with the microblades. Two dates from the charcoal were circa 11,660 ± 70 B.P. (Beta 56667, CAMS-4252) and 11,660 ± 60 B.P. (Beta 71372, CAMS-12389) (Holmes et al. 1996:321). However, Hamilton and Goebel (1999) suggest that the microblades, and presumably other artifacts, may have been mixed with older charcoal immediately after the deposition of a pebbly colluvial layer and immediately before the loess above it began to accumulate. Additional research at Swan Point is essential to resolve concerns about the age of the early microblade component and its relationship to the Nenana complex.

The Healy Lake Village site located in the upper Tanana Valley was excavated in the late 1960s and early 1970s by John Cook. In the lower levels, Cook discovered distinctive teardrop-shaped bifaces that he called Chindadn points (pronounced Chin-da-din, an Athapaskan word meaning ancestor) (Cook 1969, 1996). Although most archeologists agree that artifacts from the lower levels of this shallow site were stratigraphically mixed, the regional nomenclature has retained the name for the artifact type. Chindadn points are generally small and occasionally heavily ground on one lateral edge, suggesting they were dulled for hafting and possibly were used as knives (Figure 7.4). This very distinctive artifact type occurs in Nenana complex type sites, as well as other sites throughout the Tanana Valley.

The relationship between the Nenana complex and somewhat earlier Tanana Valley sites has not been satisfactorily defined. Preliminary data suggest that both groups of sites share a number of common traits. They are perhaps

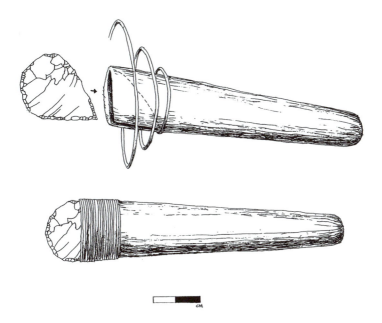

Figure 7.4 Line drawing illustrating the probable method of hafting Chindadn knives. (Graphic by Eric Parrish.)

slightly different regional and temporal representatives of a larger tradition or complex. For example, all appear to be relatively small camps that lack permanent structures. With the notable exception of the Swan Point site, all lack evidence of microblade technology. All share the occurrence of small triangular bifacially flaked projectile points, some of which have concave bases and are basally thinned. Many of the sites also contain distinctive pointed ovate Chindadn bifaces.

Although the geographic distribution of sites ascribed to the Nenana complex can be expected to increase with additional field research, they are currently restricted to interior Alaska's Tanana and Nenana River Valleys. These early inhabitants of eastern Beringia may have been confined to interior Alaska prior to the melting of Brooks Range glaciers (Hamilton and Goebel 1999). The Nenana complex appears to be restricted in time from circa 11,600–10,000 B.P. If the preliminary dating of the microblade component at Swan Point is correct, a co-tradition with the Nenana complex may be represented or an earlier cycle of occupation of interior Alaska by microblade using people prior to circa 11,600 B.P. could possibly be suggested.

Except for the few gastroliths, the original evidence from Dry Creek suggests that Nenana complex people were big game hunters primarily hunting elk and sheep. However, additional data from the Broken Mammoth site demonstrates a more generalized opportunistic gathering economy that included harvesting waterfowl, gathering eggs, and hunting and/or trapping small mammals. Large mammal hunting, particularly bison, elk, and sheep, was important. Proboscidean remains (mammoth or mastodon ivory) possibly result from collecting fossil ivory rather than mammoth or mastodon hunting.

Other than controversial evidence suggesting that possible mammoth blood residue has been preserved on some northern Paleoindian projectile points (Loy and Dixon 1998), there is little evidence for mammoth predation in eastern Beringia. Two radiocarbon dates on mammoth bone from two different locales in Alaska have been reported by Harington (1978) of 10,150 ± 100 B.P. (I-9998) and Vinson (1988) of 11,360 ± 100 B.P. (Beta 13811). Although at first glance these determinations suggest that mammoth and humans were contemporaneous in eastern Beringia, neither of these samples was subject to rigorous chemical pretreatments that are now known to be necessary in order to accurately date bone and ivory. In all likelihood, these dates are much more recent than they should be and cannot be used reliably to demonstrate that humans and mammoth were contemporaneous in eastern Beringia.

Trace element analysis indicates that obsidian from the Wrangell Mountains occurs in the lowest levels at Broken Mammoth and Walker Road sites. Obsidian from the Batza Tena source on the south side of the Brooks Range also occurs in Tanana Valley Nenana complex sites. These discoveries demonstrate that a widespread trade network was already in place in interior Alaska possibly as early as circa 11,700 B.P. (Hamilton and Goebel 1999).

All sites ascribed to the Nenana complex were small camps generally located on bluffs with panoramic views. They appear to have been occupied by only a few individuals for relatively short periods of time. No human remains or evidence of permanent structures has yet been found in association with Nenana complex sites. In most cases, fires appear to have been built directly on the surface of the ground with little or no preparation of the area. Charcoal is generally scattered and relatively scarce for dating purposes. Minute unidentifiable calcined bone fragments have been recovered frequently from these hearths, suggesting bone was burned as fuel, for spiritual purposes, or to keep camps clean. Red ochre, an iron oxide that can be made into powder by grinding to form the basis for a pigment or paint, has been reported associated with several Nenana complex occupations (Goebel and Powers 1989; Holmes et al. 1996; Phippen 1988:118; Powers and Hoffecker 1998:281).

Because little evidence has been found to indicate structures, most sites were probably open-air camps using skin tents or temporary tent-like structures. Evidence for possible tent-like structures has been reported only for the Walker Road site. The spatial distribution of more than 130 artifacts around a circular clay-lined hearth dug into the underlying gravels at the base of the loess were interpreted to be the location of a circular tent approximately 5 m (16 ft) in diameter (Goebel and Powers 1989; Powers et al. 1990). Based on these fragmentary data, it is apparent that the full range of the Nenana complex settlement pattern and subsistence cycle is still poorly understood.

American Paleoarctic Tradition (circa 10,500–8,000 B.P.)

Douglass Anderson (1970:69, 1988) first defined the American Paleoarctic tradition to include the Akmak and Band 8 assemblages from the Onion Portage site, the early microblades from the Trail Creek Caves, and various undated assemblages from the Brooks Range characterized by wedge-shaped microblade cores and microblades. Since that time, the American Paleoarctic tradition has been used to lump a wide variety of early microblade and microcore assemblages that are widely dispersed throughout eastern Beringia. These sites and site components extend westward into Eurasia, eastward into Canada's Yukon Territory, and south along the Northwest Coast of North America as far as the state of Washington (Figure 7.5).

As a result of this broad application, the term American Paleoarctic tradition has lost much of its descriptive utility. It no longer defines specific geographic and economic characteristics. Further confusion has been introduced by West's (1981, 1996a) term Beringian tradition. Geographically, the Beringian tradition encompasses microblade sites in the vast areas of northern Eurasia and northwestern North America dating between 35,000–7,500 B.P. It lumps together such a wide variety of sites from diverse environments that the term has little archeological utility except possibly at a very broad global level of description.

Since Anderson's original definition, archeologists have classified many regional variants and different economic systems under the American Paleoarctic tradition. As a result, its current use is confusing, and it no longer defines a tradition in classic definition of the term. For the purposes of this analysis, it has been divided into three basic units: (1) the American Paleoarctic tradition, (2) the Denali complex, and (3) the Northwest Coast Microblade tradition.

The first retains Anderson's original name, the American Paleoarctic tradition. The diagnostic lithic artifacts associated with this tradition include wedge-shaped microblade cores, microblades, blades and blade cores, core bifaces, antler arrow points slotted to receive microblades, grooved stone abraders, and waste flakes. The geographic distribution includes the coastal margins of Bering and Chukchi Seas and the Arctic Ocean and adjacent terrestrial environments. It extends south to roughly the limit of winter sea ice. Economically, it probably had two aspects: (1) marine mammal hunting, possibly including winter sea ice hunting and (2) exploitation of adjacent noncoastal regions to fish and hunt for terrestrial mammals. When moving inland from the coast, it is difficult to iden-

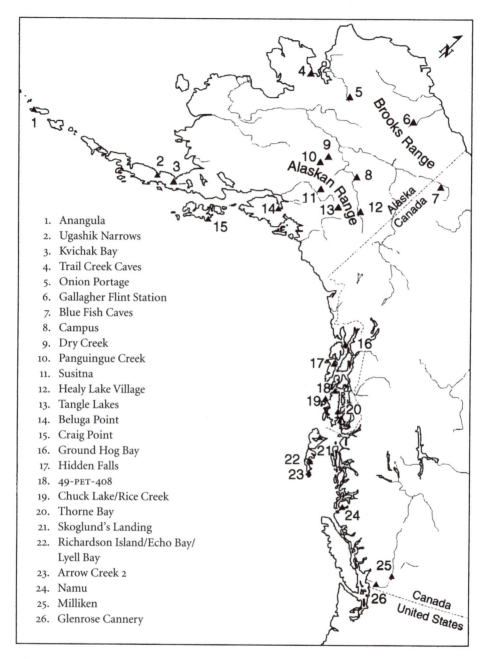

1. Anangula
2. Ugashik Narrows
3. Kvichak Bay
4. Trail Creek Caves
5. Onion Portage
6. Gallagher Flint Station
7. Blue Fish Caves
8. Campus
9. Dry Creek
10. Panguingue Creek
11. Susitna
12. Healy Lake Village
13. Tangle Lakes
14. Beluga Point
15. Craig Point
16. Ground Hog Bay
17. Hidden Falls
18. 49-PET-408
19. Chuck Lake/Rice Creek
20. Thorne Bay
21. Skoglund's Landing
22. Richardson Island/Echo Bay/
    Lyell Bay
23. Arrow Creek 2
24. Namu
25. Milliken
26. Glenrose Cannery

Figure 7.5 Map illustrating the location of important archeological sites ascribed to the American Paleoarctic and Northwest Coast Microblade traditions.

tify where economies based solely on interior environments begin and coastal economic practices are abandoned. Perhaps these different economies are best viewed as gradational with greater and greater reliance placed on nonmarine resources as one moves away from the coast toward the interior.

The archeological record is difficult to interpret along the coasts of the Bering and Chukchi Seas because rising sea level during the Birch Interval has submerged the coastal archeological record. However, the persistence of the American Paleoarctic tradition is suggested along the Bering Sea coast. Anderson (1986:313) suggests that the Lower Bench site at Cape Krusenstern may be a transitional microblade assemblage between the American Paleoarctic tradition and the Arctic Small Tool tradition (an Arctic tradition characterized by delicately flaked stone tools, burins, and microblades dating between circa 4,300–1,600 B.P. (Anderson 1968). Shortly after the sea level stabilized, there is widespread recognition of the Arctic Small Tool tradition along the Bering Sea and Chukchi Sea coasts. In regions where tectonic uplift or isostatic rebound has outpaced sea level rise, such as Anangula Island at the tip of the Alaska Peninsula (Laughlin 1967, 1975), it is clear from the physical location of the sites adjacent to the sea that they were adapted to a marine economy.

A single ^{14}C determination from Locality I at the Gallagher Flint Station suggests that American Paleoarctic populations may have been in place in interior areas adjacent to the coast possibly as early as circa 10,500 B.P. (Dixon 1975). On the Alaska Peninsula, Paleoarctic tradition occupations are documented from the lowest levels of the Ugashik Narrows site and at Kvichak Bay (Dumond 1977; Dumond et al. 1976; Henn 1978). Five radiocarbon determinations indicate that these assemblages range between circa 9,000–7,000 B.P. The Ugashik Narrows site is located along a river with a major salmon run, where large mammals such as caribou and moose may easily cross the river. The location suggests that fishing and large-mammal hunting may have been important economic activities at the site.

The Denali Complex (10,500–8,000 B.P.)

Throughout interior Alaska and the Yukon Territory, a number of archeological sites have been documented that date between circa 10,500 and 8,000 B.P. They contain bifacial biconvex knives, end scrapers, large blades and blade-like flakes, prepared microblade cores, core tablets, microblades, burins, burin spalls, worked flakes, and retouched flakes (Figure 7.6). This suite of artifacts was defined by Fredrick West (1967) as the Denali complex. Since that time, the list of associated lithic traits has been increased to include large blade cores, straight and convex based projectile points with constricting sides, elongated bifaces, spokeshaves, and abraders. The term Denali complex is retained here because it has priority in the literature and is applied to a restricted region (interior regions of eastern Beringia lacking a coastal/marine economic component).

West (1967:378) originally suggested an age for the Denali complex between circa 15,000–10,000 B.P. based on typological comparisons with Siberian assemblages. He later revised this assessment and estimated the age of the Denali complex to be between circa 10,000–8,000 B.P. (West 1975). This later estimate has proven to be very close to subsequent radiocarbon dating and stratigraphic analyses of Denali complex sites. Component II at Dry Creek, which was occupied by Denali complex people, suggests that the Denali complex first appears in interior Alaska circa 10,690 ± 250 B.P.(SI-1561) based on the overall site stratigraphy and ^{14}C dating (Powers and Hoffecker 1989). Component II at nearby Panguingue Creek is another Denali complex occupation located in the Nenana Valley. Several ^{14}C determinations bracket this occupations between 8,500–7,500 B.P. (Goebel and Bigelow 1996; Powers and Maxwell 1986).

Numerous sites have been reported from glacial terrain in the Tangle Lakes region of the south-central Alaska Range (West 1996b, 1996c, 1996d; West, Robinson, and Curran 1996; West, Robinson, and Dixon 1996; West, Robinson, and West 1996). These sites contain typical Denali complex assemblages. All are relatively shallow sites (less than 50 cm [20 inches] deep) primarily situated on the top of glacial features, some of which appear to have reliable radiocarbon determinations dating Denali complex occupations between circa 10,500–8,000 B.P. Numerous other sites containing Denali complex occupations have been reported throughout the interior including the Healy Lake Village site (Cook 1969; Cook and McKennan 1970).

In the upper Susitna River drainage, Dixon and Smith (1990) identified six sites that they ascribe to the Denali complex based on typological traits, stratigraphic position within a series of regional tephras (deposits of volcanic ash), and radiocarbon dating. Because all these sites were located on high overlooks and some contained fragmentary faunal remains attributed to medium to large mammals, an economic emphasis on terrestrial mammal hunting was postulated. The Campus site, located on the campus of the University of Alaska-Fairbanks was once thought to date to the late Pleistocene or early Holocene and was classified as one of the Denali complex sites. Although the site may have a Denali complex component, it is now considered by many northern archeologists to be late Holocene in age based on a reevaluation of the site and associated artifacts by Charles Mobley (1991, 1996).

Numerous Denali complex sites have been reported from a variety of ecological settings throughout interior eastern Beringia. The ecological setting of interior sites indicate an economy that included large mammal hunting and freshwater aquatic resources. Faunal remains from Component II at Dry Creek include bison and sheep. Many of the sites in the Alaska Range and Susitna River

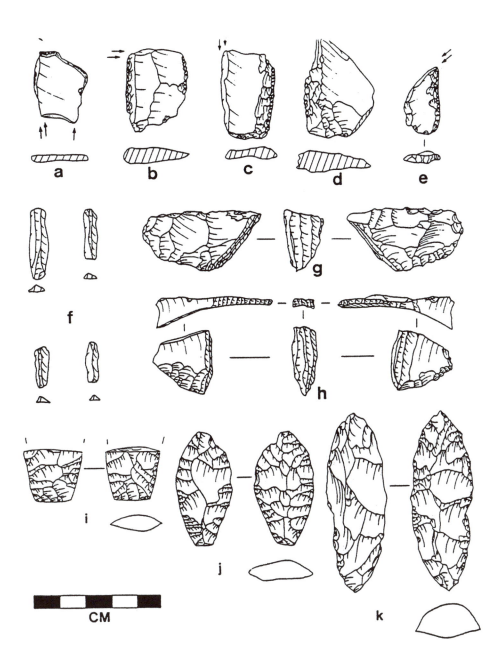

Figure 7.6 Denali complex artifacts, component II, Dry Creek: (a)–(e) burins; (f) micro-blades; (g)–(h) microblade cores; (i)–(k) bifaces (Dixon 1993:59, courtesy of Roger Powers and Ted Goebel).

drainage are ideally situated for caribou hunting. Although data are sketchy, most sites are relatively small and lack evidence of structures or other features that might be indicative of permanent or semi-permanent settlement. Organic artifacts are rare to nonexistent. Little is known about these early residents of interior Alaska except what can be learned from their lithic technology and site locations.

The Northwest Coast Microblade Tradition
(>9,000–<8,500 B.P.)

This tradition was first called the Early Boreal tradition (Borden 1969, 1975) and later was given a variety of names, including the Early Coast Microblade complex (Fladmark 1975), the Microblade tradition (Carlson 1979), Early Coast and North Coast Microblade complex (Fladmark 1982), the Marine Paleoarctic tradition (Davis 1989), and the Maritime Paleoarctic tradition (Jordan 1992). Rather than add to the confusing nomenclature, this presentation simply uses the term Northwest Coast Microblade tradition, which is keeping with Fladmark (1975) and descriptively includes both the geographic area and hallmark technological trait. These sites extend from the Kodiak Archipelago southeastward along the Pacific Rim through Southeast Alaska, British Columbia, Washington, and Oregon.

These sites all share the use of microblade technology. A maritime economy is indicated for most sites by their ecological settings and preserved faunal remains. The northern geographic limit of this tradition is impossible to ascertain based on the limited data available, but it could conceivably be extended to include the south side of the Alaska Peninsula where there is no winter pack ice. It is presumed that south of the Alaska Peninsula the adaptation to marine subsistence is different from that farther north because marine subsistence is not constrained by winter sea ice. Maritime subsistence in the Northwest Coast Microblade tradition is adapted to harvesting salmon, saltwater fishing, marine mammal hunting, and gathering intertidal shellfish and other resources. These people were experienced at navigating year-round open water along rugged forested coastlines characterized by fjords, islands, rocky headlands, and calving glaciers.

Only a few types of lithic artifacts document the material culture. These are: blocky microblade cores; microblades; utilized, notched, and waste flakes; flake cores; constricting base and leaf shaped bifaces; scrapers; gravers; and choppers. Obsidian was traded widely. The use of watercraft is inferentially demonstrated by the widespread trade in obsidian, fishing for offshore bottom fish, and the location of sites on islands and other settings primarily accessible from the sea. Although rising sea level inundated most coastal areas older than circa 9,500 B.P., the earliest radiocarbon dates suggest the Northwest Coast Microblade tradition first appears sometime between 9,500–9,000 B.P. and persists into mid-Holocene times.

Beluga Point in Cook Inlet is estimated to be between 8,000–7,000 B.P. based on typological comparisons with other sites (Reger 1996:434). Craig Point in the Kodiak archipelago is dated to 7,790 ± 620 B.P. (Beta 20123) (Jordan 1992). Although one radiocarbon determination from component III of the Ground Hog Bay 2 site near Juneau, Alaska is 10,180 ± 800 B.P.(WSU-412), it is not regarded as a reliable basal date for human occupation because of its large standard deviation and because it does not conform with the other ^{14}C determinations from the site (Ackerman 1996b; Ackerman et al. 1979). Another ^{14}C determination, 9,130 ± 130 B.P.(SI-6304), from the same level is believed to more accurately date the cultural occupation. The artifact assemblage from component III at Ground Hog Bay 2 is small, consisting of two obsidian biface fragments, one scraper, and five lithic flakes.

Another early site from Southeast Alaska is Hidden Falls, Component 1, dating to circa >9,000 B.P. (Davis 1989:194). Like component 2 at Ground Hog Bay 2, it contains microblades, microblade cores, and a variety of other lithic artifacts. Obsidian from both Hidden Falls and Ground Hog Bay 2 is from Sumez Island (adjacent to Prince of Wales in the Alexander Archipelago) and Mt. Edziza (upper Sitkine River, northern British Columbia) (Nelson 1976 cited in Ackerman 1996c:126). Several authors observe that this early trade in obsidian required the use of watercraft (Ackerman 1992; Davis 1989; Erlandson et al. 1992). It also implies that the region must have been occupied earlier in order to discover these obsidian sources and develop trade networks.

Locality 1 at the Chuck Lake site on Heceta Island, immediately west of Prince of Wales Island (Okada et al. 1989), has been dated to circa 8,200 B.P. This site is important because it has preserved faunal remains. Shellfish, bottom fish, and rock fish were the most abundant subsistence resources. Terrestrial and marine mammals and water fowl constituted a small percentage of the diet. This demonstrates maritime adaptation during the early Holocene. Like the trade in obsidian, this maritime economy required the use of watercraft. Near Rice Creek on Heceta Island, Ackerman et al. (1985) describe a cluster of flakes that rest on a glaciomarine deposit provisionally dated to circa 9,400 B.P. Ackerman (1996c:127, 130) suggests the cultural occupation may be circa 9,000 B.P. The Thorne River site, located on the eastern side of Prince of Wales Island, is dated to circa 7,500 B.P. based on several radiocarbon determinations (Holmes 1988a; Holmes et al. 1989). Like other sites, it contains microblades, microblade cores, and other lithic artifacts types. It lacks organic preservation other than charcoal.

In the Queen Charlotte Islands, several sites containing microblades and microblade cores have been reported that date between circa 9,300–9,000 B.P. (Fedje et al. 1996). A conical microblade core was recovered from the Arrow

Creek 2 site located in the southern Queen Charlottes that has been ^{14}C dated to circa 9,200 B.P. The Lyell Bay site, which contains microblade cores, is estimated to be between 9,400–9,000 B.P. based on its geologic context (Fedje et al. 1996). Farther south at the Namu Site, microblades do not occur until shortly after 9,000 B.P., probably about 8,500 B.P. (Carlson 1996). This suggests that the use of microblades in the Queen Charlotte Islands and British Columbia began very shortly after this tradition appeared in Southeast Alaska.

The Northwest Coast Microblade tradition is distinctively different and appears later than microblade traditions elsewhere. The northern microblade industries (American Paleoarctic tradition and Denali complex) predate the earliest evidence of this technology in Southeast Alaska by a least 1,000 years. The Northwest Coast microblade cores lack the detailed preparation known from the Denali complex and American Paleoarctic tradition. The Northwest Coast microblades are irregular in shape and are frequently struck from unprepared blocky and conical flakes, nodules, and even split pebbles.

The only human skeletal remains from the region dating to this time period are those from 49-PET-408 (Chapter 5). Although the sample from this site is small, the microblade technology is associated with the human remains. Isotope analysis indicates that this individual had a diet consisting almost entirely of marine foods when he was growing up. This further demonstrates adaptation to a maritime economy circa 9,200 B.P. by people using microblades along the Northwest Coast (Dixon et al. 1997).

The preliminary evidence suggests that microblade technology was incorporated into the tool kit of people already living along the Northwest Coast. Several sites have been discovered that apparently lack microblades but predate the microblade tradition. Although the data are sparse, what appear to be premicroblade occupations are reported from Ground Hog Bay (Ackerman et al. 1979), Skoglund's Landing (Fladmark 1990), Milliken (Mitchell and Pokotylo 1996), Richardson Island and Echo Bay sites (Fedje et al. 1996), and Namu (Carlson 1996), and possibly 49-PET-408.

Few sites are reported from Southeast Alaska and coastal British Columbia that may have been occupied prior to 10,000 B.P. (Fladmark 1979; Hobler 1978). Hobler (1978) reports flakes and flake cores from intertidal sites in the Queen Charlotte Islands that he presumed must have been deposited prior to sea level rise circa 10,000 B.P. The earliest cultural component at the Skoglund's Landing site (Fladmark 1979) is derived from a beach deposit approximately 10 m (33 ft) above modern sea level. This component is believed to have been occupied prior to sea level rise circa 9,000–8,500 B.P. (Fladmark 1979).

An artifact made from a large terrestrial mammal rib (possibly black bear based on comparison of isotope values), modified to make what appears to be a flint flaker, was recovered from 49-PET-408 in Southeast Alaska. This artifact was AMS ^{14}C dated to 10,300 B.P. ± 50 B.P. (CAMS-42381). Presuming this date is correct, this is the oldest archeological site yet reported on the Northwest Coast. The cave is approximately 110 m (360 ft) above modern sea level, suggesting early human exploitation and use of noncoastal settings.

Farther to the south, Fedje and Josenhans (personal communications 1998) have recovered a basalt blade-like flake from the continental shelf of British Columbia. Based on the local sea rise at the end of the last Ice Age, this locale would probably have been covered by the rising sea level about or shortly before 10,000 B.P., thus suggesting the site may have been occupied circa 10,300 B.P. Although these data are very preliminary, they suggest humans occupied the Northwest Coast of North America at the end of the last Ice Age when the sea level was lower prior to 10,000 B.P. There also is growing evidence for an extensive occupation of the Northwest Coast prior to the Northwest Coast Microblade tradition.

Northern Paleoindian Tradition (circa 10,500–8,500 B.P.)

Fluted projectile points and related lanceolate forms have been found throughout eastern Beringia. The fluted projectile points from eastern Beringia have come from sites that either have not been dated or for which the dating is ambiguous. Most scholars have assumed a historical relationship between Paleoindian projectile points from eastern Beringia and those from the Great Plains of western North America based on morphological similarities. Fluted projectile points have been found primarily in the northern areas of Beringia along the north and south sides of the Brooks Range. A few examples are also reported from regions in central interior Alaska. Based on the size and configuration of the projectile points most archeologists presume that the weapon used by the Northern Paleoindian tradition was the atlatl.

Numerous sites containing fluted projectile points from eastern Beringia are part of the larger Paleoindian tradition usually associated with the western United States (Figure 7.7) (Dixon 1993:15–23). By including the northern examples within the Paleoindian tradition, the underlying assumption is made that the people who used these tools in eastern Beringia were part of a larger population of people who shared a similar way of life and economic system. This assumption is reinforced because most of the northern sites appear to be situated in locales best suited for big game hunting, a strong economic focus of Paleoindians to the south.

There are three hypotheses that address the relationships between the northern and southern Paleoindian assemblages (Clark 1984). The first suggests that the northern specimens were left by the first humans to reach Alaska, who subsequently spread southward from eastern Beringia to colonize the continents. The

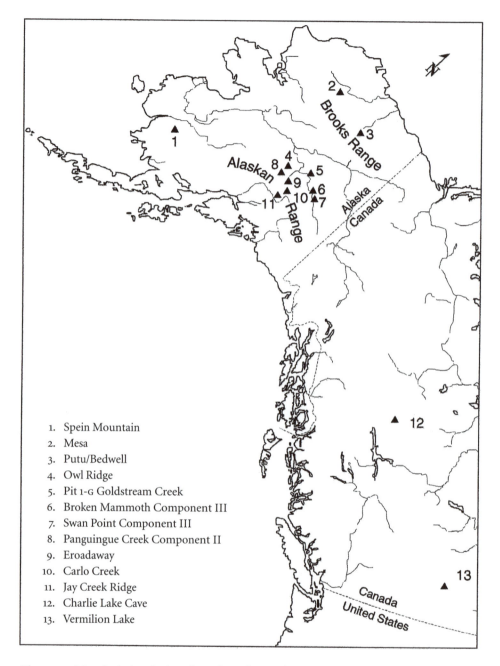

1. Spein Mountain
2. Mesa
3. Putu/Bedwell
4. Owl Ridge
5. Pit 1-G Goldstream Creek
6. Broken Mammoth Component III
7. Swan Point Component III
8. Panguingue Creek Component II
9. Eroadaway
10. Carlo Creek
11. Jay Creek Ridge
12. Charlie Lake Cave
13. Vermilion Lake

Figure 7.7 Map depicting the location of Northern Paleoindian tradition sites discussed in the text. (Graphic by Eric Parrish.)

second hypothesis proposes that fluted projectile points developed in the more southern regions of North America and spread northward into eastern Beringia. The third hypothesis suggests that fluted points were independently invented in eastern Beringia thousands of years after those to the south and that there may be no historical relationship between the two groups of artifacts. It is also possible that this technology developed rapidly from precursors to the Nenana complex and spread south from eastern Beringia (Goebel and Powers 1990; Goebel et al. 1991). While some Paleoindian sites are known to contain large blades and blade-like flakes, Paleoindian tradition people did not manufacture microblades or use side blade insets.

Several Northern Paleoindian sites have been excavated in central interior Alaska and have been dated to the interval between 9,500–8,500 B.P. These are Component I at the Carlo Creek site (Bowers 1978, 1980), the Jay Creek Ridge site (Dixon 1993:85–87), the Eroadaway site (Holmes 1988b), and Component II at the Owl Ridge site (Phippen 1988). Yesner et al. (1992) report occupations dating to circa 7,500 B.P. from the Broken Mammoth and Mead sites that also lack evidence of microblade technology but that contain bifacial stone tools. Although Component II at the Panguingue Creek site has been ascribed to the American Paleoarctic tradition, this component does not contain evidence of a microblade industry. It contains bifacial tools similar to other nonmicroblade sites, and Component II at Panguingue Creek has been dated to circa 8,600–7,000 B.P. (Powers and Hoffecker 1989:276; Powers and Maxwell 1986).

The Mesa site is located on the north side of Alaska's Brooks Range (Kunz 1982). A suite of 14 radiocarbon determinations ranging between circa 11,660–9,730 B.P. have been derived from 15 hearths at the site (Kunz and Reanier 1996). Thermal spalls resulting from artifacts being discarded in the fires demonstrate direct association between the artifacts and the hearths. Only two dates (derived from the same "split" charcoal sample) exceed 11,000 B.P. They appear to be statistical outliers, possibly resulting from burning fossil wood (Hamilton and Goebel 1999). All the remaining dates cluster around 10,000 B.P., suggesting this as a more accurate date for the Mesa occupation. Typological comparison between the Mesa site artifacts and Agate Basin projectile points from the high plains led Mike Kunz and others (Kunz and Reanier 1994, 1995, 1996; Kunz and Shelley 1994) to suggest that the Mesa culture may be ancestral to Agate Basin sites from more southern areas of North America (Frison and Stanford 1982).

The Mesa site contains lanceolate projectile points with edge ground, straight, and concave bases and constricting sides. Other artifact types include large thin bifaces (possibly knives), spurred gravers made on flakes, unifacially flaked lithic tools, scrapers, retouched flakes, flake hammer and anvil stones using stream cobbles, waste flakes, quartz crystals, and possible hematite. No faunal remains were recovered; however, the ecological setting suggests that the site was used as a look-out for large mammals where waiting hunters manufactured and repaired their projectiles and tools.

The Putu site is located on the north flank of the Brooks Range on the upper Sagavanirktok River. The site has two localities that frequently have been treated as two separate sites, the Putu site and the Bedwell site (Alexander 1974, 1987; Clark 1984; Clark and Clark 1983, 1991; Dumond 1980; Kunz and Reanier 1994; Morlan 1977). The Putu locality has two components, a lower one containing fluted projectile points and a more recent one in the sod layer containing saw-cut antler and fresh-looking bone. A single radiocarbon date of 11,470 ± 500 B.P.(SI-2382) (Alexander 1987) was originally believed to date the early occupation. After a thorough reevaluation of the Putu site, Reanier (1994, 1996) has demonstrated that two other dates of 8,450 ± 130 B.P. (WSU-1318) and 8,810 ± 60 B.P (Beta 69901, CAMS-11038) are probably more accurate. The lower component of the Putu site contains several fluted, straight, and convex-based projectile points with constricting sides. A thin triangular biface, similar to those associated with the Nenana complex, was also found.

Reanier (1994, 1996) obtained an AMS ^{14}C date on charcoal collected during the original excavation that had been curated since that time. This sample produced a date of 10,490 ± 70 B.P. (Beta 69895, CAMS-11032). Based on comparison of the lanceolate, edge ground Bedwell projectile points with similar specimens from the Mesa site, Reanier suggests this ^{14}C determination may date the Bedwell occupation. No fluted points were recovered from the Bedwell locality. There is only one concave base specimen, while the rest exhibit straight and convex bases with constricting sides.

The Spein Mountain site is located about 60 km (37 mi) east of the town of Bethel, in southwestern Alaska (Ackerman 1996d). The site is important because it extends the range of the Northern Paleoindian tradition to southwestern Alaska. A single radiocarbon date from a hearth-like depression containing charcoal and calcined bone dated to 10,050 ± 90 B.P. (Beta 64471, CAMS-8281). Pollen analysis demonstrated that there were no trees in the region and grasses were the predominant plants growing near the site at the time of occupation. The site lacks microblades or evidence of microblade technology. Artifact types include flakes, bifacial "adz blades," ovate bifaces, biface preforms, gravers, flake knives, scrapers, a whetstone/abrader, a notched flake, cobble spall scrapers, choppers, hammer stones, split cobbles, and bifacially flaked lanceolate projectile points with constricting bases. Ackerman (1996d:460) believes the Spein Mountain assemblage is similar to artifacts from the Mesa site and Bedwell complex in the Brooks Range.

It could be argued that a large geographic gap exists between Northern Paleoindian sites in the Brooks Range and Spein Mountain. However, a number of isolated surface finds that are typologically characteristic of Northern Paleo-indian tradition projectile points have been found throughout Alaska and Canada's Yukon Territory. Furthermore, other sites in interior Alaska may be related to the Northern Paleoindian tradition based on typological comparison and radiocarbon dating, albeit with somewhat younger dates.

The Jay Creek Ridge site was occupied circa 9,500 B.P., based on six AMS ^{14}C determinations run on charcoal identified as dwarf birch and willow. Concave-based projectile points manufactured on flat, thin flakes of argillite and basalt, which exhibit basal and lateral edge grinding, were found. Other artifacts include an end scraper and small triangular points or knives. There is no microblade technology. These projectile points are Folsom-like, but lack fluting. In referring to the Midland cultural complex, Frison (1983:111–114) described similar projectile forms associated with Folsom sites from the more southern areas of western North America: "unfluted Folsom projectile points, as well as pseudo-Folsom points that are simply outline forms imposed on thin, flat flakes with no interrupting flake scars, occur along with fluted points in Folsom sites" (Frison 1983:111–114).

At the Carlo Creek site, located in the Nenana River Valley, Bowers (1980) reports finding the remains of a fall/winter hunting camp where caribou, sheep, and ground squirrel were processed. The stone used to manufacture artifacts appears to have been heat treated, and the artifacts recovered include percussion-flaked elongate bifaces, biface fragments, retouched flakes, and lithic debitage. No evidence of a microblade or burin industry is associated with this assemblage, which dates to circa 8,500 B.P.

Several ^{14}C determinations on wood charcoal from Panguingue Creek Component I range between 10,200–8,200 B.P. The small artifact assemblage contains two lanceolate projectile points, a blade/flake core, a few scrapers, and waste flakes. The age, absence of evidence of microblade technology, and presence of lanceolate points suggest this component might also be related to the Northern Paleoindian tradition.

The Component II occupation at the Owl Ridge site has been dated by four ^{14}C determinations between 9,500–7,500 B.P. (Phippen 1988:3,77). Although only a few artifacts were recovered, including one ovate and one subtriangular biface, the component lacks evidence of microblade technology. The spatial distribution of cobbles has been interpreted as the remains of a possible tent ring (a ring of stones placed along the perimeter of a tent to secure it in the wind) (Phippen 1988:118–123).

The Eroadaway site has been dated by Holmes (1988b:3) to 8,640 ± 170 B.P. (WSU-3683). The site contains straight and slightly concave-based projectile points, some of which exhibit edge grinding, as well as bifaces, unifacial flake tools, and lithic debitage (Holmes 1988b) (personal communication 1990). Preserved spruce needles and burned twigs also were recovered from the site, suggesting the proximity of spruce to the site circa 8,500 B.P. (Holmes 1988b:4). This site also lacks evidence of microblade technology.

A series of four ^{14}C determinations suggests that Cultural Zone III at the Broken Mammoth site was occupied around circa 10,300 B.P. Zone III contains waste flakes, point fragments, two small "trianguloid" basally ground projectile points, large biface and point fragments, quartz hammer stones, and a small eyed bone needle. Faunal remains in addition to fossil proboscidean ivory include bison, elk, Dall sheep, canid, river otter, porcupine, marmot, ground squirrel, red squirrel, swan, goose, duck, ptarmigan, salmonoid fish scales, possibly grayling, and egg shells (Hamilton and Goebel 1999; Yesner 1996; Yesner et al. 1992).

At the Swan Point site, cultural Component III dated to 10,230 ± 80 B.P. (Beta 56666, CAMS-4252) also has no evidence of microblade technology. This occupation contains strait- and convex-based small lanceolate projectile points as well as thin triangular points. Gravers, made by chipping spurs on broken points, and quartz pebble choppers and hammer stones have also been recovered from Component III.

Two exceptionally well-preserved bone projectile points recovered from Pit 1-G on Goldstream Creek about 6 km (4 mi) downstream from the town of Fox in interior Alaska were reported by Rainey (1939:393). Two AMS ^{14}C radiocarbon determinations indicate they were probably manufactured circa 8,500 B.P. (Chapter 3). The points were not slotted to receive microblades and are probably rare organic projectile points associated with the Northern Paleoindian tradition. Similar large bone projectile points, possibly atlatl dart points, may have been an important component of Northern Paleoindian tradition weapon systems.

It is not clear what happened to the Northern Paleoindian tradition. There are several sites in Alaska, such as Carlo Creek and the Eroadaway sites, that suggest it persisted for a considerable length of time. Although it has been suggested that these more recent sites might represent a continuum from the Nenana complex in Alaska's interior (Dixon 1993), it is equally plausible that they may be later regional manifestations of the Northern Paleoindian tradition, or possibly a later blending of both Nenana complex and Northern Paleoindian tradition technological traits.

These later sites contain bifacial forms similar to Paleoindian sites elsewhere in North America and possibly similar to the earlier Nenana complex. They all lack evidence of a microblade industry. Several hypotheses may explain their occurrence: (1) ovate and triangular bifacial forms from many of these sites may bear morphological similarity to examples in the earlier Nenana complex, and these sites may represent a late manifestation of that tradition, (2) they may be late examples of the Northern Paleoindian tradition, that developed regionally from earlier fluted point forms, or (3) they may be transitional between Northern Paleoindian and Northern Archaic traditions or possibly very early examples of the Northern Archaic tradition.

In central western Canada, the continental glaciers melted, reestablishing a land connection between eastern Beringia and unglaciated areas of western North America by circa 11,000 B.P. This enabled the exchange of species between eastern Beringia and the western plains of North America. It also provided an avenue for the northward expansion of the Paleoindian tradition along the eastern flank of the western Cordillera into the Yukon Territory and northern Alaska. This newly deglaciated area possibly created an extensive parkland environmental zone consisting of high-altitude/high-latitude grasslands interspersed with shrubs and stands of conifers, possibly pine in the south and spruce in the north. High percentages of grass pollen at Spein Mountain, spruce needles preserved at the Eroadaway site, and red squirrel remains associated with grazers, such as bison, at Broken Mammoth provide evidence for parkland-like environments at several of these sites.

High-altitude adaptation to grassy parklands may have been a pre-adaptation to high latitudes. This could have facilitated rapid northward migration of southern Paleoindian people shortly after continental deglaciation. Presuming the ^{14}C dating at both Spein Mountain, Putu, and Mesa is correct, it appears that the fluted points from the Great Plains Paleoindian tradition may have arrived in eastern Beringia beginning circa 10,500 B.P., immediately following partition of the continental ice and the establishment of biological resources essential to sustain human subsistence. This hypothesis is supported by the discovery of a Clovis component at Charlie Lake Cave in northeastern British Columbia dated to circa 10,550 B.P. (Driver 1996; Driver et al. 1996; Fladmark et al. 1988). At Vermilion Lake in Banff National Park in Alberta, Canada, Fedje et al. (1995) have documented an assemblage that they consider to belong to the "Late Fluted Point tradition." Although diagnostic projectile points were not recovered, the assemblage shares other technological traits with other fluted point assemblages and possibly dates as early as 10,800 B.P. Based on ^{14}C determinations from other typologically similar sites that lack microblades, it appears that this tradition may have persisted in regions of eastern Beringia as a co-tradition with the American Paleoarctic tradition until circa 8,000 B.P.

Northern Paleoindian projectile points do not exhibit the full typological array of Paleoindian projectile points from the more southern regions of North America. Most of the early northern fluted points exhibit multiple flutes, concave bases, and edge grinding (Figure 7.8). However, large Clovis points are rare, and classic Folsom points are nonexistent. Later lanceolate forms resemble tapering stemmed forms similar to Agate Basin and Hell Gap points.

It has been suggested that there was a transition from the Northern Paleoindian tradition into the Northern Archaic tradition (characterized by notched

Figure 7.8 Fluted projectile points from eastern Beringia.

projectile points) in eastern Beringia similar to the transition to the Archaic elsewhere in North America (Dixon 1986). Wormington and Forbis (1965:183–88) and later Dixon (1976) proposed the south to north spread of Paleoindian technology based on the fact that the northern examples looked typologically later than the those found on the western Great Plains. Dixon (1976) suggested the south to north spread of this technology may have occurred circa 10,000 B.P., but data that are more recent suggest it may have been earlier, probably circa 10,500 B.P.

Summary

Humans occupied interior regions of eastern Beringia by at least 11,600 B.P. At that time, widespread trade in obsidian was already established, indicating human occupation of Alaska prior to that time. The occurrence of scavenged fossil ivory seems to be present at several sites. Although mammoth or mastodon kill sites have not been found in eastern Beringia, there is growing evidence that humans may have hunted these large elephant-like animals. What may be mammoth blood residue has been identified on fluted projectile points from eastern Beringia (Loy and Dixon 1998).

The earliest human occupation of eastern Beringia is ascribed to the Nenana complex, which is characterized by distinctive triangular bifacial projectile points and tapering ovate bifaces, probably knives. The Nenana complex persists until circa 10,500–10,000 B.P. at which time it becomes difficult to distinguish it from the Northern Paleoindian tradition in interior Alaska. This suggests a possible blending of technological traits of the Nenana complex and the Northern Paleoindian tradition.

Goebel et al. (1991) have presented an analysis comparing the lithic traits of the Nenana and Clovis complexes. Using both cumulative percentage curves and cluster analysis, they quantitatively demonstrate a close relationship between both lithic industries. Based on this analysis, they conclude that only two explanations for these similarities are possible. The first reiterates C. Vance Haynes's (1987) hypothesis that humans crossed the Bering Land Bridge sometime between 13,000–12,000 B.P. and rapidly moved south through the ice-free corridor and that both Clovis and the Nenana complexes are later regional variants of this migration. The second hypothesis is that both complexes are technologically derived from an earlier migration that hypothetically took place, this time before the closing of the ice-free corridor, sometime between circa 25,000–22,000 B.P. Currently there is little, if any, archeological evidence to support this hypothesis. The data also suggest a third hypothesis. This postulates that although both may have shared a common technological origin, the Northern Paleoindian tradition is derived from a northward movement sometime between 11,000–10,500 B.P. of the Paleoindian tradition from the Great Plains. This movement was probably associated with colonization of recently deglaciated terrain in central Canada.

Distinctive microblade technologies are introduced into eastern Beringia sometime around 10,500 B.P. The microblade technologies are contemporaneous with both the Nenana complex and Northern Paleoindian tradition. The Denali complex represents an inland adaptation by microblade using people. Because the American Paleoarctic and Northwest Coast Microblade traditions are found in ecologically very different coastal areas, they are recognized as distinct co-traditions.

The presence and absence of microblade technology and different projectile point types could result from the use of specific sites for different tasks and activities. For example, microblades may not be found in fish camps because they were not used for fishing. However, this type of explanation seems unsatisfactory because all the sites (those with and without microblades) have been inter-preted as hunting camps by their excavators. Consequently, they superficially ap-pear to be used for the same type of activities and tasks. Microblades com-monly are recovered in high frequencies probably because they are essential components of composite projectile point systems most often associated with hunting sites. It is significant that nonmicroblade bearing sites, or site compo-nents, contain bifacial lithic artifacts associated with the maintenance and repair of bifacial projectile points.

Another hypothesis is that American Paleoarctic and Denali microblade technology might constitute a winter tool kit (being a more conservative use of lithic raw material) and nonmicroblade technology might characterize a sum-mer tool kit. However, this seems unlikely because there are no compelling archeological data to separate these various sites into summer versus winter oc-cupations. Also, ^{14}C dating clusters sites containing microblades and sites that do not contain microblades into discrete periods of time. This further suggests that the presence or absence of microblades is an important indicator of cultural tradition rather than site function or season of occupation.

The American Paleoarctic and Denali microblade-using cultures sharply contrast with archeological assemblages that lack microblades and instead are typified by bifacially flaked projectile points. These two contrasting assem-blages represent radically different technological approaches to producing projectile points. The vast northern area of interior Alaska and Canada was a transitional region between more Asian oriented microblade traditions and nonmicroblade bifacial traditions characteristic of southern parts of North America. The boundaries between these technological traditions shifted re-peatedly over time, and consequently some archeological sites provide a se-quence of nonmicroblade/microblade technologies when viewed from a single geographic perspective.

In two rare cases where organic remains have been discovered in association with American Paleoarctic tradition lithic artifacts, distinctive antler arrow points slotted to receive microblade insets have been found (Ackerman 1996a; Larsen 1968a). These were first recognized by Helge Larsen (1968a), who imme-diately identified them as arrow points and compared them to examples that are more recent from Inupiak (Eskimo) sites. Nearly 30 years later, Ackerman (1996a) reports a similar artifact from Cave 1, in the Lime Hills located in the Kuskokwim River drainage in southwestern Alaska. This suggests that the bearers of the American Paleoarctic tradition may have first introduced the bow and arrow into North America from Asia possibly as early as circa 10,500 B.P. Although the American Paleoarctic tradition almost certainly used the atlatl, the introduction of the bow and arrow created a sharp contrast in the use of early weapon systems. The American Paleoarctic tradition added the bow and arrow to their weapons inventory, while the earlier Nenana and Paleoindian populations probably continued to rely on the atlatl as their primary weapon system.

Although the Denali complex and American Paleoarctic microblades appear to have been used as insets in bone and antler projectile points, the microblades used along the Northwest Coast may have functioned very differently. Microscopic analysis and replicative experiments suggest that "backed" microblades (those steeply retouched or ground along one edge) may have been hand held. Others were probably "end-hafted," or set into the end of a handle, like a modern razor, or "Xacto," knife (Hutchings 1996). Experiments demonstrate that microblades hafted in this fashion are excellent tools for cutting thin leather, soft woods such as cedar, roots, fresh bark, and other pliable materials. End hafted microblades used along the Northwest Coast may have been the tool of choice for delicate precision craft work. They also may have been used for other purposes such as intentional scarification, minor surgery, or even cutting hair (Hutchings 1996).

Some researchers (Matson and Coupland 1995:82) imply the appearance of microblade technology along the Northwest Coast may indicate a physical migration of people. However, it is equally probable that the Pebble Tool tradition (Chapter 8), already established along the coast, adopted microblade technology, added it to their existing tool kit, and produced and used microblades somewhat differently than their northern neighbors. Carlson (1996:98) notes that the tool assemblage at the Namu site in central coastal British Columbia changed very little during this period, with the exception of the addition of microblades. This adaptation of microblade technology may have resulted in less formal methods of producing microblades. Along the Northwest Coast, they were applied to different functions such as precision working soft materials, as opposed to arming projectile points. However, these different functions were probably not mutually exclusive.

Preliminary evidence suggests that the concept of the bow and arrow was introduced into North America by microblade using people. It is possible that the bow and arrow may have been adopted by late Nenana complex or Northern Paleoindian tradition people, because some of the smaller lightweight triangular stone projectile points could have functioned as arrowheads. Apparently, bow and arrow technology was not shared with the Folsom complex or Plano tradition to the south, where there is no conclusive evidence for the use of the bow and arrow prior to 8,000 B.P.

The preceding review illustrates that it is no longer practical to order the regional archeology of Alaska and the Pacific Northwest in a traditional unilinear sequence, with one tradition or complex leading to the next. The three major traditions outlined here are probably best viewed as co-traditions that, beginning about 10,500 B.P., existed together in the same geographic region. This early cultural complexity may result from Alaska's proximity to Asia, where Old World cultural traits were in contact with early New World cultural innovations, such as fluted projectile points, that were independently developed in the Americas. Future research is necessary to further identify and clarify these complex relationships and interactions.

8

The Far West and Mexico
Prior to 8,000 B.P.

Introduction

The Far West encompasses the area between the Pacific Ocean and the North American Continental Divide and from British Columbia, Canada to the Isthmus of Panama. This huge area contains a wide array of environments, ranging from coastal rain forests in the north to deserts in the south (Figure 8.1). These environmental differences became intensified at the end of the Pleistocene about 10,000–11,000 B.P. The early archeology of North America's Far West and Mexico remains an enigma to archeologists, largely because most archeological discoveries have come from surface sites or sites that are poorly stratified. These circumstances make them extremely difficult to date and interpret.

As archeological work has progressed, various archeological traditions, complexes, and phases have been defined throughout the Far West. These archeological frameworks are an outgrowth of local and regional research that enables researchers to organize their data, understand regional economic patterns, artifact types and distributions, and environmental change. Given the great technological and economic diversity throughout the region, it has not proven useful to lump these diverse technological patterns and economic systems into a single classificatory unit. It is more appropriate to use regional terminology already in the literature that best defines broad similarities in technology and economy throughout a given area during defined periods of time.

To classify some of the early archeological discoveries in the northwestern areas of the Far West, Robert Butler (1961, 1965) introduced the term Old Cordilleran culture. Sites ascribed to this early "culture" all contained leaf-shaped bifaces and projectile points. Some archeologists thought that the Old Cordilleran culture might have been as old or older than the well-documented Clovis sites east of the Rocky Mountains. However, it is now known that leaf shaped projectile points and other artifacts associated with the Old Cordilleran culture are younger. The Old Cordilleran culture is now generally believed to be derived from the preceding Windust phase, which appears to be a local manifestation of the Western Stemmed Point tradition (Carlson 1983).

Figure 8.1 Map depicting the Far West and important physiographic provinces. (Graphic by Eric Parrish.)

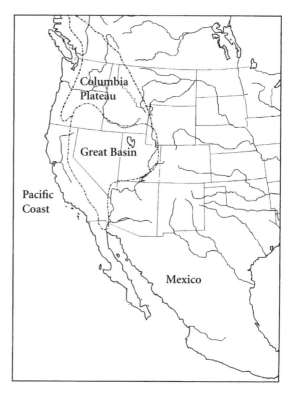

Another early attempt to help order the archeology of the Far West was made by Charles Borden (1969) who introduced the term Protowestern tradition. The term was used to distinguish between numerous Far West complexes and artifact assemblages east of the continental divide, such as Clovis and other Paleoindian complexes. The Protowestern tradition was considered to have a comparatively poorly developed lithic technology that included leaf-shaped and other projectile point types, bifacial knives, a wide variety of scrapers, pebble tools or flake cores, and blades. At the time it was proposed, some archeologists entertained the possibility that early archeological material in the Far West may have had a non-Clovis origin (Matson and Coupland 1995:66).

Steven Bedwell introduced the term Pluvial Lakes tradition to classify archeological assemblages dating between circa 11,000–8,000 B.P. from the Great Basin (Bedwell 1973). Pluvial Lakes tradition sites are located along the margins of former lakes created during periods of increased precipitation that are often correlated with glacial stages. These lakes are now dry, and archeological sites are preserved along their ancient shorelines. These sites are characterized by stemmed projectile points and crescents, and lack ground-stone artifacts. Based on their ecological setting, it is presumed that subsistence activities were directed toward lacustrine (lake) resources (Bedwell 1973; Hester 1973).

Roy Carlson (1979, 1983, 1990, 1996) has introduced and advocated the use of the term Pebble Tool tradition that he views as an early technological tradition restricted to the coastal areas of western North America between northern Oregon and Alaska. The tradition bears similarities to Borden's Protowestern tradition and is characterized by foliate, or leaf-shaped, bifaces and high frequencies of choppers and scrapers manufactured from cobbles. Many of the "choppers" are probably flake cores from which usable sharp flakes have been struck for a variety of utilitarian purposes. Many of these sites are located adjacent to the ocean which suggests subsistence based on marine resources supplemented by exploitation of the narrow adjacent coastal plain, and possibly unglaciated refugia, exposed by lower sea level at the end of the last Ice Age and early Holocene times.

Technologically the Pebble Tool tradition is similar to the Old Cordilleran described by Butler. In Carlson's (1996) view, the Pebble tool tradition was restricted to the coast while the Old Cordilleran culture was originally viewed as a terrestrial adaptation that subsequently became adapted to the coast. The two traditions share many technological similarities and perhaps the Old Cordilleran should be viewed as a somewhat later inland adaptation of the Pebble Tool tradition.

Far to the south in Mexico, José Luis Lorenzo and Lorena Mirambell have termed the period between circa 14,000–7,000 B.P. the Cenolithic (Lorenzo 1967; Lorenzo and Mirambell 1999). They have divided it into two stages. The earliest stage is the lower Cenolithic and dates between 14,000–9,000 B.P. It is followed by the upper Cenolithic that spans the interval between 9,000–7,000 B.P. Leaf shaped, stemmed, and fluted lithic projectile points, blades, and blade cores all characterize the lower Cenolithic. The upper Cenolithic exhibits a greater variety of lithic artifacts, including the introduction of ground and polished stone artifacts, particularly mortars and flat grindstones. Although leaf-shaped points persist, stemmed points and stemmed points with "ears" become more common. In addition to hunting, increased emphasis was placed on collecting wild varieties of squash, avocado, chile, amaranth, corn, and perhaps beans during the upper Cenolithic (Lorenzo and Mirambell 1999). This terminology does not have wide recognition or application outside of Mexico. Consequently, terms more familiar to most North American archeologists are used in following analysis.

In an effort to concisely present the regional archeology and reduce confusion the following terms are used in the subsequent presentation: (1) The Western Fluted Point tradition (circa 11,500?–10,500? B.P.) following the example of other researchers (Beck and Jones 1997; Grayson 1993) in an attempt to avoid confusion arising from the use of terms, such as Clovis or Paleoindian. (2) The Western Stemmed Point tradition, circa 11,500?-11,000–7,000 B.P. in Washington,

Oregon, Nevada, Utah, and Idaho (Bryan 1980, 1988; Carlson 1983), and (3) San Dieguito/Sulphur Spring complexes 10,000–8,000 B.P. in southern California, southern Nevada, Arizona, and northern Mexico (Sayles and Antevs 1941; Warren 1967). Figure 8.2 depicts the location of important sites discussed in the text.

Western Fluted Point Tradition (circa 11,500?–10,500? B.P.)

Fluted, concave-based, and edge ground projectile points similar to Clovis points found in the western Great Plains have been reported throughout the Columbia Plateau (Carlson 1988:319), from interior and coastal California (Erlandson 1994), throughout the Great Basin (Willig and Aikens 1988), from Ari-

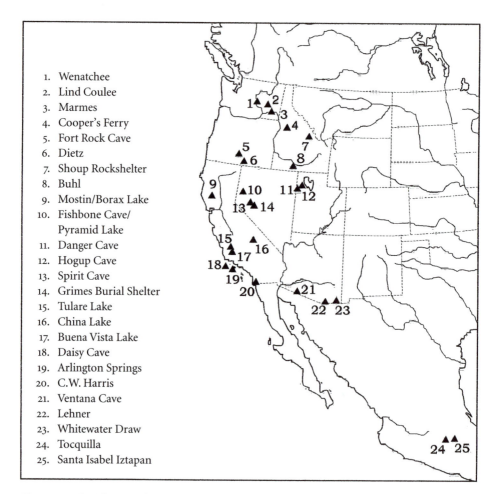

1. Wenatchee
2. Lind Coulee
3. Marmes
4. Cooper's Ferry
5. Fort Rock Cave
6. Dietz
7. Shoup Rockshelter
8. Buhl
9. Mostin/Borax Lake
10. Fishbone Cave/
    Pyramid Lake
11. Danger Cave
12. Hogup Cave
13. Spirit Cave
14. Grimes Burial Shelter
15. Tulare Lake
16. China Lake
17. Buena Vista Lake
18. Daisy Cave
19. Arlington Springs
20. C.W. Harris
21. Ventana Cave
22. Lehner
23. Whitewater Draw
24. Tocquilla
25. Santa Isabel Iztapan

Figure 8.2 Significant early archeological sites located in the Far West. (Graphic by Eric Parrish.)

zona (Martin and Plog 1973; Irwin-Williams 1979), and south into Mexico (LeTourneau 1995; Wormington 1957) and Central America (MacNeish 1983; Mayer-Oakes 1986), possibly extending as far south as Panama (Bird and Cooke 1978). The geographic range of the Western Fluted Point tradition in the Far West extends from the Pacific Coast in the west to the Great Plains in the east and from British Columbia in the north to the Isthmus of Panama in the south.

Despite this vast geographic distribution, the age of this tradition remains ambiguous. Because Clovis is the earliest widely recognized bifacial stone projectile point type elsewhere in North America, some archeologists suggest this is also the case in the Far West. Willig and Aikens (1988:12) have attempted to resolve this problem by comparing radiocarbon dates from Western Stemmed tradition sites to those from Western Fluted Point tradition sites. This led them to suggest that western fluted projectile points are older than the stemmed forms. They (Willig and Aikens 1988) hypothesize that a technological change from fluted to stemmed points may have occurred possibly as early as circa 11,000 B.P.

However, other researchers question whether Western Fluted points are older than Western Stemmed projectile points in the Far West or are contemporary with them. Bryan and Tuohy (1999) believe adequate field data exist to indicate that stemmed points may predate fluted ones in the northern sector of the Far West. Most fluted points have been isolated surface finds or have been found in other contexts that have not enabled researchers to reliably date them. Stemmed projectile points have also been found throughout the Far West, including the Great Basin and Columbia Plateau, and many of these discoveries appear to be in contexts equal in age to Clovis points found elsewhere. Based on a rigorous analysis of early archeological sites in the Great Basin, Beck and Jones (1997:187) suggest that some more gracile forms of fluted points may persist possibly as late as circa 10,300 B.P. in the Great Basin.

The Wenatchee, or Richie-Roberts, site is located in central Washington. This site is important because it firmly documents the Clovis complex in the Far West. Furthermore, it is the only cache of spectacular Clovis lithic artifacts that has been discovered in situ and excavated and analyzed by scientists. The site contains Clovis projectile points, bifaces, and bone foreshafts. Two of the artifacts, described as fluted knives, exhibit red ochre staining. Ochre on these specimens is restricted to the hafting area, implying that they may have been hafted in wooden handles painted red (Gramly 1996:19) (see Chapter 9).

Unfortunately, the Wenatchee site has not been adequately dated. Mehringer and Foit (1990) reported that the artifacts rested on volcanic ash from the Glacier Peak eruption dating to circa 11,000 B.P., suggesting that they had been deposited shortly after the eruption. Three ^{14}C determinations on samples of "artifactual" bone have apparently been run, but only one date of 5,215 ± 90 B.P.

is reported (Gramly 1996:19). Given the geologic dating by Mehringer and Foit and the distinctive typological characteristics of the collection, this date is clearly too recent. It is probable that the sample lacked the rigorous chemical pre-treatment required to obtain reliable ^{14}C determinations on bone.

To the south of Wenatchee lies the Great Basin, which is a vast inland area encompassing most of the state of Nevada and parts of Oregon, California, and Utah. In the Great Basin, the early cultural chronology is still poorly understood. Basin and range topography continues south of the Great Basin through Arizona, southwestern New Mexico, and to central Mexico. From a purely archeological perspective, this southern area is considered an extension of the Great Plains cultural sequence (Chapter 9) following the chronology beginning with Clovis, followed by Folsom, and continuing with the Plainview complex (Irwin-Williams et al. 1973).

Although Folsom sites tend to be concentrated east of the Arizona-New Mexico border (Irwin-Williams 1979), fluted and Clovis-like points have been reported from a number of sites throughout Mexico, possibly extending as far south as Panama (Bird and Cooke 1978). Lorenzo and Mirambell (1999) report approximately 26 locations in Mexico where Clovis-type projectile points have been found. Although most are from surface sites and are undated, two fishtail points in association with a fluted point have been dated by radiocarbon and obsidian hydration to between 9,700–8,000 B.P. from a site in the state of Chiapas, bordering Guatemala in southern Mexico (Santamaria 1981:64 cited in Lorenzo and Mirambell 1999).

Projectile points have been found in direct association with mammoth remains at the Santa Isabel Iztapan site not far from Mexico City (Aveleyra Arroyo de Anda 1956; Aveleyra Arroyo de Anda and Maldonado-Koerdal 1953) (Figure 8.3). Although the projectile points are not typically Clovis nor are they fluted, they are similar to the three subgroups of Clovis points defined by Lorenzo and Mirambell (1999). The subgroups are typical pentagonal and concave-sided forms. Martinez del Rio (1952 paraphrased in Wheat 1971) theorized that the Santa Isabel mammoths may have been wounded by thrusting spears, later dying from loss of blood in a shallow lake where they may have sought refuge after being mortally wounded.

There are also several sites in Mexico that may document human association with extinct late Pleistocene animals. These sites are similar to other sites reported throughout North America that contain deposits of Ice Age mammal bone that has been modified in ways that might suggest human hunting or scavenging. Tocquilla, a site near Mexico City, has been partially excavated and contains the remains of several mammoths that have been preserved in situ (Figure 8.4). Many of the bones have been flaked and modified in ways similar to bones that have been worked by humans. A single radiocarbon date on mam-

Figure 8.3 Reconstruction of the Santa Isabel Iztapan mammoth kill site in the National Museum of Anthropology, Mexico City, Mexico. The numbers designate the locations where stone projectile points were discovered.

moth bone from this site of 11,100 ± 80 B.P. (OxA-7746) (Arroyo-Cabrales, personal communication 1998) suggests that it is contemporaneous with Clovis sites documented elsewhere in North America. As of 1998, no artifacts had been found in association with the mammoth bones at Tocuila.

Unlike classic Clovis sites from the Great Plains, there is little evidence for large mammal predation from most Western Fluted Point tradition sites. Pleistocene fauna and Western Fluted points have not been found in direct association in the Far West United States. However, at several locales around China Lake in the Mojave Desert, Emma Lou Davis (1975, 1978) has reported possible associations of extinct Pleistocene mammals from erosional contexts. However, it has not been possible to firmly establish that the faunal remains and artifacts deposited at the same time. Many archeologists regard all reported archeological associations of fluted projectile points with extinct fauna from the Great Basin as equivocal (Beck and Jones 1997:182). With the possible exception of the problematic association of humans and dwarf mammoths on the Channel Islands off the coast of southern California (Orr and Berger 1966), there is no firm evidence of humans hunting extinct Pleistocene species in the northern sector of the Far West.

Toward the end of the Pleistocene, between 13,000–10,500 B.P., many of the large deep lakes in the Far West began to dry up because evaporation exceeded

Figure 8.4 Paleontologists Russ Graham (right) and Jaquien Arroyo examine mammoth remains at Tocquilla, Mexico, 1998.

rainfall. This process was not uniform throughout the region. Conditions varied between lakes, and water levels fluctuated within specific lakes. The greatest number of fluted points seems to be associated with these rapidly disappearing bodies of water. The largest concentrations of fluted projectile points are reportedly associated with ancient shorelines. There may have been a brief period of increased precipitation about 11,000 B.P. (Beck and Jones 1997:170). At several sites, including the Dietz site in Oregon (Willig 1989, 1996), Western Fluted Point tradition occupations have been discovered on dry lake shorelines that are lower than those occupied by later Western Stemmed Point tradition and Archaic period occupations.

The ecological settings of many Western Fluted Point tradition sites indicate that lake-marsh margins and associated streams were preferred subsistence locales (Willig 1996). This suggests that the economy of the people who made and used fluted points was based on exploitation of resources, such as fish, waterfowl, and plants, as well as large and small mammals. This adaptation is viewed by Willig (1996) as unique to the Western Fluted Point tradition because it de-emphasized big game hunting more characteristic of many Clovis sites in the western Great Plains. Willig (1989, 1990, 1991, 1996) suggests that early Western Fluted Point tradition people were primarily general foragers rather than big game hunters.

Beaton (1991b) describes an early cultural occupation dated by a ^{14}C determination of 11,450 ± 340 B.P. (Beta 39545) from the lowest levels of a rockshelter adjacent to Pleistocene Tulare Lake near the California-Oregon border. Faunal remains associated with this occupation include fish, birds (probably waterfowl), and mammals. Preliminary analysis suggests that the economic emphasis was on the periodic taking of fish and waterfowl by people foraging along the lakeshores. However, it is not clear which lithic tradition is associated with this early site.

Although caves and rockshelters were used by people who made and used fluted points, their utilization appears to be more a matter of "availability rather than preference" (Wheat 1971:23). Perishable artifacts have been found at Fishbone Cave in western Nevada (Orr 1956). The well-preserved skin of a young pelican, a piece of fine netting, six basketry fragments, several pieces of cordage, and a piece of matting dating to circa 11,500–11,000 B.P. were found associated with human remains (Chapter 5). This rare find demonstrates that early people had a rich organic material culture including woven mats, baskets, and bags. However, in the absence of diagnostic projectile points, it is impossible to ascribe this occupation to a specific lithic tradition.

There is increasing evidence for a possible coastal aspect of the Western Fluted Point tradition. Matson and Coupland (1995:67) suggest that Clovis people also used the coast because the Richie-Roberts Clovis Cache near Wenatchee, Washington is less than 150 km (93 mi) from the ocean. Fluted points have also been reported from coastal sites in California. One point is reported from Mendocino County (Simons et al. 1985); another was recovered near Santa Barbara (Erlandson et al. 1987). An isolated find has been reported from central Baja California near a spring draining toward the west coast (Aschmann 1952).

Although it is possible that people associated with fluted points made and used watercraft and were adapted to a maritime way of life, there is no firm archeological evidence to support this hypothesis. Rising sea level has inundated the late Pleistocene shoreline along most of the west coast of North America. If people had been living along the coast at that time, most archeological sites documenting that occupation are now under water. Human remains from Arlington Springs on Santa Rosa Island off the coast of southern California date to circa 11,000 B.P. This provides evidence for one of the oldest reliably dated humans in North America (see Channel Islands, Chapter 3; and Arlington Man, Chapter 5). Santa Rosa Island was not connected to mainland North America during the last Ice Age (Erlandson 1994:183; Moratto 1984). The ^{14}C age for Arlington Man is within the age range of fluted point sites elsewhere in North America. Although it is possible that Arlington Man may be associated with this technological tradition, fluted points have not been found at this site.

Jon Erlandson (1994) discusses archeological research along the California coast documenting early occupation beginning by at least 10,500 B.P. Coastal occupation continues well into the middle Holocene based on analysis of faunal remains from several sites. These sites have very few flaked stone tools, and it appears that shellfish constitute a major proportion of the diet (Erlandson 1994). Minimal lithic technology and poor organic preservation make these sites difficult to detect, classify, and interpret.

Fitzgerald and Jones (1998) have reported a coastal habitation site from central California dated to circa 10,500 B.P. Farther south, Erlandson (1994; Erlandson and Moss 1996; Erlandson et al. 1998) document sites off the coast of southern California. An occupation at Daisy Cave on San Miguel is characterized by a shell midden dated to circa 9,100 B.P. (Figure 8.5). About 40–45 cm (16–18 inches) below this level, there is evidence of an earlier, less extensive occupation dating to about 10,400 B.P. Another site, CA-SRI-6, also documents maritime subsistence by 9,300 B.P. on Santa Rosa Island (Erlandson et al. 1998).

The obvious maritime focus of many of these early sites demonstrates that people had already adapted to coastal environments when the sea level began to stabilize at the end of the Pleistocene. About 10,000 B.P. when people in the Great Basin and western California were making an important subsistence shift toward plant collection, the people along the California coast were already adjusted to a similar semisedentary way of life based on stable economic resources of shellfish and other marine foods.

Figure 8.5 Excavations at Daisy Cave, San Miguel Island, California. (Photograph courtesy of Jon Erlandson.)

Western Stemmed Point Tradition (11,000–7,000 B.P.)

Roy Carlson (1983) lumps a variety of projectile point types with stems and constricting sides toward the base into what he terms the Western Stemmed Point tradition. Charlotte Beck and George Jones (1988) have demonstrated that much of the variation among Western Stemmed points results from resharpening points and from reducing bifaces during the manufacturing process. This tradition is not only characterized by a wide variety of stemmed and shouldered stone projectile points, but also includes stone crescents; ovoid, domed, and keeled scrapers; gravers; and drills. The chipped-stone crescents characteristic of the Great Basin have not been found farther north than the Columbia Plateau (Carlson 1988:320). The function of these curious artifacts remains unknown. There appears to be no clearly defined and dated stratigraphic sequence that chronologically orders the variety of constricting-base, shouldered, and stemmed forms (Musil 1988:382; Willig and Aikens 1988).

Although the coastal archeological data are sketchy along the west coast south of the Strait of Juan de Fuca, beginning by at least 8,500 B.P. the Old Cordilleran tradition appears to extend along the west coast of North America from Vancouver Island in the north to the area of the California/Oregon border (Matson and Coupland 1995). Lithic artifacts include leaf-shaped projectile points and bifaces, contracting stem points, and a high percentages of cobble tools and flakes, unifacial and bifacial choppers and chopping tools, scraper planes, hammer stones, stone abraders, and miscellaneous fragments of ground stone. Organic artifacts recovered from the Glenrose Cannery site include antler wedges, an antler punch, a nondetachable barbed-bone projectile point, a tooth pendant, and several bone awls (Matson and Coupland 1995:70–73). Faunal remains consist of an interesting blend of terrestrial as well as marine mammals and include: elk, deer, canid, and harbor seal. In spite of the coastal setting, terrestrial mammals (elk and deer) were the most abundant. The primary types of fish taken at Glenrose were salmon, sturgeon, flatfish, eulachon, and sticklebacks indicating a spring and early summer occupation. Shellfish, primarily bay mussels, were also harvested in large numbers (Matson and Coupland 1995:73–74).

The Mostin site is located along an inland stream flowing into Clear Lake in northern California. In addition to containing several human burials (Chapter 5), the site also provides important evidence about the lives of early people in the Far West. Stratum 5 at the site was 5.3 m (17 ft) below the valley floor and consisted of a black layer 20–30 cm (8–12 inches) thick containing obsidian flakes and tools, mammal bones, what are probably poorly preserved fish and bird bones, charcoal, and fragments of freshwater shells. Charcoal from this level was radiocarbon dated to 11,250 ± 240 B.P. (UCLA-2165) (Kaufman 1980:102). However, the accuracy of the radiocarbon dates from this site have been questioned, and they possibly could be several thousand years too old as a result of contamination by older carbon transported by ground water (Fredrickson and White 1988).

The stone tools from the Mostin site are difficult to compare with those from other sites dating to about the same time period. Projectile point forms include leaf-shaped and ovate bipointed types and points with constricting edges. Many of the projectile points have straight or convex bases. This may suggest that the inhabitants of the site used bifacial projectile points and knives more similar in form to those of the Pacific Northwest and practiced an inland subsistence pattern based on hunting and foraging. Presuming the dating of the site is correct, the very early occurrence of ground-stone pestles and a possible mano associated with burial 1978-1 (Chapter 5) implies processing seeds and other foods may have been important economic activities.

The Borax Lake site is located approximately 150 km (93 mi) north of San Francisco. Fluted projectile points and crescents have been found around the lakeshore, suggesting that the people who made these artifacts were economically focused toward the resources of the lake, rather than hunting big game. Based on an analysis of the local geology and obsidian hydration studies, Meighan and Haynes (1970) suggested that the fluted points dated between 12,000–10,000 B.P. They were further able to compare the hydration thickness of the obsidian from which the fluted points were made with that of the stemmed points also found on the margins of Borax Lake. Based on their analysis, the hydration rim thicknesses were generally greater for the fluted points, suggesting that they may be older.

Western Fluted points and Lake Mohave projectile points have also been recovered from several areas along the southern shore of Tulare Lake, a large shallow lake and marshland (Wallace and Riddell 1988). Tulare Lake is located in central California's San Joaquin Valley between San Francisco and Los Angeles. Lake Mohave points are leaf-shaped projectile points with constricting bases, which are believed to be associated with flaked-stone crescents. At nearby Buena Vista Lake, what appears to be Lake Mohave/San Dieguito type artifacts were recovered associated with the remains of shellfish, birds, turtles, fish, and deer (Fredrickson and Grossman 1977) suggesting a generalized foraging economy. Similarities with San Dieguito points and specimens from Buena Vista Lake suggest that Lake Mohave-type artifacts may be younger than the Clovis-like points and possibly date between 10,000–8,000 B.P. (Wallace and Riddell 1988).

If the Western Stemmed Point tradition evolved from the Western Fluted Point tradition, there should be a period of time when both stemmed and fluted points were in use. It would be expected that people in areas remote from the center of change would still be using fluted points after others had already begun making stemmed points (Carlson 1988:321). Fluted points were still in use circa

10,500 B.P. in the more northerly areas of British Columbia and nearby Alberta, Canada, at the same time stemmed points were being manufactured and used at Marmes Rockshelter and other sites farther to the south (Carlson 1988; Fedje 1996; Fladmark et al. 1988; Rice 1972; Wilson 1996). A number of undated projectile point types that could be typologically intermediate between the Western Fluted Point tradition and Western Stemmed Point tradition have been found throughout the Far West (Willig and Aikens 1988:21). The obsidian hydration and very limited ^{14}C data are confusing and in some cases contradictory. Additional research is necessary to firmly resolve this problem.

The Cooper's Ferry site is located along the lower Salmon River near Grangeville, Idaho. Although the site has been known for some time, it has recently been reinvestigated by Loren Davis who reports discovering a pit containing a cache of artifacts, including stemmed points, from the lowest stratigraphic levels at the site. Two AMS radiocarbon dates, one run on bone and another on charcoal dated 12,020 ±170 B.P. (Beta 114806) and 11,370 ± 70 B.P. (Beta 224949), respectively (Wisner 1998:4–5). However, another radiocarbon date derived from charcoal apparently collected from the same stratigraphic level dates to circa 7,300 (no lab number reported) (Wisner 1998:5). If the early dates from this site accurately date the projectile points, this would indicate that the early Western Stemmed points predate fluted points in the region.

The origins of the Western Stemmed Point tradition are unclear. Carlson (1983:82) suggests that the tradition could have been derived from Asia and draws tentative comparisons to the Ushki Lake site, Level VII, where stemmed points have been recovered and controversially ^{14}C dated to circa 14,000 B.P. (see Chapter 3). However, current data suggest that early microblade assemblages containing constricting-based bifaces first appear in eastern Beringia circa 10,500 B.P. If this preliminary dating withstands the test of time, a transition to stemmed points in the Far West may precede the introduction of constricting-based projectile points in eastern Beringia by several hundred years. This might suggest that this hafting technique is an independent New World innovation, possibly originating in the Great Basin where experimentation may have led to a wide variety of forms.

People of the Western Stemmed Point tradition continued to live around the drying lakes throughout much of the Far West. Adaptation to the lakes and their resources is clearly documented by artifacts and coprolites (fossil feces) associated with human burials (see Chapter 5) in the Great Basin. The best examples of the organic material culture are preserved in the dry caves along the margins of these lakes. These sites contain rare and important discoveries that provide unique insights into the lives and aesthetics of early Americans living in the Far West.

People living around these drying lakes made diamond-plaited matting that has been found at Grimes Burial Shelter associated with a burial dating to circa 9,500 B.P. and at Spirit Cave dating to circa 9,400–9,300 B.P. At Spirit Cave, a metate, a small twined bag of split tules, and a close twined bag of hemp all dating to circa 9,000 B.P. were found in association with human cremations. Further evidence of adaptation to lake and marsh environments has been documented by Tuohy (1988:212). From the north end of Pyramid Lake, near Reno, Nevada, he reports finding two-ply sagebrush fishing line dated to 9,660 ± 170 B.P. (GX-13744). Associated organic artifacts included fragments of two twined baskets and one piece of a compound bone fishhook.

Based on excavation at Fort Rock Cave, where fiber sandals dated to circa 9,000 B.P. were recovered, Cressman (1981:28) suggested that almost no leather clothing was worn in the northern Great Basin during this time. However, widespread use of tailored skin clothing prior to and after this time is suggested by the occurrence of eyed bone needles recovered from the Shoup Rockshelters in Idaho (Swanson and Sneed 1966), Lind Coulee in eastern Washington (Daugherty 1956; Irwin and Moody 1978), and the Buhl burial in Idaho (Green et al. 1998). At Spirit Cave, there is evidence of leather in the form of three-piece leather moccasins, puckered around the toes and sides, hair side out, circa 9,400 B.P. These moccasins were sewn with two-ply fiber cordage, rather than sinew or leather (Tuohy and Dansie 1997b).

Manos and metates appear in the archeological record before 10,000 B.P. A metate is a large, flat stone upon which seeds are placed and ground using a mano, which is a grinding stone held in the hands. These artifacts generally indicate seed collecting and processing. They signal a major economic shift toward reliance on plant products for food. The earliest specimens are reported from Fort Rock Cave in the northern Great Basin where they are believed to date slightly older than 10,000 B.P. At Danger Cave, grinding stones and pickleweed chaff first appear in Level II, which is dated to circa 9,800 B.P.(Jennings 1957). At Hogup Cave, slab metate fragments were recovered from Stratum I dated to circa 8,400 B.P., and pickleweed chaff and pollen were recovered from human coprolites (Aikens 1970).

Jesse Jennings attempted to provide unity to many of these sites by advancing the concept of Desert Culture (Jennings 1964:152–153), which he later came to realize was a western expression of the American Archaic stage (Jennings 1978b:29). The Archaic stage is generally considered a level of economic, social, and political development consisting of band-size social units depending on scheduled, seminomadic foraging. It is viewed by many North American archeologists as a stage of cultural development immediately following the Paleoindian stage, which is also characterized by band-level social organization and an economy based primarily on big game hunting and gathering. Stones for grinding seeds into flour are important technological innovations necessary for the development of agriculture, and it is significant that their first widespread appearance in North America is in the Far West.

San Dieguito/Sulphur Spring Complexes (10,000–8,000 B.P.)

The San Dieguito complex was defined by Claude N. Warren (1967) to include a number of regional archeological assemblages throughout the area of southern Nevada and southern California and probably extending into northwestern Mexico. Lithic artifacts that characterize the San Dieguito complex are leaf-shaped knives, small leaf-shaped projectile points, stemmed and shouldered projectile points, ovoid large domed and rectangular end and side scrapers, engraving tools, and crescents (Warren 1967:177). Most San Dieguito sites have been reported from mesas and ridges where they have been eroded and lack midden material. Other site locales include lake terraces, the margins of stream and drainage channels, and near water holes. In addition to interior sites, San Dieguito sites are also documented along the southern California coast.

Three radiocarbon determinations from the C. W. Harris site (a type site for the San Dieguito complex) ranging between circa 9,000–8,500 B.P., coupled with geologic evidence, and ^{14}C dates from other San Dieguito sites, led Warren (1967:179–180) to determine that the San Dieguito complex spans the interval of 10,000–8,000 B.P. However, no coastal sites ascribed to the San Dieguito complex are older than about 9,000 B.P. (Erlandson 1994:44).

The origins of the San Dieguito complex are obscure. Erlandson (1994:45) offers two hypotheses regarding the coastal aspect: (1) that coastal San Dieguito adaptations developed from interior San Dieguito populations, and (2) that the coastal San Dieguito complex derived from earlier late Pleistocene coastal populations or coastal migration. As yet, there is not enough archeological data to resolve these questions, although the occurrence of crescents commonly associated with the Western Stemmed Point tradition to the north might suggest inland ties.

At Ventana Cave, located in southern Arizona, Emil Haury (1950) discovered the remains of contemporary and extinct fauna in association with artifactual remains that he called the Ventana complex. The Ventana lithic assemblage consisted of projectile points, a hammer stone, a hand stone, knives, scrapers, gravers, choppers, and planes. Haury (1950:531–532) viewed the cave as a meeting ground where there was a blending between the San Dieguito complex from the Far West with the Folsom complex farther east. At that time, the Folsom complex appeared to be contemporaneous with the earlier phase of the San Dieguito complex. The Ventana assemblage only contained two projectile points. The correlation to Clovis/Folsom points was based primarily on only one of them that resembled

Folsom points in general outline but not in manufacturing technique (Haury and Hayden cited in Haury 1975:v). The occurrence of marine shells in the same stratigraphic unit with the Ventana complex and similarity of the artifacts to those of the San Dieguito complex suggested greater affinity to the San Dieguito complex than to the Folsom complex.

Archeologist E. B. Sayles, working with geologist Ernst Antevs, defined Cochise culture in the area of Whitewater Draw in southern Arizona. Cochise culture was interpreted by them to be the predecessor of later regional sedentary ceramic-making people (Sayles and Antevs 1941). Cochise culture was divided into three phases; the oldest was the Sulphur Spring phase. Sayles described the Sulphur Spring phase as being characterized by milling stones, percussion flaked-stone tools, scrapers, axes, and hammer stones (Sayles and Antevs 1941: 12–13).

Faunal remains associated with the artifacts from Whitewater Draw included bison, pronghorn antelope, coyote, and extinct Pleistocene species including mammoth, horse, and dire wolf. Many of the bones appeared to have been burned and fractured, presumably to extract the marrow. Antevs estimated the age of the Sulphur Spring stage to be older than 10,000 B.P. based on the association of the artifacts with Pleistocene fauna, its relative position within the regional stratigraphy, and the presumed geologic age of the deposits from which the artifacts were recovered (Sayles and Antevs 1941:46–48).

For many years, the Sulphur Spring phase of Cochise culture was viewed as a troubling anomaly because Pleistocene fauna were associated with milling stones. Some archeologists (Berry and Berry 1986) refute the existence of a Sulphur Spring phase. The milling stones suggest a strong emphasis on seed gathering and grinding, which is characteristic of later periods. The work of Sayles and Antevs began in 1936 and was published in 1941, before the discovery and development of radiocarbon dating. Consequently, they were forced to rely on faunal associations and geologic and paleoenvironmental correlations.

Whitewater Draw was subsequently reanalyzed by Michael Waters (1986a). Waters discovered that the bones of mammoth, horse, camel, and dire wolf had been eroded from older sediments and redeposited along with the younger Sulphur Spring phase artifacts. Even though the deposits contained the remains of extinct Ice Age animals, they dated to between 10,400–7,000 B.P. This demonstrated that the Sulphur Spring phase of Cochise culture was more recent than the Clovis and Folsom complexes. Excavations at the Lehner site (Haynes 1982) revealed what is possibly a Cochise occupation that is stratigraphically above the Clovis level. This discovery supports Waters' research conclusion, and Cochise culture is now recognized as dating to the early Holocene.

Some researchers believe that the early San Dieguito complex is similar to the Ventana complex (Hayden 1976; Rogers 1958, 1966) and that there is also a strong relationship to the Sulphur Spring phase (Irwin-Williams 1979; Waters 1986a). Waters (1986a:62) postulated that the absence of ground stone in early San Dieguito sites could result from a relative lack of seeds and plant products because there was less local precipitation. Greater emphasis on grinding, as indicated by grinding stones used during the Sulphur Spring phase, could be a local variation resulting from greater precipitation.

Regardless of the cultural and economic relationships between these complexes, there does appear to be chronological agreement that beginning about 10,000 B.P. San Dieguito, Ventana, and Sulphur Spring complex people practiced generalized foraging and possessed a lithic tool kit that de-emphasized the manufacture of bifacial projectile points. These complexes appear to rely on a wide array of local resources depending on availability. The ephemeral nature of most of these sites suggests that they represent the remains of relatively small, mobile human groups with a foraging-based economy.

Although the archeological record in northern Mexico is not clear, it is probable that San Dieguito/Sulphur Spring complexes occur throughout the region following Clovis times. The general foraging pattern of these cultures, which appears to emphasize seed collection and grinding, may have provided the foundation upon which subsequent plant domestication was developed, ultimately giving rise to the complex societies of Mesoamerica.

However, Michael Moseley (1975; Moseley and Feldman 1988) theorizes that in South America the roots of Andean civilization are derived from rich marine resources that enabled humans to live in sedentary settlements. Maritime resources were so plentiful that large sedentary populations could be supported. This in turn led to complex social organization that found expression in the design and construction of monumental architecture and other public works. This hypothesis has been modified to suggest that maritime adaptations may also explain the origins of American plant domestication (Stothert 1998). Succinctly stated, horticulture may have its origins in sedentary coastal settlements where people would have had the opportunity to plant, care for, and protect plants growing adjacent to settlements. In other words, sedentism resulting from maritime adaptation may have led to plant domestication rather than plant domestication ultimately leading to sedentism.

Summary

The very early archeological data from Mexico and the Far West remain somewhat sketchy, and additional research is desperately needed. Although some researchers favor the hypothesis that the first settlement of Far West North America was by people who manufactured and used fluted projectile points, this remains unclear (Figure 8.6). Some sites suggest that some people were using bi-

pointed and stemmed projectile points at the same time others were manufacturing and using fluted points. Perhaps, like the archeology of Alaska and
the Pacific Northwest, co-traditions existed. The data may indicate that people
throughout this vast region made and used both stemmed and fluted projectile
points and other types of tools during the same time period. Regardless of
the technology employed, the limited evidence suggests that people practiced
a generalized foraging economy, exploiting a wide variety of locally available
plants, animals, and fish depending upon the area in which they lived.

Unlike the Clovis complex in the Great Plains that is commonly associated with
Pleistocene mammals, the Western Fluted Point tradition displays greater typological variation and possibly greater adaptation to foraging. In many respects, the
typological variability exhibited by fluted projectile points from the Far West is
similar to that demonstrated by specimens from eastern Beringia. This might suggest that, like the northern specimens, they are somewhat younger than they are

Figure 8.6 Fluted projectile
points from the Zacoalco
Basin, Jalisco Province,
Mexico. (Line drawings
courtesy of Frederico
Solorzano.)

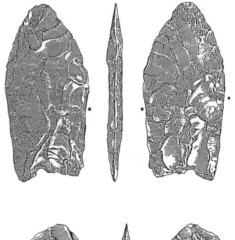

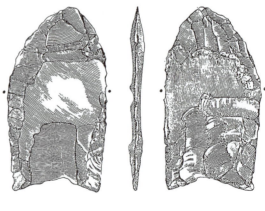

on the Plains. However, this could also be attributed to a more sedentary life on the margins of lakes and rivers, or possibly other factors.

The origins of the Western Stemmed Point tradition remain unclear. It appears to be too old to have been derived from the microblade traditions to the north, where tapering, or stemmed bifaces first appear about 10,500 B.P. The Western Stemmed points also appear to predate similar examples from the Great Plains. A possibility that needs to be seriously considered is that the Western Stemmed Point tradition may be derived from an earlier, yet poorly defined, phase of the Old Cordilleran/Pebble Tool traditions of the Northwest Coast. Additional research is required to explain its origins and subsequent development.

As the climate began to change at the end of the last Ice Age, aridity increased and lakes continued to dry up. Although the evidence remains unclear, the Western Stemmed Point tradition may be contemporaneous with the Western Fluted Point tradition in the Great Basin. Although it has been suggested that a change in projectile point types from the Western Fluted Point tradition to Western Stemmed Point tradition in the Great Basin began about 11,000 B.P., the practice of fluting projectile points may have persisted longer in some areas. The extensive use of manos and metates in the Western Stemmed Point tradition indicates increased reliance on seed collecting and processing.

In southern California, southern Arizona, and probably much of Mexico, there seems to have been less emphasis on lithic projectile points and more emphasis on collecting plant products and seed grinding. However, mammoth hunting is documented in Arizona and Mexico. Along the California coast, there appears to be a well-documented coastal adaptation beginning by at least 10,500 B.P., and possibly earlier.

Two hypotheses have emerged, both of which suggest that the origins of American agriculture may have its roots in the early lifeways of people living in the Far West. One suggests that collection of seeds and a greater reliance on plant products that began in the Far West at the end of the last Ice Age led to plant domestication. The other hypothesis theorizes that the abundant resources of the sea enabled coastal people to be sedentary. Sedentism enabled them to nurture and protect plants, thus making plant domestication possible.

9 The Great Plains Prior to 8,000 B.P.

Introduction

Some archeologists refer to Great Plains archeology as projectile point archeology because so much attention has been devoted to making distinctions between projectile point types. To an outsider, the regional nomenclature and distinctions between projectile point types can be confusing. It is a matter of regional pride that avocational archeologists can date and classify projectile points by the multitude of types. Some projectile point types have been named after land owners and collectors who originally reported them to archeologists. In the state of Texas, for example, more than 50 different point types are recognized by local collectors and professionals.

The regional proliferation of "traditions" and "complexes" may result in part from an overemphasis on projectile point types that may not mark the beginning or end of a tradition or complex. A change in projectile point type does not necessarily correspond to a change in economy and/or other elements of material culture. Dennis Stanford (1999) suggests that Great Plains archeology may also be complicated by an assumption that all regional complexes and traditions must be ordered in a unilinear sequence while ignoring the possibility that co-traditions or co-complexes may exist. In eastern Beringia, regional adaptations were already well underway by 11,000–10,000 B.P., and there is little reason to assume that similar processes were not occurring on the Great Plains as well.

Viewed from a continental perspective, this is microclassification that over emphasizes typology and tends to undermine its usefulness as a horizon marker and indicator of function. If artifact typology is to be effectively used to address archeological problems over a broad geographic region, the artifacts must reflect a collective mental template shared by members of the society who repeatedly produce similar artifacts over a broad geographic area during a specific interval of time. In other words, point types must be an integral part of economic systems and lifeways in keeping with the archeological concepts of tradition and complex.

To simplify and unify the profusion of point types, the Paleoindian archeology of the western Great Plains is commonly divided into two traditions and several complexes. The Paleoindian tradition includes the Clovis complex (11,500–10,900 B.P.) and Folsom complex (10,900–10,200 B.P.) (Frison 1991; Haynes 1992; Stanford 1999). The Goshen complex is characterized by unfluted projectile points that are morphologically similar to Clovis and Folsom points and spans the same period of time. The Plano tradition 10,200–8,000 B.P. encompasses the Plainview complex in the southern Great Plains, as well as the Agate Basin, Hell Gap, and Cody complexes in the northern Great Plains (Figure 9.1). While a variety of other complexes and cultures are used in the literature, for the purposes of clarity, this chapter will attempt to follow the above terminology whenever possible.

Figure 9.1
Diagnostic projectile point types found on the Great Plains: (a) Clovis, (b) Folsom, (c) Plainview, (d) Agate Basin, (e) Hell Gap, and (f) Cody. (Graphic by Eric Parrish.)

(a)

(b)

(c)

(d)

(e)

(f)

0   5CM

Clovis Complex (circa 11,500–10,900 B.P.)

The Clovis complex assumes its name from the location of the type site, Blackwater Draw, near Clovis, New Mexico. It was at Blackwater Draw that distinctive Clovis stone projectile points (Figure 9.2) were documented firmly associated with mammoth remains. These distinctive fluted projectile points are lanceolate in form with concave bases and are edge ground near the base to facilitate hafting. These projectile points were used to tip atlatl darts. It has been demonstrated repeatedly that this weapon system was capable of killing mammoths and that Clovis tools were adequate to dismember and butcher them (Frison 1976, 1989, 1991; Stanford, Bonnichsen, and Morlan 1981). Because there is so little physical evidence of atlatls preserved in the archeological record, some archeologists have questioned whether atlatls were used by Clovis and other Paleoindian hunters. However, Hutchings (1997) has demonstrated its use by Paleoindian hunters based on analysis of projectile point fracture patterns (see Chapter 6).

Other artifact types are frequently associated with the Clovis complex. Although organic artifacts are rare, they include shaft wrenches, bone and ivory foreshafts, and beveled based bone points. Stone artifacts are better preserved and more common and include large thin bifaces, large blades struck from true blade cores, blade cores, end and side scrapers, spokeshaves, spurred gravers, a variety

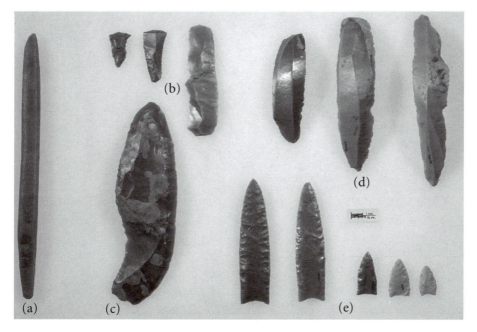

Figure 9.2 Diagnostic Clovis artifact types: (a) bone foreshaft, (b) scrapers, (c) knife, (d) blades, and (e) projectile points. (Photograph courtesy of Dennis Stanford.)

retouched flakes, flake cores, hammer stones, and waste flakes. End scrapers are frequently made from blades or blade fragments. Blades frequently exhibit retouch suggesting their use as knives and subsequent reshaping into other tools. Clovis people valued high-quality glassy stone as raw material from which to manufacture their artifacts. High-quality lithic raw material was traded over vast areas. Fluted projectile points similar to those found on the Great Plains have been reported from Mexico (LeTourneau 1995) and as far north as Alberta and eastern British Columbia, Canada (Fladmark et al. 1988; Gryba 1985).

Clovis is the only firmly documented New World archeological complex positively associated with mammoth procurement. However, only about twelve archeological sites have been reported where Clovis projectile points are associated with the bones of these large extinct elephant-like creatures (G. Haynes 1991:197–197, 206). At many other sites, the association of humans with mammoth remains has not been firmly established. Although there is no doubt that some Clovis people hunted mammoth and possibly mastodon, current research suggests that these rather spectacular kill sites are probably not typical of Clovis culture. Important Clovis sites are illustrated in Figure 9.3.

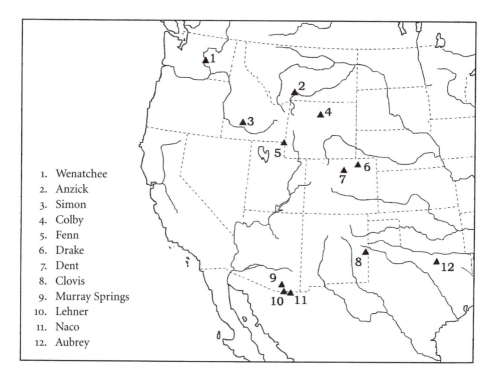

1. Wenatchee
2. Anzick
3. Simon
4. Colby
5. Fenn
6. Drake
7. Dent
8. Clovis
9. Murray Springs
10. Lehner
11. Naco
12. Aubrey

Figure 9.3 Map depicting the location of significant Clovis sites. (Graphic by Eric Parrish.)

Many Paleoindian sites are situated in close proximity to water sources (Wheat 1971). However, this general observation does not encompass all sites, and there are notable exceptions, such as the Kincaid Rockshelter in Texas (Collins et al. 1989) and the Colby site in northern Wyoming (Frison and Todd 1986). Except for the Colby site, mammoth kill sites appear to be associated with springs. It is presumed that animals were ambushed when they came to drink and feed on vegetation around the water source. It is also possible in some instances that animals wounded elsewhere eventually died at watering holes. At both Blackwater Draw, New Mexico and the Lehner site in Arizona, bison bones were recovered along with mammoth remains.

At the Dent site in Colorado, three Clovis points were found associated with the remains of 11 mammoth cows and one mammoth bull (Figgens 1933; Wormington 1957). It has been suggested that the animals may have been driven over a bluff and that the mammoths that were not killed in the fall from the bluff were dispatched with Clovis points and stunned with boulders (Haynes 1966). Other hypotheses have also been suggested to explain the site. For example, the projectile points may result from animals that had been wounded and escaped from previous hunts, or the animals may have drowned in the adjacent river and carcasses may have been scavenged by humans. Many of the skeletons remained articulated or semiarticulated.

At Blackwater Draw, six mammoths were taken, probably ambushed while coming to the spring for water (Sellards 1952; Warnica 1966). At the Naco site located in southern Arizona, an articulated mammoth skeleton missing the hind legs, pelvic girdle, and lumbar vertebrae was found with eight Clovis points (Haury 1953; Wormington 1957). One point was found at the base of the skull, and another on the atlas vertebra could have severed the spinal column. One point was near the left scapula, and two others were wedged between ribs. At the Murray Springs site, which is also located in Arizona, the remains of a young female mammoth were recovered, and only two limbs were partially disarticulated (C. V. Haynes 1991:438–39). Thirteen Clovis points were recovered from the Lehner site, which contained a large bone bed and two associated hearths. In addition to mammoth remains, the bones of tapir, bison, and horse were also recovered; however, it is not certain that all the faunal remains result from the cultural occupation.

The Colby site in northern Wyoming is not associated with a water source (Frison and Todd 1986). At the Colby site, the left front-quarter was removed from the mammoth carcass and placed on the arroyo bank. The meat and bones were then covered with long bones of other animals that had been killed earlier. Frison (1990:103) hypothesizes that the cache was then covered with semifrozen slush that froze and protected it from scavengers and decomposition.

Although this cache was never opened by the people who created it, a second one located nearby was reopened by Clovis people.

The probocideans (mammoth and mastodon) may not have been the primary economic foundation of the Clovis complex. However, there can be little doubt that when one or more mammoths were killed, there was an immediate food surplus. Mammoth kill sites, such as Blackwater Draw, Murray Springs, and Colby, are characterized by mammoth bones in partial articulation. Many of the bones have not been broken and do not have butchering marks. This demonstrates that animals were not completely butchered, and probably only portions were consumed. This may be attributable to the shear volume of meat available and an inability to move or roll over such large carcasses after the animals were killed.

The Aubrey site is one of the most significant Clovis sites to be discovered in recent years (Ferring 1989, 1990, 1995). It is a deeply buried (7.5–9 m [25–30 ft] below the surface) campsite containing well-preserved faunal remains, and the site has been professionally excavated and analyzed. Located in north-central Texas on the upper Elm Fork of the Trinity River, the site was attractive because of a spring pool that was formed in an older cutoff river channel. The site is only partially excavated, and as of 1998, the analysis was not yet complete. It is not possible to ascertain with certainty whether all of the animal remains found at the site result from human activity or if some might result from natural mortality of animals that happened to die near the spring. The following species have been reported: ground sloth, bison, white-tailed deer, ground squirrel, bog lemming, muskrat, several species of rabbits, fishes, turtles, and birds.

Reid Ferring (1990, 1995) describes two Clovis complex camp areas (B and F) that have been excavated at the Aubrey site. Each area contains hearths, work areas, and faunal remains. Camp B contains more than 8,000 waste flakes, many of which were very small chips resulting from manufacturing bifaces and sharpening and repairing stone tools. The stone used to make the tools was from distant sources, the most common being Tecovas quartzite, probably from a source about 380 km (236 mi) west of the site. Stone tools included spurred end scrapers, a notched end scraper, a burin, and retouched flakes and blades. Fires were built directly on the ground surface. Based on evidence of burning and spatial proximity to the activity areas, large numbers of mammal bone appear to have been deposited by humans. Species that could be identified from Camp B include bison, deer, and turtle.

Camp F contains about 3,500 lithic artifacts, mostly waste flakes. Also found were two scraper fragments, two gravers, burin spalls, and a flake core, also of Tecovas quartzite. Faunal remains from Camp F include four partial mammoth or mastodon ribs. Based on the use of the same lithic sources for the manufacture of stone tools and the close stratigraphic position, Ferring (1995:

279) suggests that these two camps may have been occupied simultaneously or at very nearly the same time.

The reinvestigation of the Lewisville site (Chapter 3) also demonstrates the incredible economic diversity that characterized Clovis life. In addition to the remains of small mammals, Stanford (1995) reports egg shells, reptiles, amphibians, roasted mud dauber wasp nests, and hackberry seeds. At the Aubrey site, turtle procurement and processing is documented along with the use of other species including deer, rabbit, squirrel, and fish (Ferring 1995:280).

Although rare, tools presumably used to grind vegetal products have been recovered from early Paleoindian and Plano contexts, including Blackwater Draw (Warnica 1966), the Lime Creek site in Kansas (Davis 1962), and the Hell Gap site in Wyoming (Irwin 1968 cited in Wheat 1971). As additional evidence becomes available, the interpretation of Clovis people as generalized gatherers rather than big game specialists is becoming better understood. This diverse subsistence strategy is difficult to document because Clovis campsites might appear to be somewhat nondescript and ephemeral in the absence of proboscidean remains and Clovis projectile points. Furthermore, well-preserved Clovis camps are rare, and many are probably deeply buried. Although this would provide a favorable setting for interdisciplinary studies, it also makes discovery difficult and excavation time consuming and expensive.

While camps have been recognized adjacent to kill sites at Blackwater Draw (Hester 1972) and Murray Springs (C. V. Haynes 1991), these appear to have been occupied briefly during the kill and while some of the carcasses were being processed and consumed. Clovis band size is difficult to determine. It probably varied seasonally and over longer periods of time. Based on our limited knowledge of the archeological record and extrapolation from ethnographic studies, it is reasonable to postulate that bands may have fragmented into groups as small as a family or two during times of scarce resources. At specific locales where resources were abundant, it may have been possible for people to form aggregates possibly as large as 30 to 60 individuals.

Two types of caches of Clovis artifacts have been reported throughout western North America. One type is utilitarian, which contains tools and lithic raw material commonly associated with the tasks of everyday life. The nonutilitarian Clovis caches are hoards of magnificent artifacts manufactured from the finest known lithic materials. These caches must have represented extraordinary wealth at the time they were made. The quality of the lithic material is unsurpassed; it was exquisitely prepared and was transported long distances. Thus far, the most spectacular caches have been reported from the northern areas occupied by Clovis people, but it is difficult to determine the significance, if any, of this geographic distribution.

The first reported discovery of a Clovis cache was made in 1961 in south-central Idaho (Butler 1963; Butler and Fitzwater 1965; Woods and Titmus 1985) where 34 spectacular bifaces coated with ochre were found. This cache was named the Simon site. The exact origin of another spectacular find, the Fenn Cache, is not entirely clear, but the find was apparently made in the vicinity where the state boundaries of Idaho, Utah, and Wyoming converge. The cache contained 56 stone artifacts (Frison 1991; Wilke et al. 1991), including large bifacial flake cores and finished Clovis projectile points.

The Anzick site located in Montana appears to be the largest and most spectacular of all the caches discovered to date. According to Lahren and Bonnichsen (1974:186), the artifact assemblage includes fluted stone projectile points, ovoid and lanceolate bifaces, a blade, an end scraper, utilized flakes, and bone foreshafts. Lahren and Bonnichsen (1974) believe the foreshafts were associated with the Paleoindian tradition, Clovis period burial based on typological comparison of these artifacts with Clovis sites. A detailed analysis of many of the Anzick artifacts has been undertaken by Wilke et al. (1991). They use the lithic artifact assemblage to describe the stages of lithic reduction in producing Clovis stone tools. They also suggest that at least some of the distinctive "foreshafts" were handles for composite flint flakers.

Stanford and Jodry (1988) describe the Drake Cache (Figure 9.4), located in north-central Colorado. The cache contained a chert hammer stone and 13 Clovis projectile points. All 13 points are complete, sharp, and ready-to-use. Although six of the points had been used and resharpened, the remaining seven had never been used. No ochre or bone was found at the Drake Cache, but a few very small ivory fragments were recovered. Originally, Stanford and Jodry (1988) suggested that the Simon and Drake Caches might reflect Clovis mortuary practices similar to those at Anzick. However, they have reevaluated the Drake Cache and believe it most probably represents a cache of hunters' equipment (Stanford, personal communication 1998).

All five Clovis caches (including the Richie-Roberts Cache in Washington, Chapter 8) were found accidentally during various types of earth moving activities. While the caches could possibly be mortuary offerings, there is no definitive evidence of human burial in at least four cases. With the exceptions of the Drake and Richie-Roberts Cache, all are associated with red ochre. Both the Richie-Roberts and Anzick sites contained bone foreshafts. Although red ochre is commonly associated with Paleoindian period burials, it may have other significance or functions when used in conjunction with cached artifacts. It remains unclear whether these spectacular collections of artifacts were more than caches, or hoards, of valuable material stored for later use, or if they were possibly prepared as offerings in a spiritual or metaphysical context.

Caches that appear to be purely utilitarian are more common. Hofman (1995) reports the Busse Cache located in northwestern Kansas that he believes

Figure 9.4 Artifacts from the Drake Cache. (Photograph courtesy of Dennis Stanford.)

is Clovis in age based on typological comparison with other Clovis caches and sites. Although red ochre has been applied to one side of many of the artifacts, Hofman suggests it is different than other Clovis caches because many of the artifacts have been used and the cache contained broken tools that had been repaired and reused. This, coupled with the large volume of material weighing 7.4 kg (16.4 lbs), suggests that it may have been cached merely because it was too heavy to carry. Hofman (1995) suggests that the items may not have been cached for spiritual, ritual, or metaphysical reasons and that Clovis people intended to retrieve it later.

Earl Green (1963) describes a cache of Clovis blades at Blackwater Draw, and more recently additional examples have been recovered from the same site (Montgomery and Dickenson 1992). Mallouf (1994) reports another cache of what are almost certainly Clovis blades near the Cimarron River in Kansas. The cache contained 10 cores, 151 blades and flakes, and five unifacial tools all manufactured from water-worn cobbles of "agate," from the Alibates flint quarry in Texas. The weight of the assemblage, 20.5 kg (45.2 lbs), led Mallouf (1994:46) to suggest that it was unlikely that it had been transported by only one person. Young and Collins (1989) also report a cache of 14 Clovis blades from Navarro County in northeastern Texas. They note flake scars and nicked edges suggesting damage from use. These are also characteristic of the Clovis blades recovered from Blackwater Draw, suggesting that the blades may have been used as knives and cutting tools until broken or damaged and then served as cores from which subsequent artifacts, such as end scrapers, were manufactured.

C. Vance Haynes (1991) has hypothesized that there was a period of aridity at the end of Clovis times that he calls the Clovis drought. This is believed to have been a significant paleoclimatic event that may have contributed to the extinction of the mammoth and the demise of Clovis culture. The drought is believed to have begun circa 10,900 B.P. and ended circa 10,750 B.P. Its beginning is marked by a dramatic drop in the water table at a number of important Clovis sites, including Murray Springs, Blackwater Draw, Lange/Ferguson, Aubrey, and other sites. Clovis people resorted to digging wells at Blackwater Draw and the Aubrey sites. In the Far West, a pronounced drop in lake levels is documented at about this same time. Clovis artifacts and sites are found along shorelines associated with the lower lake levels. C. Vance Haynes (1991) theorizes that some species of Pleistocene fauna, particularly mammoths, were placed under extreme stress by the drought and became easy prey to Clovis hunters because the mammoths were forced to concentrate around the few remaining watering holes. He concludes that the combination of environmental factors (drought) and human predation were the cause for mammoth extinction in western North America. However, regional analysis of stratigraphy and fossils preserved in valleys and draws in the southern high Plains suggests that there is little evidence of drought in this area during the late Pleistocene and early Holocene (Holliday 1995:88–89).

What happened to Clovis people, their remarkable technology, and way of life? The transition to the following archeological complex, Folsom, appears to have happened rapidly, perhaps in less than a hundred years. There are not yet adequate data to fully and adequately explain the end of the Clovis lifeway on the Great Plains. One possibility is that environmental change coinciding with the extinction of mammoths quickly brought an end to the Clovis lifeway. Although the Folsom people that followed continued a general pattern of foraging supplemented by big game hunting, they began to place greater emphasis on bison hunting, often killing many animals in a single hunt.

Folsom Complex (circa 10,900–10,200 B.P.)

Throughout the North American Great Plains, the Clovis way of life and its distinctive lithic technology was replaced by Folsom. The hallmark of Folsom culture is the Folsom projectile point, which is recognized throughout the Americas for its unique design, exceptional workmanship, and the high-quality raw materials from which they are manufactured. Like their Clovis predecessors, Folsom flint knappers valued high-quality, fine grained, vitreous (glassy) lithic raw material from which to manufacture their tools. Many North American archeologists consider Folsom lithic technology to represent some of the finest examples of stone working known anywhere in the world. Frison (1991:50) describes the duration of Folsom culture in the northern Great Plains from circa 10,900–10,200 B.P. In a more recent chronostratigraphic analysis of the Lipscom and Waugh sites, Hofman (1995) has bracketed the age of Folsom occupations in the southern Great Plains to the same time period (10,900–10,200 B.P.).

The Folsom technological complex extends eastward from the Rocky Mountains across the Great Plains and from North Dakota southward to northern Mexico. There is no direct association of mammoth with Folsom artifacts, and it is clear that by Folsom times mammoth had become extinct. The primarily focus of the Folsom economy was bison hunting (Figure 9.5). The archeological evidence indicates that Folsom hunters commanded exceptional knowledge of bison behavior. Although other species were hunted, from Folsom times until the end of the Plano tradition, taking bison in mass-kill settings became the single most important subsistence strategy on the North American Great Plains.

Analysis and calibration of ^{14}C determinations from the Folsom and Clovis sites suggests that the replacement of Clovis by Folsom was rapid, possibly occurring within a period of a hundred years or less (Haynes et al. 1984; Taylor et al. 1996). This rapid change may explain why there is little evidence of the tech-

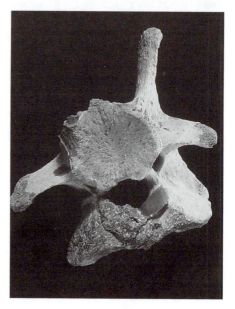

Figure 9.5 (*above*) Folsom projectile point resting between bison ribs, recovered from the Folsom type site, Folsom, New Mexico (Denver Museum of Natural History Photograph) and (*right*) Folsom projectile point lodged in a bison vertebra, from the Lindenmeier site, Colorado (Photograph on file, Denver Museum of Natural History, courtesy of the Smithsonian Institution).

nological transition from Clovis to Folsom. Given the rapidity of the change, it is likely that very few artifacts were manufactured, deposited, and preserved that document this technological change.

George Frison (1990, 1991) suggests that Goshen points may be transitional between Clovis and Folsom. Goshen points are typologically unfluted Clovis points and appear to date at some sites to the critical time period at the end of the Clovis and the beginning of the Folsom (probably between circa 10,900–

10,800 B.P.) (Frison 1990:104). Frison (1991:46) hypothesizes that because Goshen projectile points resemble later Plainview points, archeologists may have traditionally ascribed them to a later time period and, as a result, failed to recognize them as transitional between Clovis and Folsom.

Goshen points have been found stratigraphically below Folsom and above Clovis at the Hell Gap site in Wyoming (Irwin-Williams et al. 1973). Excavations and radiocarbon dating at the Mill Iron and Carter/Kerr-McGee sites in Wyoming also suggest that Goshen points may fit chronologically between Clovis and Folsom. However, it is difficult to understand why the technology would change from fluting (Clovis) to nonfluting (Goshen) and back to fluting (Folsom) (Frison 1990:106). Stanford (1999) expanded the definition of Goshen to include later Plainview points. In this combined category called Goshen/Plainview, the points are defined as generally exhibiting concave bases that have been thinned by well-developed flute-like pressure flakes from the base. Based on radiocarbon dates from several sites, Goshen points chronologically overlap with Clovis and by lumping Goshen with later Plainview points they can be seen to persist well into later Plano times (Stanford 1999). Stanford (1999) further suggests that there may be a north-south time transgressive distribution of Goshen/Plainview projectile points on the Great Plains. This hypothesis is supported by the early use of Agate Basin and Hell Gap projectile points rather than Goshen/Plainview points in the northern Plains and the later persistence of Goshen/Plainview in the southern Plains.

Rather than representing a distinct archeological complex, the Goshen/Plainview pattern of projectile point manufacture may simply suggest that some individuals did not make fluted projectile points during the same time period that others did. Individual members of society that shared the same way of life, and possibly even the same language, may have chosen to manufacture projectile points in slightly different ways than others. The differences are minor and all the points appear to have been manufactured to serve as end blades in the split-shaft hafting tradition. Goshen/Plainview type projectile points persist from Clovis to late Plano times and are possibly little more than unfluted variants of Clovis projectile points that persist into Plainview times.

It is presumed that Folsom people used a weapon system similar to that of their Clovis predecessors, except that the atlatl dart head was tipped with a Folsom point instead of the earlier Clovis point. Other lithic artifacts include characteristic channel flakes resulting from creating the flutes of the Folsom point, preforms, ultra-thin bifacial knives, flake knives, gravers, spokeshaves, drills, end and side scrapers, flakes, flake cores, choppers, abrading stones, various mineral pigments, and pigment grinding stones. Large bifaces probably served as flake cores from which large thin flakes were struck to manufacture Folsom points (Hofman 1992; Stanford and Broilo 1981).

Folsom people ushered in a new era where the primary economic focus was bison hunting. They skillfully employed the use of natural topographic features to entrap these animals in large numbers, and this strategy lay the foundation for much larger bison kills that were to follow in later times. On the relatively flat plains, arroyo headcuts provide ideal ambush sites. Because the Great Plains are relatively featureless regions, downcutting resulting from water erosion provides some of the best topographic settings for big game hunting. Bison are naturally attracted to arroyos because increased moisture provides higher quality vegetation and intermittent opportunities for fresh water. Once in an arroyo, the animals can be driven toward the constricting arroyo head. Hunters waited in relative safety on the edge of the plateau and ambushed the animals when they are concentrated below. Arroyo traps accounted for most of the bison taken by communal hunts during Paleoindian times (Frison 1990:107). However, bison were also ambushed at springs and trapped in parabolic sand dunes (Frison 1992:331; Jodry and Stanford 1992).

Evidence from the Lindenmeier campsite in northern Colorado demonstrates that, like their Clovis predecessors, Folsom people also practiced a generalized foraging subsistence economy. In addition to bison, the Folsom people camped at Lindenmeier also used deer, rabbit, antelope, fox, wolf, coyote, turtle, prairie dog, and possibly camel (Wilmsen and Roberts 1978:46).

At the Stewart's Cattle Guard site in southern Colorado, Pegi Jodry and Dennis Stanford (1992:113–16) (personal communication 1998) report a minimum of forty bison were trapped and killed in a parabolic sand dune. By conducting an excellent spatial analysis in relation to other features, Jodry demonstrates that after primary processing of front and hind quarters, people carried the rib slabs, and some axial elements to the camp. Some of these bones were then redistributed to another area of the site where they were scavenged and possibly gnawed by domestic dogs or wild scavengers (Jodry and Stanford 1992) (Jodry, personal communication 1997).

Faunal remains from a Folsom bison kill at the Agate Basin site in Wyoming (Frison 1982) consist of only eight animals taken during the late winter in an arroyo trap. An associated camp was located on the arroyo floodplain near the bison remains. Frison (1990:106) suggests that frozen meat was cashed and that the settlement was used possibly only during the winter because the arroyo would flood during other times of the year. At the Lindenmeier kill site, at least nine individual bison were killed in a low marshy area of the valley, where the bison were disarticulated. Burned bone suggests that some meat was cooked at the kill site. At the Cooper site in northwestern Oklahoma, bison were trapped in an arroyo on two separate occasions. Both kills were in the late summer or early fall. The upper bone bed contains the remains of at least 13 animals, many of which are mostly articulated (Bement 1994). Ultra-thin bifacial knives recovered at several Folsom sites were possibly used to cut long thin slices of meat for drying (Jodry, personal communication 1997).

It is presumed that Folsom people lived primarily in open-air camps. At the Lindenmeier site, a campsite spatially separated from the kill site exhibits no evidence of structures. However, artifacts and faunal remains were distributed around ash lenses and hearths. Subsequent examination of the Lindenmeier artifact assemblage identified distinct activity areas and suggested that stylistic variation in projectile points might indicate that people from different areas congregated at Lindenmeier for communal bison hunting (Wilmsen and Roberts 1978:179).

There can be little doubt that Folsom people wore tailored skin clothing. A serrated bone flesher made from bison long bone and another made from camel bone were recovered from the Folsom level at the Agate Basin site (Frison and Stanford 1982). These tools were probably used to prepare hides for tanning and subsequent skin working. Numerous eyed bone needles were recovered from the Lindenmeier campsite (Wilmsen and Roberts 1978:131). A needle midsection was recovered from Steward's Cattle Guard (Jodry, personal communication 1997), and needles are reported from the Folsom level at the Agate Basin site, as well as other Folsom sites. Beads recovered from Lindenmeier suggest that clothing and other objects may have been beaded.

Curious bone objects decorated with "ticked" edges are reported from a number of Folsom sites, including Lindenmeier and Agate Basin (Figure 9.6). The function of these objects, which exhibit short incised lines around the margins, is conjectural. The incised lines could be decorative; the objects could be gaming pieces (Frison 1982:169); or they may be counting, recording, or communicating devices of some type. The Buhl burial in Idaho dating to circa 10,600 B.P. contains a "ticked" bone object as well as a projectile point that has been attributed to the Western Stemmed Point tradition (Green et al. 1998). This site is contemporaneous with Folsom sites, but located in the Far West, and suggests that art or cultural symbols may have been shared by people in different regions participating in different ways of life.

Although traditionally thought of as a Great Plains bison hunting culture, there is evidence that Folsom people also occupied the Rocky Mountain high country. Folsom points have been reported from several high-altitude locations along the eastern front of the Rocky Mountains. Jodry et al. (1996) report a Folsom hunting camp high in the San Juan Mountains in southern Colorado. Located at 3,096 m (10,160 ft) above sea level, the site appears to be a seasonally-occupied hunting camp where natural topographic constrictions funneled game near the site. Farther north, two additional Folsom sites have been reported to the Denver Museum of Natural History from South Park, central Colorado (the term park refers to high-altitude grassland interspersed with pine). Benedict

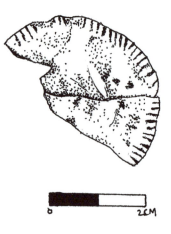

Figure 9.6 Line drawing of a "ticked" bone object recovered from the Lindenmeier site, Denver Museum of Natural History collections. (Graphic by Eric Parrish.)

(1992:347) reports another Folsom point from another high-altitude setting in northern Colorado. Other Folsom points from Colorado have been reported as far west as the Uncompahgre Plateau (Huscher 1939), Grand Junction (Steward 1933), and Montrose County (Wormington 1957). Based on these discoveries, there can be little doubt that Folsom people explored and exploited the high-altitude resources of the Rocky Mountains.

Plano Tradition (circa 10,000–8,000 B.P.)

Plano is a term that lumps a variety of lanceolate projectile point styles dating to the period immediately following Folsom (circa 10,200–8,000 B.P.). This archeological tradition is more complex than the proceeding period when fluted points were in vogue. The Plano projectile point styles exhibit greater regional and temporal variation, and there appear to be greater regional economic differences. Plano incorporates a wide variety of lanceolate projectile points that were hafted differently and occur over a vast geographic area between 10,200–8,000 B.P. As with the change from Clovis to Folsom, the change from Folsom to Plano appears to have been abrupt.

The Great Plains may be subdivided into two broad geographic regions each of which is characterized by somewhat different technology following Folsom times. Gleichman and Gleichman (1989) suggest that the South Platte River drainage in central Colorado was the zone of interaction between northern complexes and southern complexes, of the Plano tradition. This geographic boundary provides a useful conceptual devise for discussing Great Plains archeology, however, artifacts characteristic of the northern Great Plains have been reported from the southern Great Plains (Collins et al. 1997:15–17).

In the southern Great Plains, the Plainview complex postdates Folsom and remains relatively unchanged until the beginning of the Archaic period (circa 8,000 B.P.). Based on the limited archeological data available, it appears that immediately following Folsom times, the split-shaft hafting technique persisted in the southern Great Plains. In the southern sector, bison were typically hunted near springs and watering holes.

In the northern Great Plains, many names are used to describe a variety of projectile point types that are frequently equated with complexes and cultures. The names of these point types are often derived from individuals who discovered them or the places near where they were found. Some of the types include Agate Basin, Hell Gap, Cody, Angostura, Jimmy Allen, Frederick, Eden, Scottsbluff, San Jon, Firstview, and Kersey. Consensus has not been reached among Great Plains archeologists as to the number of projectile point types, their ages, or relationships. In the northern Great Plains, bison were more frequently trapped and killed in arroyos. Figure 9.1 illustrates some of the most important projectile point types from the northern Great Plains.

Projectile points with sides constricting toward the base, such as Agate Basin and Hell Gap points, have been discovered stratigraphically above fluted Clovis and Folsom points. At the Agate Basin site in Wyoming, Agate Basin type projectile points, characterized by basally constricting sides with slightly rounded bases, immediately overlay the Folsom level (Frison and Stanford 1982). This suggests that northern Plano abruptly abandoned the split-shaft hafting technique practiced during Folsom times in favor of hafting using sockets or beds.

Stanford (1999) suggests that Agate Basin-like projectile points may have their origin in the Far West where they appear earlier in northern Basin and Range and Plateau environments before appearing on the northern Plains. It is also possible that they may have diffused southward from American Paleoarctic/Denali complex populations in eastern Beringia in contact with Northern Paleoindian people who in turn had contact with the Paleoindians of the northern Great Plains beginning about 10,500 B.P. Denali complex people manufactured and used constricting-based projectile points as early as circa 10,500 B.P. The Hell Gap complex at the Hell Gap site in Wyoming exhibits reliance on Knife River flint derived from North Dakota. This may suggest cultural ties to the north or more northerly group movements (Irwin-Williams et al. 1973:48)

Radiocarbon dates for the Agate Basin complex range from 10,430 ± 570 B.P. (RL-557) to 9,340 ± 450 B.P. (O-1252) (Frison and Stanford 1982:178–180). Agate Basin like points are also reported from the Packard complex, defined from a site located in northeastern Oklahoma (Wyckoff 1985) and from the north in Canada (Clark 1987; Wright 1976, 1981). The Hell Gap complex immediately follows the Agate Basin complex and is thought to range in age between 10,200–9,500 B.P. (Irwin-Williams et al. 1973:48; Stanford 1999). The Hell Gap

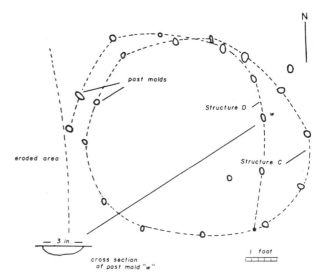

Figure 9.7 Post molds depicting small, approximately 2 m diameter, Agate Basin period structures found at Hell Gap, Wyoming (directly from Irwin-Williams, Figure 10, 1973:41, with permission from *Plains Anthropologist*).

post molds

Structure D

eroded area

Structure C

3 in.

cross section
of post mold "w"

1 foot

N

points are believed to be derived from the earlier Agate Basin points. There is a gradual change from constricting- and round-based points to straighter-based points with more pronounced shoulders.

Evidence of three Agate Basin period structures was noted at the Hell Gap site. They were relatively small structures identified by a series of post molds. The structures average slightly more than 2 m (6.6 ft) in diameter. If these were tents or skin covered lodges, they could not have accommodated more than a few people, possibly a nuclear family. Two of the post mold patterns are illustrated in Figure 9.7.

The archeological evidence suggests that following communal kills, bands would camp near the kill site while processing the meat. If the kill occurred in late fall or winter, when the cool or frozen meat could last a considerable length of time. Frison and Stanford (1982) document possible caching of frozen meat at the Agate Basin site during Agate Basin and Hell Gap times, suggesting that people camped near frozen carcasses and caches.

The Jones-Miller site in northeastern Colorado is a spectacular bison kill located adjacent to a former channel of the Arikaree River (Figure 9.8). The site presents interpretative challenges because geologic analysis demonstrated that unlike most Paleoindian kill sites, it was not a natural trap. What appear to be two consecutive bison kills, consisting of about 150 animals each, probably occurred during a single winter (Stanford, personal communication 1998). Because of the absence of natural topographic features characteristically used to trap bison, Stanford (1974, 1975, 1978, 1979a) suggests that an artificial impoundment constructed of snow and possibly brush was used to drive the animals into a low area, possibly using water to create an icy down-hill entry that would pre-

Figure 9.8 The bone bed at the Jones-Miller site, northeastern Colorado. (Photograph on file at the Denver Museum of Natural History, courtesy of Dennis Stanford and the Smithsonian Institution.)

vent the animals from climbing back up the slippery slope. Once driven into the impoundment, they were dispatched by darts tipped with Hell Gap type projectile points. The bison were all females and calves, indicating that these were winter nursery herds.

A post mold was identified within the impoundment. Around it were found several unusual artifacts not normally associated with kill sites. They include what appears to be a fragment of a flute made of antler, a miniature stone projectile point less than one inch in length, and the bones of a butchered wolf or dog. These items suggested to Stanford (1979a) that this feature could possibly reflect activities similar to those recorded for some northern Native American tribes, including the Cree and Assiniboin, who placed offerings around a post or tree near the center of the trap. Farther south at the Lake Theo site in Briscoe County, Texas (Harrison and Smith 1975:82) report finding a cluster of bison mandibles, which they suggest could have been used as shims to support a post near the center of this Folsom kill site (Figure 9.9). At the Cooper site, located in northwestern Oklahoma, Bement (1997) reports a bison skull painted with red ochre zig-zag-like lines was recovered within the arroyo kill impoundment. These discoveries suggest that ritual activity associated with communal hunts may have persisted over a large geographic area for a long period of time.

Except for kill sites and a few associated encampments, little is known about the lifeway of these people. Benedict (1992) notes that Agate Basin and Hell Gap type projectile points are commonly found along high-altitude passes or valleys that lead to passes. This suggests that in addition to hunting on the Great Plains, these people regularly used the high country for transmountain travel. The Gordon Creek burial, located in northern Colorado (Anderson 1966) (Chapter 5) has been ^{14}C dated to Agate Basin times. This individual may have been associated with the Agate Basin complex. The red ochre covering the bones and artifacts associated with the burial could imply that cultural beliefs may have been passed on to Agate Basin people from earlier Clovis and Folsom populations.

The parallel-stemmed Alberta, Scottsbluff, and Eden projectile point types follow the earlier constricting-based points of the Agate Basin and Hell Gap complexes of the northern Plano tradition. Alberta (stemmed) points may overlap temporally with constricting-based points. Parallel-sided shouldered points, including those from the Alberta and Cody complexes, occur later circa 9,500–8,400 B.P. (Agenbroad 1978; Frison 1983, 1984, 1991; Musil 1988; Wheat 1972). These types of points are frequently associated with Cody knives. These distinctive stemmed knives were sometimes manufactured from broken stemmed projectile points and are the hallmark of the Cody complex. Ruthann Knudson (1983) suggests a possible connection between Plainview technology and the Cody complex based on flaking techniques.

Figure 9.9 Photograph of bison mandibles removed and preserved at the Plains-Panhandle Museum, from the Lake Theo Site, Texas.

Presuming Musil's (1988) correlation between hafting technique and projectile point typology is correct, the transition from socket hafting techniques employed by Agate Basin people back to split-shaft hafting techniques by Cody complex people might suggest influence from the southern Great Plains. During this period, the split-shaft technique apparently persisted in the southern Great Plains as the Plainview complex. However, it is not clear that all northern Plano stemmed points were hafted by the split-shaft technique. It is possible that parallel-sided stemmed forms, particularly those with thick stems, may have been hafted in sockets.

Midland points are essentially identical to Folsom points except that Midland points are not fluted. However, it does not appear that Midland points are transitional from Folsom to later northern Plano point types, and they are similar to later southern Plano types. Amick et al. (1989) have recovered numerous Folsom and Midland points at the Shifting Sands site in Texas, where the two point types appear to be contemporaneous. Hofman (1992:195) presents an analysis showing that about 25 percent of the completed points from the Lindenmeier site are not fluted, about 34 percent from Blackwater Draw are unfluted, and 16 percent from the Elida site are unfluted. This suggests that Midland points are essentially unfluted Folsom points and that the transition from Folsom to southern Plano may have occurred as a result of a change from Folsom to Midland. Judge (1970) has suggested that the only difference between the two types was the flint knappers' abilities to control the original size and thickness of the flake from which the points were manufactured. Only the thicker flakes were suitable for the manufacture of Folsom points. However, Hester (1972) believes that the exceptional skill of Folsom flint knappers would have enabled them to produce the required flake from which to manufacture Folsom points and suggests that the two types may reflect different functions.

Another possible explanation has been offered by Hofman (1992) who suggests that as time passed and projectile points were lost and broken, the bifacial flake cores used to produce the flakes from which Folsom points were manufactured became exhausted. As less raw material was available, hunters were forced to use smaller and thinner flakes, which in turn resulted in an inability to flute the preform. Consequently, a greater and greater percentage of the points would, of necessity, be unfluted until a fresh supply of flakable stone could be obtained. Social and environmental factors, such as interruption of trade networks, warfare, or floods, also could have made sources of lithic raw material rare or difficult to obtain during certain periods of time.

In the southern Great Plains, Folsom is followed directly by Plainview. Plainview received its name from a large bison kill site containing the remains of about 100 bison discovered during road construction in 1944 near Plainview, Texas (Wormington 1957). Plainview is characterized by projectile points similar in shape to Folsom points but lacking fluting. They are lanceolate points with concave bases and are basally edge ground. Because they share the split-shaft hafting method and are morphologically similar to Folsom and Midland points, they may represent a transition from Folsom to later Plano types. The full temporal span is poorly understood. Chronostratigraphic studies suggest Plainview occupation in the southern Great Plains centers around 10,000 B.P. (Bamforth 1988; Holliday and Johnson 1986).

The Firstview complex was defined by Joe Ben Wheat (1972) at the Olsen-

Chubbock site in Colorado. Firstview points are lanceolate/leaf shaped projectile points with straight bases that occasionally have stems that are made by grinding the lower edges of the point to create slight shoulders. There are more pronounced examples called San Jon points that tend to be shorter and narrower. San Jon points occasionally have stems produced by chipping and edge grinding and are probably retooled Firstview points (Wheat 1975). The Firstview complex also includes Milnesand points that are also lanceolate points with bases that range from slightly convex to straight and concave. In the southern Great Plains, the continuation of the split-stem hafting tradition may have persisted until circa 8,000 B.P.

When Joe Ben Wheat excavated the Olsen-Chubbock site on the plains of eastern Colorado between 1958–1960, he ushered in a new era in Great Plains archeology. This arroyo kill site contained the bones of about 190 bison. By analyzing the bones and their spatial distribution, Wheat (1972) was not only able to estimate the total number of animals killed, but he was also able to reconstruct the nature and season of the kill, estimate the quantity of butchered meat, describe the butchering methods, and extrapolate from these data an estimate that about 150 to 200 people were involved in the bison harvest. Since this classic study, Great Plains archeology has devoted increased attention to the nature, composition, and character of faunal remains in interpreting Paleoindian subsistence patterns and activities.

Located in Colorado, the Jurgens site dates to circa 9,100 B.P. The site contains an extensive array of faunal remains, including deer, moose, antelope, elk, rabbit, beaver, muskrat, canid, birds, turtle, fish, and at least 31 bison (Wheat 1979). The Jurgens site was a campsite apparently occupied on two different occasions, once as a short-term camp and another time as a long-term camp. An area was used to process food resources brought to the site. In addition to the vast array of fauna, it also contains stone slabs for grinding seeds and plants. Significantly, a bone atlatl hook and stone tube, inferred by Wheat (1979) to be a pipe, were also found.

Plainview projectile points have been recovered at Horn Shelter 2, near Waco, Texas (Chapter 5). This important site also documents further evidence of a diverse diet and foraging pattern by Plano people. Associated with a double human burial were bones and bone fragments of turtle, deer, bird, rodent, snake, frog, and at least three species of fish. The burials date to circa 9,650 B.P. and further demonstrate that Plano people continued to practice a broad, generalized foraging economy in addition to large communal hunts.

Three early sites, Lime Creek, Red Smoke, and Allen, are located in the Central Plains adjacent to Lime Creek in Frontier County, Nebraska. Projectile points from the earliest occupation (Zone I) at the Lime Creek site are characteristic of the Plano tradition. A log located about .3 m (1 ft) below Zone I was dated to 9,524 ± 450 (C-471) (Libby 1955:107). Faunal remains from Zone I include beaver, antelope, deer, elk, prairie dog, pocket gopher, jackrabbit, raccoon, coyote or dog, and few rare bison bones (Davis 1962; Wedel 1986). At the Red Smoke site, subsistence activities focused primarily on bison hunting and hide processing. Both the Lime Creek and Red Smoke sites are located near an outcrop of jasper that was quarried to manufacture stone tools.

Two of three radiocarbon dates from the Allen site appear to very roughly establish the time of the cultural occupation at 8,274 ± 500 B.P. (C-108a) and 10,493 ± 1,500 B.P. (C-470) (Libby 1955). Artifacts included concave based projectile points, scrapers, lanceolate and ovoid bifaces, drills, grinding and abrading tools, eyed bone needles, awls, a possible fish gorge, and a grooved stone. Faunal remains included bison, antelope, deer, coyote, rabbit, mice, rats, birds, and fresh water mussels and fish. Burned mud dauber wasp nests suggest a summer occupation (Wedel 1986:70-71).

Just as Paleoindian traits appear in eastern Beringia shortly after the establishment of a deglaciation corridor between the Great Plains and Yukon Territory, distinctively northern technological traits appear south of the continental ice about the same time. Frison (1991:67–79) presents a variety of projectile point types primarily characterized by concave, tapering, and occasionally stemmed bases exhibiting oblique flaking that he refers to as Foothills-Mountain Paleoindian "groups" or "manifestations." Most of these sites are located in high altitude areas that may have also played an important role in animal procurement using nets. Frison et al. (1986) report the discovery of a large net probably used to trap deer or mountain sheep in the Absaroka Mountains of Wyoming. The net, made of juniper, was radiocarbon dated to 8,860 ± 170 B.P. (RL-396).

Farther south in the high mountains of southwestern Colorado, Bonnie Pitblado (1999) analyzed the distribution of Paleoindian projectile point types in relationship to their frequency, altitude, and type of stone from which they were manufactured. She grouped point types (believed to date between 10,000–7,500 B.P.) similar to those described by Frison into to the Foothills-Mountain Paleoindian complex. Her analysis indicates that occupation of this high altitude region was sparse during Clovis and Folsom times, prior to circa 10,000 B.P. Acknowledging that the increase in the number of late Paleoindian projectile point types could result from a greater time span, she suggests that the mountains may have been occupied more intensively between 10,000–7,500 B.P. than they were prior to 10,000 B.P. She further suggests that the high frequency of points similar to those of the Western Stemmed Point tradition may support Kevin Black's (1991) hypothesis that high altitude Paleoindian technology might have originated in the Far West, possibly in the region of the Great Basin.

James Benedict (1992:348) notes the high frequency of "burinated" points (points struck from one end using a special technique called a "burin blow" to detach a flake along an edge) and obliquely flaked lanceolate points found above timberline in the Rocky Mountain Front Range of Wyoming and Colorado. Burin blows on projectile points and oblique pressure flaking are typical technological traits commonly found in eastern Beringia. These technological traits appear to date to between about 10,000–7,500 B.P. in the Rocky Mountains. Many of these sites document the use of high latitude subsistence techniques such as stone game drive lines and rock slab hunting blinds. Benedict (1992: 357) suggests that people with strong ties to the mountains used parallel-oblique flaked lanceolate projectile points, relied more heavily on local resources (including stone—particularly orthoquartzite), and were less mobile than their counterparts to the east on the plains who also frequented the mountains.

These data may indicate that shortly after continental deglaciation, contact was established between people in eastern Beringia and the Rocky Mountains. Eastern Beringia subsistence practices may have been adapted to high altitude settings where environmental conditions were very similar. By adapting northern subsistence strategies to southern high altitude habitats, people may have been able to occupy the mountainous regions of western North America year round for the first time.

At this same time, there appears to be a shift in settlement pattern, with more people concentrating in the foothill-mountain regions along the eastern flank of the Rocky Mountains. Benedict (1979, 1981) has suggested that areas, such as Colorado's Front Range (the eastern edge or front of the Rocky Mountains), may have provided refugia where water and other resources occurred in quantities sufficient to support late Plano tradition populations in this period of drought. In these regions, early lithic technology appears to have continued later than on the Great Plains. Benedict (1992:357) notes that these people used collaterally flaked stemmed projectile points manufactured from high-quality glassy rocks obtained from distant sources, suggesting they were more mobile or had wide trade networks.

In these areas, the late Paleoindian tradition people may have developed Archaic tradition technology and subsistence strategies. Based on principals of stylistic change of projectile point types, Benedict (Benedict 1981; Benedict and Olson 1973) suggests that Paleoindian projectile point types, such as obliquely-flaked Jimmy Allen and Pryor Stemmed points, developed into early Archaic point types, such as McKean Lanceolate and Duncan points, respectively.

The long-lived Plano tradition disappears from the Great Plains at the onset of a period of severe drought and climatic change, referred to as the Altithermal (Antevs 1955). Even though it is difficult to establish a strict beginning and end to the Altithermal, it probably culminated shortly after 8,000 B.P. (Frison 1991: 67) and persisted until about 5,000 B.P. (Meltzer 1995:349). During this time, the discharge from springs decreased, surface water became scarce, and there was increased deflation resulting from less plant cover necessary to stabilize sediments (Holliday 1995:89-90). Although life on the Great Plains did not come to an end, the era of large communal bison hunts drew to a close. The paucity of archeological evidence from the Great Plains immediately following the Paleoindian period is probably attributable to a dramatic drop in animal and human populations. Other factors, such as large scale regional erosion, may explain the rarity of early Archaic sites on the Great Plains (Frison 1991:79).

Summary

The major Paleoindian weapon system was the atlatl. It probably included the spear thrower (the atlatl), an atlatl hook, a wooden dart shaft, a bone fore shaft, a wooden or bone harpoon head, a stone projectile point, and a shaft wrench to periodically straighten the darts. Although the foreshafts are known from several sites, the dart heads are extremely rare, probably because they were made of more perishable materials such as locally available hardwoods. Unlike the stone points, the organic dart heads would rapidly decompose when lost. The shaft wrench is a tool type that appears to persist from Clovis times and continued into the Paleoindian and Plano traditions.

The various styles of stone projectile points used to tip the atlatl darts have been employed by archeologists as the primary method to classify the prehistoric cultures of the region. Although Clovis people are frequently stereotyped as mammoth hunters, contemporary research demonstrates that they were general foragers who supplemented their foraging economy with occasional big game hunting, including mammoth. The extinction of the mammoth on the Great Plains appears to correlate with a period of aridity. Human predation may have played a role in the extinction of these animals as they were forced to concentrate at ever diminishing sources of water where they could be ambushed.

Throughout Paleoindian times, the repeated use of red ochre suggests red was an important, and possibly spiritually powerful, color. Evidence from the Riche-Roberts Cache implies that some tool handles may have been painted red. Red, the color of blood, may have been associated with the excitement, exhilaration, and danger of the hunt. The use of ochre may have heighten the potency, aesthetic quality, and possibly metaphysical qualities of artifacts associated with hunting. Perhaps red ochre and aesthetically made stone artifacts were a sign of respect to the animals being hunted; expressing humility and encouraging animals to give themselves to humans. Perhaps of all the cultural pursuits, large mammal hunting became emphasized and significant because of the tremendous food surplus that immediately became available if successful. This success was followed by a period of relative economic prosperity, temporary sedentary lifestyle, and comfort.

Anyone who has had the opportunity to examine Great Plains Paleoindian lithic artifacts, particularly Clovis and Folsom collections, is impressed by the intrinsic beauty of these specimens. It results from the exceptionally high quality of raw material they chose and their incredible craftsmanship. These early flint knappers took advantage of the unique qualities of the stone they were working, often incorporating banding, highlighting colors, and accentuating contours and textures of the stone to enhance the aesthetic beauty of the lithic artifacts. This highly refined mobile form of art culminated in the manufacture of the projectile point, possibly the single most important subsistence artifact and cultural symbol.

Because of poor preservation of organic artifacts, it is not known whether this sense of aesthetics manifest itself in other areas of material culture and life. However, at the Gault site located in southwestern Bell County, Texas, elaborately engraved stones have been found associated with Clovis artifacts (Collins and Hester 1998; Collins et al. 1991). Although these specimens may be unique to the Gault site, the engraving is difficult to detect, and it is possible that similar specimens may have been unrecognized at other Clovis sites. The engraved pebbles and exquisitely flaked stone artifacts provide a glimpse into the exceptional aesthetic life of Paleoindian people and have left a nonperishable legacy for all to appreciate. Mammoths became extinct at the end of Clovis times, and the role that humans may have played in their extinction remains unclear. However, the available data suggest that climatic change may have been more important than human predation in causing extinction of the mammoth.

A transition from fluted to constricting-base shouldered projectile points occurs sometime around 10,200–10,000 B.P. in the northern Great Plains. In the northern areas of the Far West, Carlson (1988:321) indicates a transition to stemmed points may occur about the same time (between 10,500–9,500 B.P.). Additional research is necessary to determine whether this transition in projectile point types has it origins to the west or to the north in eastern Beringia. The preliminary data suggest that constricting-base and shouldered projectile points are younger in the Great Plains than they are in eastern Beringia and the Far West. In the southern Great Plains most people did not make the transition to constricting based and shouldered projectile points and continued to manufacture Goshen/Plainview projectile points similar to earlier Clovis and Folsom points, but lacking flutes.

Some ecological settings proved to be excellent hunting locales and were repeatedly used by Paleoindian people over several millennia. At the Hell Gap site, several distinct complexes were found stratigraphically superimposed on one another beginning with Goshen and Midland and followed by Agate Basin, Hell Gap, Alberta/Cody, Frederick, and Lusk (Irwin-Williams et al. 1973). This sequence resulted from repeated entrapment and ambush of bison in this narrow valley. The Carter/Kerr-McGee site, also in Wyoming, provides an excellent example where bison and other large mammals were repeatedly trapped near the upper end of an arroyo, first by Clovis/Goshen, then Folsom, followed by Agate Basin/Hell Gap, and finally by Cody complex people. The Agate Basin site also records successive Folsom and Agate Basin arroyo entrapments. Topography was an important factor in site selection (Albanese 1977), and these sites clearly document that some favored locales were used repeatedly. However, there are no known sites that were occupied by Paleoindian people through all seasons year after year.

Robert Kelly and Larry Todd (1988) suggest that Folsom and Clovis people practiced a land use pattern different than that of later foragers. They suggest that the lack of regional point styles implies frequent shifts in ranges. The rather ephemeral nature of many of the sites leaves very little accumulation of archeological debris. Camps containing a wider array of artifacts are frequently associated with kill sites, suggesting entire bands moved from kill to kill. There was a wide distribution of high-quality lithic material, as opposed to greater use of local sources in later times. There is an apparent lack of caches or processing areas where meat surpluses might be stored or prepared for storage. Incomplete utilization of kills is suggested by the fact that relatively few bones are missing and frequently carcasses have not been fully disarticulated and processed.

Following Clovis and Folsom times, there were ever increasing numbers of bison taken in communal hunts with increasing numbers of people involved. However, evidence from the Lime Creek sites, Horn Shelter 2, the Jurgens site, and other sites demonstrate that the tradition of general foraging still persisted. The first discernible domestic structures have been recognized at the end of Folsom times, and this suggests that skin tents or lodges were supported by poles and possibly staked down along their margins. From the Folsom component at the Agate Basin site, Frison and Stanford (1982) report two pieces of bison rib driven into the sediment at an angle suggesting they were used at tent pegs. The size and configuration of these early shelters suggest that they probably housed nuclear families.

Although the archeology of high-altitude regions in the eastern Rockies is poorly understood, recent research indicates that high-altitude habitats were exploited by Paleoindian people beginning by at least Folsom times and probably earlier. High altitude habitats are recognized as important environments in the development of subsistence adaptations at the close of the Paleoindian period.

However, high altitude alone may have been less important than the topographic and environmental diversity characteristic of mountainous regions.

Mountainous terrain has some specific environmental advantages over regions with little topographic relief. For example, diverse habitats ranging from alpine tundra, coniferous forests, parklands, and brushy stream valleys can all be concentrated in restricted geographic area, such as a single mountain valley. Relatively short vertical movement within these restricted areas enables humans to access diverse resources available at different times of the seasonal cycle (Pitblado 1998:343). Glaciers and snow fields provide predictable and reliable sources of fresh water, and the aspect of slopes relative to the changing position of the sun throughout the seasons create numerous diverse microhabitats. Cooler temperatures and specific locales (such as north facing slopes) provide opportunities to preserve seasonal surpluses of foods, which in turn can create greater economic stability. More intense exploitation of diverse resources is viewed by many archeologists as the single most important economic factor characterizing the transition from the Paleoindian to the Archaic period.

The available archeological data suggest that on the Great Plains communal Paleoindian bison kills began in Folsom times and continued with increasing intensity. They appear to be seasonal occurrences, most commonly in the fall and winter when the cold weather would preserve meat for long periods of time. Groups of people congregated to cooperate and participate in the kill. During these occasions, they processed the meat and hides and enjoyed a brief period of sedentary life. As meat supplies were depleted, or became tainted, these larger groups dispersed across the landscape. As smaller groups, possibly only a family or two, they survived based on more diverse resources and a broader foraging and hunting pattern. These communal undertakings were probably strongly reinforced by social and economic factors, including opportunities to trade, find marriage partners, and to share knowledge about changing environmental and social conditions. A prolonged period of drought beginning shortly after about 8,000 B.P. appears to have brought an end to this early way of life and ushered in an new era of economic and cultural change on the Great Plains.

10 Summary and Speculation

Introduction

This book has reviewed possible pre-11,500 B.P. archeological sites in North and South America, the Pleistocene deglaciation of North America, early human skeletal remains, and the regional archeology of western North America. These summaries underscore many of the constraining factors relevant to the first colonization of the Americas and what in some cases appear to be confusing facts. For example, how can human occupation in South America occur 800 years prior to the first firm archeological evidence of human occupation in Alaska? If an ice-free corridor did not exist until about 11,000 B.P., how can we explain well-documented Clovis sites south of the continental ice 300 years prior to that time? If people were not south of the ice sheets prior to the end of the last glaciation, why do reliably dated human remains occur at far flung localities, such as coastal California, Nevada, and Montana, by circa 11,000 B.P.? Is there a unifying concept that can explain these diverse and seemingly conflicting facts? How many colonizing events may there have been?

Ongoing archeological research makes it increasingly clear that the colonization of the Americas was very complex and remains poorly understood. Genetic evidence suggests that there were at least four, or five, founding lineages. This evidence can be interpreted to suggest anywhere from one to five or more migration events. Cranial morphology suggests at least two populations, an earlier "long-headed" and a later more "round-headed" people. Dental evidence has been interpreted to suggest that there were three different populations. Linguistic data have been interpreted to suggest at least three, and possibly more, distinct linguistic groups populated the Americas.

The technological evidence is also difficult to interpret and largely depends on whether one wishes to "lump" technological traditions and complexes together or to "split" them based on a variety of criteria. For example, three distinct technological traditions can be identified in North America by about 11,000 B.P. The Nenana complex has been recognized in eastern Beringia, the Western Stemmed Point tradition appears to occur contemporaneously with Western

Fluted Points in the Far West, and the Clovis complex is well documented on the Great Plains.

This concluding chapter is intended to be provocative. It attempts to provide some speculative and alternative concepts and interpretations for explaining the early archeological record of western North America. It is intended to challenge traditional ideas, stimulate fresh thinking, and provoke debate. Because it is speculative, it abstracts data to levels that may be uncomfortable for some scientists. As working hypotheses and propositions, these concepts are not presented as rigorously proven and tested scientific fact.

Beringia and the Ice-free Corridor

The apparently conflicting lines of archeological evidence are only inconsistent if one accepts the traditional Beringian mammoth hunting model for human colonization of the Americas. The Bering Land Bridge has been a cornerstone in American paleontology and archeology for hundreds of years. In addition to explaining the exchange of plants and large terrestrial mammals between Asia and North America, it is presumed that hunters of large terrestrial mammals probably first entered North America from Asia via the Bering Land Bridge. The traditional explanation is that humans then moved south through central western Canada sometime about 11,500 B.P. either through a hypothetical ice-free corridor or after the continental glaciers melted. According to this theory, the pattern of Old World mammoth hunting was transposed to North America near the end of the last Ice Age by people using Clovis, or Clovis-like, technology.

The Bering Land Bridge–Ice-free Corridor model explaining New World human colonization has intellectually dominated the study of New World prehistory for the past several hundred years. One result has been the relative neglect of archeological investigations attempting to document and understand the first peopling of the Americas in the maritime regions of northeast Asia and along the western coasts of the Americas. Like many scientific theories that have been presented persuasively and frequently, this paradigm has become dogma. An outspoken Native American scholar Vine Deloria (cited in Thomas 1993:28) has gone so far as to describe the Bering Land Bridge theory as a "triumph of doctrine over facts." He suggests that as a theory, it provides an example of how Christian religious doctrine could have been transformed to scientific theory. While many scientists would forcefully disagree, there is wisdom in Deloria's observation.

European ethnocentrism may be inherent in the predominance of the Bering Land Bridge theory in explaining the initial colonization of the Americas. The New World has largely been interpreted as an extension or repetition of the patterns identified in Old World archeology, particularly from late Pleistocene archeological sites in central Eurasia. However, analogous environments, species, and economic pursuits may have led to the development of functionally similar tool kits requiring similar types of artifacts. Independently developed subsistence strategies based on large terrestrial mammal predation may have emphasized well-made lithic projectile points and cutting implements. Similar economic systems also tend to create similarities in band size and settlement patterns. In other words, similarities between Old World Paleolithic and New World Paleoindian lithic technology may result from convergent evolution (the process by which unrelated cultures develop similar technological adaptations in response to similar environmental conditions), rather than linear evolution that requires a historic relationship resulting from migration from Asia.

There is some, albeit equivocal, evidence for mammoth predation by humans in Beringia from Berelyoth, Broken Mammoth, Mead, and Swan Point sites, and the analysis of residue from some stone projectile points. However, mammoth hunting does not appear to be the primary, or possibly even an important, economic focus in Beringia. It has been suggested (Yesner 1996) that in some cases mammoth remains may have been scavenged more than a thousand years after the animals had died. Perhaps some enigmatic sites south of the ice sheet, such as Lamb Spring, Dutton, Selby, and La Sena, may be ephemeral examples of a foraging tradition that incorporated scavenging mammoth bone from noncultural bone accumulations or individual skeletons.

Gary Haynes (1991:208–13) has demonstrated that the only places where there is firm evidence for mammoth hunting are on both sides of Beringia, not Beringia itself. There is little evidence to support the traditional paradigm of mammoth hunters expanding from the Asian steppe into Beringia and southward through what is now interior Canada into more southern regions of the Americas. It is equally plausible that New World proboscidean hunting represents an independent invention historically not related to Old World mammoth hunting.

North American glacial chronology establishes maximum and minimum limiting dates for human colonization of North America. Deglaciation along the Northwest Coast of North America was sufficiently advanced to enable human settlement by at least 13,000 B.P. However, the interior Bering Land Bridge–midcontinental route was not deglaciated until circa 11,000 B.P.

The Bering Land Bridge–Ice-free Corridor migration model requires an economy based on hunting large terrestrial mammals, possibly freshwater fishing, and pedestrian travel. On the other hand, the coastal hypothesis suggests an economy based on marine mammal hunting, saltwater fishing and shellfish gathering, and the use of watercraft. It is important to address these hypotheses because each requires different types of cultural adaptations by the New World founding populations, and the nature of this adaptation set the stage for subsequent New World cultural development.

Origins

The interior Bering Land Bridge model for the first peopling of the Americas has traditionally been viewed as a unidirectional (first west to east and then north to south) terrestrial migration beginning about 12,000 B.P. The theory has further been refined to require rapid spread of the human population across the two American continents and a wide variety of environmental zones in less than 1,000 years. This has been necessary to explain the widespread distribution of Clovis sites and Pleistocene mammalian extinctions. However, recent research on the dating of late Pleistocene deglaciation suggests that terrestrial connections between eastern Beringia and areas south of the continental ice were not reestablished until about 11,000 B.P. (Chapter 2). Additionally, review of several regional archeological sequences demonstrates that by circa 11,500–11,000 B.P. there already exist several distinctive regional adaptations in North America. At this time in Alaska, there is the Nenana complex; while in the Far West, the Western Fluted Point and early Stemmed Point traditions exist; and Clovis is well documented on the Great Plains. For these regional variations to have developed so early, initial colonization must have occurred earlier than Clovis times.

Although strong similarities exist between the lithic technology of the Nenana complex of eastern Beringia and the Clovis complex in more southern regions of North America, there are also striking differences. For example, Clovis lacks the distinctive teardrop-shaped Chindadn knives, and the Nenana complex lacks the distinctive Clovis fluted projectile points. While general similarities between the two complexes may be derived from the same technological tradition, or common technological ancestor, they are sufficiently different to imply that they have been separated from each other for a considerable amount of time.

These observations support a hypothesis (Carlson 1990; Dixon 1993; Jordan 1992) that early bifacial industries may have preceded the spread of the Northwest Coast Microblade tradition along the Northwest Coast of North America. According to this hypothesis, both the Nenana and Clovis complexes represent later inland adaptations of an earlier (circa 13,000 B.P.) occupation of the Pacific Coast by people without microblades. The Nenana complex represents human adaptation to the subarctic of eastern Beringia, while the Clovis complex represents a different and slightly later adaptation to temperate regions of interior North America. This hypothesis is strengthened by the fact that the Northern Paleoindian tradition is derived from south of the continental ice and does not appear in eastern Beringia until circa 10,500 B.P. This demonstrates that people were south of the continental ice prior to deglaciation about 11,000 B.P.

As our knowledge of Clovis lifeways increases from sites such as Aubrey, important new insight has been gained into Clovis economy. Clovis people are best viewed as generalized gatherers and secondarily as mammoth hunters. This suggests that Clovis subsistence origins lie in a more generalized gathering economy and technological tradition and is not rooted in the large mammal hunting traditions of the Eurasian Upper Paleolithic.

An Alternative Model

An alternative hypothesis for human colonization of the Americas is coastal migration with later inland movement and settlement within broad environmental zones (biomes or "megapatches") that extend from north to south throughout the Americas (Chapter 2). It is easier for people to exploit their current environmental zone, using their existing subsistence knowledge, than to move to adjacent foreign environmental zones. Thus, people were likely to settle the coasts before moving very far inland. Migration probably occurred in many directions at the same time. For example, some people may have been moving more rapidly southward along the Pacific Coast of the Americas while others were colonizing more slowly eastward from the coast to the interior of the continents.

This model is drastically different from the traditional interior Beringian migration and subsequent unidirectional movement from north to south cross-cutting environmental zones and a wide array of physical obstacles. Colonization along large environmental zones is more consistent with New World archeological data and enables seemingly conflicting evidence to be reconciled into a single rational model for colonization of the Americas. Figure 10.1 schematically portrays how colonization may have occurred along major environmental zones at arbitrary 500 year intervals beginning at circa 13,000 B.P. Extreme northeastern North America and Greenland were not sufficiently deglaciated to permit colonization until about 5,000 B.P.

The coastal route provided the environmental avenue essential for the initial human entry to the Americas. The coast formed part of a continuous marine coastal-intertidal ecosystem extending between northeastern Asia and northwestern North America and farther south to the southern hemisphere. It would have facilitated coastal navigation and provided similar subsistence resources in a continuous ecological zone linking Asia and North America. Old World adaptations could have facilitated rapid colonization without developing new technologies or subsistence strategies.

This alternative model proposes that initial human colonization of the Americas began around 13,500 B.P. along the southern margin of the Bering Land

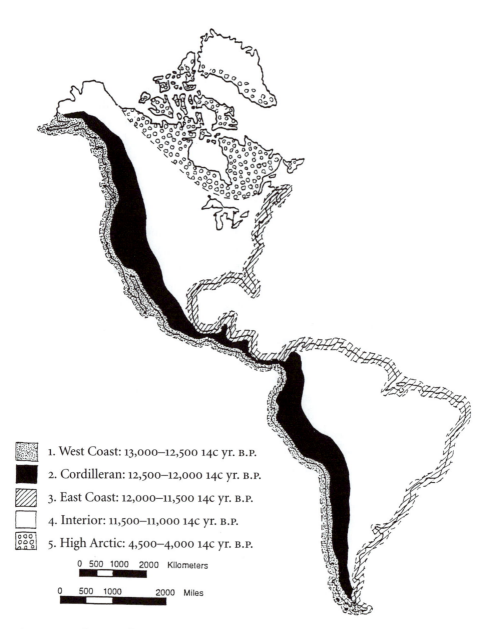

Figure 10.1 Schematic illustration of how New World colonization may have occurred along major environmental zones at arbitrary 500 year intervals. Extreme northeastern North America and Greenland were not sufficiently deglaciated to permit colonization until circa 5,000 B.P. (Graphic by Eric Parrish.)

The legend reads:

1. West Coast: 13,000–12,500 14C yr. B.P.
2. Cordilleran: 12,500–12,000 14C yr. B.P.
3. East Coast: 12,000–11,500 14C yr. B.P.
4. Interior: 11,500–11,000 14C yr. B.P.
5. High Arctic: 4,500–4,000 14C yr. B.P.

0 500 1000 2000 Kilometers

0 500 1000 2000 Miles

Bridge and then continued southward along the Pacific Coast of the Americas. With the use of watercraft, possibly skin boats, the human population moved rapidly southward along the coastal-intertidal Pacific biome, or megapatch. Although evidence of this early migration may have been obscured by rising sea level at the end of the last Ice Age, evidence might be expected to be found in adjacent areas of the interior, such as Monte Verde, which is located along a river drainage only 15 km (9 mi) northeast of the Pacific Ocean. If this model is correct, the Pacific Coast of the Americas could have been occupied thousands of years before the continental ice in North America melted.

Coastal environments provide many ecological advantages for generalized foragers, an economic adaptation best suited for colonizing populations. For example, intertidal resources, such as shellfish, may be harvested by children and the elderly, and simply eaten raw. On the other hand, the traditional interior Bering Land Bridge–Ice-free Corridor model requires human groups to be dependent on hunters specializing in large terrestrial mammals. This concept requires groups to be dependent on a few strong adults to bring down large mammals, including mammoths. This model also requires greater territorial movement and presents greater difficulty for human groups that realistically include the elderly, the very young, pregnant women, and the infirm. Current data from the earliest sites in the Americas do not indicate subsistence traditions based primarily on specialized large mammal hunting but on foraging instead.

The coastal route offers many advantages for colonization. For example, latent heat stored in the ocean results in a more equitable environment lacking both the low temperature extremes of the north and the low precipitation of the arid west. Local abundance of marine and intertidal resources and predictable runs of anadromous fish concentrated human populations in specific locales, such as sheltered bays, inlets, estuaries, and along streams in which fish spawn.

Temperate coastal technological adaptations rely heavily on readily available materials such as drift wood, marine mammal products, beach cobbles, and shell, which in many cases may have been already partially modified by noncultural processes. In such an environment, reliance on sophisticated lithic technologies was probably not as important as in other environments. For example, preshaped and prepolished sling and bola stones, the only lithic material required for two effective, deadly weapons, can be easily and efficiently collected from noncultural beach deposits. Monte Verde provides a rare glimpse into this type of technological adaptation because it de-emphasized the production and use of bifacially flaked lithic tools and placed greater reliance on simple flakes and organic materials.

From an original and theoretical maritime subsistence strategy, several adaptive trajectories were possible as humans expanded across the landscape. Survival may have been best assured by continuing a pattern of general foraging, which could be adjusted or modified based on availability of resources and increasing knowledge of local geography and biological patterns. For example, along the West Coast, people may have continued their ancient adaptation to shellfish gathering, fishing, and marine mammal hunting. In interior regions of southern California, Arizona, and Mexico, the pattern of general foraging may have led to an increasing emphasis on harvesting and processing plant products and seed grinding. In the Great Plains, general foraging persisted throughout the Paleoindian period, but people emphasized and refined large mammal hunting, particularly communal mass bison kills.

Although the initial colonization along the continental margins of the Americas may have occurred rather quickly, subsequent colonization of interior environments may have occurred more slowly. People probably moved inland from the coast along rivers. As population increased and people gradually adapted to interior environments, they possibly advanced inland along river systems; at the same time, colonization probably continued to progress along environmental zones.

Given this scenario, the western plains of North America may have been among the last places to be settled as well as one of the least hospitable environmental regions of the continent. Adaptation to the interior plains may have occurred later because they are geographically separated from the Pacific Coast by the rugged mountainous Cordillera. Classic Clovis sites such as Blackwater Draw and Murray Springs containing evidence of spectacular mammoth predation, may be representative of a rather unique cultural, technological and ecological adaptation during the late Pleistocene. In other words, the spectacular and well-publicized Clovis kill sites may be the least typical and the least useful sites for interpreting the colonization of the Americas and early New World adaptations.

Although the Clovis culture is often associated with mammoth hunting, more current data demonstrate a greater emphasis on generalized gathering by Clovis people. In fact, only twelve sites have been documented in North America where Clovis points have been found in clear association with mammoth remains (G. Haynes 1991:197–197, 206). A more realistic portrayal of Clovis economics suggests that mammoth kill sites occur in marginal habitats that may have been some of the last to be colonized. Although they may provide the earliest evidence of human occupation in the western interior of North America, this region may have been among the last to be colonized.

Technology

The lithic technology found at Monte Verde is characterized by the selection and use of naturally occurring stone and minimal modification of stones and other useful items found in the natural environment. This type of technological system probably originates from a generalized coastal economy that might have only occasional and comparatively rare need for bifacial projectile points to serve as harpoon end blades, lance points, or possibly knives.

An intriguing connection between coastal migrations and mammoth hunting may lay in understanding the primary Clovis weapon system. It is characterized by the atlatl, or spear thrower, used to propel a short light-weight spear, or dart. The dart is tipped with a bifacially flaked stone Clovis projectile point believed to be mounted in a split-shaft harpoon-like haft, that is attached to a bone foreshaft (Stanford 1996). Stanford (personal communication 1997) has suggested that the detachable projectile point might be attached by a line to a drag, which would impede the escape of wounded animals and enable them to be more easily tracked or followed by pedestrian hunters. However, very little is known about these detachable harpoon-like projectile points and the example exhibited by Stanford (1996) lacks a hole or other characteristics necessary to attach a line.

This type of sophisticated weapon system is commonly associated with marine mammal hunting. This system is effective when hunting marine mammals from watercraft because it requires only one hand to hold the atlatl and propel the dart. This frees the hunter's other hand to stabilize the watercraft using a double-bladed paddle during stalking and throwing (Figure 10.2). The detachable harpoon or projectile point is frequently attached to a line tied to a float. The float not only creates a drag that impedes the animal's progress but frequently rises to the surface prior to the emergence of a submerged animal. This enables the hunter to track the animal in the open water and position himself for another shot where the animal is expected to surface.

The end blade, harpoon, and foreshaft assembly used for marine mammal hunting is strikingly similar to the Paleoindian foreshaft, "harpoon" head, and Clovis end blade assembly suggested by Stanford (1996) (Figure 10.3). This type of weapon system is compatible with marine mammal hunting. Thus the Clovis weapon system may have its origins in coastal marine mammal hunting weapons technology, which was subsequently adapted to hunting large terrestrial mammals. When this weapon system was adapted to terrestrial hunting, there may no longer have been a need for a line hole to attach a float or retrieving line. The diagnostic trait of basal thinning and fluting early Paleoindian projectile points may be derived from thinning the base of stone projectile points to make them fit easily into slotted harpoon heads designed for marine mammal hunting. It may explain the origin of the earliest split-shaft hafting technique used in the Americas. This type of end blade assembly persisted until historic times among maritime hunters in northwestern North America and northeastern Asia.

Figure 10.2 Line drawing illustrating the use of the atlatl and detachable harpoon in open water hunting. (Graphic by Eric Parrish.)

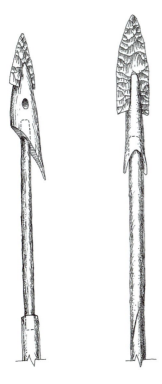

Figure 10.3 Line drawing comparing (*left*) the detachable marine mammal hunting end blade, harpoon head, and foreshaft assembly used in marine mammal hunting and (*right*) the detachable Clovis end blade, dart head, and foreshaft atlatl dart assembly. (Graphic by Eric Parrish.)

Colonization Events

From a purely technological perspective, there appear to be two major colonizing events in the Americas. The first was an early migration by the ancestors of the Clovis complex, the Nenana complex, and possibly the Western Stemmed point tradition sometime before circa 12,500 B.P. and possibly as early as circa 13,500 B.P. This group of people relied on the atlatl and darts tipped with bifacially flaked stone end blades lashed to harpoon-like heads that were seated on bone foreshafts. They did not manufacture microblades and probably did not use the bow and arrow. However, it is possible that the small triangular projectile points characteristic of the Nenana complex could also have been used to tip arrows. The atlatl remained the primary weapon system in South America and temperate and southern regions of North America until Archaic times and even later in some areas.

The second colonization event was by people bearing the American Paleoarctic tradition about, or shortly before, 10,500 B.P. These people probably also used the atlatl, and they introduced the bow and arrow. Early microblade technology included the complex technique of manufacturing composite projectile points by insetting razor sharp stone microblades along the sides of bone and antler projectile points. This type of technology appears to have been adopted about a thousand years later along the Northwest Coast where microblades appear to have been inset in handles and used primarily for precision craft work.

These two technological traditions are radically and fundamentally different. Although both populations required effective projectile points that were essential in hunter-gather societies, each developed unique approaches to manufacturing them. Nenana and Clovis peoples relied primarily on reducing a lithic core by flaking away excess rock to create a flaked stone projectile point, or biface. American Paleoarctic people engaged in a complex technological sequence of building projectile points by inserting microblades into slots carved along the sides of cylindrical bone or antler projectile points. These conceptually complex and different approaches successfully solved the same problem. These differences resulted from learned behavior passed from generation to generation. This also implies that other profound differences may have existed between these two groups, possibly including biological and linguistic traits as well as technological and social concepts.

The limited physical anthropological data also suggest at least two distinct human groups immigrated to the Americas. The first were an earlier long-headed people with smaller and relatively narrow faces and smaller more narrow nasal apertures. They were followed by a second population bearing greater resemblance to contemporary northern Asians and Native Americans. Although rapid evolutionary change could explain the differences between the earlier and later Native American populations, the physical differences more likely represent two distinct populations circa 11,000–10,000 B.P. The older group has been described as having greater similarity to early Asian people and resembles the Ainu of northern Japan. If these comparisons are accurate, then both early technological evidence and physical anthropological data might suggest a possible point of origin for the earliest Americans in the maritime regions of eastern Asia.

The data regarding the earliest skeletal evidence provide additional insight into the timing of the first colonization of the Americas. The earliest human skeletal remains have been recognized at Arlington Springs, Fishbone Cave, and Anzick circa 11,000 B.P. indicating that humans were distributed over much of North America by this time. This suggests that by circa 11,000 B.P. people were sufficiently numerous that their remains are preserved in sufficient numbers to make their subsequent discovery possible.

Conclusions

The initial colonization of the Americas used watercraft and occurred about 13,500 B.P. and possibly earlier. This hypothesis is supported by the following:

1. The earliest deglaciated route was coastal. The deglaciated West Coast of North America was first available for colonization by circa 13,500 B.P. The interior route was blocked by the continental glaciers until about 11,000 B.P. An unglaciated ice-free corridor did not exist between Beringia and the southern areas of North America until circa 11,000 B.P.

2. Several sites, including Monte Verde in South America, predate the opening of the midcontinental route. This demonstrates people were south of the continental glaciers prior to deglaciation circa 11,000 B.P.

3. Reliably dated human remains first appear in the North American archeological record by 11,000 B.P., firmly demonstrating that human colonization had occurred prior to that time.

4. By about 11,500–11,000 B.P. regional cultural adaptation was well under way in several large regions of North America, further suggesting an earlier migration.

5. The Paleoindian tradition spread from the Great Plains northward into eastern Beringia circa 10,500 B.P. indicating that people were south of the continental ice prior to deglaciation, circa 11,000 B.P.

6. Paleoindian subsistence data indicate an economic system rooted in general foraging, not specialized big game hunting.

7. The New World's first weapon system, the foreshaft/harpoon/end-blade atlatl dart assembly, may trace its origins to coastal marine mammal hunting, rather than large terrestrial mammal hunting.

8. Evidence from other regions of the world demonstrates that humans had watercraft and the ability to navigate near-shore ocean waters prior to 14,000 B.P., and possibly more than 40,000 B.P.

9. Technological evidence suggests at least two major colonizing events. The first occurred about 13,500 B.P. or earlier and used the atlatl. The second was about 10,500 B.P. and introduced the bow and arrow. However, the relationships, if any, between human physical types, language families, or genetic groups and the two major technological traditions is not clear.

At the present time, this model seems to best fit the archeological data. However, it is imperative that New World archeologists keep their minds open to earlier human colonization of the Americas, continue to consider different types of colonization processes, evaluate new evidence, and apply new methods of analysis. The limited data from the lower level at Monte Verde and controversial discoveries at Pedra Furada, Meadowcroft Rockshelter, and other sites are not considered adequate by many archeologists to demonstrate with certainty colonization earlier than 13,500 B.P. A stronger suite of evidence will be required to convince most scientists of an earlier (circa 30,000 B.P.) date for human colonization of the Americas.

The intellectual dominance of the interior Beringian colonization model has resulted in little archeological research being directed toward searching for evidence of New World colonization along the coastal regions of northeastern Asia and the West Coast of the Americas. As research advances, additional sites will be located to test this model. Earlier theories were developed when science lacked the archeological and geologic evidence available today. Geologic research over the past two decades has made reinterpretation possible. It has documented the relatively ice-free character of the Northwest Coast of North America beginning about 13,500 B.P. and the persistence of the interior continental glaciers of North America until about 11,000 B.P. Ethnographic research has provided greater understanding of hunting and gathering societies and has provided archeologists with more realistic models of how early people may have operated within their environments. Other scientific advances that have contributed to our ability to reinterpret archeological evidence are reliable methods for the AMS ^{14}C dating and isotopic analysis of bone.

Although this synthesis suggests alternative avenues for interpretation and future research, it represents only a small contribution to the ongoing process of Paleoindian research. It is important for archeologists to continue to address the timing and processes of colonization of the Americas because the cultural adaptations of the New World founding populations established the foundation for all subsequent New World cultural development. The initial colonization is analogous to the concept of the "Big Bang" in physics—it is the starting point from which the great cultural diversity and complexity of the Americas began. This research also provides important insight into humans as colonizers.

The new environments of the Americas helped shape New World cultural development, producing entirely new and unique cultural configurations. These early adaptations lay the foundations for subsequent cultural development throughout western North America and established the basis for the diverse economic systems and lifeways that followed. Understanding the nature, timing, and character of the initial peopling of the Americas is essential if we are to accurately interpret the processes that later transformed founding New World populations into the vast array of resourceful and diverse cultures that ultimately occupied the Americas.

Bibliography

Abbot, C.

1876   Antiquity of Man. *The American Naturalist* 10:51–52.

1883   Evidences of Glacial Man. *Science* 2:437–438.

1889   Evidence of the Antiquity of Man in Eastern North America. *Proceedings of the American Association for the Advance of Science* 37:293–315.

1892   Paleolithic Man in America. *Science* 20:270–271.

Ackerman, R. E.

1992   Earliest Stone Industries on the North Pacific Coast of North America. *Arctic Anthropology* 29(2):18–27.

1996a   Lime Hills, Cave 1. In *American Beginnings: The Prehistory and Palaeo-ecology of Beringia*, edited by Frederick Hadleigh West, pp. 470–478. University of Chicago Press, Chicago.

1996b   Ground Hog Bay, Site 2. In *American Beginnings: The Prehistory and Palaeoecology of Beringia*, edited by Frederick Hadleigh West, pp. 424–429. University of Chicago Press, Chicago.

1996c   Early Maritime Culture Complexes of the Northern Northwest Coast. In *Early Human Occupation in British Columbia*, edited by Roy L. Carlson and Luke Dalla Bona, pp. 123–132. University of British Columbia Press, Vancouver.

1996d   Spein Mountain. In *American Beginnings: The Prehistory and Palaeo-ecology of Beringia*, edited by Frederick Hadleigh West, pp. 456–460. University of Chicago Press, Chicago.

Ackerman, R. E., T. D. Hamilton, and R. Stuckenrath

1979   Early Culture Complexes on the Northern Northwest Coast. *Canadian Journal of Archaeology* 3:195–208.

Ackerman, R. E., K. C. Reid, J. D. Gallison, and M. E. Roe

1985   *Archaeology of Heceta Island: A Survey of 18 Timber Harvest Units in the Tongass National Forest, Southeastern Alaska.* Center for Northwest Anthropology, Washington State University, Pullman.

Acosta, J. de

1604   *The Naturall and Morall Historie of the East and West Indies.* Translated by Edward Grimston. Reprinted by Bart Franklin, New York, by permission of the Haakluyt Society.

Adovasio, J. M.

    1993   The Ones That Will Not Go Away: A Biased View of Pre-Clovis Populations in the New World. In *From Kostenki to Clovis,* edited by Olga Soffer and N. D. Praslov, pp. 199–218. Plenum Press, New York.

Adovasio, J. M., J. D. Gunn, J. Donahue, and R. Stuckenrath

    1977   Meadowcroft Rockshelter: Retrospect 1976. *Pennsylvania Archaeologist* 47(2–3): 1–93.

    1978   Meadowcroft Rockshelter, 1977: An Overview. *American Antiquity* 43:632–651.

Adovasio, J. M., J. D. Gunn, J. Donahue, R. Stuckenrath, J. Guilday, and K. Lord

    1978   Meadowcroft Rockshelter. In *Early Man in America from a Circum-Pacific Perspective,* edited by Alan Lyle Bryan, 140–180. Occasional Papers No. 1. Department of Anthropology, University of Alberta, Edmonton.

Adovasio, J., J. D. Gunn, J. Donahue, R. Stuckenrath, J. E. Guilday, and K. Volman

    1980   Yes Virginia, It Really Is That Old: A Reply to Haynes and Mead. *American Antiquity* 45:588–595.

Adovasio, J. M. and D. C. Hyland

    1993   Paleo-Indian Perishables from Pendejo Cave: A Brief Summary. Paper presented at the 48th Annual Meeting of the Society for American Archaeology, St. Louis.

Agenbroad, L. D.

    1978   *The Hudson-Meng Site: An Alberta Bison Kill in the Nebraska High Plains.* University Press of America, Washington, D. C.

Agenbroad, L. D., J. I. Mead, and L. W. Nelson (editors)

    1990   *Megafauna and Man: Discovery of America's Heartland.* Scientific Papers, Vol. 1. The Mammoth Site of Hot Springs, Hot Springs, South Dakota; and Northern Arizona University, Flagstaff.

Ager, T. A. and L. Brubaker

    1985   Quaternary Palynology and Vegetational History of Alaska. In: *Pollen Records of Late Quaternary North American Sediments,* edited by V. M. Bryant and R. G. Holloway, pp. 353–384. American Association of Stratigraphic Palynologists, Dallas.

Agogino, G. A. and B. Ferguson

    1978   The Angus Mammoth: Was It a Valid Kill Site? *Anthropological Journal of Canada* 16(3):7–9.

Aikens, C. M.

    1970   *Hogup Cave.* University of Utah Anthropological Papers 93, Salt Lake City.

Akazawa, T. and E. J. E. Szathmáry (editors)

    1996   *Prehistoric Mongoloid Dispersals.* Oxford University Press, Oxford.

Albanese, J. P.

    1977   Paleotopography and Paleoindian Sites in Wyoming and Colorado. In *Pa-*

leoindian Lifeways, edited by E. Johnson, pp. 28–47. The Museum Journal XVII. Texas Tech University.

Alexander, H. L.

1974   The Association of Aurignacoid Elements with Fluted Point Complexes in North America. In *International Conference on the Prehistory and Paleoecology of Western North American Arctic and Subarctic*, edited by S. Raymond and P. Schlederman, pp. 21–31. University of Calgary Archaeological Association, Calgary.

1987   *Putu: A Fluted Point Site in Alaska*. Publication 17, Department of Archaeology, Simon Fraser University, Burnaby, British Columbia.

Allen, J., C. Gosden, R. Jones, and J. P. White

1988   Pleistocene Dates for Human Occupation of New Ireland, Northern Melanesia. *Nature* 331:707–709.

Allen, J., C. Gosden, and J. P. White

1989   Pleistocene New Ireland. *Antiquity* 63(240):548–560.

Alsoszatai-Petheo, J.

1986   An Alternative Paradigm for the Study of Early Man in the New World. In *New Evidence for the Pleistocene Peopling of the Americas*, edited by Alan Lyle Bryan, pp. 15–26. Center for the Study of Early Man, University of Maine at Orono.

Amick, D. S., J. L. Hofman, and R. O. Rose

1989   The Shifting Sands Folsom-Midland Site in Texas. *Current Research in the Pleistocene* 6:1–3.

Anderson, D. C.

1966   The Gordon Creek Burial. *Southwestern Lore* 32:1–9. Gunnison, Colorado.

Anderson, D. D.

1968   A Stone Age Campsite at the Gateway to America. *Scientific American* 218(6):24–33.

1970   Akmak: An Early Archeological Assemblage from Onion Portage, Northwest, Alaska. *Acta Arctica*, Fasc 16, Copenhagen.

1986   The Settlement and Cultural Development of Eskimos Around Kotzebue Sound. In *Beach Ridge Archeology of Cape Krusenstern*, edited by J. L. Giddings and D. D. Anderson, pp. 311–325. Publications in Archeology 20. National Park Service, U. S. Department of the Interior, Washington, D.C.

1988   *Onion Portage: The Archaeology of a Stratified Site from the Kobuk River, Northwest Alaska*. Anthropological Papers of the University of Alaska 22(1–2). University of Alaska Press, Fairbanks.

Antevs, E.

1929   Maps of the Pleistocene Glaciation, *Bulletin of the Geological Society of America*, 40:631–720.

1936   The Occurrence of Flints and Extinct Animals in Pluvial Deposits near

Clovis, New Mexico, II, Age of Clovis Lake Beds. *Proceedings of the Philadelphia Academy of Natural Sciences* 87:304–311.

1937   Climate and Early Man in North America. In *Early Man*, edited by G. G. MacCurdy, pp. 125–132, J. D. Lippincott, Philadelphia.

1955   Geologic-Climatic Dating in the West. *American Antiquity* 20:317–335.

Armenta, C. J.

1959   Hallazgo de un Artefacto Asociado con Mammut en al Valle de Puebla. *Mexico Instituto Nacional Antropologia e Historia, Direcion Prehistoria* 7:7–25.

1978   *Vestigios de Labor Humana en Huesos de Animales Extinctos de Valsequillo, Puebla Mexico.* Consejo Editorial del Gobierno del Estado de Puebla, Puebla, Mexico.

Aschmann, H.

1952   A Fluted Point from Central Baja California. *American Antiquity* 17:262–263.

Aveleyra Arroyo de Anda, L.

1956   The Second Mammoth and Associated Artifacts at Santa Isabel Iztapan, Mexico. *American Antiquity* 22:12–28.

Aveleyra Arroyo de Anda, L. and M. Maldonado-Koerdal

1953   Association of Artifacts with Mammoth in the Valley of Mexico. *American Antiquity* 18:332–340.

Bada, J. L., R. A. Schroeder, and G. F. Carter

1974   New Evidence for the Antiquity of Man in North America Deduced from Aspartic Acid Racemization. *Science* 184:791–793.

Bahn, P. G.

1993   50,000-year-old Americans of Pedra Furada. *Nature* 362:114–115.

Bailliet, G., F. Rothhammer, F. R. Carnese, C. M. Bravi, and N. O. Bianchi

1994   Founder Mitochondrial Haplotypes in Amerindian Populations. *American Journal of Human Genetics* 54:27–33.

Bamforth, D. B.

1988   *Ecology and Human Organizations on the Great Plains.* Plenum, New York.

Barnosky, C. W., P. W. Anderson, and P. J. Bartlein

1987   The Northwestern U. S. During Deglaciation: Vegetational History and Paleoclimatic Implications. In *North American and Adjacent Oceans During the Last Deglaciation*, edited by W. F. Ruddiman and H. E. Wright, pp. 289–321. The Geology of North America, Vol. K-3. Geological Society of America, Boulder.

Barry, R. G.

1982   Approaches to Reconstructing the Climate of the Steppe-Tundra Biome: 195–204. In *Paleoecology of Beringia*, edited by David M. Hopkins, John V. Matthews, Jr. Charles E. Schweger, and Steven B. Young, pp. 195–204. Academic Press, New York.

Beaton, J. M.

    1991a   Colonizing Continents: Some Problems for Australia and the Americas. In *The First Americans: Search and Research*, edited by Tom D. Dillehay and David J. Meltzer, pp. 209–230. CRC Press, Boca Raton, Florida.

    1991b   Paleoindian Occupation Greater than 11,000 yr B.P. at Tule Lake, Northern California. *Current Research in the Pleistocene* 8:5–7.

Beck, C. and G. T. Jones

    1988   Western Pluvial Lakes Tradition Occupation in Butte Valley, Eastern Nevada. In *Early Human Occupation in Far Western North America: The Clovis-Archaic Interface*, edited by Judith A. Willig, C. Melvin Aikens, and John L. Fagan, pp. 273–301. Nevada State Museum Anthropological Papers No. 21. Carson City.

    1997   The Terminal Pleistocene/Early Holocene Archaeology of the Great Basin. *Journal of World Prehistory* 11(2):161–236.

Bedwell, S. R.

    1973   *Fort Rock Basin Prehistory and Environment*. University of Oregon Books, Eugene.

Beebe, B. F.

    1983   Evidence of Carnivore Activity in a Late Pleistocene/Early Holocene Archaeological Site (Blue Fish Cave 1), Yukon Territory, Canada. In *A Question of Bone Technology*, edited by G. M. LeMoine and A. S. MacEachern, pp. 1–14. The Archaeological Association of the University of Calgary, Calgary.

Behrensmeyer, A. K. and A. P. Hill

    1980   *Fossils in the Making. Vertebrate Taphonomy and Paleoecology*. University of Chicago Press, Chicago.

Bement, L. C.

    1994   The Cooper Site: A Stratified Paleoindian Bison Kill in Northwest Oklahoma. *Current Research in the Pleistocene* 11:7–9.

    1997   Ritual and the Hunt: A Painted Skull from a Folsom Bison Kill in NW Oklahoma. In *Program and Abstracts*, 55th Annual Plains Anthropological Conference 24. Boulder, Colorado, November 19–22, 1997.

Benedict, J. B.

    1979   Getting Away from It All: A Study of Man, Mountains, and the Two-Drought Altithermal. *Southwestern Lore* 45(3):1–12. Gunnison, Colorado.

    1981   *The Fourth of July Valley: Glacial Geology and Archeology of the Timberline Ecotone*. Center for Mountain Archeology Research, Report No. 2, Ward, Colorado.

    1992   Along the Great Divide: Paleoindian Archaeology of the High Colorado Front Range. In *Ice Age Hunters of the Rockies*, edited by Dennis J. Stanford and Jane S. Day, pp. 343–359. Denver Museum of Natural History.

Benedict, J. B. and B. L. Olson

    1973   Origin of the McKean Complex: Evidence from Timberline. *Plains Anthropologist* 18(62):323–27.

Berger, R.

    1975   Advances and Results in Radiocarbon Dating: Early Man in America. *World Archaeology* 7:174–184.

    1980   Early Man on Santa Rosa Island. In *The California Islands: Proceedings of a Multidisciplinary Symposium,* edited by D. M. Power, pp. 73–78. Santa Barbara Museum of Natural History, Santa Barbara.

    1982   The Woolly Mammoth Site, Santa Rosa Island, California. In *Peopling of the New World,* edited by J. E. Ericson, R. E. Taylor, and R. Berger, pp. 163–170. Anthropological Papers 23. Ballena Press, Los Altos, California.

Berger, R. and P. C. Orr

    1966   The Fire Areas on Santa Rosa Island, California, II. *Proceedings of the National Academy of Sciences* 56:1678–1682.

Berger, R. and R. Protsh

    1989   UCLA Radiocarbon Dates XI. *Radiocarbon* 31:55–67.

Berry, C. F. and M. S. Berry

    1986   Chronological and Conceptual Models of the Southwestern Archaic. In *Anthropology of the Desert West: Essays in Honor of Jesse D. Jennings,* edited by C. J. Condie and D. D. Fowler, pp. 253–327. University of Utah, Salt Lake City.

Binford, L. R.

    1981   *Bones: Ancient Men and Modern Myths.* Academic Press, New York and London.

Bird, J. B.

    1938   Antiquity and Migrations of the Early Inhabitants of Patagonia. *Geographical Review* 28(2):250–275.

    1946   The Archaeology of Patagonia. In *Handbook of South American Indians,* Vol. 1, edited by J. H. Steward, pp. 7–24. Bulletin 143 of the Bureau of American Ethnology. Smithsonian Institution, Washington, D.C.

    1988   *Travels and Archaeology in South Chile.* University of Iowa Press, Iowa City.

Bird, J. B. and R. Cooke

    1978   The Occurrence in Panama of Two Types of Paleo-Indian Projectile Points. In *Early Man in America from a Circum-Pacific Perspective,* edited by Alan Lyle Bryan, pp. 263–272. Occasional Papers No. 1. Department of Anthropology, University of Alberta, Edmonton.

Birdsell, J. B.

    1957   Some Population Problems Involving Pleistocene Man. Cold Spring Harbor Symposium. *Quantitative Biology* 22:47–69.

    1977   The Recalibration of a Paradigm for the First Peopling of Greater Australia. In *Sunda and Sahul*, edited by J. Allen, G. Golson, and R. Jones, pp. 113–166. Academic Press, London.

Black, K. D.
  1991   Archaic Continuity in the Colorado Rockies: The Mountain Tradition. *Plains Anthropologist* 36(133):1–29.

Blaise, B., J. J. Clague, and R. W. Mathewes
  1990   Time of Maximum Late Wisconsin Glaciation, West Coast of Canada. *Quaternary Research* 34:282–295.

Bliss, W. L.
  1940a   A Chronological Problem Presented by Sandia Cave, New Mexico. *American Antiquity* 5:200–201.
  1940b   Sandia Cave. *American Antiquity* 6:77–78.

Boas, F.
  1964   *The Central Eskimo*. University of Nebraska Press, Lincoln, Nebraska.

Bobrowsky, P. T., N. R. Catto, J. W. Brink, B. E. Spurling, T. H. Gibson, and N. W. Rutter
  1990   *Archaeological Geology of Sites in Western and Northwestern Canada*. Centennial Special Vol. 4, Chapter 5, pp. 87–122. Geological Society of America, Boulder.

Bonnichsen, R.
  1978   Critical Arguments for Pleistocene Artifacts from the Old Crow Basin, Yukon: A Preliminary Statement. In *Early Man in America from a Circum-Pacific Perspective*, edited by Alan Lyle Bryan, pp. 102–118. Occasional Papers No. 1. Department of Anthropology, University of Alberta, Edmonton.
  1979   *Pleistocene Bone Technology in the Beringian Refugium*. National Museum on Man, Mercury Series, Archaeological Survey of Canada Paper 89. Ottawa.

Bonnichsen, R., M. T. Beatty, M. D. Turner, and M. Stoneking
  1996   What Can be Learned from Hair? A Hair Record from the Mammoth Meadow Locus, Southwestern Montana. In *Prehistoric Mongoloid Dispersals*, edited by Takeru Akazawa and Emőke J. E. Szathmáry, pp. 201–213. Oxford University Press, New York.

Bonnichsen, R., M. T. Beatty, M. D. Turner, J. C. Turner, and D. Douglas
  1992   Paleoindian Lithic Procurement at the South Fork of Everson Creek, Southwestern Montana: A Preliminary Statement. In *Ice Age Hunters of the Rockies*, edited by Dennis J. Stanford and Jane S. Day, pp. 285–321. Denver Museum of Natural History.

Bonnichsen, R., C. W. Bolen, M. D. Turner, J. C. Turner, and M. T. Beatty
  1993   Hair from Mammoth Meadow II, Southwestern Montana. *Current Research in the Pleistocene* 9:75–78.

Bonnichsen, R., D. Douglas, M. Beatty, M. D. Turner, J. C. Turner, and B. Stanyard
  1990   New Paleoindian Discoveries at Mammoth Meadow, Southwestern Montana. *Current Research in the Pleistocene* 7:3–5.

Borden, C. E.

1969   Early Population Movements from Asia into Western North America.
        Syesis 2:113.

1975   Origins and Development of Early Northwest Coast Culture to about
        3,000 B.C. Canada National Museum of Man, Mercury Series. Archaeo-
        logical Survey of Canada Paper 45. Ottawa.

Borrero, L. A.

1982   Arqueologia del Seno de la Ultima Esperanza Magallanes (Chile). *Con-
        greso Nacional de Arqueologia* 7:11–16. Montevideo.

1989   Spatial Heterogeneity in Fuego-Patagonia. In *Archaeological Approaches
        to Cultural Identity*, edited by S. J. Shennan, pp. 258–266. Unwin Hyman,
        London.

1995   The Archaeology of the Far South of America—Patagonia and Tierra del
        Fuego. In *Ancient Peoples and Landscapes*, edited by Eileen Johnson, pp.
        207–215. Museum of Texas Tech University, Lubbock.

Bousman, C. B.

1998   Late Paleoindian Archeology. In *Wilson-Leonard, An 11,000-year Archeo-
        logical Record of Hunter-Gathers in Central Texas*, assembled and edited by
        Michael B. Collins, Chapter 8, pp. 161–210. Studies in Archeology 31, Texas
        Archeological Research Laboratory, University of Texas at Austin, and
        Archeological Studies Program, Report 10, Texas Department of Trans-
        portation, Environmental Affairs Division. Austin.

Bowers, P. M.

1978   Research Summary: 1977 Investigations of the Carlo Creek Archaeological
        Site, Central Alaska. Report submitted to the University of Alaska Mu-
        seum, Fairbanks. Laboratory of Anthropology, Arctic Research Section,
        Washington State University, Pullman. Ms. 24 1. January.

1980   *The Carlo Creek Site: Geology and Archaeology of an Early Holocene Site in
        the Central Alaska Range*. Anthropology and Historic Preservation, Coop-
        erative Park Studies Unit, Occasion Paper No. 27. Fairbanks, Alaska.

Brain, C. K.

1981   *The Hunters or the Hunted? An Introduction to African Cave Taphonomy*.
        University of Chicago Press, Chicago.

Brand, D. D.

1940   Regarding Sandia Cave. *American Antiquity* 5:339.

Breternitz, D. A., A. C. Swedlund, and D. C. Anderson

1971   An Early Burial from Gordon Creek, Colorado. *American Antiquity*
        36:170–182.

Bright, R. C.

1966   Pollen and Seed Stratigraphy of Swan Lake, Southeastern Idaho: Its Rela-
        tion to Regional Vegetational History and to Lake Bonneville History.
        Tebiwa: Journal of the Idaho State University Museum 9(2):1–47.

Bryan, A. L.

1978   An Overview of Paleo-American Prehistory from a Circum-Pacific Perspective. In *Early Man in America from a Circum-Pacific Perspective*, edited by Alan Lyle Bryan, pp. 306–327. Occasional Papers No. 1. Department of Anthropology, University of Alberta, Edmonton.

1979   The Stratigraphy of Taima-Taima. In *Taima-Taima: A Late Pleistocene Paleo-Indian Kill Site in Northernmost South America—Final Reports of the 1976 Excavation*, edited by Claudio Ochsenius and Ruth Gruhn, pp. 41–52. Germany.

1980   The Stemmed Point Tradition: An Early Technological Tradition in Western North America. In *Anthropological Papers in Memory of Earl H. Swanson, Jr.*, edited by L. B. Harten, C. N. Warren, and D. R. Tuohy, pp. 77–107. Idaho Museum of Natural History, Pocatello.

1983   South America. In *Early Man in the New World*, edited by R. Shutler, Jr., pp. 137–147. Sage Publications, Beverly Hills.

1986   Paleoamerican Prehistory as Seen from South America. In *New Evidence for the Pleistocene Peopling of the Americas*, edited by A. L. Bryan, pp. 1–14. Center for the Study of Early Man, University of Maine, Orono.

1988   The Relationship of the Stemmed Point and Fluted Point Traditions in the Great Basin. In *Early Human Occupation in Far Western North America: The Clovis-Archaic Interface*, edited by J. A. Willig, C. M. Aikens, and J. L. Fagan, pp. 53–74. Nevada State Museum Anthropological Papers No. 21, Carson City.

Bryan, A. L. (editor)

1978   *Early Man in America from a Circum-Pacific Perspective*. Occasional Papers No. 1. Department of Anthropology, University of Alberta, Edmonton.

1986   *New Evidence for the Pleistocene Peopling of the Americas*. Center for the Study of Early Man, University of Maine at Orono.

Bryan, A. L., R. M. Casamiquela, J. M. Cruxent, R. Gruhn, and C. Ochsenius

1978   An El Jobo Mastodon Kill at Taima-Taima, Venezuela. *Science* 200:1275–1277.

Bryan, A. L. and R. Gruhn

1979   The Radiocarbon Dates of Taima-Taima. In *Taima-Taima: A Late Pleistocene Paleo-Indian Kill Site in Northernmost South America—Final Reports of the 1976 Excavation*, edited by Claudio Ochsenius and Ruth Gruhn, pp. 53–58. Germany.

Bryan, A. L. and D. R. Tuohy

1999   Prehistory of the Great Basin/Snake River Plain to About 8500 Years Ago. In *Ice Age Peoples of North America*, edited by R. Bonnichsen. Oregon University Press for the Center for the Study of the First Americans, Corvalis.

Burns, J. A.

    1990   Paleontological Perspectives on the Ice-free Corridor. In *Megafauna and Man: Discovery of America's Heartland*, edited by Larry D. Agenbroad, Jim I. Mead, and Lisa W. Nelson, pp. 61–66. Scientific Papers, Vol. 1. The Mammoth Site of Hot Springs, Hot Springs, South Dakota; and Northern Arizona University, Flagstaff.

    1996   Vertebrate Paleontology and the Alleged Ice-free Corridor: The Meat of the Matter. *Quaternary International* 32:107–112. Great Britain.

Butler, B. R.

    1961   *The Old Cordilleran Culture in the Pacific Northwest*. Occasional Papers of the Idaho State College Museum, No. 3, Pocatello.

    1963   An Early Man Site at Big Camas Prairie, South-Central Idaho. *Tebiwa: Journal of the Idaho State University Museum* 6(1):22–33.

    1965   A Report on Investigation of an Early Man Site near Lake Channel, Southern Idaho. *Tebiwa: Journal of the Idaho State University Museum* 8(1):1–20.

Butler, B. R. and R. J. Fitzwater

    1965   A Further Note on the Clovis Site at Big Camas Prairie, South-Central Idaho. *Tebiwa: Journal of the Idaho State University Museum* 8(1)38–40.

Byers, D. S.

    1942   Concerning Sandia Cave. *American Antiquity* 4:408–409.

Cardich, A.

    1978   Recent Excavations at Lauricocha (Central Andes) and Los Toldos (Patagonia). In *Early Man in America from a Circum-Pacific Perspective*, edited by Alan Lyle Bryan, pp. 296–300. Occasional Papers No. 1. Department of Anthropology, University of Alberta, Edmonton.

Carlson, R. L.

    1979   The Early Period on the Central Coast of British Columbia. *Canadian Journal of Archaeology* 3:211–228.

    1983   The Far West. In *Early Man in the New World*, edited by Richard Shutler, Jr., pp. 73–96. Sage Publications, Beverly Hills.

    1988   The View from the North. In *Early Human Occupation in Far Western North America: The Clovis-Archaic Interface*, edited by Judith A. Willig, C. Melvin Aikens, and John L. Fagan, pp. 319–324.

    1990   Cultural Antecedents. In *Northwest Coast*, edited by W. Suttles, pp. 60–69. Handbook of North American Indians, Vol. 7, W. C. Sturtevant, general editor. Smithsonian Institution, Washington, D.C.

    1996   Introduction to Early Human Occupation in British Columbia. In *Early Human Occupation in British Columbia*, edited by Roy L. Carlson and Luke Dalla Bona, pp. 3–10. University of British Columbia Press, Vancouver.

1997 Early Maritime Adaptations on the Northwest Coast. Paper presented in the Early Maritime Adaptations in North America 10,000 to 4,500 B.P. Symposium at the 1997 Annual Meeting of the American Association for the Advancement of Science, Seattle, Washington.

Carlson, R. L. and L. D. Bona (editors)
1996 *Early Human Occupation in British Columbia.* University of British Columbia Press, Vancouver.

Carter, G. F.
1952 Interglacial Artifacts from the San Diego Area. *Southwest Journal of Anthropology* 8(4):444–456.
1957 *Pleistocene Man at San Diego.* Johns Hopkins Press, Baltimore.
1980 *Earlier than You Think.* Texas A and M Press, College Station.

Cassells, E. S.
1997 *The Archaeology of Colorado,* revised edition. Johnson Books, Boulder.

Caulk, G.
1988 *Examination of Some Faunal Remains from the Marmes Rockshelter Floodplain.* Master's thesis, Department of Anthropology, Washington State University, Pullman.

Chatters, J. C.
1997 Encounter with an Ancestor. *American Anthropological Association Newsletter* 9–10, January.

Chisholm, B. S.
1986 *Reconstruction of Prehistoric Diet in British Columbia Using Stable-carbon Isotope Analysis.* Ph.D. dissertation in Archaeology, Department of Archaeology, Simon Fraser University, Burnaby, British Columbia.

Chisholm, B. S. and D. E. Nelson
1983 An Early Human Skeleton from South Central British Columbia: Dietary Inference from Carbon Isotopic Evidence. *Canadian Journal of Archaeology* 7(1):396–398.

Chlachula, J.
1994 A Paleo-American (Pre-Clovis) Settlement in Alberta. *Current Research in the Pleistocene* 11:21–23.

Chrisman, D.
1997 Reply to Shaffer and Baker. *American Antiquity* 62:561.

Chrisman, D., R. S. MacNeish, and G. Cunnar
1997 Reply to Dincauze. *American Antiquity* 62:556–558.

Chrisman, D., R. S. MacNeish, J. Mavalwala, and H. Savage
1996 Late Pleistocene Human Friction Skin Prints from Pendejo Cave, New Mexico. *American Antiquity* 61:357–376.

Cinq-Mars, J.
1979 Blue Fish Cave I: A Late Pleistocene Eastern Beringian Cave Deposit in the Northern Yukon. *Canadian Journal of Archaeology* 3:1–32.

Clague, J. J., J. M. Ryder, W. H. Mathews, O. L. Hughes,
N. W. Rutter, and C. M. MacDonald

    1989   Quaternary Geology of the Canadian Cordillera. In *Quaternary Geology of Canada and Greenland*, edited by R. J. Fulton, Chapter 1, pp. 17–96. Geological Society of Canada, Geology of Canada, No. 1. Ottawa.

Clark, D. W.

    1984   Northern Fluted Points: Paleo-Eskimo, Paleo-Arctic, or Paleo-Indian. *Canadian Journal of Anthropology* 4(1):65–81

    1987   *Archaeological Reconnaissance at Great Bear Lake.* Archaeological Survey of Canada Paper No. 136. Mercury Series. Canadian Museum of Civilization, Ottawa.

Clark, D. W. and A. M. Clark

    1983   Paleo-Indians and Fluted Points: Subarctic Alternatives. *Plains Anthropologist* 1:283–92.

    1991   *Batza Téna Trail to Obsidian: Archaeology at an Alaskan Obsidian Source.* Archaeological Survey of Canada, Mercury Series Paper 147. Canadian Museum of Civilization, Hull, Quebec.

Clausen, C. J., H. K. Brooks, and A. B. Wesolowsky

    1975   The Early Man Site at Warm Mineral Springs, Florida. *Journal of Field Archaeology* 2(3):191–213.

Clausen, C. J., A. D. Cohen, C. Emiliani, J. A. Holman, and J. J. Stipp

    1979   Little Salt Spring, Florida: A Unique Underwater Site. *Science* 203:609–614.

Clements, T.

    1979   The Geology of the Yermo Fan. In Pleistocene Man at Calico, edited by Walter C. Schuiling. *Quarterly of San Bernardino County Museum Association* 26(4):21–30

Clutton-Brock, J.

    1988   The Carnivore Remains Excavated at Fell's Cave in 1970. In *Travels and Archaeology in South Chile*, edited by J. B. Bird, pp. 188–195. University of Iowa Press, Iowa City.

Cockrell, W. A. and L. Murphy

    1978   Pleistocene Man in Florida. *Archaeology of Eastern North America* 8:1–13.

Coffin, R.

    1937   *Northern Colorado's First Settlers.* Colorado State College, Fort Collins.

Collins, M. B. (editor)

    1998   *Wilson-Leonard, An 11,000-year Archaeological Record of Hunter-Gathers in Central Texas, assembled and edited by Michael B. Collins.* Studies in Archeology 31. Texas Archeological Research Laboratory, University of Texas at Austin, and Archeological Studies Program, Report 10, Texas Department of Transportation, Environmental Affairs Division. Austin.

Collins, M. B. and T. D. Dillehay

    1986   The Implications of the Lithic Assemblage from Monte Verde for Early Man Studies. In *New Evidence for the Pleistocene Peopling of the Americas,* edited by Alan Lyle Bryan, pp. 339–355. Center for the Study of Early Man, University of Maine at Orono.

Collins, M. B., G. L. Evans, T. N. Campbell, M. C. Winans, and C. E. Mear

    1989   Clovis Occupation at Kincaid Shelter, Texas. *Current Research in the Pleistocene* 6:3–4.

Collins, M. B. and T. R. Hester

    1998   Introduction to the Gault Site. Texas Archeological Research Laboratory Research Notes 6(1):4. University of Texas at Austin.

Collins, M. B., T. R. Hester, D. Olmstead, and P. J. Headrick

    1991   Engraved Cobbles from Early Archaeological Contexts in Central Texas. *Current Research in the Pleistocene* 8:13–15.

Collins, M. B., D. J. Stanford, J. L. Hofman, M. A. Jodry,

R. O. Rose, L. C. Todd, K. Kibler, and J. M. Blackmar

    1997   Cody Down South: the Seminole-Rose Site in West Texas. *Current Research in the Pleistocene* 14:15–17.

Cook, J. P.

    1969   *The Early Prehistory of Healy Lake, Alaska.* Ph.D. dissertation, Department of Anthropology, University of Wisconsin, Madison.

    1996   Healy Lake. In *American Beginnings: The Prehistory and Palaeoecology of Beringia*, edited by Frederick Hadleigh West, pp. 323–327. University of Chicago Press, Chicago.

Cook, J. P. and R. A. McKennan

    1970   The Village Site at Healy Lake, Alaska: An Interim Report. Paper presented at the 35th Annual Meeting of the Society for American Archeologists, Mexico City, Mexico.

Correal Urrego, G.

    1981   Evidencias Culturales y Megafauna Pleistocénica en Columbia. *Fundacion de Investigaciones Arqueologicas Nacionales* 12:1–148. Bogota.

Cotter, J. L.

    1935   A Report of the Fieldwork of the Colorado Museum of Natural History at the Lindenmeier Folsom Campsite. On file, Archives, Denver Museum of Natural History.

    1937   The Occurrence of Flints and Extinct Animals in Pluvial Deposits near Clovis, New Mexico. Report on the Excavations at the Gravel Pit in 1936. *Proceedings of the Philadelphia Academy of Natural Sciences* (4)89:2–16.

    1938   The Occurrence of Flints and Extinct Animals in Pluvial Deposits near Clovis, New Mexico. Report on Field Season of 1937. *Proceedings of the Philadelphia Academy of Natural Sciences* (6)90:113–117.

    1991   Update on Natchez Man. *American Antiquity* 56:36–39.

Coulter, H. W., D. M. Hopkins, T. N. V. Karlstrom,

T. L. Pewe, C. Wahrhaftig, and J. R. Williams

    1965   Map showing extent of glaciations in Alaska. U. S. Geological Survey Miscellaneous Geologic Investigations Map, 1-415, scale 1:2,500,00.

Crane, H. R.

    1955   Antiquity of the Sandia Culture: Carbon-14 Measurements. *Science* 122:689–690.

Cressman, L. S.

    1977   *Prehistory of the Far West.* University of Utah Press, Salt Lake City.

    1981   *The Sandal and the Cave: The Indians of Oregon.* Reprint of Beaver Books, 1962 by Oregon State University Press, Eugene.

Crook, W. W. and R. K Harris

    1957   Hearths and Artifacts of Early Man near Lewisville, Texas and Associated Faunal Material. *Bulletin of the Texas Archaeological Society* 28:7–97.

    1962   Significance of a New Radio-carbon Date from the Lewisville Site. *Bulletin of the Texas Archaeological Society* 32:327–330.

Cruxent, J.

    1956   Discovery of a Lithic Industry of Paleo-Indian Type in Venezuela. *American Antiquity* 22:172–179.

    1957   Further Comments on the Finds at E. Jobo, Venezuela. *American Antiquity* 22:412.

    1970   Projectile Points with Pleistocene Mammals in Venezuela. *Antiquity* 49(175):223–225.

Cruxent, J. M. and C. Ochsenius

    1979   Paleo-Indian Studies in Northern Venezuela: Brief Review. In *Taima-Taima, A Late Pleistocene Paleo-Indian Kill Site in Northernmost South America—Final Reports of 1976 Excavations,* edited by Claudio Ochsenius and Ruth Gruhn, pp. 9–14. Germany.

Cushing, J., A. M. Wenner, E. Noble, and M. Daily

    1986   A Groundwater Hypothesis for the Origin of "Fire Areas" on the Northern Channel Islands. *Quaternary Research* 26:207–217.

Cwynar, L. C.

    1982   A Late-Quaternary Vegetation History from Hanging Lake, Northern Yukon. *Ecological Monographs* 52:1–24.

Cybulski, J. S., D. E. Howes, J. C. Haggarty, and M. Eldridge

    1981   An Early Human Skeleton from Southcentral British Columbia: Dating and Bioarchaeological Inference. *Canadian Journal of Archaeology* 5:59–60.

Dansie, A. J.

    1997a   Early Holocene Burials in Nevada: Overview of Localities, Research and Legal Issues. *Nevada Historical Society Quarterly* 40(1):1–14.

    1997b   Note on Textiles Associated with the Spirit Cave Burials. In Cave Burials Near Fallon, Nevada, by S. M. Wheeler. *Nevada Historical Society Quarterly* 40(1):17–23.

Daugherty, R. D.

    1956   Archaeology of the Lind Coulee Site, Washington. *Proceedings of the American Philosophical Society* 100(3):223–278.

Davies, D. M.

1978   Some Observations on the Otavalo Skeleton from Imbabura Province, Ecuador. In *Early Man in America from a Circum-Pacific Perspective*, edited by Alan Lyle Bryan, p. 273. Occasional Papers No. 1. Department of Anthropology, University of Alberta, Edmonton.

Davis, E. L.

1975   The "Exposed Archaeology" of China Lake, CA. *American Antiquity* 40:39–53.

1978   Associations of People and a Rancholabrean Fauna at China Lake, California. In *Early Man in America from a Circum-Pacific Perspective*, edited by Alan Lyle Bryan, pp. 183–217. Occasional Papers No. 1. Department of Anthropology, University of Alberta, Edmonton.

Davis, E. M.

1962   *Archaeology of the Lime Creek Site in Southwestern Nebraska.* Special Publication of the University of Nebraska State Museum, 3. Lincoln.

Davis, S. D.

1989   Cultural Component I. In *The Hidden Falls Site*, edited by Stanley D. Davis, pp. 159–198. Alaska Anthropological Association, Monograph Series No. 5, Aurora.

Dawson, G. M.

1894   Geological Notes on Some of the Coasts and Islands of Bering Sea and Vicinity. *Geological Society of America Bulletin* 5:117–146.

Deetz, J.

1967   *Invitation to Archaeology.* American Museum Science Books. The Natural History Press, Garden City, New York.

Delibrias, G. N., N. Guidon, and F. Parenti

1988   The Toca do Boqueirao do Sitio da Pedra Furada: Stratigraphy and Chronology. In *Early Man in the Southern Hemisphere*, pp. 3–11. Supplement to Archaeometry: Australasian Studies, J. R. Prescott, Adelade.

Desert Research Institute News

1996   Discovery May Link Old, New Worlds. The Newsletter of the Desert Research Institute, Winter, p. 5. Reno.

Dikov, N. N.

1977   *Arkheologicheshie pamyatniki Kamchctki, Chukotki i Verkhnej Kolymy* (Archeological Monuments of Kamchatka, Chukotka, and the Upper Kolyma). Nauka, Moscow.

1979   *Drevnie kul'tury Severo-Vostochnoj Azii* (Ancient Cultures of Northeast Asia). Nauka, Moscow.

1993   *Asia at the Juncture with America in Antiquity.* Russian Academy of Sciences (RAS), Department of History Far-Eastern Branch of RAS Northeastern Interdisciplinary Research Institute, Nauka, St. Petersburg, Richard L. Bland, translator. Published in 1997 by the U.S. Department of the Interior, National Park Service, Beringia Program, Anchorage, Alaska.

Dikov, N. N. and E. E. Titov

 1984 Problems of the Stratification and Periodization of the Ushki Sites. *Arctic Anthropology* 21(2):69–80.

Dillehay, T. D.

 1984 A Late Ice-Age Settlement in Southern Chile. *Scientific American* 251(4): 100–109.

 1985 A Regional Perspective of Preceramic Times in the Central Andes. *Reviews in Anthropology* 12:193.

 1986 The Cultural Relationships of Monte Verde: A Late Pleistocene Settlement in the Sub-Antarctic Forest of South-Central Chile. In *New Evidence for the Pleistocene Peopling of the Americas*, edited by Alan Lyle Bryan, pp. 319–337. Center for the Study of Early Man, University of Maine at Orono.

 1988 How New is the New World? *Antiquity* 62:94–97.

 1991 Disease Ecology and Initial Human Migration. In *The First Americans: Search and Research*, edited by Tom D. Dillehay and David J. Meltzer, pp. 231–264. CRC Press, Boca Raton, Florida.

 1996 Letter to Science. *Science* 274:1824–1825.

 1997 *Monte Verde: A Late Pleistocene Settlement in Chile*. Smithsonian Series in Archaeological Inquiry, Washington, D.C.

Dillehay, T. D. and M. Collins

 1988 Early Cultural Evidence from Monte Verde in Chile. *Nature* 332:150–152.

Dillehay, T. D. and D. J. Meltzer (editors)

 1991 *The First Americans: Search and Research*. CRC Press, Boca Raton, Florida.

Dillehay, T. D., M. Pino Q., E. M. Davis, S. Valastro, Jr.,

A. G. Varela, and R. Casamiquela

 1983 Monte Verde: radiocarbon dates from an Early Man site in south–central Chile. *Journal of Field Archaeology* 9:547–549.

Dincauze, D. F.

 1981 The Meadowcroft Papers (Adovasio, Gunn, Donahue, Stuckenrath, Guilday, Lord, Volman; Haynes, Mead)", *Quarterly Review of Archaeology* 2:3–4.

 1997 Regarding Pendejo Cave: Response to Chrisman et al. *American Antiquity* 62:554–555.

Dixon, E. J.

 1975 The Gallagher Flint Station, An Early Man Site on the North Slope, Arctic Alaska and Its Role in Relation to the Bering Land Bridge. *Arctic Anthropology* 12(1):68–75.

 1976 The Pleistocene Prehistory of Arctic North America. In *Colloque XVII Habitats Humains. Anterieurs a l'Holocene en Amerique*, edited by J. B. Griffin, pp. 168–198. Proceedings of the 9th International Congress of Anthropological Sciences, Nice, France.

 1983 Pleistocene Proboscidean Fossils from the Alaskan Continental Shelf. *Quaternary Research* 20:113–119.

1984   Context and Environment in Taphonomic Analysis: Examples from Alaska's Porcupine River Caves. *Quaternary Research* 22:201–215.

1985   Cultural Chronology of Central Interior Alaska. *Arctic Anthropology*. 22(1):47–66.

1986   The Northern Paleoindian/Northern Archaic Transition in Alaska. Paper presented at the 13th Annual Meeting of the Alaska Anthropological Association, Fairbanks, Alaska.

1993   *Quest for the Origins of the First Americans.* University of New Mexico Press, Albuquerque.

1995   The Fabulous Baker Family. *Museum Quarterly* 4(1). Denver Museum of Natural History.

Dixon, E. J., T. H. Heaton, T. E. Fifield, T. D. Hamilton, D. E. Putnam, and F. Grady

1997   Late Quaternary Regional Geoarchaeology of Southeast Alaska Karst: A Progress Report. *Geoarchaeology: An International Journal* 12(6): 689–712.

Dixon, E. J., D. C. Plaskett, and R. M. Thorson

1985   *Cave Deposits, Porcupine River Alaska.* National Geographic Society Research Reports, 1979 Projects, Washington, D.C.

Dixon, E. J. and G. S. Smith

1986   Broken Canines from Alaskan Cave Deposits: Re-evaluating Evidence for Domesticated Dog and Early Humans in Alaska. *American Antiquity* 51: 341–351.

1990   *A Regional Application of Tephrochronology in Alaska.* Centennial Special Vol. 4, Chapter 21:383–398. Geological Society of America, Boulder.

Dixon, E. J. and R. M. Thorson

1984   Taphonomic Analysis and Interpretation in North American Pleistocene Archaeology. *Quaternary Research* 22:155–159.

Driver, J. C.

1996   The Significance of the Fauna from the Charlie Lake Cave Site. In *Early Human Occupation in British Columbia*, edited by Roy L. Carlson and Luke Dalla Bona, pp. 21–28. University of British Columbia Press, Vancouver.

Driver, J. C., M. Handly, K. R. Fladmark, D. E. Nelson, G. M. Sullivan, and R. Preston

1996   Stratigraphy, Radiocarbon Dating, and Culture History of Charlie Lake Cave, British Columbia. *Arctic* 49(3):265–277.

Dumond, D. E.

1962   Blades and Cores in Oregon. *American Antiquity* 27:419–420.

1977   *The Eskimos and Aleuts.* Thames and Hudson, London.

1980   The Archeology of Alaska and the Peopling of America. *Science* 209:984–991.

1982   Trends and Traditions in Alaskan Prehistory: The Place of Norton Culture. *Arctic Anthropology* 19(2):39–51.

Dumond, D. E., W. Henn, and R. Stuckenrath

    1976   Archaeology and Prehistory on the Alaska Peninsula. *Anthropological Papers of the University of Alaska* 18(1):17–29.

Duvall, J. G. and W. T. Venner

    1979   A Statistical Analysis of Lithics from the Calico Site (SBCM 1500A), California. *Journal of Field Archaeology* 6:455–462.

Easton, N. A.

    1992   Mal de Mer above Terra Incognita, or "What Ails the Coastal Migration Theory." *Arctic Anthropology* 29:28–42.

Edgar, H. J. H.

    1997   Paleopathology of the Wizards Beach Man (AHUR 2023) and the Spirit Cave Mummy (AHUR 2064). *Nevada Historical Society Quarterly* 40(1):57–61.

Edwards, M. E. and P. W. Dunwiddie

    1985   Dendrochonological and palynological observations on *Populus balsamifera* in northern Alaska, U.S.A. Arctic and Alpine Research, 17:271–278.

Eiselt, B. S.

    1997   Fish Remains from the Spirit Cave Paleofecal Material: 9,400 Year Old Evidence or Great Basin Utilization of Small Fishes. *Nevada Historical Society Quarterly* 40(1):117–139.

Elias, S. A., S. K. Short, C. H. Nelson, and H. H. Birks

    1996   Life and Times of the Bering Land Bridge. *Nature* 382:60–63.

Elias, S. A., S. K. Short, and R. L. Phillips

    1992   Paleoecology of Late Glacial Peats from the Bering Land Bridge, Chukchi Sea Shelf Region, Northwestern Alaska. *Quaternary Research* 38:371–378.

Ericson, J. E. and R. Berger

    1974   Late Pleistocene American Obsidian Tools. *Nature* 249(5460):824–825.

Ericson, J. E., R. E. Taylor, and R. Berger (editors)

    1982   *Peopling of the New World.* Anthropological Papers 23. Ballena Press, Los Altos, California.

Erlandson, J. M.

    1991   Early Maritime Adaptations on the Northern Channel Islands, California. In *Hunter-Gathers of Early Holocene Coastal California*, edited by J. M. Erlandson and R. Colten, pp. 101–111. Perspectives in California Archaeology 1. Institute of Archaeology, University of California, Los Angeles.

    1994   *Early Hunter-Gatherers of the California Coast.* Plenum Press, New York and London.

Erlandson, J. M., T. Cooley, and R. Carrico

    1987   A Fluted Projectile Point Fragment from the Southern California Coast: Chronology and Context at CA-SBA-1951. *Journal of California and Great Basin Anthropology* 9:120–128.

Erlandson, J. M. and M. L. Moss

    1996   The Pleistocene-Holocene Transition along the Pacific Coast of North

America. In *Humans at the End of the Ice Age: The Archaeology of the Pleistocene-Holocene Transition*, edited by L. G. Straus, B. V. Eriksen, J. M. Erlandson, and D. R. Yesner, pp. 277–301. Plenum, New York.

Erlandson, J. M., M. L. Moss, and R. E. Hughes

1992   Archaeological Distribution and Trace Element Geochemistry of Volcanic Glass from Obsidian Cove, Sumez Island, Southeast Alaska. *Canadian Journal of Archaeology* 16:89–95.

Erlandson, J. M., T. C. Rick, R. L. Vellanoweth, and D. J. Kenneth

1998   Maritime Subsistence Patterns at CA-SRI-6: A 9300 Year Old Shell Midden from Santa Rosa Island, California. *Journal of Field Archaeology* in review.

Fagan, B. M.

1987   *The Great Journey: The Peopling of Ancient America.* Thames & Hudson, London.

Farrand, W. R.

1961   Frozen Mammoths and Modern Geology. *Science* 133:729–735.

Fedje, D. W.

1996   Early Human Presence in Banff National Park. In *Early Human Occupation in British Columbia*, edited by Roy L. Carlson and Luke Dalla Bona, pp. 35–44. University of British Columbia Press, Vancouver.

Fedje, D. W., A. P. Mackie, J. B. McSporran, and B. Wilson

1996   Early Period Archaeology in Gwaii Haanas: Results of the 1993 Field Program. In *Early Human Occupation in British Columbia*, edited by Roy L. Carlson and Luke Dalla Bona, pp. 133–150. University of British Columbia Press, Vancouver.

Fedje , D. W., J. M. White, M. C. Wilson, D. E. Nelson, J. S. Vogel, and J. R. Southon

1995   Vermilion Lakes Site: Adaptations and Environments in the Canadian Rockies During the Latest Pleistocene and Early Holocene. *American Antiquity* 60:81–108.

Ferring, C. R.

1989   The Aubrey Clovis Site: A Paleoindian Locality in the Upper Trinity Drainage Basin, Texas. *Current Research in the Pleistocene* 6:9–11.

1990   The 1989 Investigations at the Aubrey Clovis Site, Texas. *Current Research in the Pleistocene* 7:10–12.

1995   The Late Quaternary Geology and Archaeology of the Aubrey Site, Texas: A Preliminary Report. In *Ancient Peoples and Landscapes*, edited by Eileen Johnson, pp. 273–281. Museum of Texas Tech University, Lubbock.

Fiedel, S.

1996   Letter to Science. *Science* 274:1823–1824.

Figgins, J. D.

1924   *Annual Report of the Colorado Museum of Natural History.* Colorado Museum of Natural History, Denver.

1927   The Antiquity of Man in America. *Natural History* 27(3):229–239.

1931   An Additional Discovery of the Association of a "Folsom" Artifact and Fossil Mammal Remains. *Proceedings of the Colorado Museum of Natural History* 10(2):23–24.

1933   A Further Contribution to the Antiquity of Man in America. *Proceedings of the Colorado Museum of Natural History* 12(2):4–10.

1935   New World Man. *Proceeding of the Colorado Museum of Natural History* 14(1):1–5.

Finley, M. P.

1995   The (Eight Thousand Year) Old Man. *Falcon* 3(2):24–27.

Fitzgerald, R. and T. Jones

1998   Coastal Lifeways During the Pleistocene Holocene Interface: A New Perspective from Central California. Paper presented at the 63rd Annual Meeting of the Society for American Archaeology, Seattle, Washington.

Fladmark, K. R.

1975   *A Paleoecological Model for Northwest Coast Prehistory.* Archaeological Survey of Canada Paper 43. National Museum of Man, Mercury Series, Ottawa.

1979   Routes: Alternative Migration Corridors for Early Man in North America. *American Antiquity* 44:55–69.

1982   An Introduction to the Prehistory of British Columbia. *Canadian Journal of Archaeology* 6:95–156.

1983   Times and Places: Environmental Correlates of Mid-to-Late Wisconsin Human Population Expansion in North America: In *Early Man in the New World*, edited by Richard Shutler, pp. 13–42. Sage Publications, Beverly Hills.

1986   Getting One's Berings. *Natural History* 95(11):8–19.

1990   Possible Early Human Occupation in the Queen Charlotte Islands. *Canadian Journal of Archaeology* 14:183–97.

Fladmark, K. R., J. C. Driver, and D. Alexander

1988   The Paleoindian Component at Charlie Lake Cave (HbRf 39), British Columbia. *American Antiquity* 53:371–384.

Folsom, F. and G. Agogino

1975   New Light on an Old Site: Events Leading Up to the Discovery of the Folsom Type Site. *Anthropological Journal of Canada* 13(3): 2–5.

Forrester, R. E.

1985   Horn Shelter Number 2: The North End: A Preliminary Report. *Central Texas Archeologist 10,* edited by S. Alan Skinner, pp. 21–35. Baylor University Press, Waco, Texas.

Fredrickson, D. A. and J. W. Grosman

1977   A San Dieguito Component at Buena Vista Lake, California. *Journal of California Anthropology* 4(2):173–190.

Fredrickson, D. A. and G. G. White

1988   The Clear Lake Basin and Early Complexes in California's North Coast

Ranges. In *Early Human Occupation in Far Western North America: The Clovis-Archaic Interface*, edited by J. A. Willig, C. M. Aikens, and J. L. Fagan, pp. 75–86. Nevada State Museum Anthropological Papers No. 21. Carson City.

Frison, G. C.

1976   Cultural Activity Associated with Prehistoric Mammoth Butchering and Processing. *Science* 194:728–730.

1978   *Prehistoric Hunters of the High Plains*, 1st edition. Academic Press, New York.

1982   Paleo-Indian Winter Subsistence Strategies on the High Plains. In *A Collection of Essays in Honor of John C. Ewers and Waldo R. Wedel*, edited by D. H. Ubelaker and H. J. Viola, pp. 293–300. Smithsonian Contributions to Anthropology 30. Smithsonian Institution, Washington, D.C.

1983   The Western Plains and Mountain Region. In *Early Man in the New World*, edited by Richard Shutler, Jr., pp. 109–124. Sage Publications, Beverly Hills.

1984   The Carter/Kerr-McGee Paleoindian Site: Cultural Resource Management and Archaeological Research. *American Antiquity* 49:288–414.

1989   Experimental Use of Clovis Weaponry and Tools on African Elephants. *American Antiquity* 54:766–784.

1990   Clovis, Goshen, and Folsom: Lifeways and Cultural Relationships. In *Megafauna and Man: Discovery of America's Heartland*, edited by L. D. Agenbroad, J. I. Mead, and L. W. Nelson, pp. 100–108. Scientific Papers, Vol. 1. The Mammoth Site of Hot Springs, Hot Springs, South Dakota; and Northern Arizona University, Flagstaff.

1991   *Prehistoric Hunters of the High Plains*, 2nd edition. Academic Press, New York.

1992   The Foothills-Mountains and the Open Plains: The Dichotomy in Paleoindian Subsistence Strategies Between Two Ecosystems. In *Ice Age Hunters of the Rockies*, edited by Dennis J. Stanford and Jane S. Day, pp. 323–342. Denver Museum of Natural History.

Frison, G. C., R. L. Andrews, J. M. Adovasio, R. C. Carlisle, and R. Edgar

1986   A Late Paleoindian Animal Trapping Net from Northern Wyoming. *American Antiquity* 51:352–361.

Frison, G. C. and D. Stanford

1982   *The Agate Basin Site: A Record of the Paleoindian Occupation of the Northwestern High Plains*. Academic Press, New York.

Frison, G. C. and L. C. Todd

1986   *The Colby Mammoth Site: Taphonomy and Archaeology of a Clovis Kill in Northern Wyoming*. University of New Mexico Press, Albuquerque.

Fryxell, R., T. Bielicki, R. D. Daugherty, C. E. Gustafson, H. T. Irwin, and B. C. Keel

1968   A Human Skeleton from Sediments of Mid-Pinedale Age in Southeastern Washington. *American Antiquity* 33:511–514.

Fryxell, R., T. Bielicki, R. D. Daugherty, C. E. Gustafson,
H. T. Irwin, B. C. Keel, and G. S. Krantz

    1968   Human Skeletal Material and Artifacts from Sediments of Pinedale (Wisconsin) Glacial Age in Southeastern Washington, United States. *Ethnology and Archaeology*, pp. 176–181. Proceedings of the 7th International Congress of Anthropological and Ethnological Sciences, Vol. III, Tokyo and Kyoto.

Gibbons, J. R. H., G. A. U. Clunie

    1985   Sea Level Changes and Pacific Prehistory: New Insight into Early Human Settlement of Oceania. *The Journal of Pacific History* 20:58–82.

Giddings, J. L.

    1964   *The Archaeology of Cape Denbigh.* Brown University Press, Providence.

    1967   *Ancient men of the Arctic.* Alfred Knoph, New York.

Gifford, J. A. and G. Rapp, Jr.

    1985   The Early Development of Archaeological Geology in North America. In *Geologists and Ideas: A History of North American Geology*, edited by Ellen T. Drake and William M. Jordan, pp. 409–422. Centennial Special Vol. 1. Geological Society of American, Boulder, Colorado.

Giles, R. E., H. Blanc, H. M. Cann, and D. C. Wallace

    1980   Maternal Inheritance of Human Mitochondrial DNA. *Proceedings of the National Academy of Science* 77:6715–6719.

Gillio, D. A.

    1970   A Reexamination of the Gordon Creek Burial Lithic Material. *Southwestern Lore* 36:12–14. Gunnison, Colorado.

Glassow, M. A.

    1977   *An Archaeological Overview of the Northern Channel Islands, California.* Department of Anthropology, University of California, Santa Barbara.

    1980   Recent Developments in the Archaeology of the Channel Islands. In *The California Islands: Proceedings of a Multidisciplinary Symposium*, pp. 79–81. Santa Barbara Museum of Natural History.

Gleichman, P. J. and C. L. Gleichman

    1989   Prehistoric Paleo-Indian Cultures of the Colorado Plains, Multiple Property Listing. Native Cultural Services, 308 Pearl Street, Boulder, Colorado.

Goebel, F. E. and W. R. Powers

    1990   Early Paleoindians in Beringia and the Origins of Clovis. In *Chronostratigraphy of the Paleolithic of North, Central and East Asia and America*, p. 173. Academy of Sciences of the USSR Institute of History, Philology and Philosophy, Siberian Branch of the Academy of Sciences. Novosibersk, USSR.

Goebel, F. E., W. R. Powers, and N. Bigelow

    1991   The Nenana Complex of Alaska and Clovis Origins. In *Clovis Origins and Adaptations*, edited by R. Bonnichsen and K. Turnmire, pp. 49–79. Center for the Study of the First Americans, Oregon State University, Corvalis.

Goebel T. and N. H. Bigelow

1996   Panguingue Creek. In *American Beginnings: The Prehistory and Paleoecology of Beringia*, edited by Frederick Hadleigh West, pp. 366–371. University of Chicago Press, Chicago.

Goebel, T. and W. R. Powers

1989   A Possible Paleoindian Dwelling in the Nenana, Alaska: Spatial Analysis at the Walker Road Site. Paper presented at the 16th Annual Meeting of the Alaska Anthropological Association.

Graham, R. W.

1981   Preliminary Report on Late Pleistocene Vertebrates from the Selby and Dutton Archaeological/Paleontological Sites, Yuma County, Colorado. *Contributions to Geology* 20:33–56. University of Wyoming, Laramie.

1990   Evolution of new ecosystems at the end of the Pleistocene. in *Megafauna and Man: Discovery of Americas Heartland*, L. D. Agenbroad, J. I. Mead and L. W. Nelson eds., pp. 54–60. The Mammoth Site of Hot Springs, South Dakota, Inc. Scientific Papers 1.

in preparation   An Analysis of the Pleistocene Fauna from Valsequillo, Mexico. Unpublished manuscript in possession of the author, Denver Museum of Natural History.

Gramly, R. M.

1996   The East Wenachee Clovis Site (Richey-Roberts Site): Summary of Findings and Current Status. *Current Research in the Pleistocene* 13:19–20.

Grayson, D. K.

1993   *The Desert's Past: A Natural Prehistory of the Great Basin*. Smithsonian Institution Press, Washington, D.C.

Green, F. E.

1963   The Clovis Blades: An Important Addition to the Llano Complex. *American Antiquity* 29:145–165.

Green, T. J., B. Cochran, T. Fenton, J. C. Woods, G. Titmus,
L. Tieszen, M. A. Davis, and S. Miller

1998   The Buhl Burial: A Paleoindian Woman from Southern Idaho. *American Antiquity* 63:437–456.

Greenberg, J. H.

1987   *Language in the Americas*. Stanford University Press, Stanford.

1996   Beringia and New World Origins: The Linguistic Evidence. In *American Beginnings: The Prehistory and Palaeoecology of Beringia*, edited by Frederick Hadleigh West, pp. 525–536. University of Chicago Press, Chicago.

Greenberg, J. H., C. G. Turner II, and S. L. Zegura

1986   The Settlement of the Americas: A Comparison of the Linguistic, Dental, and Genetic Evidence. *Current Anthropology* 27(5):477–97.

Griffin, J. B.

1979   The Origin and Dispersion of American Indians in North America. In *The First Americans: Origins, Affinities, and Adaptations*, edited by

William S. Laughlin and Albert B. Harper, pp. 43–56. Gustav Fischer, New York.

Gruhn, R.

1961 *The Archaeology of Wilson Butte Cave, South–central Idaho.* Occasional Papers of the Idaho State College Museum, 6. Pocatello.

1965 Two Early Radiocarbon Dates from the Lower Levels of Wilson Butte Cave, South–central Idaho. *Tebiwa: Journal of the Idaho State University Museum* 8:57.

1979a Description of the 1976 Excavations at Taima-Taima. In *Taima-Taima, A Late Pleistocene Paleo-Indian Kill Site in Northernmost South America— Final Reports of 1976 Excavations*, edited by Claudio Ochsenius and Ruth Gruhn, pp. 31–34, South American Quaternary Documentation Program, printed in the Federal Republic of Germany.

1979b Synthesis: A Reconstruction. In *Taima-Taima, A Late Pleistocene Paleo- Indian Kill Site in Northernmost South America—Final Reports of 1976 Excavations*, edited by Claudio Ochsenius and Ruth Gruhn, pp. 109–110, South American Quaternary Documentation Program, printed in the Federal Republic of Germany.

1987 On the Settlement of the Americas: South American Evidence for an Ex- panded Time Frame. *Current Anthropology* 28:363–364.

1988 Linguistic Evidence in Support of the Coastal Route of Earliest Entry into the New World. *Man* 23:77–100.

1991 Stratified Radiocarbon-dated Archaeological Sites of Clovis Age and Older in Brazil. In *Clovis Origins and Adaptations*, edited by R. Bonnich- sen and K. L. Turnmire, pp. 283–286. Peopling of the Americas Publica- tions, Oregon State University, Corvallis.

1994 The Pacific Coast Route of Initial Entry: An Overview. In *Methods and Theory for Investigating the Peopling of the Americas*, edited by Robson Bonnichsen and D. Gentry Steele, pp. 249–256. Center for the Study of the First Americans, Oregon State University, Corvallis.

1995 Results of New Excavations at Wilson Butte Cave, Idaho. *Current Research in the Pleistocene.* 12:16–17.

1997 The South American Context of the Pedra Pintada Site in Brazil. *Current Research in the Pleistocene* 14:29–32.

Gruhn, R. and A. Bryan

1998 Chac Mool Conference, Calgary, Alberta, Field Excursion, Site Summaries EgPn415 Bowmont Park, EgPn413 Varsity Estates. University of Alberta, Canada.

Gryba, E. M.

1985 Fluted Point Occurrences at the Sibbald Creek Site in Alberta. *Current Research in the Pleistocene* 2:15–16.

Guidon, N.

1986 Las Unidades Culturales de Sao Raimundo Nonato-Sudeste del Estado de

Piaui-Brasil. In *New Evidence for the Pleistocene Peopling of the Americas*, edited by Alan Lyle Bryan, pp. 157–171. Center for the Study of Early Man, University of Maine at Orono.

Guidon, N. and G. Delibrias

  1986   Carbon-14 Dates Point to Man in the Americas 32,000 Years Ago. *Nature* 321:769–771.

Gustafson, C. E., D. Gilbow, and R. D. Daugherty

  1979   The Manis Mastodon Site: Early Man on the Olympic Peninsula. *Canadian Journal of Archaeology* 3:157–164.

Guthrie, R. D.

  1990   Frozen Fauna of the Mammoth Steppe. University of Chicago Press, Chicago.

Haley, S. D. and F. Solorzano

  1991   The Lake Chapala First Mexicans Project, Jalisco, Mexico. *Current Research in the Pleistocene* 8:20–22.

Hall, D. A.

  1995   Ice-Age Wisconsin People Left Unique Cultural Record. *Mammoth Trumpet* 10(2):5–8. Center for the Study of the First Americans, Oregon State University, Corvallis.

Hamilton, T. D. and T. Goebel

  1999   Late Pleistocene Peopling of Alaska. In *Ice Age Peoples of North America*, edited by R. Bonnichsen. Oregon University Press for the Center for the Study of the First Americans, Corvalis.

Harington, C. R.

  1978   *Quaternary Vertebrate Faunas of Canada and Alaska and Their Suggested Chronological Sequence.* Canadian National Museum of Natural Sciences, Syllogeus 15, Ottawa.

  1989   Pleistocene Vertebrate Localities in the Yukon. In *Late Cenozoic History of the Interior Basins of Alaska and the Yukon*, edited by L. D. Carter, T. D. Hamilton, and J. P. Galloway, pp. 93–98. U. S. Geological Survey Circular 1026. U. S. Government Printing Office, Washington, D.C.

Harington, C. R., R. Bonnichsen, and R. E. Morlan

  1975   Bones Say Man Lived in Yukon 27,000 Years Ago. *Canadian Geographical Journal* 91(2):42–48.

Harrison, W. R. and H. C. Smith

  1975   A Test Excavation of the Lake Theo Site, Briscoe County, Texas. *Panhandle-Plains Historical Review* 67:70–106. Panhandle-Plains Historical Society, Canyon, Texas.

Hassan, A. A. and P. E. Hare

  1978   Amino Acid Analysis in Radiocarbon Dating of Bone Collagen. Advances in Chemistry Series 171. *Archeological Chemistry* 11:109–116.

Hassan, A. A. and D. J. Ortner

    1977   Inclusions in Bone Material as a Source of Error in Radiocarbon Dating. *Archaeometry* 19:131–135.

Haury, E. W.

    1950   *The Stratigraphy and Archaeology of Ventana Cave, Arizona.* University of Arizona Press, Tucson, and University of New Mexico Press, Albuquerque.

    1953   Artifacts with Mammoth Remains, Naco, Arizona. *American Antiquity* 19:1–14.

    1975   *The Stratigraphy and Archaeology of Ventana Cave, Arizona.* University of Arizona Press, Tucson.

Hayden, J. D.

    1976   Pre-Altithermal Archaeology in the Sierra Pinacate, Sonora, Mexico. *American Antiquity* 41:274–289.

Haynes, C. V., Jr.

    1964   Fluted Projectile Points: Their Age and Dispersion. *Science* 145:14098–14113.

    1966   Elephant-Hunting in North America. In *Early Man in America, readings from Scientific American,* compiled by Richard S. MacNeish, pp. 44–52. W. H. Freeman, San Francisco.

    1967   *Carbon-14 Sampling of the Tlapacoya Site, Mexico.* INAH Bulletin 29. Mexico City.

    1969   The Earliest Americans. *Science* 166:709–715.

    1973   The Calico Site: Artifacts of Geofacts? *Science* 181:305–310.

    1974   Paleoenvironments and Cultural Diversity in Late Pleistocene South America: A Reply to Alan L. Bryan. *Quaternary Research* 4:378–380.

    1977   When and from Where Did Man Arrive in Northeastern North America? A Discussion. In *Amerinds and Their Paleoenvironments in Northeastern North America,* edited by W. S. Newman and B. Salwen, pp. 137–160. Annals of the New York Academy of Sciences.

    1980   Paleo-Indian Charcoal from Meadowcroft Rockshelter: Is Contamination a Problem? *American Antiquity* 45:582–588.

    1982   Archaeological Investigations at the Lehner Site, Arizona. *National Geographic Society Research Reports* 13:243–251.

    1987   Clovis Origin Update. *The Kiva* 52(2):83–92.

    1991   Geoarchaeological and Paleohydrological Evidence for a Clovis-Age Drought in North America and Its Bering on Extinction. *Quaternary Research* 35:438–450.

    1992   Contributions of Radiocarbon Dating to the Geochronology of the Peopling of the New World. In *Radiocarbon After Four Decades: An Interdisciplinary Perspective,* edited by R. E. Taylor, A. Long, and R. S. Kra, pp. 355–374. Springer-Verlag, New York.

Haynes, C. V., Jr. and G. A. Agogino

    1960   *Geological Significance of a New Radiocarbon Date from the Lindenmeier Site*. Proceedings of the Denver Museum of Natural History, Series 2, No. 9, pp. 5–23.

    1986   *Geochronology of Sandia Cave*. Smithsonian Institution Press, Washington, D.C.

Haynes, C. V., Jr., D. J. Donahue, A. T. Jull, and T. H. Zabel

    1984   Application of Accelerator Dating to Fluted Point Paleoindian Sites. *Archaeology of Eastern North America* 12:184–191.

Haynes, G.

    1991   *Mammoths, Mastodonts, & Elephants: Biology, Behavior, and the Fossil Record*. Cambridge University Press, Cambridge, New York.

Heaton, T. H.

    1995   Middle Wisconsin Bear and Rodent Remains Discovered on Prince of Wales Island, Alaska. *Current Research in the Pleistocene* 12:92–95.

    1996   The Late Wisconsin Vertebrate Fauna of On Your Knees Cave, Northern Prince of Wales Island, Alaska. *Journal of Vertebrate Paleontology* 16:40A-41A.

Heaton, T. H. and F. Grady

    1993   Fossil Grizzly Bears from Prince of Wales Island, Alaska, Offer New Insights into Animal Dispersal, Interspecific Competition, and Age of Deglaciation. *Current Research in the Pleistocene* 10:98–100.

Heaton, T. H., S. L. Talbot, and G. F. Shield

    1996   An Ice Age Refugium for Large Mammals in the Alexander Archipelago, Southeastern Alaska. *Quaternary Research* 46:186–192.

Heizer, R. and R. Brooks

    1965   Lewisville-Ancient Campsite or Wood Rat Houses? *Southwestern Journal of Anthropology* 21:155–165.

Henn, W.

    1978   *Archaeology on the Alaska Peninsula: The Ugashik Drainage. 1973–1975*. University of Oregon Anthropological Papers No. 14. Eugene.

Hester, J. J.

    1972   *Blackwater Locality No. 1: A Stratified Early Man Site in Eastern New Mexico*. Fort Burgwin Research Center Publication No. 8. Fort Burgwin Research Center, Southern Methodist University, Dallas.

Hester, J. J. and J. Grady

    1982   *Introduction to Archaeology*, 2nd edition. Holt, Rinehart, and Winston, New York.

Hester, T. R.

    1973   *Chronological Ordering of Great Basin Prehistory*. Contributions of the University of California Archaeological Research Facility, No. 17. Berkeley.

Hibben, F. C.

1937   Association of Man with Pleistocene Mammals in the Sandia Mountains, New Mexico. *American Antiquity* 2:260–263.

1940   Sandia Man. *Scientific American* 163:14–15.

1941a   Sandia Cave. *American Antiquity* 6:266.

1941b   Evidence of Early Occupation in Sandia Cave, New Mexico, and Other Early Sites in the Sandia-Manzano Region. *Smithsonian Institution Miscellaneous Collections* 99(3):1–44.

1942   Pleistocene Stratification in the Sandia Cave, New Mexico. *Proceedings of the 8th American Science Congress* 2:45–48.

1955   Specimens from Sandia Cave and Their Possible Significance. *Science* 122:688–689.

1957   Comments on "Radiocarbon Dates from Sandia Cave, Correction." *Science* 125:235.

Hobler, P. M.

1978   The Relationship of Archaeological Sites to Sea Levels on Moresby Island, Queen Charlotte Islands. *Canadian Journal of Archaeology* 2:1–14.

Hofman, J. L.

1992   Recognition and Interpretation of Folsom Technological Variability on the Southern Plains. In *Ice Age Hunters of the Rockies*, edited by Dennis J. Stanford and Jane S. Day, pp. 193–224. Denver Museum of Natural History.

1995   Dating Folsom Occupations on the Southern Plains: The Lipscomb and Waugh Sites. *Journal of Field Archaeology* 22:421–437.

Holen, S. R.

1994   Did Someone Eat the La Sena Mammoth? In The Cellars of Time. *NEBRASKAland Magazine* 72(1):88–93.

Holen, S. R. and D. W. May

1996   The Angus Mammoth: Archaeology or Paleontology? *Proceedings of the Nebraska Academy of Sciences*.

Holliday, V. T.

1995   *Stratigraphy and Paleoenvironments of Late Quaternary Valley Fills on the Southern High Plains*. Geological Society of America Memoir 186. Geological Society of America, Boulder.

Holliday, V. T. and A. B. Anderson

1993   "Paleoindian," "Clovis" and "Folsom": A Brief Etymology. *Current Research in the Pleistocene* 10:79–81.

Holliday, V. T. and E. Johnson

1986   Re-evaluation of the First Radiocarbon Age for the Folsom Culture. *American Antiquity* 51:332–338.

Holliday, V. T. and D. J. Meltzer

1996   Geoarchaeology of the Midland (Paleoindian) Site, Texas. *American Antiquity* 61:755–771.

Holmes, C. E.

1988a   *Archaeological Mitigation of the Thorne River Site (CRG-177), Prince of Wales Island, Alaska.* Office of History and Archaeology, Report 15. Division of Parks and Outdoor Recreation, Alaska Department of Natural Resources, Anchorage.

1988b   An Early Post Paleo-Arctic Site in the Alaska Range. Paper presented at the 15th Annual Meeting of the Alaska Anthropological Association, Fairbanks, Alaska.

1990   The Broken Mammoth Site: Its Relevance in Alaska/Yukon Prehistory. Paper presented at the Canadian Archaeological Association Annual Meeting, Whitehorse, Yukon Territory.

1996   Broken Mammoth. In *American Beginnings: The Prehistory and Palaeoecology of Beringia,* edited by Frederick Hadleigh West, pp. 312–317. University of Chicago Press, Chicago.

Holmes, C. E., R. J. Dale, and J. D. McMahn

1989   *Archaeological Mitigation of the Thorne River Site (CRG-177).* Office of History and Archaeology, Report 15. Division of Parks and Outdoor Recreation, Alaska Department of Natural Resources, Anchorage.

Holmes, C. E., R. Vanderhoek, and T. E. Dilley

1996   Swan Point. In *American Beginnings: The Prehistory and Palaeoecology of Beringia,* edited by Frederick Hadleigh West, pp. 319–323. University of Chicago Press, Chicago.

Holmes, W. H.

1890   A Quarry Workshop of the Flaked Stone Implement Makers in the District of Columbia. *American Anthropologists* 3:1–26.

1892   Modern Quarry Refuse and the Paleolithic Theory. *Science* 20:295–297.

1893   Traces of Glacial Man in Ohio. *Journal of Geology* 1:147–163.

Hopkins, D. M.

1967   *The Bering Land Bridge.* Stanford University Press, Stanford.

1973   Sea Level History in Beringia During the Past 250,000 Years. *Quaternary Research* 3:520–540.

1979   Landscape and Climate of Beringia During Late Pleistocene and Holocene Times. In *The First Americans: Origins, Affinities, and Adaptations,* edited by William S. Laughlin and Albert B. Harper, pp. 15–41. Gustav Fischer, New York.

1982   Aspects of the Paleogeography of Beringia During the Late Pleistocene In *Paleoecology of Beringia,* edited by D. M. Hopkins, J. V. Matthews, Jr., C. E. Schweger, and S. B. Young, pp. 3–28. Academic Press, New York.

Horai, S., R. Kondo, S. Sonoda, and K. Tajima

1996   The First Americans: Different Waves of Migration to the New World Inferred from Mitochondrial DNA Sequence Polymorphisms. In *Prehistoric Mongoloid Dispersals,* edited by Takeru Akazawa and Emőke J. E. Szathmáry, pp. 270–283. Oxford University Press, Oxford.

Howard, E. B.

    1935   Evidence of Early Man in North America. *The Museum Journal*, University of Pennsylvania Museum XXIV(2–3).

    1943   The Finley Site: Discovery of Yuma Points, in Situ, near Eden, Wyoming. *American Antiquity* 8:224–234.

Hrdlička, A.

    1912   *Early Man in South America.* Bureau of American Ethnology Bulletin 52. Washington, D.C.

    1925   *The Origins and Antiquity of the American Indian.* Smithsonian Report for 1923, Publication 2778. Smithsonian Institution, Washington, D.C.

    1928   The Origin and Antiquity of Man in America. *New York Academy of Medicine Bulletin* 4(7):802–816.

    1937   Early Man in America: What Have the Bones to Say? In *Early Man, as Depicted by Leading Authorities at the International Symposium at the Academy of Natural Sciences, Philadelphia, March 1937*, edited by G. G. MacCurdy, pp. 93–104. J. B. Lippincott, Philadelphia.

Huscher, H.

    1939   Influence of the Drainage Pattern of the Uncompahgre Plateau on the Movements of Primitive Peoples. *Southwestern Lore* 5(2). Gunnison, Colorado.

Hutchings, K. W.

    1996   The Namu Obsidian Industry. In *Early Human Occupation in British Columbia*, edited by Roy L. Carlson and Luke Dalla Bona, pp. 167–176. University of British Columbia Press, Vancouver.

    1997   *The Paleoindian Fluted Point: Dart or Spear Armature? The Identification of Paleoindian Delivery Technology Through the Analysis of Lithic Fracture Velocity.* Ph.D. dissertation, Department of Archaeology, Simon Fraser University, Burnaby, British Columbia.

    1998   The Identification of Paleoindian Fluted Point Delivery Technology Through the Analysis of Lithic Fracture Velocity. Paper presented at the 63rd Annual Meeting of the Society for American Archaeology, Seattle.

Irving, W. N. and C. R. Harington

    1973   Upper Pleistocene Radiocarbon-dated Artifacts from the Northern Yukon. *Science* 179:335–340.

Irving, W. N., A. V. Jopling, and B. F. Beebe

    1986   Indications of Pre-Sangamon Humans near Old Crow, Yukon, Canada. In *New Evidence for the Pleistocene Peopling of the Americas*, edited by Alan Lyle Bryan, pp. 49–63. Center for the Study of Early Man, University of Maine at Orono.

Irving, W. N., J. T. Mayhall, F. J. Melbye, and B. F. Beebe

    1977   A Human Mandible in Probable Association with a Pleistocene Faunal Assemblage in Eastern Beringia: A Preliminary Report. *Canadian Journal of Archaeology* 1:81–93.

Irwin, A. M. and U. Moody

    1978   *The Lind Coulee Site (45-GR-97)*. Project Report 56. Washington Archaeological Research Center, Washington State University, Pullman.

Irwin, G.

    1989   Against, Across and Down the Wind: A Case for the Systematic Exploration of the Remote Pacific Islands. *The Journal of the Polynesian Society* 98(2):167–106.

Irwin, G., S. Bickler, and P. Quirke

    1990   Voyaging by canoe and computer: experiments in the settlement of the Pacific Ocean. Antiquity 64(242):34–50.

Irwin, H. T.

    1971   Developments in Early Man Studies in Western North America. *Arctic Anthropology* 8(2):42–67.

Irwin-Williams, C.

    1967   Association of Early Man with Horse, Camel and Mastodon at Hueyatlaco, Valsequillo (Puebla Mexico). In *Pleistocene Extinctions*, edited by P. S. Martin, pp. 337–347. Yale University Press, New Haven.

    1969   Comments on the Associations of Archeological Materials and Extinct Fauna in the Valsequillo region, Puebla, Mexico. *American Antiquity* 34:82–83.

    1973   *The Oshara Tradition: Origins of Anasazi Culture.* Contributions in Anthropology 5(1). Eastern New Mexico University, Portales.

    1978   Summary of Archaeological Evidence from the Valsequillo Region, Puebla, Mexico. In *Cultural Continuity in Mesoamerica*, edited by D. L. Browman, pp. 7–22. Mouton, The Hague.

    1979   Post-Pleistocene Archeology, 7000–2000 B.C. In *Southwest*, edited by A. Ortiz, pp. 31–42. Handbook of North American Indians, Vol. 9, W. C. Sturtevant, general editor. Smithsonian Institution, Washington, D.C.

    1981   Commentary on Geologic Evidence for Age of Deposits at Hueyatlaco Archeological Site, Valsequillo, Mexico. *Quaternary Research* 16:258.

Irwin-Williams, C., H. Irwin, G. Agogino, and C. V. Haynes, Jr.

    1973   Hell Gap: Paleo-Indian Occupation on the High Plains. *Plains Anthropologist* 18(59):40–53.

Jackson, L. E., Jr. and A. Duk-Rodkin

    1996   Quaternary Geology of the Ice-free Corridor: Glacial controls on the Peopling of the New World. In *Prehistoric Mongoloid Dispersals*, edited by Takeru Akazawa and Emőke J. E. Szathmáry, pp. 214–227. Oxford University Press, New York.

Jackson, L. E., Jr., E. C. Little, E. R. Loboe, and P. J. Holme

    1996   A re-evaluation of the Paleoglaciology of the Maximum Continental and Montane Advances, Southwestern Alberta. In *Current Research 1996-A; Geological Survey of Canada*, pp. 165–173.

Jackson, L. E., Jr., F. M. Phillips, K. Shimamura, and E. C. Little

  1997   Cosmogenic ^{36}Cl Dating of the Foothills Erratics Train, Alberta, Canada.
          Geology 25(3):195–198.

James, S. R.

  1989   Hominid Use of Fire in the Lower and Middle Pleistocene. A Review of
          the Evidence. *Current Anthropology* 30:1–26.

Jantz, R. L. and D. W. Owsley

  1997   Pathology, Taphonomy, and Cranial Morphometrics of the Spirit Cave
          Mummy (AHUR 2064). *Nevada Historical Society Quarterly* 40(1):62–84.

Jenks, A. E.

  1937   *Minnesota's Browns Valley Man and Associated Burial Artifacts.* Memoirs
          of the American Anthropological Association, Number 49. Menasha,
          Wisconsin.

Jenness, D. (editor)

  1933   *The American Aborigines, Their Origin and Antiquity.* A Collection of
          Papers by Ten Authors Assembled and Edited by Diamond Jenness. Pub-
          lished for presentation at the Fifth Pacific Science Congress. Canada.
          Cooper Square Publishers, New York, 1973.

Jennings, J. D.

  1957   *Danger Cave.* University of Utah Anthropological Papers 27. Salt Lake
          City

  1964   The Desert West. In *Prehistoric Man in the New World*, edited by J. D. Jen-
          nings and E. Norbeck, pp. 149–174. University of Chicago Press, Chicago.

  1978a   Origins. In *Ancient Native Americans*, edited by Jesse D. Jennings, pp.
          1–42. W. H. Freeman and Company, San Francisco.

  1978b   *Prehistory of Utah and the Eastern Great Basin.* Anthropological Papers of
          the University of Utah 98. Salt Lake City.

Jodry, M. A. and D. J. Stanford

  1992   Stewart's Cattle Guard Site: An Analysis of Bison Remains in a Folsom
          Kill-Butchery Campsite. In *Ice Age Hunters of the Rockies*, edited by Den-
          nis J. Stanford and Jane S. Day, pp. 101–168. Denver Museum of Natural
          History.

Jodry, M. A., M. D. Turner, V. Spero, J. C. Turner, and D. J. Stanford

  1996   Folsom in the Colorado High Country: The Black Mountain Site. *Current
          Research in the Pleistocene* 13:25–27.

Johnson, E. and P. Shipman

  1993   Scanning Electron Microscope Analysis of Bone Modifications at Pendejo
          Cave, New Mexico. *Current Research in the Pleistocene* 10:72–75.

Johnson, F.

  1957   Radiocarbon Dates from Sandia Cave, Correction. *Science* 125:234–235.

Johnston, W. A.

  1933   Quaternary Geology of North America in Relation to the Migration of
          Man. In *The American Aborigines, Their Origins and Antiquity*, edited by

Diamond Jenness, pp. 9–46. A Collection of Papers by Ten Authors Assembled and Edited by Diamond Jenness. Published for presentation at the Fifth Pacific Science Congress. Canada. Cooper Square Publishers, New York, 1973. University of Toronto Press, Toronto.

Jones, K. B. and G. H. Johnson

    1997   Geology of the Cactus Hill Archaeological Site (44sx202) Sussex County, Virginia. In *Archaeological Investigations of Site 44sx202, Cactus Hill, Sussex County, Virginia*, J. M. McAvoy and L. D. McAvoy, authors, Appendix C. Virginia Department of Historic Resources, Research Report Series No.8. Sandston, Virginia.

Jones, R.

    1989   East of Wallace's Line: Issues and Problems in the Colonization of the Australian Continent. In *The Human Revolution*, edited by P. Mellars and C. Stringer, pp. 743–782. University of Edinburgh Press, Edinburgh and University of Princeton Press, Princeton.

Jones, S. and R. Bonnichsen

    1994   The Anzick Clovis Burial. *Current Research in the Pleistocene* 11:42–43.

Jopling, A. V., W. N. Irving, and B. F. Beebe

    1981   Stratigraphic, Sedimentological and Faunal Evidence for the Occurrence of Pre-Sangamonian Artifacts in Northern Yukon. *Arctic* 34(1):3–33.

Jordan, R. H.

    1992   *A Maritime Paleoarctic Assemblage from Kodiak Island, Alaska.* Anthropological Papers of the University of Alaska (24). Fairbanks.

Josenhans, H. W., D. W. Fedje, K. W. Conway, and J. E. Barrie

    1995   Post Glacial Sea-Levels on the Western Canadian Continental Shelf: Evidence for Rapid Change, Extensive Subaerial Exposure, and Early Human Habitation. *Marine Geology* 125:73–94.

Josenhans, H. W., D. W. Fedje, R. Pienitz, and J. Southon

    1997   Early Humans and Rapidly Changing Holocene Sea Levels in the Queen Charlotte Islands-Hecate Strait, British Columbia, Canada. *Science* 277: 71–74.

Judge, W. J.

    1970   Systems Analysis of the Folsom-Midland Question. *Southwestern Journal of Anthropology* 26:40–51.

    1973   *Paleoindian Occupation of the Central Rio Grande Valley in New Mexico.* University of New Mexico Press, Albuquerque.

Kaestle, F.

    1997   Molecular Analysis of Ancient Native American DNA from Western Nevada. *Nevada Historical Society Quarterly* 40(1):85–96.

Kaplan, D. and R. A. Manners

    1972   *Culture Theory.* Prentice-Hall, Englewood Cliffs, New Jersey.

Kaufman, T. S.

    1980   Early Prehistory of the Clear Lake Area, Lake County, California. Unpublished Ph.D. dissertation, University of California, Los Angeles. University Microfilms International, Ann Arbor.

Keefer, D. K., S. D. deFrance, M. E. Moseley, J. B. Richardson III, Dennis R. Satterlee, A. Day-Lewis

1998   Early Maritime Economy and el Niño Events at Quebrada Tacahuay, Peru. *Science* 281:1833–1835.

Kelly, R. L.

1996   Ethnographic Analogy and Migration to the Western Hemisphere. In *Prehistoric Mongoloid Dispersals*, edited by Takeru Akazawa and Emőke J. E. Szathmáry, pp. 228–240. Oxford University Press, New York.

Kelly, R. L. and L. C. Todd

1988   Coming into the Country: Early Paleoindian Hunting and Mobility. *American Antiquity* 53:231–244.

King, M. L. and S. B. Slobodin

1996   A Fluted Point from the Uptar Site, Northeastern Siberia. *Science* 273:634–636.

Kirner, D. L., R. Burky, K. Selsor, D. George, R. E. Taylor, and J. R. Southon

1997   Dating the Spirit Cave Mummy: The Value of Reexamination. *Nevada Historical Society Quarterly* 40(1):54–56.

Knudson, R.

1983   Organizational Variability in Late Paleoindian Assemblages. Washington State University, Laboratory of Anthropology, Reports of Investigations 60.

Krantz, Grover S.

1979   Oldest Human Remains from the Marmes Site. *Northwest Anthropological Research Notes* 13(2):159–174.

Krieger, A. D.

1947   Certain Projectile Points of the Early American Hunters. *Bulletin of the Texas Archaeological Paleontological Society* 18:7–27.

1957   Sandia Cave in Notes and News. *American Antiquity* 22:435–438.

1964   Early Man in the New World. In *Prehistoric Man in the New World*, edited by J. D. Jennings and Edward Norbeck, pp. 23–81. University of Chicago Press, Chicago.

Kroeber, A. L.

1962   The Rancho La Brea Skull. *American Antiquity* 27:416–417.

Kunz, M. L.

1982   The Mesa Site: An Early Holocene Hunting Stand in the Iteriak Valley, Northern Alaska. *Anthropological Papers of the University of Alaska* 20(1–2):113–122.

Kunz, M. L. and R. E. Reanier

1994   Paleoindians in Beringia: Evidence from Arctic Alaska. *Science* 263: 660–662.

1995 The Mesa Site: A Paleoindian Hunting Lookout in Arctic Alaska. *Arctic Anthropology* 32(1):5–30.

1996 The Mesa Site, Iteriak Creek. In *American Beginnings: The Prehistory and Palaeoecology of Beringia*, edited by Frederick Hadleigh West, pp. 497–504. University of Chicago Press, Chicago.

Kunz, M. L. and P. H. Shelley

1994 The Mesa Complex: A Possible Beringian Precursor to the Agate Basin Culture. Paper presented at the 52nd Annual Plains Anthropological Conference, Lubbock, Texas.

Lahren, L. L. and R. Bonnichsen

1974 Bone Foreshafts from a Clovis Burial in Southwestern Montana. *Science* 186:147–150.

Larsen, H.

1968a Trail Creek, Final Report on the Excavation of Two Caves at Seward Peninsula, Alaska. *Acta Arctica* 15:7–79. Copenhagen.

1968b The Eskimo Culture and Its Relationship to Northern Eurasia. In *Proceedings of the 8th International Congress of Anthropological and Ethnological Sciences*, pp. 337–340.

Laughlin, W. S.

1967 Human Migration and Permanent Occupation in the Bering Area. In *The Bering Land Bridge*, edited by D. M. Hopkins, pp. 409–450. Stanford University Press, Stanford.

1975 Aleuts: Ecosystem, Holocene History, and Siberian Origin. *Science* 189:507–515.

Leakey, L. S. B., R. D. Simpson, and T. Clements

1968 Archaeological Excavations in the Calico Mountains, California: Preliminary Report. *Science* 181:305–310.

Leboe, E. R.

1995 Quaternary Geology and Terrain Inventory, Eastern Cordillera NATMAP Project. Report 2: Surficial Geology and Quaternary Stratigraphy, Pincher Creek and Brocket Map Areas, Alberta. In *Current Research 1995-A; Geological Survey of Canada*, pp. 167–175.

Lee, R. B. and I. DeVore

1968 Problems in the Study of Hunters and Gatherers. In *Man the Hunter*, edited by R. B. Lee and I. DeVore, pp. 3–12. Aldine, Chicago.

LeTourneau, P.

1995 Quaternary Studies in Northern Chihuahua. *Current Research in the Pleistocene* 12:29–31.

Lev, D.

1987 Balsam Poplar (*Populus balsamifera*) in Northern Alaska: Ecology and Growth Response to Climate. Master's thesis, University of Washington, Seattle.

Libby, W. F.

1955   *Radiocarbon Dating*, 2nd edition. University of Chicago Press, Chicago.

Liddicoat, J. C., R. S. Coe, P. W. Lambert, H. E. Malde and V. Steen-McIntyre

1981   Paleomagnetic Investigation of Quaternary Sediment at Tlapacoya,
        Mexico, and at Valsequillo, Puebla, Mexico. *Geofisica Internacional*
        20(3):250–262.

Lorenz, J. G. and D. G. Smith

1996   Distribution of Four Founding mtDNA Haplogroups Among Native
        North Americans. *American Journal of Physical Anthropology* 101:307–323.

Lorenzo, J. L.

1967   *La Elapa Litica en Mexico*. Departmento de Prehistoria, 20 INAH, Mexico
        City, Mexico.

Lorenzo, J. L. and L. Mirambell

1986   35,000 Anos de Historia del Lago de Chalco. Coleccion Cientifica, Insti-
        tuto Nacional de Anthropologia e Historia. Mexico, D.F.

1999   The Inhabitants of Mexico During the Upper Pleistocene. In *Ice Age Peo-
        ples of North America*, edited by R. Bonnichsen. Oregon University Press
        for the Center for the Study of the First Americans, Corvalis.

Loy, T. H. and E. J. Dixon

1998   Blood Residues on Fluted Points from Eastern Beringia. *American Antiq-
        uity* 63:21–46.

Lynch, T. F.

1974   The Antiquity of Man in South America. *Quaternary Research* 4:356–377.

1980   *Guitarreo Cave: Early Man in the Andes*. Academic Press, New York.

1983   The Paleo-Indian. In *Ancient South Americans*, edited by J. D. Jennings,
        pp. 87–137. Freeman, San Francisco:

1990   Glacial-age Man in South America? A Critical Review. *American Antiquity*
        55:12–36.

1991a   Lack of Evidence for Glacial-Age Settlement of South America. Reply to
        Dillehay and Collins and to Gruhn and Bryan. *American Antiquity*
        56:348–355.

1991b   Paleoindians in South America: A Discrete and Identifiable Cultural
        Stage? In *Clovis: Origins and Adaptations*, edited by R. Bonnichsen and
        K. Turnmire, pp. 225–259, Center for the Study of the First Americans,
        Oregon State University, Corvallis.

MacDonald, G. M.

1987a   Postglacial Development of the Subalpine-Boreal Transition Forest of
        Western Canada. *Journal of Ecology* 75:303–320.

1987b   Postglacial Vegetation History of the Mackenzie River Basin. *Quaternary
        Research* 28:245–262.

MacNeish, R. S.

1971   Early Man in the Andes. *Scientific American* 224:36–48.

1979   The Early Man Remains from Pikimachay Cave, Ayacucho Basin, High-

land Peru. In *Pre-Llano Cultures of the Americas: Paradoxes and Possibili-*
ties, edited by R. L Humphrey and D. Stanford, pp. 1–47. Anthropological
Society of Washington, Washington, D.C.

1983   Mesoamerica. In *Early Man in the New World,* edited by Richard Shutler,
Jr., pp. 125–136. Sage Publications, Beverly Hills.

1991   *The Fort Bliss Archaeological Project by* AFAR *Excavation of Pintada and*
Pendejo Caves near Orogrande, New Mexico. 1991 Annual Report. Unpublished report, Andover Foundation for Archaeological Research, Andover.

1992   *The 1992 Excavations of Pendejo and Pintada Caves near Orogrande, New*
Mexico—An AFAR *and Fort Bliss Archaeological Project.* Unpublished Report, Andover Foundation for Archaeological Research, Andover.

MacNeish, R. S. (editor)

1980   *Prehistory of the Ayacucho Basin, Peru. Nonceramic Artifacts,* Vol. 3. University of Michigan Press, Ann Arbor.

MacNeish, R. S., G. Cunnar, G. Jessop, and P. Wilner

1993   *A Summary of the Paleo-Indian Discoveries in Pendejo Cave near Oro-*
grande, New Mexico. The Annual Report of AFAR for 1993. Andover Foundation for Archaeological Research, Andover.

MacPhee, R. D. E. and P. A. Marx

1997a   Disease and Mammalian Extinctions in the Late Quaternary. In *Program*
and Abstracts, Beringian Paleoenvironments Workshop. Florissant,
Colorado.

1997b   Lightning Strikes Twice: Blitzkrieg, Hyperdisease, and Global Explanations of Late Quaternary Catastrophic Extinctions. In *Presentation Sum-*
maries, Humans and Other Catastrophes: Explaining Past Extinctions and
the Extinction Process. Center for Biodiversity and Conservation, American Museum of Natural History, New York.

Malde, H. E.

1968   *The Catastrophic Late Pleistocene Bonneville Flood in the Snake River*
Plain, Idaho. Professional Paper No. 596. U. S. Geological Survey, Washington, D.C.

Malde, H. E. and V. Steen-McIntyre

1981   Reply to Comments by C. Irwin-Williams: Archeological Site, Valsequillo,
Mexico. *Quaternary Research* 16:418–425.

Mallouf, R. J.

1994   Sailor-Helton: A Paleoindian Cache from Southwestern Kansas. *Current*
Research in the Pleistocene 11:44–46.

Mandryk, C. A.

1990   Could Humans Survive the Ice-free Corridor?: Late-Glacial Vegetation
and Climate in West Central Alberta. In *Megafauna and Man: Discovery of*
America's Heartland, edited by Larry D. Agenbroad, Jim I. Mead, and Lisa
W. Nelson, pp. 67–79. The Mammoth Site of Hot Springs, South Dakota,
Inc. Scientific Papers, Vol. 1. Hot Springs, South Dakota.

Mann, D. H. and D. M. Peteet

    1994   Extent and Timing of the Last Glacial Maximum in Southwestern Alaska. *Quaternary Research* 42:136–148.

Markgraf, V.

    1988   Fell's Cave: 11,000 Years of Changes in Paleoenvironments, Fauna, and Human Occupation. In *Travels and Archaeology in South Chile*, edited by J. B. Bird, pp. 196–201. University of Iowa Press, Iowa City.

Martin, P. S.

    1967   Prehistoric Overkill. In *Pleistocene Extinctions: The Search for a Cause*, edited by P. S. Martin and H. E. Wright, pp. 75–120. Yale University Press, New Haven.

    1973   The Discovery of America. *Science* 179:969–974.

    1982   Pattern and Meaning of Holarctic Mammoth Extinction. In *Paleoecology of Beringia*, edited by D. M. Hopkins, J. V. Matthews, Jr., C. E. Schweger, and S. B. Young, pp. 399–408. Academic Press, New York.

    1984   Prehistoric Extinctions: The Global Model. In *Quaternary Extinctions: A Prehistoric Revolution*, edited by P. S. Martin and R. G. Klein, pp. 354–403. University of Arizona Press, Tucson.

Martin, P. S. and F. Plog

    1973   *The Archaeology of Arizona*. Doubleday-Natural History Press, Garden City, New York.

Mason, R. J. and C. Irwin

    1960   An Eden-Scottsbluff Burial in Northeastern Wisconsin. *American Antiquity* 26:43–57.

Matson, R. G. and G. Coupland

    1995   *The Prehistory of the Northwest Coast*. Academic Press, London.

Mayer-Oakes, W. J.

    1986   Early Man Projectile Points and Lithic Technology in the Ecuadorian Sierra. In *New Evidence for the Pleistocene Peopling of the Americas*, edited by Alan Lyle Bryan, pp. 133–156. Center for the Study of Early Man, University of Maine at Orono.

McAvoy, J. M. and L. D. McAvoy

    1997   *Archaeological Investigations of Site 44sx202, Cactus Hill, Sussex County, Virginia*. Virginia Department of Historic Resources, Research Report Series No.8. Sandston, Virginia.

McCartney, P. H.

    1980   Taphonomy and Archaeology of a Cody Bison Kill in Colorado. Department of Archaeology, University of Calgary, Alberta, Canada.

McKennan, R. A.

    1969   Athapaskan Groupings and Social Organization in Central Alaska. Anthropological Series 84. *National Museum of Canada Bulletin* 228:93–115.

McManus, D. A., J. S. Creager, R. J. Echols, and M. L. Holmes

    1983   The Holocene Transgression of the Arctic Flank of Beringia: Chukchi Valley to Chukchi Estuary to Chukchi Sea. In *Quaternary Coastlines and Marine Archeology*, edited by P. M. Masters and M. C. Flemming, pp. 365–388. Academic Press, New York.

Mead, J. I.

1980   Is It Really That Old? A Comment About the Meadowcroft Rockshelter "Overview." *American Antiquity* 45:579–582.

Meggers, B. J.

1996   Letter to Science. *Science* 274:1825.

Mehringer, P. J., Jr. and F. F. Foit, Jr.

1990   Volcanic Ash Dating of the Clovis Cache at East Wenatchee, Washington. *National Geographic Research* 6(4):495–503.

Meighan, C. W. and C. V. Haynes

1970   The Borax Lake Site Revisited. *Science* 167:1213–1221.

Meltzer, D. J.

1989   Why Don't We Know When the First People Came to North America? *American Antiquity* 54:471–490.

1991   On "Paradigms" and "Paradigm Bias" in Controversies Over Human Antiquity in America. In *The First Americans: Search and Research*, edited by Tom D. Dillehay and David J. Meltzer, pp. 13–49. CRC Press, Boca Raton, Florida.

1995   Modeling the Prehistoric Response to Altithermal Climates on the Southern High Plains. In *Ancient Peoples and Landscapes*, edited by Eileen Johnson, pp. 349–368. Museum of Texas Tech University, Lubbock.

Meltzer, D. J., D. K. Grayson, G. Ardila, A. W. Barker, D. F. Dincauze, C. V. Haynes, F. Men, L. Nuñez, and D. J. Stanford

1997   On the Pleistocene Antiquity of Monte Verde, Southern Chile. *American Antiquity* 62:659–663.

Mengoni Goñalons, G. L.

1986   Patagonian Prehistory: Early Exploitation of Faunal Resources (13,500–8,500 B.P.). In *New Evidence for the Pleistocene Peopling of the Americas*, edited by A. L. Bryan, pp. 271–279. Center for the Study of Early Man, University of Maine, Orono.

Merriwether, D. A., F. Rothhammer, and R. E. Ferrell

1995   Distribution of the Four Founding Lineage Haplotypes in Native Americans Suggests a Single Wave of Migration for the New World. *American Journal of Physical Anthropology* 98(4):411–430.

Michael, H. N.

1984   Absolute Chronologies of Late Pleistocene and Early Holocene Cultures of Northeastern Asia. *Arctic Anthropology* 21(2):1–68.

Mirambell, L.

1978   Tlapacoya: A Late Pleistocene Site in Central Mexico. In *Early Man in America from a Circum-Pacific Perspective*, edited by Alan Lyle Bryan, pp.

221–230. Occasional Papers No. 1. Department of Anthropology, University of Alberta, Edmonton.

Mitchell, D. and D. L. Pokotylo

1996   Early Period Components at the Milliken Site. In *Early Human Occupation in British Columbia*, edited by Roy L. Carlson and Luke Dalla Bona, pp. 51–64. University of British Columbia Press, Vancouver.

Mobley, C. M.

1991   *The Campus Site: A Prehistoric Camp at Fairbanks, Alaska.* University of Alaska Press, Fairbanks.

1996   Campus Site. In *American Beginnings: The Prehistory and Palaeoecology of Beringia*, edited by Frederick Hadleigh West, pp. 296–301. University of Chicago Press, Chicago.

Mochanov, Y. A.

1977   *Drevnejshie Etapy Zaseleniya Chelovekom Severo-Vostochnoj Azii* (Ancient-most Stages of the Settlement by Man of Northeast Asia). Nauka, Novosibirsk.

Montané, J.

1968   Paleo-Indian Remains from Laguna de Tagua Tagua, Central Chile. *Science* 161(2):1137–1138.

Montgomery, J. and J. Dickenson

1992   Additional Blades from Blackwater Draw Locality No. 1, Portales, New Mexico. *Current Research in the Pleistocene* 9:32–33.

Moratto, M. J.

1984   *California Archaeology.* Academic Press, New York.

Morell, V.

1998   Genes May Link Ancient Eurasians, Native Americans, *Science* 280:520

Morlan, R. E.

1977   Fluted Point Makers and the Extinction of the Arctic-Steppe Biome in Eastern Beringia. *Canadian Journal of Archaeology* 1:95–108.

1978   Early Man in Northern Yukon Territory: Perspectives as of 1977. In *Early Man in America from a Circum-Pacific Perspective*, edited by Alan Lyle Bryan, pp. 78–95. Occasional Papers No. 1. Department of Anthropology, University of Alberta, Edmonton.

1979   A Stratigraphic Framework for Pleistocene Artifacts from Old Crow River, Northern Yukon Territory. In *Pre-Llano Cultures in the Americas: Paradoxes and Possibilities*, edited by R. L. Humphrey and D. Stanford, pp. 125–145. Anthropological Society of Washington, Washington, D.C.

1980   *Taphonomy and Archaeology in the Upper Pleistocene of the Northern Yukon Territory: A Glimpse of the Peopling of the New World.* National Museum of Man Mercury Series, Archaeological Survey of Canada Paper No. 94. Ottawa.

1983   Spiral Fractures on Limb Bones: Which Ones Are Artificial? In *Carnivores, Human Scavengers, and Predators: A Question of Bone Technology,* edited by G. Le Moine and A. S. MacEachern, pp. 241–269. University of Calgary, Calgary.

Morlan, R. E. and J. Cinq-Mars

1982   Ancient Beringians: Human Occupation in the Late Pleistocene of Alaska and the Yukon Territory. In *Paleoecology of Beringia*, edited by David M. Hopkins, John V. Matthews, Jr. Charles E. Schweger, and Steven B. Young, pp. 353–381. Academic Press, New York.

Morris, D. H.

1975   Warm Mineral Springs Man. Unpublished manuscript on file, Division of Historical Research, Department of State, Tallahassee.

Moseley, M. E.

1975   *The Maritime Foundations of Andean Civilization*. Cummings Publishing, Philippines.

Moseley, M. E. and R. A. Feldman

1988   Fishing, farming, and the foundations of Andean civilization, In *The Archaeology of Prehistoric Coastlines*, Chapter 11 pp. 125–134. Cambridge University Press, Cambridge.

Mossimann, J. E. and P. S. Martin

1975   Simulating Overkill by Paleoindians. *American Scientists* 63:304–313.

Mulvaney, D. J.

1964   The Pleistocene Colonization of Australia. *Antiquity* 38:263–267.

Musil, R. R.

1988   Functional Efficiency and Technological Change: A Hafting Tradition Model for Prehistoric North America. In *Early Human Occupation in Far Western North America: The Clovis-Archaic Interface*, edited by J. A. Willig, C. M. Aikens, and J. L. Fagan, pp. 373–387. Nevada State Museum Anthropological Papers No. 21. Carson City.

Napton, K. L.

1997   The Spirit Cave Mummy: Coprolite Investigations. *Nevada Historical Society Quarterly* 40(1):97–104.

Nasmith, H. W.

1970   Pleistocene Geology of the Queen Charlotte Islands and Southern British Columbia. In *Early Man and Environments in Northwestern North America*, edited by R. A. Smith and J. Smith, pp. 5–9. University of Calgary, Calgary.

Nelson, D. E., R. E. Morlan, J. S. Vogel, J. R. Southon, and C. R. Harington

1986   New Dates on Northern Yukon Artifacts: Holocene Not Upper Pleistocene. *Science* 232:749–51.

Nelson, N. C.

1933   The Antiquity of Man in America in the Light of Archaeology. In *The American Aborigines, Their Origin and Antiquity*, edited by Diamond Jenness, pp. 85–130. A Collection of Papers by Ten Authors Assembled and Edited by Diamond Jenness. Published for presentation at the Fifth

Pacific Science Congress. Canada. Cooper Square Publishers, New York, 1973.

1935　Early Migration of Man to America. *Natural History* 35(4):356.

1937　Notes on Cultural Relations Between Asia and America. *American Antiquity* 2:267–272.

New Dates at Old Site

1997　*Mammoth Trumpet* 12(3):8. Center for the Study of the First Americans, Oregon State University, Corvallis.

Nichols, J.

1990　Linguistic Diversity and the First Settlement of the New World. *Language* 66(3):475–521.

Oakley, K. P.

1963　Relative Dating of Arlington Springs Man. *Science* 141:1172.

Ochsenius, C. and R. Gruhn (editors)

1979　*Taima-Taima, A Late Pleistocene Paleo-Indian Kill Site in Northernmost South America—Final Reports of 1976 Excavations.* Germany.

O'Connor, J. E.

1990　*Hydrology, Hydraulics and Sediment Transport of Pleistocene Lake Bonneville Flooding on the Snake River, Idaho.* Ph.D. dissertation, University of Arizona. University Microfilms, Ann Arbor.

Odum, E. P.

1975　*Ecology: The Link Between the Natural and the Social Sciences,* 2nd edition. Holt, Rinehart, and Winston, New York.

Okada, H., A. Okada, Y. Kotani, K. Yajima, W. M. Olson, Y. Nishimoto, and S. Okino

1989　*Heceta Island, Southeastern Alaska Anthropological Survey in 1987.* Department of Behavioral Science, Faculty of Letters. Hokkaido University, Sapporo, Japan.

Orr, P. C.

1951　Ancient Population Centers of Santa Rosa Island. *American Antiquity* 16:221–226.

1956　Pleistocene Man in Fishbone Cave, Pershing County, Nevada. Department of Archaeology, *Nevada State Museum Bulletin* 2:1–20. Carson City.

1962　The Arlington Springs Site, Santa Rosa Island, California. *American Antiquity* 27:417–419.

1965　Radiocarbon Age of a Nevada Mummy. *Science* 148:1466–1467.

1967　Geochronology of Santa Rosa Island, California. *Proceedings of the Symposium on the Biology of the California Islands,* edited by R. N. Philbrick, pp. 317–325. Santa Barbara Botanic Garden, Santa Barbara.

1968　*Prehistory of Santa Rosa Island.* Santa Barbara Museum of Natural History, Santa Barbara.

Orr, P. C. and R. Berger

1966　The Fire Areas on Santa Rosa Island, California. *Proceedings of the National Academy of Sciences* 56(5):1409–1416.

Overstreet, D. F.

1993 *Chesrow: A Paleoindian Complex in the Southern Lake Michigan Basin.*
Great Lakes Archaeological Press, Milwaukee.

1998 Late Pleistocene Geochronology and the Paleoindian Penetration of the
Southwestern Lake Michigan Basin. *The Wisconsin Archeologist,* 79(1):
28–52. The Wisconsin Archeological Society, Milwaukee.

Overstreet, D. F., D. J. Joyce, K. F. Hallin, and D. Wasion

1993 Cultural Contexts of Mammoth and Mastodon in the Southwestern Lake
Michigan Basin. *Current Research in the Pleistocene* 10:75–77.

Overstreet, D. F., D. J. Joyce, and D. Wasion

1995 More on Cultural Contexts of Mammoth and Mastodon in the Southwestern Lake Michigan Basin. *Current Research in the Pleistocene*
12:40–42.

Overstreet, D. F. and T. W. Stafford, Jr.

1997 Additions to a Revised Chronology for Cultural and Non-Cultural Mammoth and Mastodon Fossils in the Southwestern Lake Michigan Basin.
Current Research in the Pleistocene 14:70–71.

Parenti, F., N. Mercier, and H. Valladas

1990 The Oldest Hearths of Pedra Furada, Brazil: Thermoluminesence Analysis of Heated Stones. *Current Research in the Pleistocene* 7:36–38.

Peyre, E.

1993 *Nouvelle Decouverte d'un Homme Prehistorique Americain: Une Femme
de 9 700 Ans au Bresil. Paleontologie Humaine* (Human Paleontology).
C. R. Acad. Sci. Paris, t. 316, Serie II: 839–842.

Phippen, P. G.

1988 *Archaeology at Owl Ridge: A Pleistocene-Holocene Boundary Age Site in
Central Alaska.* Master's thesis, University of Alaska, Fairbanks.

Pitblado, B.

1998 Peak to Peak in Paleoindian Time: Occupation of Southwest Colorado.
Plains Anthropologist 43(166):333–348.

Politis, G. G., J. L. Prado, and R. P. Beukens

1995 The Human Impact in Pleistocene-Holocene Extinctions in South America—The Pampean Case. In *Ancient Peoples and Landscapes,* edited by
Eileen Johnson, pp. 187–205. Museum of Texas Tech University, Lubbock.

Powell, J. F and D. G. Steele

1994 Diet and Health of Paleoindians: An Examination of Early Holocene
Human Dental Remains. Center for Archaeological Investigations, Occa-
sional Paper No. 22, edited by K. D. Sobolik, pp. 178–194. Southern Illinois
University, Carbondale.

Powers, W. R.

1973 Paleolithic Man in Northeast Asia. *Arctic Anthropology* 10(2):1–106.

1990 The People of Eastern Beringia. In *Prehistoric Mongoloid Dispersals,* No. 7.
Special Issue. University Museum, University of Tokyo.

Powers, W. R., T. Goebel, and N. H. Bigelow

    1990   Late Pleistocene Occupation at Walker Road: New Data on the Central Alaskan Nenana Complex. *Current Research in the Pleistocene* 7:40–43.

Powers, W. R. and J. F. Hoffecker

    1989   Late Pleistocene Settlement in the Nenana Valley, Central Alaska. *American Antiquity* 54:263–287.

Powers, W. R. and H. E. Maxwell

    1986   *Lithic Remains from Panquinque Creek: An Early Holocene Site in the Northern Foothills of the Alaska Range.* Alaska Historical Commission, Anchorage.

Prest, V. K.

    1969   *Retreat of Wisconsin and Recent Ice in North America.* Geological Survey of Canada Map 1257A.

Preston, D.

    1995   The Mystery of Sandia Cave. *New Yorker* 12 June:66–69.

Purdy, B. A.

    1991   *The Art and Archaeology of Florida's Wetlands.* CRC Press, Boca Raton.

Rainey, F.

    1939   Archaeology in Central Alaska. *Anthropological Papers of the American Museum of Natural History* 36(4):351–405.

Rancier, J. G., G. Haynes, and D. Stanford

    1981   Investigations of Lamb Spring, *Southwestern Lore.* Gunnison, Colorado.

Reanier, R. E.

    1994   The Putu Site: Pleistocene or Holocene? *Current Research in the Pleistocene* 11:148–150.

    1996   Putu and Bedwell. In *American Beginnings: The Prehistory and Palaeoecology of Beringia,* edited by Frederick Hadleigh West, pp. 505–511. University of Chicago Press, Chicago.

Redder, A. J.

    1985   Horn Shelter Number 2: The South End, A Preliminary Report. In *Central Texas Archeologist* 10, edited by S. Alan Skinner, pp. 37–65. Baylor University Press, Waco, Texas.

Reeves, B., J. M. D. Pohl, and J. W. Smith

    1986   The Mission Ridge Site and the Texas Street Question. In *New Evidence for the Pleistocene Peopling of the Americas,* edited by Alan Lyle Bryan, pp. 65–80. Center for the Study of Early Man, University of Maine at Orono.

Reger, D. R.

    1996   Beluga Point. In *American Beginnings: The Prehistory and Palaeoecology of Beringia,* edited by Frederick Hadleigh West, pp. 433–436. University of Chicago Press, Chicago.

Report of Dickeson Exhibit

    1846   *Proceedings of the Academy of Natural Sciences of Philadelphia* 3(5):106–107.

Rice, D. G.

1972   *The Windust Phase in Lower Snake River Region Prehistory*. Laboratory of Anthropology, Report of Investigations 50. Washington State University, Pullman.

Ritchie, J. C.

1984   *Past and Present Vegetation of the Far Northwest of Canada*. University of Toronto Press, Toronto.

Ritchie, J. C. and L. C. Cwynar

1982   The Late Quaternary Vegetation of the North Yukon. In *Paleoecology of Beringia*, edited by D. M. Hopkins, J. V. Matthews, Jr., C. E. Schweger, and S. B. Young, pp. 113–126. Academic Press, New York.

Ritchie, J. C., L. C. Cwynar, and R. W. Spear

1983   Evidence from North-West Canada for an Early Holocene Milankovitch Thermal Maximum. *Nature* 305:126–128. London.

Roberts, F. H. H., Jr.

1935   A Folsom Complex: Preliminary Investigations at the Lindenmeier Site in Northern Colorado. *Smithsonian Miscellaneous Collections* 94(4). Smithsonian Institution, Washington, D.C.

1937   New World Man. *American Antiquity* 11:172–177.

1940   Development on the Problem of the North American Paleo-Indian. *Smithsonian Miscellaneous Collections* 100:51–116. Smithsonian Institution, Washington, D.C.

Rogers, M. J.

1958   San Dieguito Implements from the Terraces of the Rincon-Pantano and Rillito Drainage System. *The Kiva* 24:1–23.

1966   *Ancient Hunters of the Far West*. The Union-Tribune, San Diego.

Rogers, R. A.

1985a   Glacial Geography and Native North American Languages. *Quaternary Research* 23:130–137.

1985b   Wisconsinan Glaciation and the Dispersal of Native Ethnic Groups in North America. *Woman, Poet, Scientist; Essays in New World Anthropology Honoring Dr. Emma Louise Davis*, edited by T. C. Blackburn, pp. 104–113. Anthropological Papers No. 29. Ballena Press, Los Altos.

Rogers, R. A., L. A. Rogers, R. S. Hoffmann, and L. D. Martin

1991   Native American Biological Diversity and the Biogeographic Influence of Ice Age Refugia. *Journal of Biogeography* 18:623–630.

Romer, A. S.

1933   Pleistocene Vertebrates and Their Bearing on the Problem of Human Antiquity in North America. In *The American Aborigines: Their Origin and Antiquity*, pp. 47–84. A collection of Papers by Ten Authors Assembled and Edited by Diamond Jenness. Published for presentation at the Fifth Pacific Science Congress. Canada. Cooper Square Publishers, Inc., New York, 1973.

Roosevelt, A. C.

    1995   Response. *Science* 274:1825–1826.

Roosevelt, A. C., M. Lima da Costa, C. Lopes Machado, M. Michab,
N. Mercier, H. Valladas, J. Feathers, W. Barnett, M. Imazio da Silveira,
A. Henderson, J. Sliva, B. Chernoff, D. S. Reese, J. A. Holman,
N. Toth, and K. Schick

    1996   Paleoindian Cave Dwellers in the Amazon: The Peopling of the Americas. *Science* 272:373–384.

Rouse, I. and J. Cruxent

    1963   *Venezuelan Archaeology.* Yale University Press, New Haven.

Royal, W. and E. Clark

    1960   Natural Preservation of Human Brain, Warm Mineral Springs, Florida. *American Antiquity* 26:285–287.

Rutter, N. W.

    1984   Pleistocene History of the Western Canadian Ice-free Corridor. In *Quaternary Stratigraphy of Canada—A Canadian Contribution to IGCP Project 24,* edited by R. J. Fulton, pp. 49–56. Geological Survey of Canada, Paper 84–10.

Sandweiss, D. H., H. McInnis, R. L. Burger, A. Cano, B. Ojeda,
R. Paredes, M. C. Sandweiss, and M. D. Glascock

    1998   Quebrada Jaguay: Early South American Maritime Adaptations. *Science* 281:1830–1832.

Sattler, R. A.

    1991   Paleoecology of A Late Quaternary Cave Deposit in Northeast Alaska. Master's thesis, University of Alaska, Fairbanks.

Sayles, E. B. and E. Antevs

    1941   *The Cochise Culture.* Medallion Papers 29. Gila Pueblo, Globe.

Schuiling, W. C. (editor)

    1979   Pleistocene Man at Calico. *Quarterly of San Bernardino County Museum Association* 26(4).

Schurr, T. G., S. W. Ballinger, Y. Gan, J. A. Hodge, D. A. Merriwether, and
D. N. Lawrence

    1990   Amerindian Mitochondrial DNA's Have Rare Asian Mutations at High Frequencies, Suggesting They Derived from Four Primary Maternal Lineages. *American Journal of Human Genetics* 46:613–23.

Schwacheim, C.

    1926   Field note copies, on file, Denver Museum of Natural History, Denver.

Schweger, C.

    1982   Primary Production and Pleistocene Ungulates—The Productivity Paradox. In *Paleoecology of Beringia,* edited by David M. Hopkins, John V. Matthews, Jr. Charles E. Schweger, and Steven B. Young, pp. 95–112. Academic Press, New York.

Scott, G. R.

    n.d.   Geology of the Lamb Spring Site. Unpublished report on file, United
    States Geological Survey, Denver Colorado and Department of Anthro-
    pology, Smithsonian Institution, Washington, D.C.

Scott, W. E., W. D. McCoy, R. R. Shroba, and M. Ruben

    1983   Reinterpretation of the Exposed Record of the Last Two Cycles of Lake
    Bonneville, Western United States. *Quaternary Research* 20:261–285.

Sellards, E. H.

    1917   On the Association of Human Remains and Extinct Vertebrates at Vero,
    Florida. *Journal of Geology* 25(1):4–24.

    1952   *Early Man in America*. University of Texas Press, Austin.

Shaffer, B. S. and B. W. Baker

    1997   How Many Epidermal Ridges per Linear Centimeter? Comments on Pos-
    sible Pre-Clovis Human Friction Skin Prints from Pendejo Cave. *Ameri-
    can Antiquity* 62:559–560.

Sheppard, J. C., P. E. Wigand, C. E. Gustafson, and M. Rubin

    1987   A Reevaluation of the Marmes Rockshelter Radiocarbon Chronology.
    American Antiquity 52:118–125.

Shutler, R., Jr. (editor)

    1983   *Early Man in the New World*. Sage Publications, Beverly Hills.

Simons, D. D., T. N. Layton, and R. Knudson

    1985   A Fluted Point from the Mendocino County Coast, California. *Journal of
    California and Great Basin Anthropology* 7:260–269.

Simpson, R. D.

    1979   The Calico Mountains Archaeological Project. In Pleistocene Man at Cal-
    ico, edited by Walter C. Schuiling. *Quarterly of San Bernardino County
    Museum Association* 26(4):9–20.

Simpson, R. D., L. W. Patterson, and C. A. Singer

    1986   Lithic Technology of the Calico Mountains Site, Southern California. In
    New Evidence for the Pleistocene Peopling of the Americas, edited by Alan
    Lyle Bryan, pp. 89–105. Center for the Study of Early Man, University of
    Maine at Orono.

Skow, J.

    1986   This Florida Spa Holds a Surprising Lode of Prehistory. *Smithsonian*
    17(9):73–83.

Slayman, A. L.

    1997   A Battle over Bones. *Archaeology* 50(1):16–23.

Smith, B. H.

    1984   Patterns of Molar Wear in Hunter-Gatherers and Agriculturists. *American
    Journal of Physical Anthropology* 69:39–56.

Solorzano, F. A.

    1990   Pleistocene Artifacts from Jalisco, Mexico: A Comparison with Some Pre-

Hispanic Artifacts. In *Bone Modifications*, edited by R. Bonnichsen and M. H. Sorg, pp. 499–514. The Center for the Study of the First Americans, Orono.

Specht, J., I. Lilley, and J. Normu

    1981   Radiocarbon Dates from West New Britain, Papua, New Guinea. *Australian Archaeology* 12:13–15.

Stafford, T. W., Jr.

    1994   Radiocarbon Dating of Bone Using Accelerator Mass Spectrometry: Current Discussions and Future Directions. In *Method and Theory for Investigating the Peopling of the Americas*, edited by. R. Bonnichsen and D. G. Steele, pp. 45–55. Center for the Study of the First Americans, Oregon State University, Corvallis.

    1998   Radiocarbon Chronostratigraphy. In *Wilson-Leonard, An 11,000-year Archeological Record of Hunter-Gathers in Central Texas*, assembled and edited by Michael B. Collins, Chapter 25, pp. 1039–1066. Studies in Archeology 31, Texas Archeological Research Laboratory, University of Texas at Austin, and Archeological Studies Program, Report 10, Texas Department of Transportation, Environmental Affairs Division. Austin.

Stafford, T. W., Jr., P. E. Hare, L. Currie, A. J. T. Jull, and D. Donahue

    1990   Accuracy of North American Human Skeleton Ages. *Quaternary Research* 34:111–120.

    1991   Accelerator Radiocarbon Dating at the Molecular Level. *Journal of Archaeological Science* 18:35–72.

Stafford, T. W., Jr. and R. A. Tyson

    1989   Accelerator Radiocarbon Dates on Charcoal, Shell, and Human Bone from the Del Mar Site, California. *American Antiquity* 54, 389–395.

Stalker, A. M.

    1969   Geology and Age of the Early Man Site at Taber, Alberta. *American Antiquity* 34:425–428.

Stanford, D. J.

    1974   Preliminary Report of the Excavation of the Jones-Miller Hell Gap Site, Yuma County, Colorado. *Southwestern Lore* 40:29–36. Gunnison, Colorado.

    1975   The 1975 Excavations at the Jones-Miller Site, Yuma County, Colorado. *Southwestern Lore* 41:34–38. Gunnison, Colorado.

    1978   The Jones-Miller Site: An Example of Hell Gap Bison Procurement Strategy. In *Bison Procurement and Utilization: A Symposium*, pp. 90–97. Plains Anthropologist Memoir 14.

    1979a   Bison Kill by Ice Age Hunters. *National Geographic* 155(1):114–121.

    1979b   The Selby and Dutton Sites: Evidence for a Possible Pre-Clovis Occupation of the High Plains. In *Pre-Llano Cultures of the Americas: Paradoxes and Possibilities* edited by R. L. Humphrey and D. Stanford, pp. 101–123. The Anthropological Society of Washington, Washington, D.C.

1979c   Afterward: Resolving the Question of New World Origins. In *Pre-Llano Cultures of the Americas: Paradoxes and Possibilities*, edited by R. L. Humphrey and D. Stanford, pp. 147–152. Anthropological Society of Washington, Washington, D.C.

1983   Pre-Clovis Occupation South of the Ice Sheets. In *Early Man in the New World*, edited by Richard Shutler, Jr., pp. 65–72. Sage Publications, Beverly Hills.

1995   Early Paleoindian Diet Breadth as Seen from the Lewisville Site, Texas: Critter Buffet as an Alternative to Mammoth Barbeque. Paper presented at the 60th Annual Meeting of the Society for American Archaeology, May 3–7, Minneapolis, Minnesota.

1996   Foreshaft Sockets as Possible Clovis Hafting Devices. *Current Research in the Pleistocene* 13:44–46.

1999   Paleoindian Archeology and Late Pleistocene Environments in the Plains and Southwestern United States. In *Ice Age Peoples of North America*, edited by R. Bonnichsen. Oregon University Press for the Center for the Study of the First Americans, Corvalis.

Stanford, D. J., R. Bonnichsen, and R. E. Morlan

1981   The Ginsberg Experiment: Modern and Prehistoric Evidence of a Bone-Flaking Technology. *Science* 212:438–440.

Stanford, D. J. and F. Broilo

1981   Frank's Folsom Campsite. *The Artifact* 19:1–13.

Stanford, D. J. and M. A. Jodry

1988   The Drake Clovis Cache. *Current Research in the Pleistocene* 5:21–22.

Stanford, D. J., W. R. Wedel, and G. R. Scott

1981   Archaeological Investigations of the Lamb Spring Site. *Southwestern Lore* 47:14–27. Gunnison, Colorado.

Steele, D. G.

1998   Human Biological Remains. In *Wilson-Leonard, An 11,000-year Archeological Record of Hunter-Gathers in Central Texas*, assembled and edited by Michael B. Collins, Chapter 31, pp. 1441–1458. Studies in Archeology 31, Texas Archeological Research Laboratory, University of Texas at Austin, and Archeological Studies Program, Report 10, Texas Department of Transportation, Environmental Affairs Division. Austin.

Steele, D. G. and J. F. Powell

1992   Peopling of the Americas: Paleobiological Evidence. *Human Biology* 64(3):303–336.

Steen-McIntyre, V., R. Fryxell, and H. E. Malde

1981   Geologic Evidence for Age of Deposits at Hueyatlaco Archeological Site, Valsequillo, Mexico. *Quaternary Research* 16:1–17.

Stevens, D. E. and G. A. Agogino

1975   Sandia Cave: A Study in Controversy. *Eastern New Mexico University Contributions to Anthropology* 7(1).

Steward, J. H.

    1933   *Archaeological Problems of the Northern Periphery of the Southwest.* Museum of Northern Arizona Bulletin 5. Flagstaff.

Stewart, T. D.

    1946   A Re-examination of the Fossil Human Skeletal Remains from Melbourne, Florida in Further Data on the Vero Skull. *Smithsonian Miscellaneous Collections* 106(10), Washington, D.C.

Stothert, K.

    1998   An Early Holocene Maritime Adaptation in Southwest Ecuador: New Perspectives on the Las Vegas Evidence. Paper presented at the 63rd Annual Meeting of the Society for American Archaeology, Seattle.

Stryd, A. R. and M. K. Rousseau

    1996   The Early Prehistory of the Mid Fraser-Thompson River Area. In *Early Human Occupation in British Columbia*, edited by Roy L. Carlson and Luke Dalla Bona, pp. 177–204. University of British Columbia Press, Vancouver.

Swanson, E. H. and P. G. Sneed

    1966   *The Archaeology of the Shoup Rockshelters in East-Central Idaho.* Occasional Papers of the Idaho State University Museum 17. Birch Creek Papers No. 3. Pocatello.

Swanton, J. R.

    1938   Historic Use of the Spear-Thrower in Southeastern North America. *American Antiquity* 3:356–358.

Szabo, B. J., H. E. Malde, and C. Irwin-Williams

    1969   Dilemma Posed by Uranium-Series Dates on Archaeologically Significant Bones from Valsequillo, Puebla, Mexico. *Earth and Planetary Science Letters* 6:237–244.

Szathmáry, Emőke J. E.

    1996   Ancient Migrations from Asia to North America. In *Prehistoric Mongoloid Dispersals*, edited by Takeru Akazawa and Emőke J. E. Szathmáry, pp. 149–164. Oxford University Press, Inc., New York.

Taylor, R. E.

    1992   Radiocarbon Dating of Bone: To Collagen and Beyond. In *Radiocarbon after Four Decades: An Interdisciplinary Perspective*, edited by R. E. Taylor, A. Long, and R. S. Kra, pp. 375–402. Springer-Verlag, New York.

Taylor, R. E., C. V. Haynes, Jr., and M. Stuiver

    1996   Clovis and Folsom Age Estimates: Stratigraphic Context and Radiocarbon Calibration. *Antiquity* 70(269):515–525.

Taylor, R. E., L. A. Payen, C. A. Prior, P. J. Slota, Jr., R. Gillespie, J. A. J. Gowlett, R. E. M. Hedges, A. J. T. Jull, T. H. Zabel, D. J. Donahue, and R. Berger

    1985   Major Revisions in the Pleistocene Age Assignments for North American Human Skeletons by c-14 Accelerator Mass Spectrometry: None Older Than 11,000 c-14 Years B.P. *American Antiquity* 50:136–140.

Thomas, D. H.

1978   Arrowheads and Atlatl Darts: How the Stones Got the Shaft. *American Antiquity* 43:461–472.

1993   Part One: The World as It Was. In *The Native Americans: An Illustrated History*, pp. 23–97. Turner, Atlanta.

Thompson, R. W.

1948   Notes on the Archeology of the Utukok River, Northwestern Alaska. *American Antiquity* 14:62–65.

Thorson, R. M. and R. D. Guthrie

1984   River Ice as a Taphonomic Agent: An Alternative Hypothesis for Bone "Artifacts." *Quaternary Research* 22:172–188.

Thorson, R. M. and T. D. Hamilton

1977   Geology of the Dry Creek Site: A Stratified Early Man Site in Interior Alaska. *Quaternary Research* 7:149–176.

Torroni, A., T. G. Schurr, C. Yang, E. J. E. Szathmáry, R. C. Williams, and M. S. Schanfield

1992   Native American Mitochondrial DNA Analysis Indicates that the Amerind and the Na-dene Populations Were Founded by Two Independent Migrations. *Genetics* 130:153–62.

Toth, N.

1991   The Material Record. In *The First Americans: Search and Research*, edited by Tom D. Dillehay and David J. Meltzer, pp. 53–76. CRC Press, Boca Raton, Florida.

Tuohy, D. R.

1988   Artifacts from the Northwestern Pyramid Lake Shoreline. In *Early Human Occupation in Far Western North America: The Clovis-Archaic Interface*, edited by, J. A. Willig, C. M. Aikens, and J. L. Fagan, pp. 201–216. Nevada State Museum Anthropological Papers No. 21. Carson City.

Tuohy, D. R. and A. J. Dansie

1997a   Papers on Holocene Burial Localities Presented at the 25th Great Basin Anthropological Conference. *Nevada Historical Society Quarterly* 40(1): 1–3.

1997b   New Information Regarding Early Holocene Manifestations in the Western Great Basin. *Nevada Historical Society Quarterly* 40(1):24–54.

Turner, C. G., II

1983   Dental Evidence for the Peopling of the Americas. In *Early Man in the New World*, edited by Richard Shutler, Jr., pp. 147–158. Sage Publications, Beverly Hills.

1985   The Dental Search for Native American Origins. In *Out of Asia: Peopling the Americas and the Pacific*, edited by Robert Kirk and Emőke Szathmáry. Journal of Pacific History, Canberra, Australia.

1992   New World Origins: New Research from the Americas and the Soviet Union. In *Ice Age Hunters of the Rockies*, edited by Dennis J. Stanford and Jane S. Day, pp. 7–50. Denver Museum of Natural History.

Vereshchagin, N. K.

1977   Berelyokhskoye "Kladbische" Mamontov. *Trudi Zoologicheskovo Instituta* 72:5–50.

Vinson, D. M.

1988   Preliminary Report on Faunal Identifications from Trail Creek Caves. In *The Bering Land Bridge National Preserve: An Archeological Survey*, edited by J. Schaaf, Vol. 1, pp. 410–438. National Park Service, Anchorage.

1993   *Taphonomic Analysis of Faunal Remains from Trail Creek Caves, Seward Peninsula, Alaska.* Unpublished Master's thesis. University of Alaska, Fairbanks.

Wallace, W. J. and F. A Riddell

1988   Archaeological Background of Tulare Lake, California. In *Early Human Occupation in Far Western North America: The Clovis-Archaic Interface*, edited by J. A. Willig, C. M. Aikens, and J. L. Fagan, pp. 87–101. Nevada State Museum Anthropological Papers No. 21. Carson City.

Warnica, J. M.

1966   New Discoveries at the Clovis Site. *American Antiquity* 31:345–357.

Warren, C. N.

1967   The San Dieguito Complex: A Review and Hypothesis. *American Antiquity* 32:168–185.

Waters, M. R.

1985   Early Man in the New World: An Evaluation of the Radiocarbon Dated Pre-Clovis Sites in the Americas. In *Environments and Extinctions: Man in the Late Glacial North America*, edited by Jim I. Mead and David J. Meltzer, pp. 125–143. Center for the Study of Early Man, University of Maine at Orono.

1986a   *The Geoarchaeology of Whitewater Draw, Arizona.* Anthropological Papers of the University of Arizona No. 45. University of Arizona Press, Tucson.

1986b   Sulphur Springs Woman: An Early Human Skeleton from Southeastern Arizona. *American Antiquity* 51:361–365.

Wedel, W.

1965   Investigations at the Lamb Spring site, Colorado, Manuscript on file at the National Science Foundation, Washington, D.C.

1986   Central Plains Prehistory, University of Nebraska Press, Lincoln, Neb. 280 pages.

Wendorf, F. and A. Krieger

1959   New Light on the Midland Discovery. *American Antiquity* 25:66–78.

Wendorf, F., A. Krieger, and C. C. Albritton

1955   *The Midland Discovery.* University of Texas Press, Austin.

West, F. H.

1967   The Donnelly Ridge Site and the Definition of an Early Core and Blade Complex in Central Alaska. *American Antiquity* 32:360–382.

1975   Dating the Denali Complex. *Arctic Anthropology* 12:76–81.

1981   *The Archaeology of Beringia.* Columbia University Press, New York.

1996a   Beringia and New World Origins II. In *American Beginnings: The Prehistory and Palaeoecology of Beringia*, edited by Frederick Hadleigh West, pp. 537–559. University of Chicago Press, Chicago.

1996b   South Central Alaska Range: Tangle Lakes Region. In *American Beginnings: The Prehistory and Palaeoecology of Beringia*, edited by Frederick Hadleigh West, pp. 375–380. University of Chicago Press, Chicago.

1996c   Reger Site. In *American Beginnings: The Prehistory and Palaeoecology of Beringia*, edited by Frederick Hadleigh West, pp. 399–403. University of Chicago Press, Chicago.

1996d   Other Sites in the Tangle Lakes. In *American Beginnings: The Prehistory and Palaeoecology of Beringia*, edited by Frederick Hadleigh West, pp. 403–408. University of Chicago Press, Chicago.

West, F. H. (editor)

1996   *American Beginnings: The Prehistory and Paleoecology of Beringia.* University of Chicago Press, Chicago.

West, F. H., B. S. Robinson, and M. L. Curran

1996   Phipps Site. In *American Beginnings: The Prehistory and Palaeoecology of Beringia*, edited by Frederick Hadleigh West, pp. 381–386. University of Chicago Press, Chicago.

West, F. H., B. S. Robinson, and R. G. Dixon

1996   Sparks Point. In *American Beginnings: The Prehistory and Palaeoecology of Beringia*, edited by Frederick Hadleigh West, pp. 394–398. University of Chicago Press, Chicago.

West, F. H., B. S. Robinson, and C. F. West

1996   Witmore Ridge. In *American Beginnings: The Prehistory and Palaeoecology of Beringia*, edited by Frederick Hadleigh West, pp. 386–394. University of Chicago Press, Chicago.

Wheat, J. B.

1971   Lifeways of Early Man in North America. *Arctic Anthropology* 8(2):22–31.

1972   *The Olsen-Chubbock Site, a Paleo-Indian Bison Kill.* Society of American Archaeology, Memoir 26.

1975   Artifact Life Histories: Cultural Template, Typology, Evidence, and Inference. In *Primitive Arts and Technology*, edited by J. S. Raymond, B. Loveseth, and G. Reardon. Chacmool, The Archaeological Association, University of Calgary, Calgary, Alberta.

1979   The Jurgens Site. *Plains Anthropologist*, Memoir 15. Lincoln, Nebraska.

Wheeler, S. M.

1997   Cave Burials near Fallon, Nevada. *Nevada Historical Society Quarterly* 40(1):15–23.

Whitney, J. D.

1867   Notice of a Human Skull, Recently Taken from a Shaft near Angel's,

Calaveras County. *California Academy of Natural Sciences Proceedings* 3(1893–67):277–278.

1880   Auriferous gravels of the Sierra Nevada of California, Contributions to American Geology, Vol. 1. Memoir of the Museum of Comparative Zoology, pp. 288–321. Cambridge.

Wickler, S. and M. Spriggs

1988   Pleistocene Human Occupation of the Solomon Island, Melanesia. *Antiquity* 62:703–706.

Wigand, P. E.

1997   Native American Diet and Environmental Contexts of the Holocene Revealed in the Pollen of Human Fecal Material. *Nevada Historical Society Quarterly* 40(1):105–116.

Wilke, P. J., J. J. Flenniken, and T. L. Ozbun

1991   Clovis Technology at the Anzick Site, Montana. *Journal of California and Great Basin Anthropology* 14(2):242–272.

Willey, G. R. and P. Phillips

1958   *Method and Theory in American Archaeology*. University of Chicago Press, Chicago.

Williams, R. C., A. G. Steinberg, H. Gershowitz, P. H. Bennet, W. C. Knowler, D. J. Pettitt, W. Butler, R. Baird, L. Dowd-Rea, T. A. Burch, H. G. Morse, and C. G. Smith

1985   Gm Allotypes in Native Americans: Evidence for Three Distinct Migrations Across the Bering Land Bridge. *American Journal of Physical Anthropology* 66(1):1–19.

Willig, J. A.

1989   Paleo-Archaic Adaptations and Lakeside Settlement Pattern in the Northern Alkali Basin. In *Early Human Occupation in Far Western North America: The Clovis-Archaic Interface*, edited by J. A. Willig, C. M. Aikens, and J. L. Fagan, pp. 417–482. Nevada State Museum Anthropological Papers No. 21. Carson City.

1990   Western Clovis Occupation at the Dietz Site, Northern Alkali Lake Basin, Oregon. *Current Research in the Pleistocene* 7:52–56.

1991   Clovis Technology and Adaptation in Far Western North America: Regional Pattern and Environmental Context. In *Clovis: Origins and Adaptations*, edited by R. Bonnichsen and K. Turnmire, pp. 91–118. Center for the Study of the First Americans, Oregon State University, Corvallis.

1996   Environmental Context for Early Human Occupation in Western North America. In *Prehistoric Mongoloid Dispersals*, edited by Takeru Akazawa and Emőke J. E. Szathmáry, pp. 241–253.

Willig, J. A. and C. M. Aikens

1988   The Clovis-Archaic Interface in Far Western North America. In *Early Human Occupation in Far Western North America: The Clovis-Archaic Interface*, edited by J. A. Willig, C. M. Aikens, and J. L. Fagan, pp. 1–40. Nevada State Museum Anthropological Papers No. 21. Carson City.

Willig, J. A., C. M. Aikens, and J. L. Fagan (editors)

1988   *Early Human Occupation in Far Western North America: The Clovis-Archaic Interface.* Nevada State Museum Anthropological Papers No. 21. Carson City.

Wilmsen, E. N. and F. H. H. Roberts, Jr.

1978   *Lindenmeier, 1934–1974: Concluding Report on Investigations.* Smithsonian Contributions to Anthropology No. 24. Smithsonian Institution, Washington, D.C.

Wilson, D. E.

1998   Stable Isotopic Results for Wilson-Leonard Burials 1 and 2. In *Wilson-Leonard, An 11,000-year Archeological Record of Hunter-Gathers in Central Texas*, assembled and edited by Michael B. Collins, Chapter 32, pp. 1459–62. Studies in Archeology 31, Texas Archeological Research Laboratory, University of Texas at Austin, and Archeological Studies Program, Report 10, Texas Department of Transportation, Environmental Affairs Division. Austin.

Wilson, I. R.

1996   Paleoindian Sites in the Vicinity of Pink Mountain. In *Early Human Occupation in British Columbia*, edited by Roy L. Carlson and Luke Dalla Bona, pp. 29–34. University of British Columbia Press, Vancouver.

Wisner, G.

1998   Cooper's Ferry Spear Cache, One of NW's Oldest Sites. *Mammoth Trumpet* 13:1,3–6.

1999   Early Ecuador People Were Maritime Adapted. *Mammoth Trumpet* 14:1,4–11.

Woods, J. C. and G. L. Titmus

1985   A Review of the Simon Clovis Collection. *Idaho Archaeologist* 8(1):3–8.

Wormington, H. M.

1948   A Proposed Revision of Yuma Point Terminology. *Proceedings of the Colorado Museum of Natural History* 18(2): pp. 1–19. Denver.

1957   *Ancient Man in North America*, 4th edition. Denver Museum of Natural History Popular Series No. 4. Denver Museum of Natural History, Denver.

1960   Foreword. In *Geological Significance of a New Radiocarbon Date from the Lindenmeier Site*, Vance Haynes and George Agogino. The Denver Museum of Natural History, Proceedings, 9:3. Denver.

1983   Early Man in the New World: 1970–1980. In *Early Man in the New World*, edited by Richard Shutler, Jr., pp. 191–195. Sage Publications, Beverly Hills.

Wormington, H. M. and D. Ellis (editors)

1967   *Pleistocene Studies in Southern Nevada.* Nevada State Museum Anthropological Papers No. 13. Carson City.

Wormington, H. M. and R. G. Forbis

    1965   *An Introduction to the Archaeology of Alberta, Canada.* Proceedings of the Denver Museum of Natural History 11.

Wright, J. V.

    1976   *The Grant Lake Site, Keewatin District, N.W.T. Archaeological Survey of Canada Paper 47.* Mercury Series. National Museum of Man, Ottawa.

    1981   Prehistory of the Canadian Shield. In *Subarctic,* edited by June Helm, pp. 86–96. Handbook of North American Indians, Vol. 6, W.C. Sturtevant, general editor. Smithsonian Institution, Washington, D.C.

Wyckoff, D. G.

    1985   The Packard Complex: Early Archaic Pre-Dalton Occupations on the Prairie-Woodlands Border. *Southeastern Archaeology* 4:1–26.

Yesner, D. R.

    1996   Human Adaptation at the Pleistocene-Holocene Boundary (circa 13,000 to 8,000 B.P.) in Eastern Beringia. In *Humans at the End of the Ice Age: The Archaeology of the Pleistocene-Holocene Transition,* edited by Lawrence Guy Straus, Berit Valentin Eriksen, Jon M. Erlandson, and David R. Yesner, pp. 255–257. Plenum Press, New York.

Yesner, D. R., C. E. Holmes, and K. J. Crossen

    1992   Archaeology and Paleoecology of the Broken Mammoth Site, Central Tanana Valley, Interior Alaska, USA. *Current Research in the Pleistocene* 9:53–57.

Young, B. and M. B. Collins

    1989   A Cache of Blades with Clovis Affinities from Northeastern Texas. *Current Research in the Pleistocene* 6:26–28.

Young, D. E.

    1985   The Paleoindian Skeletal Material from Horn Rock Shelter in Central Texas. *Current Research in the Pleistocene* 2:39–40.

    1988   The Double Burial at Horn Shelter: An Osteological Analysis. *Central Texas Archaeologist* 11:275–299.

Young, D. E., S. Patrick, and D. G. Steele

    1987   An Analysis of the Paleoindian Double Burial from Horn Shelter No. 2 in Central Texas. *Plains Anthropologist* 32:275–299.

Index

*Note: Numbers in **bold** refer to figures.*

49-PET-408 site, AK, **117, 174,** 180–81; human remains, **116,** 117–19, 145

Abbot, Charles, 12, 257
accelerator mass spectrometry (AMS), xx, 47, 52, 53, 89, 114, 129
Ackerman, R. E., 179, 184, 190, 257
Adovasio, James M., 67, 236, 258, 277
Agate Basin complex, **152,** 214, 226, 229; projectile points, 183, **214**
Agate Basin site, WY, 240
Agenbroad, Larry D., xiv, 258
Agogino, George A., 6, **14,** 82, 258, 283, 287
agriculture, 209, 211
Aikens, C. Melvin, xiv, 197, 258, 310
Akazawa, Takeru, xiv, 258
Alaska and Pacific Northwest, 162–63, **163,** 165–92
Albanese, John P., 84–85, 258
Alberta projectile points, 232
Alsoszatai-Petheo, John, 37, 259
The American Aborigines (Jenness), 10
American Beginnings (West), xiv
American Paleoarctic tradition, **152,** 159, 165, 173, **174,** 189–91
Amerind, 21, 22
Amick, D. S., 234, 259
AMS (accelerator mass spectrometry), xx, 47, 52, 53, 89, 114, 129
anadromous fish, 119, 126
Anangula site, AK, **174**
Ancient Man in North America (Wormington), xiii, xv, 9, 14–15
Anderson, D. D., 175, 259
Anderson, D. C., 125, 173, 259, 264
Andrews, R. L., 236, 277
Angus Mammoth site, NE, 6–7

Antevs, Ernst, 8, 10, 29, 139, 208, 259–60, 302
Anzick site, MT, **216,** 220; human remains, **116,** 121, 144
Archaic tradition, 79, 159, 187, 237–38, 241
Arctic Small Tool tradition, 175
Arlington Man, 129, 201
Arlington Springs site, CA, **196;** human remains, **116,** 129–30, 144
Armenta, Camacho J., 97, 260
Arrow Creek site, BC, Canada, **174,** 179–80
Arroyo, Jaquien, **200**
artifacts: antiquity of, 2, 12, 16, 63; created by noncultural processes, 45–46, 58, 61, 76, 79, 81, 86, 93, 96, 105, 109; with extinct fauna, 64, 67, 77, 99, 106, 109; with human remains, 119, 125, 127, 128–29, 134–35, 136, 138, 180; with redeposited extinct fauna, 208. *See also specific materials; specific artifact types*
atlatl hooks, 138, 151, 154
atlatls and darts, 151, **153,** 153–55, **154,** 159, 181, 225, 238; compared to harpoons, 251, **252, 253,** 255; transition to bow and arrows, 190–91
Aubrey site, TX, **216,** 218–19

Bahada projectile points, 82
Ballinger, S. W., 21–22, 302
Barrie, J. E., 119, 289
basketry, 68, 132, 133, 148, 201
Beaton, John M., 37, 40, 200, 261
Beck, C., 203, 261
Bedwell, Steven R., 194, 261
Bedwell projectile points, 184
Bedwell site, AK, **182,** 184
Beebe, B. F., 58, 61, 261, 286
Beluga Point site, AK, **174,** 178
Benedict, J. B., 227–28, 232, 237, 261–62

Mead site, AK, **166**, 167, 183

Megafauna and Man (Agenbroad, Mead, and Nelson), xiv

Mehringer, P. J., Jr., 197–98, 295

Meighan, C. W., 204, 295

Melbourne, FL, human remains, 139

Melbye, F. J., 58, 286

Meltzer, David J., xiv, 15, 272, 284, 295

Merriwether, D. A., 15, 21–22, 295, 302

Mesa site, AK, **182**, 183–84

metates, 132, 206, 211

microblades, 50, 118, 169–70, **177**, 191

microblade technology, 157–59, **159**, 161, 165, 178, 180, 189–90, 253–54

Microblade tradition, 178

microchips, 60

Midland Man, 116

Midland projectile points, 234

migration, northward, 187–88

Miller, S., 127–28, 279

Milliken site, BC, Canada, **174**, 180

Mill Iron site, WY, 225

Milnesand projectile points, 235

mineral staining, 77, 93, 95, 97

Minnesota man, 115

Mirambell, Lorena, 95–96, 195, 198, 292, 295–96

Mission Ridge site, CA, **47**, 76

mitochondrial DNA (mtDNA), 21–22

Mobley, Charles M., 176, 296

Monte Verde site, Chile, **92**, 101–3, **102**, 107, 108–9

Moose Creek site, AK, **166**, 167

Moratto, Michael J., xiv, 296

Morris, D. H., 138–39, 297

Moseley, Michael E., 209, 297

Moss, M. L., 202, 274

Mossimann, J. E., 35, 297

Mostin site, CA, **196**, 203–4; human remains, 116, **116**, 128–29, 145

Murray Springs, AZ, **216**, 217

Musil, Robert R., 155, 157, 233, 297

Mylodon Cave site, Chile, 106

Naco site, AZ, **216**, 217

Na-dene, 21, 22

Namu site, BC, Canada, **174**; human molars, **120**; human remains, **116**, 119, 145, 180

Native American Graves Protection and Repatriation Act (NAGPRA), 111–12; consultations, 117, 125

Nelson, D. E., 187, 275, 297

Nelson, Lisa W., xiv, 258

Nelson, Nels C., 11, 297

Nenana complex, **152**, 165, **166**, 166–73, 189; compared to Clovis complex, 189, 246; diagnostic artifacts, 167, **168**; similarities to Northern Paleoindian, 186, 189

New Evidence for the Pleistocene Peopling of the Americas (Bryan), xiv

New World context evaluated with Old World criteria, 2, 12, 16, 78, 89

noncultural processes creating artifacts, 45–46, 58, 61, 76, 79, 81, 86, 93, 96, 105; difficulty of distinguishing, 109

Nordenskiold, Erland, 10

Northern Paleoindian tradition, 165–66, 181–88, **182**

Northwest Coast Microblade tradition, 119, **152**, 178–81, 189–90

obsidian: sources, 172, 179; trade, 178, 188

obsidian hydration, 65, 97, 204

ochre, 82, 107. *See also* red ochre

Ochsenius, Claudio, 98, 265, 298

Old Cordilleran culture, 193, 195, 203

Old Crow site, YT, Canada, **47**, 58, 60, 87; flesher, **58**

Old World criteria in New World context, 2, 12, 16, 78, 89

Olsen-Chubbock site, CO, 234

Onion Portage site, AK, **174**

Orr, Phil C., 76–77, 129, 132, 262, 298

Osborne, Dick, 55

Otavalo skeleton, 115

overkill hypothesis, 35–36

Overstreet, D. F., 66, 299

Owl Ridge site, AK, **182**, 183, 185

Owsley, Douglas W., 131, 288

Ozbun, T. L., 220, 310

Pacific Northwest and Alaska, 162–63, **163**, 165–92

Paleoindian tradition, 9, 99, 150, **152**, 213–14, 238–41, 246–47; projectile points, 54–55

Paleolithic in Europe, 81–82, 246

Panguingue Creek site, AK, **174**, 176, **182**, 183, 185

Parenti, Fabio, 105, 299

Patrick, S., 136–37, 312

Pebble Tool tradition, **152**, 191, 195